THE ART OF SINGING

A Compendium of Thoughts on Singing
Published Between 1777 and 1927

by

BRENT JEFFREY MONAHAN

The Scarecrow Press, Inc.
Metuchen, N.J. & London
1978

Library of Congress Cataloging in Publication Data

Monahan, Brent Jeffrey.
    The art of singing.

    Includes bibliographies and index.
    1. Singing--Instruction and study. 2. Singing--
Quotations, maxims, etc. I. Title.
MT820.M75   784.9   78-16630
ISBN 0-8108-1155-3

TABLE OF CONTENTS

LIST OF TABLES

ACKNOWLEDGMENTS

First, appreciation must be expressed to Victor Alexander Fields, who through his pioneer work in the field provided a structure for this study; and to John Carroll Burgin, whose follow-up to the Fields volume provided additional information.

Thanks must be given to the librarians of Indiana University, especially to Ms. Kathryn Talalay, who secured from the Ohio College Library Center lists showing the whereabouts of many of the sources consulted.

Thanks are in order to Mr. William Agress and Ms. Clarissa Behr for their aid in researching the numerous sources, to Ms. Behr for the loan of her library of vocal pedagogy, and to Professor Paul Matthen for his patient supervision of the writing of this book.

Finally, especial loving thanks are given to my mother, for undertaking the prodigious task of typing the manuscript, and to my mother and father both (whom I like to call "The Monahan Foundation"), for financing not only this study, but my seemingly endless career as a music student.

B. J. M.

GUIDE TO THE REFERENCES

This appendix indicates the volume titles that correspond to the names and dates contained within brackets in the main body of this study. In a few cases, two editions of the same work were consulted and quoted, and both are indicated.

Anfossi, Maria. 18-- or 180-. Trattato teorico practico sull' arte del canto

Bach, Albert Bernhard. 1880. On Musical Education

_____. 1894. The Principles of Singing

_____. 1898. Musical Education and Vocal Culture

Bacon, Richard Mackenzie. 1824. Elements of Vocal Science

Bassini, Carlo. [ca.] 1857. Bassini's Art of Singing

_____. [ca.] 1865. Bassini's Education of the Young Voice

_____. [ca.] 1869. Bassini's New Method for Soprano and Mezzo-Soprano

Behnke, Emil. 189-. The Mechanism of the Human Voice

Bishenden, Charles James. 1875. The Voice and How to Use It

_____. 1876. How to Sing

Botume, John Franklin. 1896. Modern Singing Methods; Their Use and Abuse

_____. [ca.] 1897. Respiration for Advanced Singers

_____. 1916. Voice Production Today

vii

Broekhaven, John Andrew van. 1905. The Tone Producing
Functions of the Vocal Organs

_____. 1908. Some Unfamiliar Facts Concerning the
Functions of the Larynx in Singing

_____. 1908. The True Method of Tone Production

Brower, Harriette Moore. 1920. Vocal Mastery

Browne, Lennox. 1887 [6th ed.]. Medical Hints on the Production and Management of the Singing Voice

_____, and Behnke, Emil. 1883 [13th ed.], and 1904
[16th ed.]. Voice, Song, and Speech

Buzzi-Peccia, Arturo. 1925. How to Succeed in Singing

Caruso, Enrico. 1909. The Art of Singing

Clifton, Arthur. 1846 [3rd ed.]. Clifton's Vocal Instruction

Clippinger, David Alva. [ca.] 1910. Systematic Voice Training

_____. 1917. The Head Voice and Other Problems

Cooke, James Francis. 1921. Great Singers on the Art of
Singing

Cooke, Thomas Simpson. 1828. Singing Simplified

Corfe, Joseph. 18--. A Treatise on Singing

Corrette, Michel. 1782. Le Parfait Maître a chanter

Corri, Domenico. 1810 [Foreman reprint]; 1811 [Library of
Congress]. The Singers Preceptor

Corri, Philip Antony. [ca.] 1820. New Vocal Instructor

Costa, Andrea. 1824. Considerations on the Art of Singing
in General

_____. 1838. Analytical Considerations on the Art of
Singing

Crowest, Frederick James. 1900 [7th ed.]. Advice to
Singers

Curtis, Henry Holbrook. 1914. Voice Building and Tone
Placing

_____. 1918. Thirty Years' Experience with Singers

Daniell, William Henry. 1873. The Voice and How to Use
It

D'Aubigny von Engelbrunner, Nina. 1803. Briefe an Natalie

Day, H. W. 1839. The Vocal School

Dodds, George Robert, and Lickley, James Dunlop. 1925. The Control of the Breath

Dodds, George. 1927. Practical Hints for Singers

Douty, Nicholas. 1924. What the Vocal Student Should Know

Downing, William Bell. 1927. Vocal Pedagogy for Student, Singer, and Teacher

Drew, William Sidney. 1924. Voice Training

Duff, Sarah Robinson. 1919. Simple Truths Used by Great Singers

Duval. 1800. Méthode agréable et utile pour apprendre facilment à chanter juste, avec goût et précision

Everest, Cornelius. 1861. Everest's Vocal Instructor

Ferrari, Giacomo Gotifredi. 1818. Breve trattato de canto Italiano

_____. 1838. Giacimo [sic] G. Ferrari's Celebrated Instruction Book of the Voice

_____. 184-. Instruction Book of the Voice

Ffrangçon-Davies, David. 1904 [Pro Musica reprint, 1968], 1906. The Singing of the Future

Fillebrown, Thomas. 1911 [3rd ed.]. Resonance in Singing and Speaking

Frossard, Henri Jean. 1914. La Science et l'art du chant

Fucito, Salvatore, and Beyer, B. J. 1922. Caruso and the Art of Singing

Furtado, Charles. 18--. General Observations on the Vocal Art

Garcia, Manuel. 1849. Mémoire sur la voix humaine

_____. 1894. Hints on Singing

_____. 1924. Garcia's Treatise on the Art of Singing

_____. 1975 [Da Capo Press reprint of 1847 and 1872 editions combined]. A Complete Treatise on the Art of Singing

Greene, Herbert Wilbur. 1920. The Singer's Ladder

Guttmann, Oskar. 1885. Key to the Guttmann Tables

_____. 1887 [2nd ed.]. Gymnastics of the Voice

Hallock, William, and Muckey, Floyd S. 1896. Rational Scientific Voice-Production

Heinrich, Max. 1910. Correct Principles of Classical Singing

Henderson, William James. 1906 and 1920. The Art of the Singer

Hiller, Johann Adam. 1780 and 1798. Anweisung zum musikalischenzierlichen Gesange

_____. 1792. Kurze und erleichterte Anweisung zum Singen

Holmes, William Gordon. 1879. A Treatise on Vocal Physiology and Hygiene

_____. 1880. The Science of Voice Production and Voice Preservation

Hulbert, Henry Harper. 1903. Breathing for Voice Production

_____. 1921. Eurhythm: Thought in Action

Kirkland, Henry Stuart. 1916. Expression in Singing

Kofler, Leo. 1889. Take Care of Your Voice

_____. 1897. The Art of Breathing as the Basis of Tone Production

Lablache, Louis. 184-. A Complete Method of Singing for the Bass Voice

_____. 1860. Lablache's Complete Method of Singing

Lamperti, Francesco. 1864. Guida teorica-pratica-elementare per lo studio del canto

_____. 1883. L'arte del canto

Lamperti, Giovanni Battista. 1905. The Technics of Bel Canto

Lankow, Anna. 1901. Supplement to Vocal Art.

_____; Brömme, Adolph; and Garcia, Manuel. 1899. Kunst-gesang Schule

_____, and Garcia, Manuel. 1903 [3rd ed.]. The Science of the Art of Singing

Lanza, Francesco Giuseppe. 183-. Lanza's Abridgement of
His Work on the Art of Singing

Lanza, Gesualdo. 1813. Lanza's Elements of Singing

Lasser, Johan Baptist. 1805. Vollständige Anleitung zur
Singkunst

Lehmann, Lilli. 1906. How to Sing

Lunn, Charles. 1880. Vox populi

_____. 1888 [6th ed.]. The Philosophy of Voice

_____. 1904. The Voice: Its Downfall, Its Training and
Its Use

Mackenzie, Morell. 1886 and 1891 [7th ed.]. The Hygiene
of the Vocal Organs

Marafioti, Pasqual Mario. 1922. Caruso's Method of Voice
Production

_____. 1925. The New Vocal Art

Marchesi, Mathilde. 1901. Ten Singing Lessons

_____. 1903. The Marchesi School

Marchesi, Salvatore. 1902. A Vademecum for Singing-
Teachers and Pupils

Martens, Frederick Herman. 1923. The Art of the Prima
Donna and Concert Singer

Marx, Adolf Bernhard. 1826. Die Kunst des Gesanges

Mason, Lowell. 1847 [5th ed.]. Manual of the Boston
Academy of Music

Melba, Nellie Mitchell. 1926. Melba Method

Miller, Frank Ebenezer, and Wangemann, A. Theo. E.
1898. Observations About the Human Voice

Miller, Frank Ebenezer. 1910. The Voice; Its Production,
Care and Preservation

_____. 1912. Vocal Art-Science from the Standpoint of
the Use and Abuse of the Voice

_____. 1912 Vocal Atlas. [The title is used together
with the date of this volume to differentiate it from the
1912 Vocal Art-Science from the Standpoint of the Use and
Abuse of the Voice.]

_____. 1917. Vocal Art-Science and Its Application

Minoja, Ambrosio. 1815. Über den Gesang

Muckey, Floyd. 1915. The Natural Method of Voice Production in Speech and Song

Myer, Edmund John. 1883. Truths of Importance to Vocalists

_____. 1886. The Voice from a Practical Standpoint

_____. 1891. Vocal Reinforcement

_____. 1897 and 1911. Position and Action in Singing

_____. 1902. The Renaissance of the Vocal Art

_____. 1913. The Vocal Instructor

Nathan, Isaac. 1836 [Pro Musica reprint, 1968]. An Essay on the History and Theory of Music

Nordica, Lillian. 1923. Lillian Nordica's Hints to Singers

Novello, [Mary Sabilla]. 1856. Voice and Vocal Art

Oliver, Edward Battle. 186- or 187-. The Vocalist's Companion

Panofka, Heinrich. [ca.] 1859. Gesangs--A B C

Panseron, Auguste-Mathieu. [ca.] 1865. The A B C of Music

Parisotti, Luigi. 1911. A Treatise on Speaking and Singing

Pfeiffer, Michael Traugott, and Nägeli, Hans Georg. 1810. Gesangbildungslehre nach Pestalozzischen Grundsätzen pädagogisch begründet

_____. 1830. Auszug der Gesangbildungslehre nach Pestalozzian Grundsätzen

Proschowsky, Frantz. 1923. The Way to Sing

_____. [ca.] 1927. The Singing School of Frantz Proschowsky

Randegger, Alberto. 1912. Singing

Rogers, Clara Kathleen. 1895. The Philosophy of Singing

_____. 1910. My Voice and I

_____. [ca.] 1925. Your Voice and You

Romer, Francis. 1845. The Physiology of the Human Voice

Russell, Louis Arthur. 1904. The Body and Breath under Artistic Control for Song and Fervent Speech. [Because Russell published three pamphlets in 1904, the title will always accompany the date in citation.]

_____ . 1904. A Plain Talk with American Singers

_____ . 1904. Some Psychic Reflections for Singers

_____ . 1907 or 1912. The Commonplaces of Vocal Art

Rutz, Ottmar. 1908. Neue Entdeckungen von der menschlichen Stimme

_____ . 1911. Sprache, Gesang, und Körperhaltung

Santley, Charles. 1908. The Art of Singing and Vocal Declamation

Seiler, Emma. 1871. The Voice in Singing

Shakespeare, William. 1899 or 1910. The Art of Singing

_____ . 1924. Plain Words on Singing

Shaw, W. Warren. 1914. The Lost Art and Its Restoration

Shryock, Daniel. 1856. The Music Teacher

Sieber, Ferdinand. 1872. The Art of Singing

_____ . 1858. Kurze Anleitung zum gründlichen Studium des Gesanges

Stanley, Douglas. 1916. A few Remarks on Voice Production and Operatic Timbre

Stockhausen, Julius. 188-. Julius Stockhausen's Gesangtechnik und Stimmbildung

_____ . 1884. Julius Stockhausen's Gesang-methode

Taylor, David Clark. 1914. Self-help for Singers

_____ . 1916. New Light on the Old Italian Method

_____ . 1917. The Psychology of Singing

Tenducci, Guisto Ferdinando. 1785. Instruction of Mr. Tenducci to His Scholars

Tetrazzini, Luisa. 1909. The Art of Singing

_____ . [ca.] 1923. How to Sing

Thorp, George E., and Nicholl, William. 1896. A Text Book on the Natural Use of the Voice

Trajetta, Philipo. 1843. Rudiments of the Art of Singing

Vaccai, Niccolò. 1894. Practical Italian Vocal Method

White, Ernest G. 1918 or 1927. The Voice Beautiful in Speech and Song

Wieck, [Friedrich]. 1875. Piano and Song

Witherspoon, Herbert. [ca.] 1925. Singing: A Treatise for Teachers and Students

Wronski, Thaddeus. 1921. The Singer and His Art

I

INTRODUCTION

Singing may well be the most natural and universal of
all musical arts. It can be accomplished by almost every
normal human being with little or no thought given to the nature of its generation. However, once the concept "artistic"
is prefixed to the word "singing," there arises a bewildering
complexity of considerations. For example, man as an artistic singer is responsible not only for the aesthetic elements
that transfer the intentions of composer and poet to the audience, but also for the transfer medium itself. Whereas the
pianist may instantly improve his tonal output by acquiring a
better-made or larger piano, the singer must make do with
his natural endowment and develop it, at the cost of great
pains, to the limits of its beauty and power. This development is the slow and arduous task of first understanding the
nature of his vocal mechanism and then learning, psychologically and physically, to control this intricate apparatus. To
be sure, there are other artistic genres such as drama and
ballet that require the performer to serve as both medium
and interpreter of the art. In singing, however, the generating mechanism is hardly open to direct observation. Much
that is learned must be done by inner sensations, governed
by subjective evaluations. In addition, the singer's performance is subjectively perceived by his audience, and, in
the case of the so-called "sophisticated" audience, their ap-
prehension of the singer's level of artistry is based on a
predetermined, traditional set of criteria regarding timbre,
dynamic control, phrasing, emotion and the like.

It is little wonder, therefore, that there is much to
be discussed concerning the teaching of artistic singing in
Western culture, and that the subjective nature of the study
allows for many opinions.

A milestone in the gathering of the wealth of concepts
of singing is Victor Alexander Fields' Training the Singing

Voice (New York: King's Crown Press, 1947). In his study, under the heading "Aims and Purposes," Fields has written:

> There is certainly no lack of printed material on the subjects of singing and voice culture. But it is inaccessible to teachers because it is extremely diversified and fragmentary and rather diffusely distributed throughout a variety of books, periodicals, scientific papers, reports of experiments and published interviews that have never been correlated from the standpoint of a definite vocal pedagogy. Furthermore, what is written about the singing voice is so often overlaid and interwoven with conflicting theories and extravagant conjectures that misrepresentation is inevitable. Where there is abundant verbal testimony to support a given procedure there is not one shred of documentary or experimental evidence. Teachers of singing fall an easy prey to unscientific writings on voice for want of orientation in the foundational principles of their subject and much inherited misinformation is thus perpetuated....
>
> An analytical study and comparison of the many recent contributions to vocal pedagogy would facilitate the appraisal of teaching methods, old and new. Both pedagogy and research would be benefited by the juxtaposition and classification of the principal ideologies pursued by the singing profession. The findings of such a study would provide the vocal scientist with a background of useful knowledge against which to formulate and test his theories. The teacher would enjoy the counsel and caution of his contemporaries through an exchange of ideas gathered from a range of knowledge and experience wider than his own [page 1].

If Fields has already undertaken such a study and completed it with great success, what, then, would be the purpose of another work on the same order? The answer lies in the time limitation of Fields' work. His investigations span only a 15-year period, from 1928 to 1942. In order to provide the profession with the findings of subsequent years, John Carroll Burgin published a follow-up study, almost identical in structure, covering the period 1943-1971, entitled Teaching Singing (Metuchen, N.J.: Scarecrow Press, 1973). Many early sources of vocal pedagogy have also been systematically analyzed by Philip A. Duey in his Bel Canto in Its Golden Age (New York: King's Crown Press, 1951).

Covering the years through 1777, when Mancini published his
Riflessioni pratiche al canto figurato, Duey's study is quite
thorough.   After this date, various sources from approximately the next thirty years are mentioned but not closely
examined.   Teachers, scientists, and historians of artistic
singing in Western culture have three excellent works, then,
covering three separate eras.   Until this study, however, no
work on such a scale has been attempted for the span of
time between 1777 and 1927.

It is understandable that the oldest and the newest
eras in vocal pedagogy should receive special attention.   For
more than a hundred years, authors have spoken nostalgically
about the lost art of the mysterious "bel canto" period.   Certainly the most recent investigations in voice production are
the most complete.   And yet the period between the years
1777 and 1927 also holds much of value to the singer, scien-
tist and teacher.   It is during this period that most of the
literature of recital and opera which we now call collectively
"the classical repertoire" was composed and first performed.
This material was performed by some of the most celebrated
singers in history.   Well known today are the names of Rubini, Pasta, Nourrit, Schröder-Devrient, Duprez, Grisi,
Mario, Tamburini, Patti, Malibran, Viardot, Lind, Schnorr,
Tamagno, Maurel, Sembrich, and the De Reszke brothers.
Other equally famous vocalists set down in writing their own
precepts for artistic singing.   Among these are Tenducci,
Lablache, Stockhausen, Santley, Lilli Lehmann, Melba, Nordica,
Tetrazzini, and Caruso.

Three books of the early 1920's contain interviews with
celebrated artists, giving valuable insights on singing from the
professional point of view.   The books of Harriette Moore Brower,
James Francis Cooke, and Frederick Herman Martens contain a total of 72 interviews with 56 artists of the era, including Farrar, Galli-Curci, Schumann-Heink, Maurel, and
Ponselle.

The period between 1777 and 1927 is also important
because of the writings of a number of famous teachers.
Most celebrated is the younger Manuel Garcia, the inventor
of the laryngoscope.   Also justly renowned are Anfossi, Bach,
Bacon, Hiller, Francesco and Giovanni Lamperti, Lunn,
Mackenzie, Randegger, Russell, Seiler, and Shakespeare.

Many writers regard this period as "the golden age
of singing."   But what exactly was being taught to produce

so many phenomenal voices? Are traditional concepts retained throughout the years, are they abandoned, or are they interpreted and expanded in the light of modern scientific investigation? When do concepts not mentioned in bel canto writings emerge? Do certain concepts enjoy only fleeting popularity, and is it possible to trace the history of a concept?

To some degree all of these questions can be answered by this study. First, the study spans a period of 150 years, or ten times the length of the Fields study. Such a time span aids the detection of trends in vocal pedagogic thinking. Second, the nineteenth century is the period of greatest theoretical flux in vocal pedagogy. It witnesses a changeover from the empirical observations of the "old Italian school" to careful scientific investigations in the fields of anatomy, physiology, acoustics, and orthoepy. Third, the amount of material published in this period is much greater than that of the "bel canto" era but not so prolific as to require separate analyses every twenty or so years.

GENERAL FORMAT

To coordinate the source materials of this period, the basic format of Fields' Training the Singing Voice is duplicated. Fields' study is well conceived, well executed, and has enjoyed continued success within the singing profession. When John Carroll Burgin updated Fields' study, he used fundamentally the same format. In the opinion of this author, Burgin's study benefits from the unity and clarity of Fields' organization. Hence, it would be foolish to cast about for a unique format when a highly successful one has already been developed. Furthermore, a uniformity of structure among the three compendia allows the reader to compare concepts with a minimum expenditure of time and effort.

It must be pointed out, however, that this study does not slavishly reproduce either the format or the style of Fields' study. For example, in his chapter on resonance, Fields includes a subsection which he entitles "Quality as a guide." The quotations which follow seem only marginally applicable to the teaching situation. Furthermore, in a few cases such as this, a certain understanding of Fields' definition of a concept or his reason for placing the concept in his study is necessary if the parallel area is to have coherence in a subsequent study. If sufficient purpose could not be discerned, the concept was omitted.

A number of concepts have been added to those surveyed in the studies of Fields and Burgin. These include "the singer's health" (chapter II), "the silent and unobserved breath" (chapter III), "the jaw low and free" (chapter IV), and "the expansion of the natural vocal compass" (chapter VI).

This study also differs from the works of Fields and Burgin in its presentation of concepts. The other works rely heavily on incomplete quotation or on paraphrasing. This study prefers to present, as much as possible, an author's opinions in the complete, original syntax. It is believed that the sacrifice of space and reading time is offset by the clarity afforded by direct quotation. Such a method puts less pressure on the researcher to interpret the meanings of those authors quoted. Another reason for direct quotation is that the sources of this study tend to be less obtainable by the reader than the sources of the Fields and Burgin studies.

LIMITATIONS OF THE STUDY

Before any other considerations, a number of limitations had to be established to bring this work into manageable proportions. With one exception (area 13, below), a set of limits was borrowed and is quoted from Fields:

Because of its considerable scope, the problem underlying this study was narrowed down to workable proportions by eliminating thirty adjacent vocal areas, and by including only those publications that are written in the English language. The adjacent areas not included in this study are:

1. song literature
2. technical vocal exercises and drills
3. song programs and repertoire building
4. general musicianship for singers
5. music theory for singers
6. children's singing voice
7. adolescent of changing voice
8. community singing
9. speaking voice and phonetics
10. vocal anatomy and physiology
11. vocal pathology (medical)
12. history of singing and voice culture
13. physical health and hygiene of the vocal organs

14. phonographic recordings of singers
15. singing for the radio and crooning
16. singing as a professional career
17. operatic singing and grand opera
18. biographies of famous singers
19. technical training of singing teachers
20. teaching singing in the elementary schools
21. vocal satire, humor, and fiction
22. preparing for auditions
23. how to choose a vocal teacher
24. the study of foreign languages for singing
25. qualifications of singing teachers
26. recreational and school assembly singing
27. news items on voice and singing
28. vocal acoustics
29. group training of the singing voice
30. song writing [Training the Singing Voice, pages 9-10.]

This list applies as well to the formulation of the annotated research bibliography at the back of the study. Although this period contains many valuable books of only exercises and drills, they are not listed in the bibliography. Nor is the collection of cadenzas published by Mathilde Marchesi to be found there, even though her two teaching books are included as primary reference sources. While a number of sources included in the bibliography contain sections on the areas listed above, it was not because of this that they are included.

It must also be noted that in this study sources used are not confined to those in English. Many of the most important works of the late eighteenth and early nineteenth centuries exist only in the original Italian, French, or German. If an authoritative translation was available, it was used for quotation in the study. Where possible, the original text was compared to check for accuracy.

The studies of Fields and Burgin include every book, magazine article, dissertation and scholarly report that relates to those specifically chosen areas of vocal pedagogy within their studies. This is possible since these studies encompass only 15 and 28 years respectively. In order to examine the entire period of 1777 to 1927 as one, further limits had to be placed on the sources analyzed. First, all materials that did not exist in a separately bound state, i.e., all materials other than books or pamphlets, were passed

over. This, unfortunately, eliminates rich sources of information contained in literally dozens of periodicals. Research
for this study has revealed, however, that many important
articles in journals and reviews were later incorporated into
books. A token attempt has been made to acknowledge the
importance of periodical contributions in Appendix Two.

Fields states that he read all 702 documents that appeared during the period of his research. Burgin annotates
a total of 803 documents in his bibliography. A majority of
the documents in both studies are magazine articles of perhaps three to 20 pages. In comparison, there are only 608
entries in this study, and yet it was not possible to analyze
more than one quarter of them. Except for a few pamphlets,
the average document used in this study was a book of about
150 pages.

It was decided that the works of 100 authors would be
the physical limit for this study. This allows for one author
to represent a time interval of one and a half years.

In order not to be completely arbitrary, a set of criteria was established for the selection of the representative
authors. First, all the documents were listed in chronological order. No period of more than five years would be
allowed to elapse without at least one document to represent
it. In many cases an author had published more than one
book, and in this situation the most popular of his or her
books was chosen to represent that author's "year."

Once each author had been placed chronologically,
five other criteria were used to determine the representative
authors: (1) In how many of the libraries used in this study
does at least one of the works of an author exist? (2) How
many separate volumes did the author write? (3) How many
editions of each volume were printed? (4) Into how many
languages has any volume been translated? (5) Is the author
a famous singer or singing teacher, or the pupil of a famous
teacher?

Many more books were published in the last 75 years
of the study than in the first 75 years (see "Chronological
Bibliography" in the back). Authors were selected with this
in mind as well.

Actually, a total of 108 authors' works were read to
further decide which would be most valuable. The work of

Pestalozzi, for example, is mentioned by many sources. Examination reveals, however, that Pestalozzi's book is a graded music primer for public education. It uses no verbal instruction, and is therefore useless to this study. In another case, the work of Enrico delle Sedie is regarded by this author as valuable, but this book is available in only one of the libraries consulted, and so it was not used. Two other authors of considerable reputation are John Howard and Thomas Wesley Mills. The work of these men could not be included either. Howard and Mills each published more than one work, and while one of their publications will exist in a number of libraries, in both cases other works listed in card catalogs have been found to be missing from the library shelves.

The particular hundred authors surveyed have contributed 160 documents related to this study. By coincidence, the numbers of statements presented in these documents roughly correspond to the total number of statements tallied in the studies of Fields and Burgin:

Table 1.

Subject by Chapter		Total Number of Statements		
		Fields	Burgin	Monahan
II.	Vocal Pedagogy	690	640	636
III.	Breathing	428	497	538
IV.	Phonation	463	558	434
V.	Resonance	262	274	193
VI.	Range	228	257	343
VII.	Vocal Dynamics	110	134	110
VIII.	Ear Training	157	155	131
IX.	Diction	254	331	296
X.	Interpretation	354	384	239
	GRAND TOTAL	2946	3230	2920

At the organizational level of individual concepts there is even closer agreement in figures among the three studies. This coincidence proves valuable to research on the history of individual concepts. Appreciable advances or declines in the number of statements from one study to another helps to indicate the relative importance of a concept during a particular era. Such occurrences are noted in their proper location within the body of this study.

GATHERING THE SOURCES

The first goal of this study was to find as many books

and pamphlets as possible related to vocal pedagogy published within the period 1777-1927 for a research bibliography. The second goal was to select from this totality, the volumes of the 100 "most popular" and "most available" authors.

Toward this end, seven libraries were consulted. The Library of Congress and the New York Public Library at Lincoln Center were chosen because they represent the two largest repositories of musical documents in the United States. The Boston Public Library was selected because Boston has enjoyed a long-standing musical tradition, including a number of publishing firms that printed vocal books in the 1777-1927 period. Furthermore, the Boston Public Library is a venerable institution with a considerable collection of books on the instruction of the singing voice, including many of the oldest volumes. The library of the School of Music, Indiana University, Bloomington, Indiana (in Sycamore Hall), is the parent library of this study. It is also the library of what is reputed to be the largest music school in the world, and a school that concentrates on voice training. Westminster Choir College in Princeton, New Jersey, has a relatively small enrollment, but since the school is primarily oriented toward singing, their library contains a disproportionate number of works on voice training relative to the size of the school. The libraries of Rutgers and Princeton universities in New Jersey served primarily as control factors in this study. Rutgers is a large public (state) institution with a small music school and no emphasis on voice. The library contains few books on voice training. Hence, those works selected for inclusion would tend to be popular, not obscure, editions. Princeton University is a private institution, also with a small music department that does not emphasize the training of the voice. Excellent financial endowment, however, has enabled the Firestone Library to acquire a greater number of works on the voice than an institution of its size with no voice emphasis would normally have. Except for the Library of Congress and the New York Public Library at Lincoln Center, each library was purposely selected for a different reason to best determine the most widely available works on singing.

Once the primary sources were selected, the essential task was to secure at least one edition of each source for analysis. Books were read in each of the seven above-mentioned libraries. It was possible to do much of the research in Bloomington because of a computer system called the Ohio College Library Center (OCLC). Within this computer are catalogues of the holdings of some 180 libraries throughout the United States and Canada. Through Indiana University Interlibrary Loan some forty volumes published after 1870 were secured from a number of libraries.

SELECTING, COLLECTING, AND ARRANGING THE DATA

In conformity with the organization of Fields' study, nine general areas of interest were established, as listed in Table 1. Further divisions within each area (chapter) resulted in 161 topic headings, as designated in Tables 2 through 10 on the second page of each corresponding chapter. All statements gathered for this work fall into at least one of these 161 topic headings.

Information from each source was gathered on two sheets containing a total of nine chapter areas and 161 coded subdivisions. Next to each subdivision, the page number of a corresponding statement was noted. If the statement was deemed particularly worthy of quotation, an asterisk was placed beside the page number, and the quotation was copied onto the back of one of the sheets.

Any individual concept was counted only one time for that source, regardless of how often the author repeats the idea in the course of that writing. A number of authors, however, published more than one work in the time span of this study, and statements are often repeated. At first, a method was considered wherein any author would be credited with the statement of a concept only once, whether he voiced this concept in one or ten separate volumes. It was later decided that each of the 160 sources would be treated as separate entities. There are a number of reasons for this decision. First, only one quarter of all the works of this period are analyzed here, and therefore tallies serve only as rough indicators of the popularity of individual statements. Second, an author who publishes more volumes may indeed have an advantage in influencing the public over one who publishes one book, and this advantage should be included in these tallies. Third, a number of authors who have written more than one book have changed their opinions from one publication to another. Manuel Garcia, Charles Lunn, and Mathilde Marchesi are three of the authors whom we will quote to this effect within the body of this study.

Because of the reproductive nature of this study, the majority of space is given to the quotation of other authors. Well over a thousand quotations have been included in this survey. Obviously, a standard form of footnoting would prove not only cumbersome but confusing as well. A form used in scholarly journals of scientific investigation has been borrowed. Each quotation is followed by the last name of the author, the date of the edition quoted, and the page number(s), all within brackets. In a few cases, where two authors share the same last name, the first name is included also. Three pamphlets of Louis Arthur Russell were all published in 1904, and to avoid confusion, the titles of the pamphlets precede the date.

Quick reference to the title of the publication referred to within brackets is possible by consulting the Guide to the References (which precedes this Introduction).

To further aid the researcher, a number of additional sources are added within brackets when other authors closely concur with a particular statement.

ANALYZING THE DATA

This study has been conceived primarily as a presentational and not a critical work. No attempts have been made to assess the validity or to evaluate the opinions of those authors selected for this study. Obviously the choice of which statements are "particularly worthy of quotation" involves a degree of subjectivity on the part of this author. However, the choice was made according to how lucidly a statement is presented and not on the content of that statement. Many opinions presented in this work are regarded by this author as patently ridiculous, but, since the publication in which the statement was made enjoyed a wide reading public for a number of years, at least its influence deserves to be credited.

At the end of each chapter a brief analysis and some personal comments may be found. Chapter XI provides an overview of the findings of this study, relates the period discussed with the eras immediately preceding and following it, and offers a generalized evolutionary history of the vocal training book from 1777 to 1927.

II

VOCAL PEDAGOGY

Definition. Webster defines "pedagogy" as the profession or function of teaching; the art or science of teaching, especially, instruction in teaching methods. All sophisticated methods of vocal pedagogy rely upon an admixture of concepts drawn from aesthetics and science, terms that each embody a multitude of meanings. This chapter presents a variety of concepts that arose in the period 1777 to 1927 as each writer sought a justifiable system of rules and applications toward developing the singing voice.

THEORIES : INTRODUCTORY CONCEPTS

The Voice Defined

It is startling to discover that, of the 100 authors surveyed for this study, only six feel a need to define "voice." Further, only two of these offer definitions in a manner succinct enough to allow quotation: "The definition of voice is a very simple matter. We must all admit that the voice is sound. So far as the voice is concerned sound is a sensation produced through the organ of hearing by means of air-waves. The voice then must be airwaves and can be nothing else" [Muckey, 1915, pp. 26-27]. "The human voice is composed of two instruments. The vocal or sound producing instrument and articulating instrument, or the instrument which moulds sound into speech" [Myer, 1886, p. 7].

Singing Defined

"Singing is the interpretation of text by means of mu-

Table 2.   SUMMARY OF CONCEPTS OF VOCAL PEDAGOGY

I.   Theories of vocal pedagogy

A. Introductory concepts	52
B. Preliminary considerations	
1. benefits of vocal study	6
2. prerequisites of vocal study	60
3. the vocal training period	44
C. Objectives of vocal training	18
D. Coordination as a primary physiological factor	3
E. Standardization of vocal training	
1. vocal training can be standardized	4
2. vocal training cannot be standardized	16

II.   Methods of vocal pedagogy

A. psychological approach	
1. importance of the psychological approach	26
2. voice training as habit formation	22
3. singing as a natural function	
a) the vocal act is unconscious and involuntary	18
b) spontaneity and naturalness are the characteristics	22
4. freeing the vocal mechanism	
a) relaxation a factor in vocal training	22
b) economy of effort principle	29
c) overcoming inhibitions and fears	11
5. singing as self-expression	5
6. singing and speaking compared	25
B. The technical approach	
1. technical principles and objectives	22
2. removing muscular interferences	12
3. handling beginners	
a) classifying voices	27
b) first lessons	16
4. teaching with song	
a) songs are useful as technical exercises	6
b) vocalises are preferable as technical exercises	16
5. principles and procedures used in practicing	
a) principles of vocal practice	55
b) supervision of practice	4
c) silent practicing as a device	7
d) piano accompaniment	9
e) various factors	46
6. health	33
TOTAL STATEMENTS	636

sical tones produced by the human voice" [Henderson, 1906, p. 1]. "Singing may be defined as the art of expressing emotions and sentiments by using the voice as a musical instrument: it is acting of a particular kind" [Drew, 1924, p. 10]. "The Art of Singing, in a certain degree embraces the principles of acoustics, physiology, arithmetics, metaphysics, poetry, orthoepy, and music, as well in regard of composition as of execution" [Costa, 1838, p. 1].

> Singing, as ordinarily understood, may be described as the sound of the human voice when trained to the notes of the musical scale, and it is usually associated with speech. Yet in a higher sense, we must regard singing as the art of combining tune and speech in such a way that the notes are started in fulness and purity exactly on the pitch intended; the words are prolonged, yet sound as natural as the most expressive talking, and every tune conveys the emotion desired by the singer [Shakespeare, 1910, p. 7].

Everyone Can Sing

"To the general rule, that everyone may learn to sing, if he commences in season and continues in practice, there is probably not more than one exception in five hundred" [Day, 1839, Introduction]. "All voices are naturally beautiful. All ugliness in vocal tone is the result of transferred habits acquired by the artificial use of voice in speech" [Lunn, 1880, p. 7].

Applying Method to the Natural Voice

"To become master of one's art is, in the first place, to become master of oneself" [Rogers, 1910, p. 9]. "The favourable properties of the organs may be, although they rarely are, entirely the gift of nature. But when ... they are found unfavourable (which not unfrequently happens), art, unfolding its vast resources, may, in many cases, admirably supply the defect" [Costa, 1838, p. 2].

> The term, Science, in its particular acceptation, when applied to singing, appears to be very difficult to define. Its universal and constant use exhibits one instance of the indiscriminate adoption of words, into which people are apt to fall, without affixing to them

any precise idea. Every one talks of 'the science' of
a singer, but there are few who have ever stopped to
consider what they purpose to express. Science appears to me to imply the perfect union of taste and
knowledge--the complete combination of style and man-
ner--a thorough acquaintance with the rules of art,
and a power of reducing them to first practice [Bacon,
1824, p. 86].

The Multiplicity of Methodologies

The research of this study proves that there are as
many methods as there are books on the voice. Most methods, however, can be placed in one of three broad categories,
as described by David Taylor:

It will be recalled that the review of the topics of
model vocal instruction covered three distinct types
of materials. First, the purely mechanical doctrines,
commonly regarded as the only strictly scientific principles of Voice Culture. These are, the rules for the
management of the breath, of the registers, of laryngeal
action, and of the resonance cavities, and also the directions for attacking the tone, and for forward emission. The second class of materials is held by strict
adherents of the scientific idea to be purely empirical:
this class includes the traditional precepts of the old
Italian school, and also all the topics of instruction
based on the singer's sensations. A third class of
materials is found in the attempts to interpret the empirical doctrines in the light of the scientific analysis
of the vocal action [1917, p. 97].

The scientific methods. A preface by Kobbé to Miller's
Vocal Art-Science and Its Application states that the author
holds that "neither art nor science alone suffices, but that
art must be achieved through strict adherence to scientific
rules" [Miller, 1917, vii]. "Every art has its origin, to a
greater or less degree, in some science.... There can be
no voice without a functioning vocal apparatus, the physiological activity of which gives origin not only to the voice, but
to the correct mechanism of its production, which establishes
the scientific foundation of singing" [Marafioti, 1925, p. 14].
"The study of physiology is indispensable to the vocal teacher"
[Kofler, 1897, p. 20]. "The subject of the mechanism of
voice culture is one of muscular control" [Russell, 1912, p.
7]. Too lengthy and involved for quotation here, but one of

the earliest and most effective arguments for a physiological method is that found in Brown and Behnke's Voice, Speech and Song, 1883, pp. 9-13.

The empirical, anti-physiological methods. "The art of singing is an aesthetic art, not an anatomical study. It begins with an ideal dwelling in the realm of the conception of tonal beauty, not in the domain of correct movement of muscles" [Henderson, 1906, p. 69].

> I hold ... that a knowledge of physiology is of little practical value to the singer, as such. Nay, more: that such knowledge, unless its limitations are fully appreciated, is deceptive, often misleading. A fore-man in a piano factory who is thoroughly acquainted with the whole mechanism of a pianoforte, in detail, as a whole, and its relation to quality of sound ... is nevertheless, no better equipped for a pianist than any raw youth who does not know the difference between the hammer and the dampers [Rogers, 1895, p. 68].

"From beginning to end of vocal production the tone concept is the only guide ... the most important part of the teacher's work is that of forming the pupil's taste in tone quality ... the tone is the thing, and ... how it sounds is his [the pupil's] primary concern" [Clippinger, 1910, p. 7].

The combinative method. "The three--nature, phys-iology and psychology--must be combined in any book that professes to offer a synthetic method of voice-production" [Miller, 1910, p. 5]. In defining the use of sensation for guidance in tonal development, Taylor states, "an understand-ing of the muscular processes of singing is not sufficient to furnish a complete method of instruction" [1917, p. 67].

Other thoughts on teaching systems. "Any method giving good results is a good method, the name of the method matters but little,--what we want is results" [Proschowsky, 1923, p. 3].

> The whole matter of voice training has been clouded by controversy. The student advocates of various sys-tems, each of them 'the only true method,' have in their disputes overcast the subject with much that is irrelevant, thus obscuring its essential simplicity.
>   The 'scientific' teachers, at one extreme, have paid too exclusive attention to the mechanics of the

voice. The 'empiricists' have gone to the other extreme in leaving out of account fundamental facts in
acoustics, physiology, and psychology.

The truth is that no purely human function, especially one so subtle as singing, can be developed me-
chanically; nor, on the other hand, can the mere ipse
dixit of any teacher satisfy the demands of the modern
spirit [Fillebrown, 1911, p. 4].

THEORIES : PRELIMINARY CONSIDERATIONS

Benefits of Vocal Study

Many authors assume that the reader is interested in
a professional singing career. A few consider the non-pro-
fessional benefits:

Vocal training ... tends to promote health, physical
and intellectual.... Singing has a refining effect on
the moral feelings; it promotes health of body and
vigor of mind; affords an agreeable relaxation when
worn down by labor or wearied by study [Day, 1839,
p. 13].

Advantages of the early and continued cultivation of
vocal music.

I.   It improves the voice, in speaking and reading,
     by giving smoothness, volume and variety to the
     tone.
II. Vocal Music conduces to health....
IV. Vocal Music tends to produce social order and
     happiness in a family....
V.   The course of instruction pursued in the Manual,
     is intellectual and disciplinary [Mason, 1847, p.
     18].

Miller [1917, p. 196] recommends singing for hygienic
reasons, and Bishenden speaks of its benefit to health [1876,
Preface] and humor alike [1875, p. 28].

Prerequisites of Vocal Study

A number of physical and mental abilities are considered valuable or indispensable to success in singing. Some
authors require many skills and talents:

Study and diligence, however, where the aim is only
to please may lead to sufficient proficiency in a comparatively short time, with the following requisites:
1stly, a correct ear; 2ndly, a tolerably good voice;
3rdly, a knowledge of the language; 4thly, a suscep-
tibility of feeling; 5thly, an acquaintance with the rudiments of the pianoforte.

But those who aspire to become first-rate singers,
besides the above, must possess the six following:
1stly, not merely a fine voice, but one of that description which possesses firmness as well as expansion,
with sufficient powers of execution to perform with
delicacy and precision, any piece composed for the
particular voice of the individual. 2ndly, a long continued discipline, according to the best Italian method.
3rdly, a knowledge of musical declamation.... 4thly,
the capacity of singing with precision the grandest or
most brilliant conceptions of the composer or poet,
and thus identifying himself with the character to be
represented. 5thly, a creative genius to vary and
embellish any given subject. 6thly, a knowledge of
the theory of harmony [Anfossi, 180-, p. 8].

It is presumed that the pupil purposing to study by
this work is already a performer of the Piano Forte,
possessing a good ear, and sufficient indicator of
Voice, to warrant a course of vocal exercise [Cooke,
1828, Introduction].

The qualities with which a merely correct singer ought
to be endowed are, --A just intonation, a voice of
either a silvery or flute-like character, ... a scru-
pulous precision in the time prescribed by the music,
--the vowel sounded with that exact conformation of
the mouth and throat which respectively belongs to
them, --a regular ... articulation of the consonants;
and lastly, a symmetrical and agreeable form and
movement of the mouth.

A sublime singer ought to enjoy the following attributes, --a method, or style of singing original and
elevated, joined to a natural vivacity of expression.
Then comes the last and greatest requisite of all --
genius --genius --genius! [Costa, 1838, p. 30].

'To sing, three things are necessary, and they are
Voice, Voice, Voice. '---Rossini
'A donkey also has a voice. '---Simon Mayr

'Sing on the interest, and conserve the capital of the voice.'---Rubini....

Rossini claims that to be a singer, natural vocal qualities are necessary. Mayr asserts that intelligence is of just as great importance. Rubini advises work and study which will develop a person's artistic qualities with a certain sense of economy, --a process tending to avoid the exposure of vocal organs to any kind of overwork (forcing) [Wronski, 1921, xv, xviii].

The voice. Wronski is only one of many who quote Rossini's famous aphorism. Lamperti uses the original Italian: "Voce, voce e poi voce" [1883, p. 18]. Marafioti, however, in 1925, warns that the age in which the only requirement was "'voice, voice, and more voice' is gone forever" [p. 10]. Despite the lengthy quotation of Anfossi on the subject (see above), voice seems to have been the major criterion of a singer to the exclusion of many attributes required in the late nineteenth and early twentieth centuries. D'Aubigny, for example, states that the primary factor among "die Naturgaben eines grossen Sänger [ist] eine Stimme"/ the natural gifts of a great singer is a voice [1803, p. 123], while Furtado relies on a statement of Reina, a tenor of some renown, to make the point: 'I know but little of music.... If you want to sing, it is not studying harmony and the piano--power and flexibility of the voice is your chief aim' [18--, p. 4].

The musical ear and intonation. 'Hearing' is the only rival to 'voice' in the early years dealt with in this study as the prime requisite to becoming a singer:

Kurz, alle Naturfehler, die der guten Stimme hinderlich sind, können durch Fleiss, Uebung, und Geduld verbessert werden [ausser denen, denen es] gänzlich am musikalischen Gehöre fehlt/ In short, all natural failings that hinder a good voice can, by industry, practice and patience, be improved [except in those who] completely lack a musical ear [Hiller, 1780, p. 4].

A singer ought to have a good ear, which is a most important and indispensable requisite [Corri, 1811, p. 1].

If the ear is defective, or in other words, the Scholar cannot sing in tune, the prospect then is dreary and discouraging [Clifton, 1846, p. 4].

Bassini [1857, p. 9] and Minoja [1815, p. 15] both agree that intonation is most important and its lack the greatest possible fault.   Corfe recognizes both requirements:

> That rules may be given towards obtaining this most desirable object [learning to sing], there is no doubt although there is an old proverb mentioned by Tosi, that an hundred perfections are requisite in an excellent singer, but he that has a fine voice is possessed of ninety-nine of them.   To sing in tune, with a good intonation and expression, a proper regard to the time, and delivery of the words, are the chief constituents of a good taste in singing [18--, p. 3].

Others who recognize a musical ear as a prime requisite in later years include Daniell [1873, p. 97] and Rutz [1908, p. 151].

Ear training.   Rogers [1910, p. 18] and Taylor believe that every student must work on improving his sense of hearing.   "There is only one way that the musical ear can be trained; this is by attentive listening to musical sounds" [Taylor, 1914, p. 7].

Sight singing.   Bishenden makes a plea in his book for sight singing courses "for all our private and public schools," in England, just as was done in his time in Germany.   This, he thinks, gave German singers a distinct advantage over beginning singers in England [1875, p. 24].

Health.   Bacon is the earliest of those who recognize the need for good health in this athletic art: "One of the capital tests of the ability to make a professional singer, I apprehend to be such a natural structure of the organs of sound as will sustain the wear and tear of the continual stress from the necessary practice" [1824, p. 96].

The study of music.   "The person who sings without a knowledge of music is as much a singer as he is a painter, who confines his pictorial art study to the copying of 'Etudes aux deux Crayons'" [Browne, 1887, p. 7].   "The singer's training must include the same subjects that form the training of every musician" [Taylor, 1917, p. 5].   Henderson suggests studying the piano, foreign languages, sight reading, and the principles of musical analysis [1906, pp. 258-268].   Duff also suggests piano and the study of harmony [1919, p. 3].

Extra-musical knowledge.   "I think that perhaps the

most important thing for every ambitious young vocal student to remember is that underlying all great art in song is the widest possible knowledge of other things besides music. The broader her cultural outlook, the greater her mental development, the wider her circle of human and intellectual interests, the better she will sing" [Sophie Braslau in Martens, 1923, p. 31].

Forgo choral singing. "There is the tendency to shout louder than your neighbour, to use yourself to the bad habits of those on each side of you" [Crowest, 1900, p. 69].

The Vocal Training Period

Training should begin early. Statements on early vocal training range from 1811, when Corri writes, "A singer ought to be instructed at a very early period in life, and the practice ought to be gradual" [p. 2] to 1923, when Proschowsky writes, "Of all the arts, none is more dependent on an early beginning" [pp. 2-3]. In between there are Browne, who suggests that the pupil start "as soon as he can read.... [T]he earlier the teaching is commenced the greater will be the mechanical success" [1887, p. 47]; Seiler, who believes that 9 or 10 years is a good starting age [1871, pp. 174-180]; and among others Clifton, who suggests that girls may begin at 10 or 11 [1846, p. 4].

Some sanction early training but warn against training boys during mutation: "Children cannot commence too soon [but] ... men [should] avoid singing during mutation" [Nathan, 1836, p. 111]. Lablache also suggests interruption of study during mutation [184-, p. 3], while Pfeiffer and Nägeli recommend that girls begin at 15 or 16 but that boys should not begin until after mutation is complete [1830, p. 7].

Training should not begin early. Wieck is opposed to "this erroneous instruction of children in singing," stating that lessons cause children to force delicate voices [1875, p. 104]. Kofler thinks that boys should not begin before 19 or 20 and girls, before 17 or 18. However, beyond 35, "I should say it was too late" [1897, p. 104].

Singing cannot be quickly mastered. Bach warns that a complete course of study will require "several years under a master" [1880, p. 11], and Botume gives the figures, "four to seven years" [1897, p. 7]. Henderson says simply, "many years" [1906, p. 19]. Others have more to say:

> If an individual expects to train and cultivate his voice, and acquire a thorough, practical knowledge of vocal music in a short time, he may be assured that he expects what has never been accomplished by any one else [Day, 1839, pp. 7-8].

> Supposing vocal music can be taught in a few months. This is a fatal mistake and ruinous to correct execution. No one can learn to sing without active persevering, and long continued effort [Mason, 1847, p. 24; on page 26, he says this can take from six to eight years].

Emma Calvé observes that "you cannot perfect a pianist or a violinist in three months and certainly not a voice" [Martens, 1923, p. 38]. Shakespeare uses the same argument [1910, p. 177]. Wronski quotes Rubini as having said, "The study of our art is too long for our life. When young we have the voice but lack the schooling, afterward we get the schooling but lose the voice" [1921, p. 70]. "To sing finely is the work of a life. It is a profession which must be learned and exercised as the apprentice to any trade acquires and pursues his art" [Bacon, 1824, p. 50]. Mackenzie and Randegger both bemoan the result of hurried methods: "The great lack of good voices now generally complained of, is no doubt principally due to the feverish hurry and impatience of modern life which makes pupils and teachers alike more anxious for immediate success, however ephemeral" [Mackenzie, 1891, p. 124; Randegger's quotation is found in 1912, Preface].

General Objectives

Although the table for this chapter lists 18 statements under the heading "Objectives of vocal training," there are actually almost as many objectives as there are methodological approaches, literally dozens, contained in the sources surveyed. In most cases the objectives are so complex and dispersed throughout the books that quotation is impossible. For example, reading Browne and Behnke's Voice, Speech and Song for only a few pages will indicate to the reader that the objective of this book is to use physiological coordination to improve the voice. The objective of Ffrangçon-Davies' The Singing of the Future may be summarized as "relaxation."

Nine statements have been chosen which represent popular objectives throughout the period of this study:

Überhaupt kann Lehrenden und Lernenden die Regel nicht genung empfohlen werden, dass man in Erlerning des Gesanges der Natur nichts abzwingen, sondern alles nur nach und nach, durch überlegten und anhaltenden Fleisse, von ihr erhalten müsse/ Most of all, the rule cannot be recommended enough to teachers and pupils that in learning to sing, Nature cannot be forced; rather everything must be obtained from her gradually, by carefully considered and restrained diligence [Hiller, 1780, p. 8].

The voice should be formed in the most pleasing tone possible and delivered steady and clear, without passing through the nose, or being cloaked in the throat, which are two of the greatest imperfections a singer can be guilty of [Corfe, 18--, p. 3].

We are naturally affected by sounds, and various passions and emotions are excited by means of our sense of hearing, independently of the association attached to words. Mr. Burke has observed that great or sudden or tremulous sounds produce emotions of the sublime, and he quotes the effects of soft and sweet sounds in music, as causes of the beautiful. To unite these effects of sound with the impressions conveyed by language, and by their conjoint influence to heighten those impressions, is the primary object of the art of singing [Bacon, 1824, p. 18].

In 1838, Costa lists the objectives of vocal training as developing the true character of the voice, uniting the registers, combining vowel with consonant, and perfecting the messa di voce and the portamento [p. 35].

The conditions of good vocalizing are, first, to know how to hold the mouth well; second, to breathe well; third, to form and send forth the sounds of the different registers; fourth, to pass insensibly from the sound of one register to those of another; fifth, to attack and connect sounds for forming successions [Lablache, 184-, p. 4].

In the introduction to Voice and Vocal Art (1856), Sabilla Novello lists the objectives of practice as management of the breath, correct intonation, extended compass, and beauty of tone.

Garcia, in his typical dialectic style, writes as follows:

Q. What is the object of vocal study?
A. To make the voice irreproachable in its intonation, firm, strong, flexible, extended, and to correct its faults.
Q. Is that all?
A. To teach the student the art of phrasing, to familiarize him with the different styles, and to develop his expression [1894, p. 1].

The teacher must avoid overloading the comprehensions of the pupils with long and complicated dissertations, which only produce confusion in the mind of the neophyte.... The teacher must present his explanations in a practical rather than theoretical way [S. Marchesi, 1902, p. 6].

The cultivation of the singing voice presents, at once, two obvious but distinct propositions:

1. The essential requirements, as manifested by the standard of the world's leading artists.
2. The individual characteristics, vocal (physiological) and mental, of the ambitious singer....

The proposition that at the very outset confronts teacher and pupil is to find ways and means whereby the individual characteristics of the pupil may be adapted to the demands of the art [Wronski, 1921, p. 3].

Coordination as a Primary Physiological Factor

A number of authors observe that singing is the coordination of a threefold system which consists of "1) a motor, 2) a vibratory, and 3) a resonant element" [Mackenzie, 1891, p. 26; Holmes, 1879, p. 79]. General coordination is recognized as the antithesis of local efforts by Witherspoon [1925, p. 67]: "Correct coordination of the vocal organs is dependent, first, upon correct breathing, and second, upon correct pronunciation; and that any undue attention to, or persistence in, or stress laid upon one part or 'local' [sic] ... will interfere with that coordination." To Myer, coordination signifies the ability to balance pressure and resistance:

"In the training of the voice, there are constantly two forces to be considered, pressure and resistance, the motor power or driving force and the resisting or controlling force. A right training of the voice is a study, not only to develop both of these forces, but to equalize them, to balance them, to harmonize them" [1897, p. 16].

The Standardization of Vocal Training

Standardization is possible. In this period, only four sources were uncovered that discuss the possibility of standardization in vocal training. None argue that there can be one book or method, but the arguments in favor of standardization hinge rather on the concept that there are basic truths applicable to all students, regardless of the method of inculcating these truths:

> Almost every prominent teacher believes himself to possess a method peculiarly his own; it would not be easy to find two masters who agree on every point, practical as well as theoretical. But this confusion of methods is only on the surface. All teachers draw the materials of their methods from the same sources [Taylor, 1917, xi].

> Why is it so difficult to get any twenty persons interested in the matter [of vocal pedagogy] to agree as to what is good or bad for each voice, so far as tone production is concerned? Is not this lack of unanimity largely due to the wide divergences of opinion as to how the tone itself is produced? ... To my mind it is indispensable that thousands of individual cases should be presented to give scope to the widest observation in order to furnish a solid foundation of fact on which we all can take our stand, working, each on his own lines, yet in general harmony, toward a common goal [Miller, 1917, p. 6].

Standardization is not possible. The major argument against standardization of method is that of the individuality of each singer. "It is the teacher's duty, his art, to train the voice according to its individuality" [Heinrich, 1910, pp. 21-22].

At the very outset, two points must be borne in mind:

1. Each and every voice and mentality is individual.

> 2. The artist has become a law unto himself; it
> is not possible for him to make rules for others
> [Brower, 1920, pp. 266-267].

In preparing a practical synthetic system of vocal development, it is advisable to point out clearly at the
outset that no two voices can be trained in exactly
the same manner, for the reason that all voices possess either different defects, or the same defects in
different degrees. ... Method must be utilized by
the singer and teacher to meet the requirements of
each individual case [Shaw, 1914, p. 157].

Professional singers are particularly opposed to set
methods. Only Caruso, among this group, recognizes that
some rules and concepts can be standardized:

So one may see that there are actually as many methods as there are singers, and any particular method,
even if accurately set forth, might be useless to the
person who tried it.... However, there are many
interesting and valuable things to be said about the
voice in a general way [1909, pp. 50-51].

I think all voice training methods should be individual.
I loathe methods [Ernestine Schumann-Heink, as quoted
in Martens, 1928, p. 268].

Why spend years in dreaming of theories regarding
singing when everyone knows that the theory of singing
has been the battleground for innumerable talented
writers for centuries? Even now it is apparently impossible to reconcile the vocal writers, except in so
far as they all modestly admit that they have redis-
covered the real old Italian school [Clara Butt in Cooke,
1921, p. 62].

METHODS : THE PSYCHOLOGICAL APPROACH

Importance of the Psychological Approach

Twenty-six writers noted the importance of psychology
in a thorough method, but only two of these authors are found
in the period prior to 1900: "Der Sänger leitet seine Stimme
mit seinem Willen und seiner Intelligenz"/ the singer guides

his voice with his will and his intelligence [Panofka, 1859, p. 7]. "The mind or will-power is the great controlling force or influence in the training of the voice. It is a power for evil or for good, according as it is correctly or incorrectly applied. If the teacher or pupil has not learned to think a-right, it is easy to see how the will-force may be in the direction of the wrong" [Myer, 1891, p. 97].

Primary work is done in the brain. "Let your brain work before your voice does" [Duff, 1919, p. 75]. "Singing, after all, is a mental attitude" [Wronski, 1921, p. 21]. "A tone first of all is a mental product and its pitch, power, and quality are definite mental entities" [Clippinger, 1917, p. 6]. Of the singer, Clippinger says, "He will never sing a better tone than the one he thinks" [1917, p. 43].

> Of course there is much study, much earnest work to be done, but in the main it is mental, i. e. , the establishment of proper ideals; correct appreciation of tone quality; a true conception of that subtle sensation which so plainly tells the initiated of the poise of the voice; a clear comprehension of that priceless thing almost lost to us today, legato speech in song; phrasing, nuance of force and tone color [Russell, 1912, p. 3].

Psychological sensation related to physiological knowledge.

> Both the results of modern anatomical study and the deduction of advanced psychological research should be recognized in the use of that subtle and beautiful thing, the human voice, which in its ultimate quality is a combination of physiological and psychological phenomena [Miller, 1910, p. 3].

> As the vocal instrument is essentially plastic to the will, and adapted to express whatever the mind formulates, mind becomes the ruling factor.... Yet in many cases we train the instrument only, or at least, we make it our chief consideration, instead of training the singer, who is the real motive that causes the vocal machinery to produce one effect rather than another [Rogers, 1910, p. 3].

> A note cannot be physically absolutely right without a feeling under it--without meaning. Thus we see that the work done and the consciousness must be all body.

> The singer must thus feel inside himself and express, and the more feeling, or atmosphere, or psychological force he has inside of him, the less physical and the freer and looser the voice becomes, until we arrive at the fact that the entire consciousness must be not only body but expressing [Stanley, 1916, p. 3].

Habit Formation in Vocal Training

Two major ideas are associated in habit formation; that habits can be good or bad, and that good habits restore the natural ease of the vocal act by what is termed "second nature." Myer addresses himself to the first concept when he writes, "A constantly recurring movement will develop an automatic action, either to be desired or dreaded as it may be right or wrong. It should be the aim of the pupil to develop a correct automatic action of all the parts of the voice production apparatus; an action which is the result of correct thought" [1891, p. 97]. Russell, Fillebrown and Miller also remark that habits can be good or bad.

Thirteen authors and singers believe that "l'habitude est une seconde nature"/ habit is second nature [Frossard, 1914, p. 4]. Among this group are Muckey [1915, p. 9], Fillebrown [1911, p. 77], Parisotti [1911, p. 130], Myer [1886, p. 8, p. 18], and Morgan Kingston [as quoted in Brower, 1920, p. 215]. For reason of space, only three of many valuable statements can be presented. The first and third represent the subgroup that discusses both concepts of habit formation.

> The 'let go' means let the body go with the thought, it is then not a question of making the physical nature do the thing, it is allowing the process to go into automatic action; correct habit has been so positively established upon nature's basic materials and laws, that we may now say that to do rightly, is at least second nature, as we may say of all confirmed habits of the mind and body, whether they be correct or incorrect [Russell, 1912, p. 23].

> The cry for naturalness in art-practice is an error, because it tells only the first part of the truth. Nature supplies the materials, not the methods, for art-work. The use of these materials is a matter of culture, which induces habit.... The mind then directs a con-

tinuance or a succession of correct activities till, at last, a right habit is established, and this we sometimes ... call 'second nature' [Russell, 1904, p. 7].

The very first principle of a vocal method should be to establish so correct a use of the vocal organs that nature in this respect becomes second nature. For correct action of the voice-organs can develop into a habit so perfectly acquired that the singer acts upon it automatically, and the most disastrous result of poor teaching is that a bad habit can also become second nature and it is almost impossible to eradicate [Miller, 1910, p. 6].

Singing as a Natural Function

The vocal act is unconscious and voluntary. Ffrangçon-Davies declares that the objective of practice is to achieve an unconscious art [1904, p. 67]. When Shakespeare opposes the concept of laryngeal control, he writes, "With the throat open during singing, and the breath controlled underneath, the vocal cords perform their functions unconsciously, and we know by their responding unerringly on the pitch, that their action has not been disturbed" [1924, p. 19]. "Singers ... wonder at last why their voices have so soon worn out. The answer is readily found; they have tried to discount nature, ... and endeavored to make their vocal apparatus do certain things by muscular effort, which things should have been allowed, not forced to operate" [Russell, 1904, p. 5].

Spontaneity and naturalness are primary factors. "Spontaneity is a necessity for the highest expression of our emotion in singing ... [and] to achieve spontaneity of expression should be the first and principal aim of those who desire to attain their ideal in the art of singing" [Rogers, 1895, p. 40]. "The greatest error in the cultivation of this complex and wonderful instrument, the human voice, is the attempt to take out of the hands of Nature that which Nature intended for herself" [Shaw, 1914, p. 104]. "The art of singing is the most intricate of any and yet the most simple. In other words, while the cultivated artist will have plenty of use for all his intelligence and his years of education, it is nevertheless true that his or her work is really greatly in proportion as it approaches naturalness" [Wronski, 1921, p. 3]. "There is only one way to sing correctly, and that is to sing naturally, easily, comfortably. The height of vocal art is to have no apparent method, but to be able to sing with perfect facility from one end of the voice to the other" [Tetrazzini, 1909, p. 10].

Freeing the Vocal Mechanism

Relaxation as a factor in voice training. The term "relaxation" embraces a number of concepts that aim to keep all undue effort from the body in singing. Relaxation is the major theme of Ffrangçon-Davies in The Singing of the Future (1904). In 1785, without giving the concept a name, Tenducci made it his Rule X, writing, "In the exercise of singing, never to discover any Pain or Difficulty by distortion of the Mouth or Grimace of any Kind. " For Shryock, the term is "open": "Sing with an open sound. " [1856, p. 1], while Emmy Destinn repeats the rule of the bel canto period, "When I sing I feel as if I have no throat" [as quoted by Marafioti, 1922, p. 79]. "Relaxation" is one popular twentieth-century term. "Signor Alessandro Bonci ... says: 'The great secret of voice production is relaxity. Every tone should be produced without an effort, and without any apparent stiffening of the muscles'" [White, 1909, p. 73]. "Complete relaxation of the entire body is your first principle" [Duff, 1919, p. 10]. Another early 1900's term is "freedom":

> The basic sensation of correct singing, as generally described, is a feeling of perfect poise and harmony of the whole body; this is accompanied by a sense of freedom about the throat and jaw, and firm grasp and control of the expiratory muscles.... A feeling of 'Absence of local effort' at the throat is much spoken of, or 'perfect relaxation of the vocal muscles' [Taylor, 1917, p. 79].

> The lips, tongue, lower jaw and larynx should be free from all rigidity. This does not mean that they are to be lifeless and flabby, but that they are not to be held rigidly in one position. They must be ready to respond instantly to the will of the singer, and this they will not do unless they are free from tension [Clippinger, 1910, p. 11].

Economy of effort as a factor. This seems to be one of the more universal concepts of the 150-year period. "It is a happy fact that the right way is the easiest way, and a fundamental truth that right effort is the result of right thought"

[Fillebrown, 1911, p. 56]. As early as 1780, Hiller recognized that more could be gained from the voice by coaxing than by straining [p. 8]. In the nineteenth century, Bacon notes, "Some exertion is always necessary to practice to extend the compass and enlarge the volume of the voice, but especial care should be taken to apportion this force, if so strong a word may be applied to so slight an action, with the utmost caution" [1824, pp. 95-96]. "Beware of being flattered into the belief that a strong and powerful voice is to be preferred; many persons are known to sing loudly, but few sweetly" [Cooke, 1828, Introduction]. "Perfect ease and relaxation of the body, and an entire absense of effort are necessary to produce a healthy tone" [Oliver, 186-, p. 4].

Salvatore Marchesi quotes, without acknowledgment, Rubini's aphorism, "Sing with the interest, not the principal" [1902, p. 10]. Other valuable thoughts on the subject in twentieth-century sources can be found in Rogers [1910, p. 67], Fillebrown [1911, p. 5], Brower [1920, p. 54], Wronski [1921, p. 69], and Fucito [1922, p. 122] in addition to the three statements quoted here:

> The great bane of the voice student is the idea of
> 'forcing.' He cannot believe that with primal condi-
> tions correctly established the singer's art is exqui-
> sitely simple. We are always trying to make our
> throats, our mouths, our lips do something, while
> the fact is, if we will let the stronger parts, the mus-
> cles of the body take the effort as nature intends and
> demands, the effort of singing is really as simple as
> that of fervent speech [Russell, 1904, p. 9].

> There is always a temptation to try to make low notes
> heavy and round. Yielding to this temptation results
> only in making the tones throaty and robbing them of
> their normal carrying power. Less muscular effort
> is required, the lower you sing [Taylor, 1914, p. 55].

> The full extension of the natural range of the voice is
> produced only by using the minimum tension of the
> vocal cords, and the minimum breath required for each
> tone ... freedom is the fundamental pillar of voice
> production [Marafioti, 1922, p. 50].

Overcoming inhibitions and fears. Eleven authors acknowledge the fears and inhibitions associated with public performance. "Fear, doubt and misgivings are fatal to achievement" [Rogers, 1910, p. 71]. "Conquer any alarm which may seize you on going to sing, by recollecting the general goodwill of society, and the kind reception which the public always bestows on merit; remember also that every hearer is not a judge" [Bacon, 1824, p. 51].

> In the final analysis, that lack of self-consciousness, that ease and spontaneity which we associate with the highest art, is ... the result of method and training .... Once acquired, method is merged into habit and habit into seeming instinct.... Under such favorable conditions created by a correct method of instruction, the nervousness inseparable from a debut ... is disguised by an assumption of calm, into which the poise and aspect of a trained singer naturally fall [Miller, 1910, pp. 29-30].

Fillebrown suggests the concept of quiet, deep breathing as a momentary remedy for nervousness [1911, p. 27]. Clara Rogers offers a chapter of nine pages toward dealing with fear in performance. She stresses good preparation in practice and "concentration on the song you are singing" [1925, pp. 83-91].

Singing as Self-Expression

Five authors point out to their readers that they can use singing as a vehicle for personal expression.

> In no way can personal expression find a medium so effective as through the voice, whether in the actor's interpretation of a great dramatist, a singer's rendering of a glorious composition, a speaker's enunciation of the moral law, or in the intercourse of daily life [Miller, 1917, p. 5].

> It is of the greatest importance also to remember that the art of singing is an art of self expression from beginning to end, and this fact should be observed, kept constantly in mind at every stage of training. The moment we forget the fact, we are in danger of degenerating into vocal artificiality [Shaw, 1914, p. 159].

Singing Compared to Speaking

Within the limits of this study, Bacon is the first to

compare singing and speaking. He writes, "Some ... suppose the voice in singing to imitate the tones of passion in speech, and there is undoubtedly some analogy" [1824, p. 30]. Daniell represents four writers who say, "Singing and speaking are (or should be) identical" [1873, p. 16]. There are other variations of the idea: "Correct speaking will lead to correct singing, as speaking and singing are modulations of the same function" [Wronski, 1921, p. 39] or "Singing is intensified speech; we should show no more effort about the mouth, face, shoulders, etc. , when singing, than in fervent speech" [Russell, A Plain Talk with American Singers, 1904, p. 12].

Three writers observe differences in speaking and singing:

> In the utterances of the speakers we hear the voice as an agent of the brain, as an outward expression of mental activity, making intelligible the working of the mind. Here sound follows a secondary office.... But in the tones of the singer we listen to the voice as an acoustic principle, produced mainly under a material influence. Here sound attracts us in its physical character, and in its infinite qualities of pitch, and ... arouses ... the emotional sensibilities of the brain [Holmes, 1879, p. 51].

> The kind of tones employed in speaking are different from those used in singing....
> In speaking breath is taken without any thought just as often as it is necessary to replenish the store in the lungs. In singing it is essential to look ahead and perceive where breath can be conveniently taken without disturbing the outline of the melody which is sung. Again, in speaking we do not particularly concern ourselves about the quality of our tones, but permit them to issue from the throat in their spontaneous timbre.
> In singing we aim to produce the most beautiful tones of which our throats are capable. But ... the normal operations of the lungs and throat are the foundations of good singing.... The truth is that while speaking is nature, singing is nothing more than nature under high cultivation [Henderson, 1906, pp. 67-68].

> In singing the flow of tone is unbroken between the words, but in speaking it is interrupted. In singing

tone is sustained and changed from one pitch to another by definite intervals over a wide compass that includes notes not attempted in speech. In speaking tone is unsustained, not defined in pitch, is limited to a narrow compass, and the length of the tones is not governed by the measure of music.

Notwithstanding these differences, singing and speaking tones are produced by the vocal organs in the same way, are focused precisely alike, have the same resonance, and are delivered in the same manner.... Speech may be called the prose, and song the poetry of vocalization [Fillebrown, 1911, p. 17].

METHODS : THE TECHNICAL APPROACH

Technical Principles and Objectives and Their Defense

As was already stated in this chapter, many concepts on the level of objectives are not expressed by authors per se; rather, a philosophy must be gleaned from the majority of authors as to the degree of emphasis they wish placed on aesthetics or science, physiology or psychology. Nevertheless, 22 statements have been discovered that express technical principles and objectives in succinct fashion.

Absolute technique alone renders the vocal artist able to animate every tone, giving it mental and physical expression. Vocal art, like all other arts, requires its specific technicality as a means toward the end [Lankow, 1903, p. 7].

Some have ridiculed the idea that an acquaintance with this subject [vocal physiology] is of any more use to the vocalist than is the anatomy of the hand to the pianist. But the examples are not analagous, inasmuch as the pianist obtains his instrument ready made for him, and if he wear it out or injure it he can purchase another, while the vocalist has to form his voice, and if he wrongly use it, it may be gone for ever [Browne and Behnke, 1883, pp. 1-3].

To avoid local effort is a result of advanced culture; the novice, in seeking results, must first localize his efforts [Russell, 1912, p. 8; Fillebrown concurs, 1911, p. 51].

It [singing] does not just come--there are no chances

in singing--you must know what you do and why you do it. It is based upon inviolable laws and you must master these laws [Duff, 1919, p. 7; this point is agreed upon by Lehmann and Tetrazzini].

The old Italians attached so much importance to beautiful tone that they were willing to work conscientiously for half a dozen years to obtain it. To the beautiful tone they added a faultless technique [Clippinger, 1916, p. 2].

It might help the student to look upon singing as a negative work. That is to say, the only work required is so to control the muscles that not one of them shall start or jerk [White, 1927, p. 50].

... I shall be told that tones well sung, even unconsciously, are enough. But that is not true. The least unfavorable circumstance, overexertion, an unaccustomed situation, anything can blow out the 'unconscious' one's light, or at least make it flicker badly [Lehmann, 1924, p. 30].

Removing Muscular Interferences

"Without the proper co-operation of the muscles, it is impossible to accomplish anything" [Guttmann, 1882, p. 16]. Myer writes in The Voice from a Practical Standpoint that the greater the effort to locally control muscles, the greater will be the rigidity [1886, p. 89]. In Truths of Importance to Vocalists, Myer writes:

The ability on the part of singers to place themselves upon a level, as it were, with the high notes of their voices, that peculiar movement which enables them to produce the high tone, without effort or strain, without pushing or reaching for them, is of vast importance to all voices [1883, p. 68].

There must be as little action as possible of any muscles but such as directly assist the production of voice. The hideous muscular contortions of the face and neck, and the swelling of the veins in those parts sometimes seen in singing are the result of bad habit, and prove that the natural powers are being overstrained [Mackenzie, 1891, p. 122].

Handling Beginners

      Two areas especially germane to the beginning student are the considerations of classification of the student's voice type and what to expect from first lessons.

      Classifying voices. "Before everything, it is essential that the true quality of the voice should be once and for all determined. This is the keystone of the arch.... It is not always, however, an easy matter to recognize the natural order to which a given voice belongs.... Mere pitch is not a safe guide" [Mackenzie, 1886, pp. 160-161]. Most writers of the period prior to Mackenzie's work, however, did consider pitch (or range) the primary determinate. Both Bassini [1857, p. 7] and Everest [1861, p. 28] divide the voices into three groups each for men and women and imply that a person who sings best in a particular range as indicated in a diagram will automatically be of that voice type.

      In later years, the popular determinate changed to timbre. "Remember always that the character of a voice is determined not by compass or range of notes, but by quality, or body and timbre, of tone" [Crowest, 1900, p. 29]. Other authors who consider timbre most important in determining voice type are Bach [1880, p. 63], Lunn [1904, p. 28], and Proschowsky [1923, p. 20].

      Many authors consider both range and timbre in classification. Authors who belong to this group include Holmes [1879, p. 134], Miller [1910, pp. 119-120], Randegger [1912, p. 5], Seiler [1871, p. 67], and Bacon and Tetrazzini, chosen here for their typical viewpoints:

> The voice numbers four distinct genera, which are again divided into several species.... The distinctions lie not only in the compass, or number of notes which each is capable of sounding, but in the power or volume, and in the quality [Bacon, 1824, p. 88].

> The important task of discovering whether a voice is bass, baritone, tenor, contralto, mezzo-soprano, or soprano, and the exact character of the general ranges of these voices is a matter of great delicacy, and cannot be decided at one hearing. It is largely individual, and sometimes a matter of health and circumstances....
> It is not a question of compass only but of compass in addition to the distinctive character and quality of

the voice.... Lamperti's practice was to judge not only by the notes which could be taken, but by the facility with which words could be enunciated on them at the same time [Tetrazzini, 1923, pp. 39, 40].

It should be observed (above) that Tetrazzini believes the character of the voice must be slowly and carefully determined. Stanley and Myer concur:

One does not train a voice as a soprano, or contralto, or any thing else. One merely starts poising the voice and getting it on timbre and the body under it, and then--the voice reveals itself and goes up or down and becomes deeper and richer or more brilliant, according to its individual character [Stanley, 1916, pp. 20-21].

It is not important to surely know the style or natural order of the voice at the first start of study. The untrained voice is usually in an unnatural condition, and the quality and compass cannot always be depended upon to decide surely and correctly the style or natural order of the voice. Commence study as nearly as possible about the middle of the compass of the voice, or on the best tones of the voice.... As the voice gains strength and action ... it will finally seek and find its proper level and quality [Myer, 1891, pp. 227-228].

Caruso [1909, p. 51] and Kofler [1897, p. 122] also suggest starting with the middle range of the voice.

To range and timbre, Wronski adds vocal temperament [1921, pp. 8-13], while Salvatore Marchesi includes volume and intensity [1902, pp. 31-34].

Browne and Behnke uniquely classify voices by their structure, according to the size and thickness of the vocal ligaments [1883, pp. 74-77].

A final admonition may be added by Daniell (other quotations of this order may be found in Chapter Six, Range, under "Average compass of voices"):

No singer should endeavor to distort her voice from what it was intended to be; in other words, no contralto voice should be made into a soprano; no tenor should strive to cultivate his voice to become a bass [Daniell, 1873, p. 59].

First lessons. A variety of ideas fall collectively under the heading, "first lessons." The more popular concepts are quoted:

The average student leans too much upon his instructor, and is too apt to expect to be carried along by him. My advice to students is 'learn to think' and to come at once to a realization that it is they themselves who must do the work [Russell, Some Psychic Reflections for Singers, 1904, p. 4; the same idea is expressed by Lucrezia Bori in Martens, 1923, p. 3].

It is a false idea to consider that any teacher is good enough for a beginner. It is of far greater importance that the beginning should be made under the guidance of an experienced and capable master, even though it costs more than under an inferior one [F. Lamperti, 1883, p. 18; M. Marchesi, 1901, p. 11 and Crowest, 1900, p. 50 agree].

From the first lesson the utmost attention must be given to the beauty of the tone [Panofka, 1859, p. 7].

For first studies, phrases or songs should be selected in which the emotions demand wide contrasts in colors for their expression [Kirkland, 1916, p. 74].

Teaching with Songs

Songs are useful. Only six authors in this period believe that songs have a place in developing the voice. This concept has enjoyed greater success in more recent times, as is reflected in the counts of nine and 24 statements in Burgin and Fields, respectively. Taylor believes that "daily practice in the singing of songs and arias is fully as important a part of the singer's education as the practice of technical exercises. In the study of songs the student may find an artistic pleasure which makes voice culture a subject of never failing interest" [1914, p. 18]. Kirkland recommends as the most practical means of developing expressiveness, "the study of songs in which phrases occur indicating feelings which require an exaggerated use of some particular Means of Expression in order that the means may be better understood and more fully controlled" [1916, p. 132]. Parts of songs, according to Ffrangçon-Davies, may be used to bridge the gap between vocalises and full songs. "The best way to exercise them [words] is to take a phrase out of a lyric, or out of an aria (cantilene), and to treat it as if an exercise" [1904, p. 85]. Morgan Kingston also makes technical studies out of pieces that he uses, [Brower, 1920, p. 197], as does David Bispham [Brower, 1920, p. 216].

Vocalises are preferable as technical exercises. An appreciably greater number of authors prefer to keep the student on vocalises for a considerable length of time before attempting songs. This opinion dates back at least as far as Corri, who writes, "It is a misfortune attending our art, that songs are learned and sung before the rudiments are required" [1811, p. 2]. Lunn quotes Sabilla Novello, whose book appeared in 1856, as having written "The pure vowel induces a pure tone" [1904, p. 23]. Myer asserts that "wrong effort is aggravated ten-fold by the too-early use of words" [1886, p. 17]. Later opponents to the early use of song are Julia Clausson and Marafioti:

> One of the great troubles in America is the irrepressible ambition of both teachers and pupils.... Some teachers, I am told, start in with songs at the first or second lesson, with the sad knowledge that if they do not do this they may lose the pupil to some teacher who will peddle out songs. After four or five months I was given an operatic aria; and of course, I sang it. A year of scales, exercises and solfeggios would have been far more time-saving [Julia Clausson in Cooke, 1921, p. 96].

> When I told the maestro I wanted to learn a song he smiled and said, 'Your father is a surgeon. Ask him if, after a few days of study, he thought he could learn to perform an operation' [Marafioti, 1925, p. 251].

Principles and Procedures Used in Practicing

After theorization, practice is required. About this aspect of singing, authors also have much to say.

Principles of practice. "Execution is practice and nothing but practice, though, whether it be good or bad depends upon the inculcation of the first principles" [Bacon, 1824, p. 50]. Similar views are expressed by others. "There is an old adage that 'practice makes perfect,' and so it does, but it must be right practice" [Myer, 1886, p. 17]. "The voice is not invariably subject to the law that practice makes perfect.... The mere singing of technical exercises is not enough, it is of vital importance that the exercises be sung in some particular manner" [Taylor, 1917, pp. 5-6]. Nathan [1836, p. 113] regards singing as the same as any other athletic pursuit, i. e. , it requires daily calisthenics.

That the voice is a delicate instrument is noted by many authors. Oliver states that, "too long practice at one time is injurious" [186-, p. 4]. Bishenden instructs the student to take frequent rests, so as not to tire the voice [1876, p. 17].

Wronski believes the need for repose can be determined by the state of advancement: "The necessity for repose in vocal practice depends mostly upon the expenditure of strength. It is possible to practice a long time without danger, but with small intervals of rest. The human voice can stand easily several hours' work daily, but only when the tone is free" [1921, p. 80].

Louis Arthur Russell gives a reason why no hard-and-fast rules can be laid down concerning the length of practice:

> Clock practice is not to be entirely condemned, but it can be made a very bad guide, for hours are always discounted by brains, and for what one might accomplish in an hour, another will need much more time. Therefore, absolute rules for practice by the hour cannot be safely given ... but the voice ought never to be strained in the attempt to gain endurance [A Plain Talk with American Singers, 1904, p. 4].

Nevertheless, almost four dozen authors do suggest practice time intervals and lengths of repose in between. No two authors express exactly the same opinion, and slight differences in thought make it impossible to quote any authors as typical. The quotation of a dozen statements would only serve to yield twelve marginally different viewpoints. There can, however, be a generalized concept based on an averaging of statements. Such an average philosophy might be expressed as follows: For the beginner, two or three practice sessions every day of fifteen to thirty minutes' duration each.

Intervals of repose between thirty minutes and a few hours should be observed. For the more advanced student, two or three intermittent sessions of gradually increasing length up to but not exceeding an hour each time. The professional is expected to be able to sing for a number of hours without tiring.

Supervision of practice. Bacon quotes Tosi as having written, "If the scholar should have any defects of the nose, the throat, or the ear, let him never sing but when his master is by, or somebody that understands the profession, in order to correct him, otherwise he will get an ill habit, past all remedy" [1824, p. 90].

Two authors believe that supervision is most important in the early stages of voice training:

New pupils cannot, at first, clearly understand all the explanations given by the teacher concerning the respiration, the placing of the voice, the definition of the registers, etc. It is therefore advisable that, during a few weeks, the teacher make a new pupil sing ten or fifteen minutes every day under his guidance, forbidding him or her, however, to study alone at home [S. Marchesi, 1902, p. 44].

We think it advisable, at first, to attempt exercises in breathing, and later in tone-attack, only under the teacher's personal supervision; for just at this stage much harm may be done which is hard to undo afterwards [G. B. Lamperti, 1905, p. 9].

Buzzi-Peccia declares that only so much close supervision should be necessary after a time:

One important point, that should be understood clearly, is that the school is the place where the student gets the IDEA which he must work out alone--at home. The improvement must come from his own mind!... They [pupils] do not seem to understand that the teacher is the guide who gives them the points, but that the pupil is the one who must think them out and develop them for himself [1925, p. 24].

Silent practice. Silent practice is recognized as valuable for two reasons, namely preparation and preservation. Regarding the first, Bishenden writes, "There is a method of influencing the voice styled 'The silent preparation.' It consists in mentally practicing the air of a piece of music, and studying the effect in the mind's eye" [1876, p. 28]. In many exercises, Parisotti uses the symbol "S. pr.." This indicates that he wishes the exercise to be carefully thought out first, using silent preparation [1911, pp. 142-152].

Other authors consider silent preparation good for preserving the voice. Melba writes that when the singer has a cold, he or she should practice silently [1926, p. 14]. "Much practice tires the voice," says Lamperti. "It is therefore better merely to mark the tones lightly.... However, singing mezza voce fatigues beginners in practising. It is more important to learn with the head, without using the voice" [1905, p. 34]. Shakespeare quotes Tosi as having written, "Singing demands such close application, that when one can no longer practice with the voice one must study in thought" [1924, p. 75].

Piano accompaniments. Three major ideas are associated with piano accompaniment in relation to practice. The first opposes the overuse of accompaniment by the teacher. Friedrich Wieck, a teacher of both piano and voice, writes:

> It is common for teachers to play their accompaniments as furiously as if they had to enter into a struggle for life and death of their singers. At the beginning of the lesson, the lady singer ought to commence quite piano, at first in a one-lined octave ... and yet you bang, and pound on the keys as if you had to accompany drums and trumpets.... [Y]ou induce your pupils to strain and force their voices [1875, p. 118].

Lehmann affirms that, "the constant playing of single tones or chords on the piano by the teacher during the lesson is wrong.... The teacher can hear the pupil, but the latter cannot hear himself ... and yet it is of the utmost importance that he should learn to hear himself" [1924, p. 210]. Lamperti believes that, "only when the pupil feels uncertain, should the teacher sing to her, and support her with the piano in unison" [1905, p. 11].

The second idea concerns itself with self-accompaniment in practice. Teachers are opposed to singing while seated:

> Only in a standing position can a free, deep breath be

drawn, and mind and body be properly prepared for
the exercise or the song to follow [Lehmann, 1924,
p. 210].

All the exercises for tone are to be practised while
standing.... Most of the practising of songs is also
better done in this way. Even if you can accompany
yourself on the piano, do much of your song practise
standing, only now and then striking a chord or two
to keep you on the key [Taylor, 1914, p. 32].

Crowest also believes in standing while practicing;
that it is "far better to sound the first note of each passage
therein, and master the same without any accompaniment"
and that "the attention is not divided between the pianoforte
and the voice, while it leaves the singer free to give all his
attention and care to the production of the notes which he is
endeavouring to sing artistically" [1900, p. 55].

The third idea is that the student should be able to
play the piano in order to familiarize himself with the accompaniments. "The girl with a voice who has never worked
at the piano, is greatly handicapped from the start, when she
begins her vocal studies. As she knows nothing of the piano,
everything has to be played for her; --she can never be independent of the accompanist" [Florence Easton, quoted in
Brower, 1920, pp. 131-132]. Others who concur are Downing
[1927, p. 17] and Sophie Braslau [Brower, 1920, p. 190].

Various factors. Three concepts already mentioned
indirectly deserve reiteration. "Practice singing slowly and
hearing slowly" [Lehmann, 1924, p. 189]. "The singer should
always practice standing up" [Myer, 1913, p. 9]. "Do not
work when fatigued or if you are not sure of yourself" [Wron-
ski, 1921, p. 69].

One other concept worthy of mention is that of using
a mirror for practice. Thirty-six quotations were discovered
in the course of investigation. The concept antedates this
study; Corfe acknowledges Tosi for the idea in his work [1800,
p. 13] and Tenducci [1785, Rule X], who writes, "In the exercise of singing, never to discover any Pain or Difficulty by
distortion of the Mouth or Grimace of any Kind which will be
best avoided by examining the countenance in a Looking glass."
Garcia recommends using the mirror for correcting the habits
of pushing out the lips, protruding the jaw, knitting the brows,
and opening the mouth too much or too little [1894, p. 13].

G. B. Lamperti instructs the singer to "observe in a mirror the opening of the mouth and expression of the face," but warns that "she must sing out into the room, not against the wall" [1905, p. 11].

Health. The subject of health is not considered in the works of Fields or Burgin, but it is a subject of great concern during the time span of this study. Thirty-three authors discuss health and general physical education; some of them devote entire chapters to the areas. Discussions are too varied to effectively outline, but two major thoughts arise-- first, that every singer must get exercise other than that acquired by singing, and second, that smoking is not recommended for the singer. The reader who wishes to pursue the subject of health should especially investigate the works of D'Aubigny, Ferrari, Panofka, Browne and Behnke, Santley, Caruso, Crowest, and Wronski.

ANALYSIS AND COMMENTS

Because this study spans 150 years, some evolution in pedagogic thought might be expected. This is especially true where the subject of methodologies is concerned. The period witnesses not only the continuation of the traditional schools, but the rise of the scientific schools, the reactionary psychological methods, and the combinative approaches which sought to reconcile a number of opposing viewpoints. Not surprisingly, then, we see that the group of authors who oppose the concept that vocal training can be standardized is four times larger than those who favor the idea. In Fields' work, 13 believe in standardization, while 18 oppose the concept, and in Burgin's work the majority is reversed to seven and four, respectively. This suggests at least an increasing tolerance among authors today, if not an actual beginning of standardization. The authors of the era 1860-1920 probably launch more verbal assaults on other teachers and methods than are contained in the remainder of vocal pedagogic history.

Two concepts undergo modification in the period of this study. The classification of voices shifts from mere compass as a determinate to a set of multiple criteria, including timbre, temperament, volume and the use of the middle range. Concerning the vocal training period, the beginning of a trend can be followed from Wieck's book (1875) into the present era, suggesting that it is better to commence study in the late teens. The problems associated with male vocal mutation have led a majority of authors to propose study only after this process is completed.

Many basic principles of vocal pedagogy have not changed, however. Ideas expressed in this chapter agree with the period prior to 1777 (cf. Duey) and after 1927 both (cf. Fields and Burgin). The prerequisites of a good voice and a good ear, the fact that singing cannot be quickly mastered, that relaxation and economy of effort are vital, and that singing resembles speaking all fall into the category of seemingly obvious vocal "truths. "

It should also be noted that some of the concepts selected for inclusion in this chapter are undoubtedly more universally accepted than would be indicated by the mere count of statements. Concepts such as benefits of vocal study, singing as self-expression and the importance of removing muscular interferences are no doubt regarded as self-evident by many authors.

Opposing methodologies arising in the late nineteenth century created a need in authors to explain and justify their concepts and techniques in detail. Consequently, many of the most incisive observations occur in books written after 1900. This is reflected in the greater percentage of quotations used from this period, although this should not automatically indicate to the reader that any particular concept was not already fashionable in the eighteenth or nineteenth centuries.

III

BREATHING

When breathing is related to artful singing, it can become a complex matter. "Ordinary breathing has for its end
purely and simply the physiological function of purifying the
blood" [Curtis, 1914, p. 54], but "Air taken into the lungs,
besides oxygenating the blood, also acts as a medium for
the propagation of sound" [Thorp and Nicholl, 1896, p. 23].
In all, 538 statements were gathered relating to breath in
singing.

THEORIES : THE IMPORTANCE
AND NATURE OF BREATHING

Breathing Is a Primary Consideration

No concept has enjoyed such universal agreement in
vocal pedagogy as the importance of breath and breath management.   Eighty-four sources of the total 160 discuss this concept.   "Life depends on breathing; singing on artistic breathing" [Bach, 1894, p. 120].   Tetrazzini is one of a group of
authors who recalls the old bel canto adage of Pacchiarotti:
"He who breathes properly sings properly, it has been said;
and there is not a single authority of any weight, who does
not endorse that statement.   The old Italian masters used to
say, indeed that the art of singing is the art of breathing"
[1923, p. 47].   Others who cite this adage are F. Lamperti
[1883, Preface], White [1918, p. 11] and Taylor [1914, p.
19], who also offers a saying of Crescentini's: "Singing consists of freedom about the neck and the voice on the breath."
Another common concept is that the breath is the motor of
a threefold system in which the larynx serves as vibrator and
the cavities of the neck and head as the resonator [Thorp and
Nicholl, 1896, p. 23; Mackenzie, 1891, p. 26].   So important
is this concept of breathing as a primary consideration that
a number of statements have been included, although the idea
of many is the same:

Table 3.   SUMMARY OF CONCEPTS OF BREATHING

I.   Theories of breathing

A.   The importance and nature of breathing
   1.   breathing a primary consideration   84
   2.   pre-vocal training advised   35
B.   Physiological factors
   1.   action of ribs and diaphragm   50
   2.   other coordinating factors   9

II.   Methods of cultivating breath control

A.   The psychological approach
   1.   natural breathing advised   23
   2.   singing develops breathing   3
   3.   interpretational controls
      a)   by correct phrasing   23
      b)   by synchronization with the music   3
      c)   other devices for improving breathing   12
B.   The technical approach
   1.   postural controls
      a)   through physical culture   30
      b)   through maintaining a correct chest position   66
   2.   voluntary control of breathing organs advised   26
   3.   diaphragmatic control
      a)   diaphragmatic control is essential   9
      b)   diaphragmatic control is not essential   3
   4.   orificial controls
      a)   breathing through mouth advised   11
      b)   breathing through nose advised   20
      c)   breathing through mouth and nose advised   6
   5.   quantitative factors
      a)   breath economy   36
      b)   breath pressure and support   34
      c)   breath renewal, frequency and speed   41
      d)   the silent, unobserved breath   14
                  TOTAL STATEMENTS   538

Zwey Kunststücke muss sich die Sänger so zu eigen machen, dass sie ihm zur Natur werden: er muss 1) in einer unmerklichen Augenblicke die Lunge voll Athmen nehmen, und 2) ihn sparsam, und doch mit der ganzen Kraft der Stimme wieder heraus lassen können/ Two feats the singer must make his own so that they become as nature to him; he must 1) fill the lungs with breath in the imperceptible blink of an eye, and 2) sparingly, yet with the entire power of the voice be able to let it out again [Hiller, 1780, p. 14].

Hat ein Schuler noch nicht begriffen und gelernt Athemreich zu seyn, so wird ihm selten ein solcher Ton gelingen/ If the student has not yet grasped and learned to be rich in breath, he will seldom succeed in such a tone [the beautiful tone] [D'Aubigny, 1803, p. 74].

A long and easy breath is one of the most essential qualities for the singer [Lablache, 184-, p. 4].

Breathing is an integral part of the true method of tone production; indeed it may be said ... to be the root of the matter [Ffrangçon-Davies, 1904, p. 106].

Breathing is singing.... without properly controlled breathing the best singing or speaking tone cannot be produced, for tone is but vocalized breath [Fillebrown, 1911, p. 23].

Perhaps, in Vocal Mastery, the greatest factor of all is breathing.... Here, as in everything else, perfect ease and naturalness are to be maintained [Galli-Curci in Brower, 1920, p. 58].

Beauty of singing demands a complete mastery over the breath in order to preserve the natural opening of the throat. For as long as this mastery is maintained the vocal cords tune automatically to the controlled pressure of the breath, and cause a sympathetic vibration of the air in the spaces above and behind the tongue, thus adding tone to the voice [Shakespeare, 1924, p. 3].

Pre-Vocal Training in Breathing

The second half of the nineteenth and the first two decades of the twentieth centuries formed a very popular period for pre-vocal training, i. e. , physical development of the breath muscles before the onset of vocalization exercises. Thirty-five statements were recorded from the sources surveyed. The earliest author to discuss this concept is Lablache, who writes, "We persuade the pupil to practise holding his breath for a long time, even without singing" [184-,

p. 5]. "All first movements of voice should be first studied
without notes" [Myer, 1886, p. 16]. "There can be no harm
and undoubtedly beneficial result will be gained in many cases,
by breathing exercises without phonation in the strengthening
of the breathing muscles and developing the lungs" [Shaw,
1914, p. 99]. Some of the actual methods of training are
presented from succeeding periods of the study:

> Preliminary Exercises in Breathing.
>   By the following means the student will acquire con-
> trol of the action of the Diaphragm, and steadiness:
>   1st---Inhale for a few seconds as much air as the
>   chest can well contain. In doing this, close the
>   mouth so as to leave only a very small aperture
>   for the passage of air.
>   2nd---Exhale the air very slowly and gently.
>   3rd---Fill the lungs again and keep them inflated
>   as long as possible.
>   4th---Exhale completely, and leave the chest empty
>   as long as the physical power will conveniently al-
> low [Bassini, 1865, p. 5, admitted by the author to
> be a paraphrase of Garcia in his École du Chant, Lon-
> don].

> The preliminary action in respiratory gymnastics should
> be to draw the shoulders backwards, and to advance
> the chest forwards, and upwards, by giving the spine
> a strong forward curve at the hinder part of the abdo-
> men. At the same time the arms should not be al-
> lowed to hang against the sides of the chest [Holmes,
> 1879, p. 166].

> Divest yourself of any article of clothing which at all
> interfere with the freedom of the waist. Lie down on
> your back. Place one hand lightly on the abdomen
> and the other upon the lower ribs. Inhale, through
> the nostrils, slowly, deeply, and evenly, without inter-
> ruption, or jerking. If this is done properly the abdo-
> men will, gradually and without any trembling move-
> ment, increase in size, and the lower ribs will expand
> sideways, while the upper part of the chest and the
> collar bones remain undisturbed. Now hold the breath,
> not by shutting the glottis, but by keeping the midriff
> down, and the chest walls extended, and count four
> mentally, at the rate of sixty per minute. Then let
> the breath go suddenly.... Let it be clearly under-
> stood: The inspiration is to be slow and deep, the

expiration sudden and complete. In inspiration the
abdomen and the lower part of the chest expand, and
in expiration they collapse [Behnke, 189-, p. 106].

Exercises in diaphramatic breathing may ... be made
in the sitting position, with the hands folded behind the
back of the chair, as high up as possible [Bach, 1898,
p. 34].

1.   Balance the body beyond the front foot, and become
conscious of the existence of the back muscles by extending outwards and forwards the arms, with palms
upwards and thumbs back, while keeping the elbows
in.
2.   Do the quick breaths or quiverings in and out,
through the mouth, noiselessly, until they are felt at
the soft place underneath the breastbone and under the
shoulderblades.   This gives us a full breath not felt
at the points of the shoulders, nor at the chest.
3.   Press out the breath as though warming some object with it, while mentally pronouncing a long Ah for
ten to fifteen seconds, and finally, without losing control, stop the breath by arresting it with the breath
muscles, the throat being open [Shakespeare, 1899, p.
16].

In 1903, Hulbert offers basic rules of breathing with
many exercises to develop stance, breath-taking, breath-control and breath emission.   He includes photographs [pp. 11-
16].   Clippinger proposes pulsated drills, i. e. , exercises of
detached tones in which pulsations of the diaphragm provide
the impetus for each rearticulation, providing the singer with
a better concept of the relationship of the diaphragm to breath
and sound [1910, p. 8].

The forward poise of the body eliminates a portion of
the movement involved in inspiration, the spine now
taking part and doing its share.   This can readily be
tested by holding the back straight or rigidly upright
and taking a full breath by lifting the chest.   The
physical effort will be found much greater than when
the body is slightly poised forward, and if the singer
will gradually assume that poise and again fill his
lungs with air, he will find that to do so requires less
time and less strain [Miller, 1910, p. 42].

Fillebrown presents eight exercises, including "slow

inhalation with sudden expulsion," "rapid inspiration with slow expiration," and "Farinelli's great exercise" [compare with Bassini above]:

> Sip the breath slowly and steadily through the small-
> est possible opening of the lips; hold it a few counts,
> then exhale very slowly and steadily through the small-
> est possible opening of the lips [1911, pp. 34-37].

Fillebrown cautions that this exercise is not meant for beginners.   Parisotti gives the reader exercises for expanding the
chest by lowering and drawing in the shoulders at the back
[1911, p. 14], while Myer's basic exercise involves raising
the arms to the sides while inspiring, palms up [1913, pp.
6-7].

In 1915 we find the first statement opposing pre-vocal
breathing exercises.   Muckey writes that time is "more prof-
itably employed in breaking up the association between the
action of the extrinsic and of the intrinsic muscles" [p. 105].
Proschowsky believes, "In rare cases it would be wise to
train a student in breathing gymnastics, but then only as a
general benefit to health, not as a direct use in singing"
[1923, p. 33].

THEORIES : PHYSIOLOGICAL FACTORS

Action of the Ribs, Diaphragm and Associated Muscles

Lunn quotes Garcia as having written in his 1847 edition, under Respiration, "In order to inspire freely, hold the
head straight, the shoulders thrown back without stiffness,
and the chest open.   Raise the chest by a slow and regular
motion and draw in the stomach.   The moment that you commence executing these two motions the lungs will proceed to
dilate themselves until they are filled with air" [Lunn, 1888,
p. 23].   This statement stands as a midpoint between the
simple precepts of stance and chest position used in books
prior to the middle years of the nineteenth century and the
complex discussions of breath physiology that begin in the
1870's with such books as Lennox Browne's Medical Hints on
the Production and Management of the Singing Voice (ca. 1875).
The types of breathing that most sources describe fall into
three major categories: diaphragmatic, abdominal, clavicular.
Purely abdominal breathing finds few adherents.   Some of the
sources favor a combining of diaphragmatic and abdominal
(or intercostal) techniques.

Diaphragmatic breathing. In 1883, Lamperti advises his readers to use diaphragmatic control [p. 10]. Bach writes:

> The diaphragm is the muscle of partition between the cavity of the chest and the abdomen, and plays a great part in breathing, and we dare say the most important part in singing. Ordinarily, in speaking, we breathe with the upper part of the chest. In singing, however, we must breathe with the lower portions of the lungs also, and retain the air by the diaphragm. Simple as this may appear, it is very difficult for the beginner to do it correctly [1898, p. 23].

Henderson also describes the role of the diaphragm, and adds, "When you draw in breath the diaphragm contracts and at the same time presses downward upon the abdominal cavity. This causes the abdomen naturally to expand, but it is not forcibly pushed out" [1906, p. 28]. Ffrangçon-Davies describes the feeling of diaphragmatic breathing as expansion "all round the waist" [1904, pp. 87-91]. Salvatore Marchesi and Lilli Lehmann also favor diaphragmatic breathing, Lehmann stating that the correct action is to draw in the diaphragm and then relax it [1906, p. 14].

Diaphragmatic and intercostal breathing. In 1883, Myer writes, "Diaphragmatic is the only correct singing breath" [p. 26]. In his volume of 1891, he has changed his opinion, defending diaphragmatic and intercostal breathing combined [p. 23]. This method dates back at least to Browne's Medical Hints (ca. 1885), when he writes:

> Inspiration should commence by the action of the abdominal muscles, and descent of the diaphragm; in other words by pushing forward the walls of the abdomen and chest. As the lungs inflate with the descent of the diaphragm, the inspiration, being prolonged, becomes lateral, and the ribs expand on all sides equally, but the shoulder blades and collar-bone still remain fixed; if respiration be further and unduly prolonged, it becomes clavicular [1887, p. 15].

Shakespeare gives a very detailed physiological look at the action of ribs, diaphragm and breathing muscles in his defense of diaphragmatic-intercostal breathing [1899, pp. 9-17]. Fucito explains that diaphragmatic-intercostal breathing was the method of both the old Italian masters and of Caruso [1922, p. 115]. Curtis offers a reason for the added use of abdominal muscles:

Whereas in normal respiration the pressure exercised
by the contracting diaphragm muscles pushes out the
entire abdominal wall, the singer who employs all the
resources of his art to enlarge the chest nevertheless
retracts the lower abdominal wall in taking a deep
inspiration in order to maintain a better control of
the expiratory act [1914, p. 56].

Opponents of clavicular breathing. The most positive
statement concerning clavicular breathing is that a full breath
involves clavicular, costal and diaphragmatic breathing [Kofler,
1897, p. 40]. Even Kofler admits that, "of all methods of
breathing, the clavicular or high breathing furnishes the smallest amount of air with the greatest effort" [1897, pp. 35-36].
Most authors emphatically oppose the technique of clavicular
breathing:

Clavicular breathing is a method of respiration totally
vicious and to be avoided. By it the whole part of
the chest is flattened, and drawn in, instead of being
distended, consequently the lower or larger part of
the lungs is not inflated [Browne, 1887, p. 15].

During the fatiguing collar-bone breathing the tongue
is generally retracted and the larynx depressed. The
result of this, again, is a diminution of the cavity of
the throat--a cavity which should serve as a sounding-
board for the voice.... Breathing by the elevation of
the collar-bone is extremely fatiguing, and requires
the overcoming of obstacles which do not exist in diaphragmatic breathing [Bach, 1898, p. 46].

Browne and Behnke think it important to remark the
look of correct breath-taking: "The criterion of correct inspiration is an increase of size of the abdomen and of the
lower part of the chest. Whoever draws in the abdomen and
raises the upper part of the chest breathes wrongly" [1883,
p. 142]. Other statements on the look of correct breath-
taking can be found in this chapter under the heading, "The
silent, unobserved breath."

Other Coordinating Factors

Three other factors in the coordination of breath taking
are each mentioned by more than one author. Lunn states
that there should be a pause between the end of breath taking

and the onset of vocalization to aid the feed of breath [1904, p. 34]. Henderson explains that this action must be done with the breath muscles:

> In the practise of deep breathing, after the lungs have been filled the air should be retained for two or three seconds before exhalation. This retention is not to be accomplished by closing the vent in the larynx.... The breath must be retained simply by the action of the diaphragm and rib muscles. The throat must be kept lax and open [1906, pp. 29-30].

Kofler says that this pause is beneficial for hygienic reasons [1897, p. 59], and Proschowsky uses this "moment between inhaling and producing" to give the singer the sensation of support [1923, p. 44].

> Another concept is that of the firm chest sensation:

> There is a definite reason for holding the chest firm: First, the acoustics of the voice.... During the emission of chest-tones the vibrations of the vocal ligaments cause the air-column in the windpipe to vibrate, which makes the tones fuller and richer. If the windpipe can rest against a solid chest-wall, the tones will be rounder.... The other reason is that without the assistance of the upper chest-pressure, the process of exhaling ... could not be carried out [Kofler, 1897, p. 67; similar views expressed by Shakespeare, 1924, p. 7].

> The third concept is the opposition of the abdominal and diaphragmatic muscles in exhalation. "The act of tone-production is in 'contrary motion' to that of breath-taking; the pull of the diaphragm goes parallel with the inspiration, whereas the push of the abdominal muscles is felt to oppose it" [G. B. Lamperti, 1905, p. 9; also Lunn, 1904, p. 13].

METHODS : THE PSYCHOLOGICAL APPROACH

Natural Breathing Advised

Strictly speaking, it may be said that natural breathing was advocated by the authors of the period prior to the later half of the nineteenth century, inasmuch as none of them talk of technique beyond stance, economy and renewal of breath:

If one takes the trouble to read about the teaching of
the older masters, whose pupils certainly knew how
to sing, he finds little disagreement in regard to the
matter of breathing. Most of the old teachers had
not a great deal to say about it. They seemed to believe that if one systematically practiced drawing in
deep breaths and letting them out slowly, turning every
bit into tone, the power to breathe in just that necessary way would eventually be acquired [Henderson,
1906, p. 25].

The discussion of a "natural" technique, however, is
definitely a product of the reaction to scientific methodologies
that had gained much ground in the last years of the nineteenth
century. Those who advocate natural breathing often begin
their discussion with attacks on physiologists such as Browne
and Mackenzie and those using information acquired through
science such as Seiler and Garcia. The highpoint of natural
methodologies occurs in the second decade of the twentieth
century, the most popular writers of this viewpoint being
Muckey, Parisotti, Shaw, and Taylor. An early quotation by
Myer is followed by a number of typical statements from the
decade 1910-1919:

Never take a voluntary, conscious breath in singing.
He who consciously breathes to sing unseats the voice
thereby and sings wrongly. The singer should be no
more conscious of breath-taking for singing than for
living [Myer, 1897, p. 78].

We have daily proof that our breathing apparatus serves
us without any prompting or guidance in a great variety
of ways, and that it does so according to what act we
intend to perform. If we choose to walk, run, jump,
row, or swim, do not our breathing muscles adapt
themselves to our immediate needs by working simultaneously in different degrees or modes [Rogers, 1910,
p. 25]?

Breathing in itself offers no difficulty, and therefore
needs no special direction; in fact, ordinary breathing
is an unconscious act. . . . We must experience no
more exertion in singing than in breathing [Parisotti,
1911, p. 4].

Avoid all attempts to control the breathing, and the
breath will act normally and naturally [Shaw, 1914,
p. 99].

It has never been scientifically proved that the correct
use of the voice depends in any way on the mastery
of an acquired system of breathing.... The importance
of this subject has been greatly overestimated....
Breath control is readily mastered with very little
practice [Taylor, 1917, pp. 131, 132, 133].

Authors of the twenties who advocate natural breathing
include Greene, Marafioti, and two teachers who favor natural
breathing at least to a degree:

Many of the greatest authorities insist upon the use
of a fixed system of breathing, whenever the vocalist
appears in public. The writer ... dissents from this
opinion. He agrees that the exacting practice of breathing exercises is of the utmost importance, but believes
that during public appearance ... the action of the breathing muscles should be unconscious [Douty, 1924, p. 19].

It must not be supposed that a singer's breathing is
something strange or complex, for it is nothing more
than an amplification of normal, healthy breathing.
In contrast, however, to the undisciplined casual breathing of the general public, the singer is a professional
breather [Fillebrown, 1911, p. 23].

Singing Develops Breathing

Only two authors and three statements were found to
make direct comment on the concept that singing develops
breathing. Myer writes that singing itself gives "'the singer's
sensation.' [This is something] ... the singer who sings by
local muscular effort, knows nothing of'' [1897, pp. 18-19].
Marafioti uses the same paragraph in his books of 1922 [pp.
50-51] and 1925 [p. 110]:

Breath is an indispensable factor in voice production,
but it is not the essential power which develops the
voice as it is taught today. On the contrary, the
function of singing develops the breathing apparatus
and its power ... singing develops breathing, not
breathing, singing.

Interpretational Controls

By correct phrasing. Phrasing was one of the most

important devices for regulating the breath in the eighteenth and early nineteenth centuries.

> Im Vortrag eines Stückes nun, das man nicht in einem Athem heraus bringen kann, ist es erlaubt, frischen zu nehmen:
>
> 1. Wo in dem Noten eine Pause steht, sie sey lang oder kurz.
> 2. Wo die Worte ein kleine Ruhe verstatten, wenn
> 3. ein Interpunctionszeiche steht, oder in der Poesie eine Reimzeile sich endigt. /
>
> In the execution of a piece that one cannot finish in one breath, it is allowed to take another:
>
> 1. where there is a pause in the notes, long or short.
> 2. where the words allow a little rest, and when
> 3. a punctuation mark occurs, or when the rhyme scheme of the poetry shows a possibility [Hiller, 1780, p. 15].

Such directions, however, do not profess to improve the singer's breathing. They are included as much for musicality as to help the singer regulate his breath renewals:

> The management of the breath is indeed most important to the singer. The principal rules are, to fill the chest just before beginning a strain--to take breath on the weak or unaccented part of the measure, and never at the beginning of the bar, or in the middle of a word--to sing a single strain, or musical phrase, if possible in the same breath, to prepare, by a deep inspiration, for a long passage or division--to take the opportunities short rests or pauses afford for inhaling and giving out the breath as slowly as possible.... [A]ll other rules ... must be acquired by experience [Bacon, 1824, p. 91].

Twentieth-century authors who relate breathing to phrasing include Santley [1908, p. 61], Rogers [1910, p. 125], and W. S. Drew, who writes:

> Properly devised singing exercises in themselves form breathing exercises and should be used as such, both by singing long phrases or short phrases several times over in one breath [1924, p. 17].

Synchronization with music. This concept is closely allied with that of taking breath by phrase, since phrases often form periodic rhythmic patterns in song, of a length manageable by a single breath.

Q. Where is the singer to breathe?
A. Mere common sense forbids breathing in the middle of a word or between words, intimately united by grammatical sense. So, obviously, the singer must breathe where the punctuation and music agrees [Garcia, 1894, p. 54].

The regular rhythms of physiological breathing is, of course, out of the question in singing a musical composition, but a perfect rhythmic relation between the action represented by the musical phrase and the reaction represented by the breath must invariably be preserved [Rogers, 1895, p. 82].

Other devices for improving breathing. Five concepts have been collected here that may help the singer to improve his breathing. These precepts are not all psychologically related to the voice.

Lablache suggests the image of "sending forth the breath freely, and in such a manner as not to strike against any part of the mouth on its passage: the least rubbing against the glands destroys the vibrating quality of the tone" [184-, p. 5]. Tetrazzini is one of a few who recommend that the singer's clothing fit loosely, and that the ladies should especially avoid the use of corsets [1909, pp. 11-12]. Santley talks of careful song preparation regarding breathing:

Inexperienced persons would do well to note that under the influence of nervousness they will find it more difficult to maintain a chestful of wind, and in studying they should mark places where an extra breath may be taken without interfering with the effect of their speech or song [1908, p. 62].

One common concept is that singing is an art of opposing directions, both in thought and actual movement:

Never breathe up and sing down. Always breathe down and sing up. This refers, of course, entirely to the movements of the body.... The direction of effort in ascending must never go with the tone, but always away from it.   'Sing up, think down' [Myer, 1897, pp. 72, 73].

Lunn directs the student to "Think downward to meet the tone--in other words, reverse the direction of vital force" [1904, p. 13].   He presents a diagram:

↓ direction of   ↑ direction of
   thought   breath

The higher the tones, the deeper the breathing [G. B. Lamperti, 1905, p. 12].

Two time-honored "stunts" of vocal pedagogy that have psychological implications are the use of the cold mirror and the candle flame.   Shakespeare adds, as well the use of the finger:

> Old singers judged whether the vocal cords were acting naturally, or whether they were squeezed in some way out of their right position, by two signs.   First, when rightly produced, the note could be sung with comparatively little breath, and this, combined with a proper control gave rise to the custom of practising before a lighted taper, or a mirror, or against a finger, in order to discover if the note sounded full to a breath pressure which would last at least twenty or thirty seconds without causing the candle to flicker, or tarnishing the mirror or unduly warming the finger [1910, p. 24].

Others who refer to these devices are Bach [1880, p. 30], Browne and Behnke [1883, pp. 147-148], Duff [1919, p. 15], and Cooke [1921, p. 139].

CULTIVATING CONTROL : THE TECHNICAL APPROACH

Postural Controls

Postural control through physical culture.   The concept of extra-musical physical culture predates the limits of this study.   Certain physical skills were seen to have practical purpose for the stage as well as for the singer.   "In Italy a master of ballet is engaged to instruct the young aspirants' proper carriage and judicious action.... Lastly, a master of fencing is engaged to prevent a hero drawing his sword and handling it like a toasting fork" [Furtado, 18--, p. 9].

The systematization of exercises to develop the various muscles of the body for singing probably begins with Guttmann (1860), who claims to base his gymnastics upon physiological laws.

> Most of the text-books on the training of the voice contain rules for respiratory gymnastics, and a excellent series of exercises is contained in Guttmann's Gymnastics of the Voice. Walking, fencing, swimming, dumb-bell practice, are excellent means of improving the 'wind' provided they are not pushed to the point of fatigue [Mackenzie, 1891, p. 98; Curtis concurs, almost verbatim, 1914, p. 55].

Others who propose physical culture include Bach [1894, p. 103], Kofler [1897, p. 75], and Frossard [1914, p. 131].

Postural control through correct chest position. Maintaining a correct chest position is one of the most popular and agreed upon concepts in vocal pedagogy. An evolution in the complexity of rules on stance can be traced by viewing statements in chronological order:

> The master should always make the scholar sing standing, that the voice may have all its organization free. Let him take care, whilst he sings, that he gets a graceful posture, and makes an agreeable appearance [Bacon, 1824, p. 89, quoting Tosi].

Tenducci links standing to the chest. He states that, while practicing, "if standing, so much the better for the chest" [1785, Rule XI].

> The singer ought to stand with the body erect, the head elevated, the chest thrown forward, that things may have ample room to expand [Anfossi, 180-, p. 13].

> Standing, you thus possess more strength.... Keep the Head and Body upright which gives free passage to the Voice [Corri, 1810, p. 11].

To the concepts of Corri, Cooke adds, "with the shoulders thrown back so as to expand the chest" [1828, Introduction], while Mason appends the thoughts, "the breast bending a little outwards, and the mouth duly open" [1847, p. 100].

Bassini is probably the originator of the well-known image of the military stance:

L'allievo dovrà tenersi dritto, col petto in fuori, le
spalle composte naturalmente e la testa nè troppo
alta nè troppo bassa, in una parola, nella posizione
del soldato. / The pupil must observe carefully,
[with] the chest thrown outward, the shoulders carried
naturally and the head neither too high or too low, in
a word, in the position of a soldier [1864, p. 2].

The writers of the late nineteenth century are more
disposed to give reasons for correct position. Kofler recommends a firmly held chest for reasons of richer tone and
ease of expiration [1897, p. 67; the full statement is quoted
above on page 54].

For the controlling and economizing of the breath, as
much as possible, I recommend ... this high position
of the chest without raising of the shoulders, and with
the abdomen drawn in [Lankow, 1803, p. 9].

Other twentieth-century authors who discuss the subject at length are Tetrazzini [1909, pp. 14-16, 19], Shakespeare [1910, p. 16], and Hulbert [1903, pp. 17-19 and 1921,
pp. 16-18].

Voluntary Control of Breathing Organs Advised

Some of the authors who espouse direct control of the
breathing apparatus begin their discussions with an explanation as to why natural breathing is insufficient in their esti-
mation. Among these are Miller, Russell, and Shakespeare.

The pupil is often directed to breathe naturally. Now,
a singer's respiration, like any other feat of strength,
should be apparently natural.... [B]ut in reality his
respiration is a considerable amplification of the ordinary breath-taking.... It is therefore to the breathing
that our first studies should be directed, viz. how
to take in sufficient breath, how to press it out and
yet economize it for the longest phrases, and ... how
to sing on this basis all the notes of the voice with
the throat open and unconscious [Shakespeare, 1910,
pp. 8, 9].

There are books in which the singer is told to breathe
naturally, and this direction is harped on and extolled
for its simplicity. Surely no rule could be more sim-

ple.... It does not go far enough. It leaves too
much to the individual. For obviously there will be
... nearly as many opinions among as many different
people as what constitutes natural breathing; and a
person may have become so habitualed to a faulty
method of breathing that he believes it natural, although it is not.... Correct breathing, although a
function of the body, also is an art [Miller, 1910, pp.
27-28].

Russell believes that a breath technique can be learned
either "empirically, as in the old days of voice culture ...
or rationally, as in the higher class of modern instruction,
where the student's first lesson is how to control the body
and breath leaving tonal result until later." But of natural
breathing, he writes:

One theory which is much vaunted is that 'nature
should be let alone and she will properly manage the
singer's breathe.' ... [B]ut the earnest student is
warned that nature supplies only the elementary con-
ditions--the foundation, and that without proper culture
these elementary conditions are more likely to drop
into wrong habits than into right ones; hence the resting
of one's faith upon nature alone, grows to be but an
apology for crudeness and shallowness.... Nature's
mechanism is perfect and we must rely upon it exclusively, studying its characteristics and powers; but
as the natural manifestations of this mechanism's functions are not in direct line with art purposes, we are
called upon to engraft upon these involuntary, intuitive,
natural functions, processes of voluntary control [Rus-
sell, The Body and Breath Under Artistic Control,
1904, pp. 2, 4].

A sampling of quotations is offered to represent those
authors who favor direct control of the breathing organs.

The correct management or the mis-management of
the vibratory column of air which passes from the
vocal chords into the mouth, the resonant cavity of
the voice, is, beyond question, the great secret of
the success or of the failure of singers [Myer, 1883,
p. 18].

The first step in vocal breathing is to set up a mental activity which centres itself on the lower part of
the trunk [Ffrangçon-Davies, 1904, p. 98].

The singer should breathe as easily and naturally as animals and people do when they sleep. But we are awake when we sing; correct breath control, therefore, must be carefully studied, and is the result of understanding and experience [David Bispham in Brower, 1920, pp. 214-215].

Dodds lists eight vocal advantages and nine physical advantages of control of the breathing organs. Some vocal advantages are greater breath capacity developed, greater economy of effort, and greater confidence in the control of the expiratory muscles. Physical advantages include complete and balanced expansion of the chest, improvement in blood purification, and natural massage of the abdominal organs, resulting in better digestion [1925, p. 29].

Diaphragmatic Control

Nine authors favor diaphragmatic control in singing, while three do not. Many more authors refer to the use of the diaphragm, but do not discuss use as a concept per se, i. e. , they seem unaware of any opposition to this concept.

The diaphragm, although considered an involuntary organ, can, owing to the diverse nature of its nervous fibres, be made voluntary to a certain extent; and it is this which enables us to sing and speak, as far as inspiration and expiration are concerned [Guttmann, 1887, p. 40; Kofler's thoughts closely parallel Guttmann's, 1897, p. 122].

The mode of breathing required for artistic singing is diaphragmatic breathing. It is the sole method by which a singer can conduct sufficient air tranquilly, and with a minimum of exertion, from the lungs to the vocal organs.... [O]ur first endeavor must be to strengthen diaphragmatic breathing, and this can be accomplished only by systematically developing the abdominal muscles [G. B. Lamperti, 1905, p. 5].

The three writers found to oppose direct control of the diaphragm are Shaw, Galli-Curci, and Rogers:

All attempts to control the breath or tone at the diaphragm is [sic] suicidal [Shaw, 1914, p. 100].

We are told many fallacies by vocal teachers. One is

> that the diaphragm must be held firmly in order to
> give support to the tone. It seems to me this is a
> serious mistake. I keep the diaphragm relaxed.
> Thus tone production, in my case, is made at all
> times with ease; there is never any strain [Galli-Curci
> in Brower, 1920, p. 54].

> The reversing of the diaphragm between the acts of
> breathing and singing is not a deliberate act; it will
> take place naturally if you let it [Rogers, 1925, p. 76].

Orificial Control

The singing breath can be taken through the nose, the
mouth, or through both orifices simultaneously. All three
philosophies find adherents in this study. Those who favor
nose breathing date back at least to the time of Pfeiffer and
Nägeli's volume (1810). The earliest mention of mouth breathing is found in Lablache (184-). Both opinions then find al-
lies throughout the length of the study. The concept of nose
and mouth breathing combined is relatively recent. The
first authors in the group are Shaw (1914) and Fucito (1922).

Breathing through the mouth advised. Lunn quotes
Garcia (probably the edition of 1872) as having written, "Breathe
through the open mouth, but feel no parts" [1888, p. 21].
In 1904, Lunn writes, "Never breathe through the nose in
vocal study or in song" [p. 15]. "Before taking breath--
which must be done at first only through the mouth, not
through the nose--the mouth should be opened wide enough
to permit the forefinger to pass between the upper and lower
teeth" [G. B. Lamperti, 1905, p. 7]. Parisotti declares
that either the mouth or the nose is acceptable, but the main
concern is to get the tongue and soft palate low to allow the
air to enter easily [1911, p. 22].

Breathing through the nose is advised. Most of the
authors who believe in nose breathing explain that it is best
for reasons of health:

> Breathing through the nostrils is very essential, be-
> cause not only is this less noticeable than breathing
> through the mouth, but it has also the advantage of
> not drying the mucous membranes of the oral cavity,
> the entrance of the throat, the throat itself, and the
> vocal cords ... and the moisture of these parts is

one of the most important qualities required in originating a tone [Guttmann, 1882, p. 199].

Behnke devotes four pages to the defense of nose breathing [189-, pp. 26-30]. Other articulate defenses are offered by Thorp [1896, pp. 20, 132] and Duff [1919, pp. 10-11]. Tetrazzini admits to occasional circumstances that require mouth breathing:

> Try to avoid breathing through the mouth. Inhalation through the nostrils purifies and warms the air before it reaches the throat. Breathing through the mouth dries the throat and makes the voice husky. Nevertheless, in singing declamatory music what are called half-breaths through the mouth are necessary [1923, p. 50].

Breathing through the mouth and nose is advised. The following three statements illustrate belief in this concept.

> If you breathe through the mouth and nostrils at the same time, with the throat open, the lungs will fill more quickly and more thoroughly than if you shut off either one of those passages [Rogers, 1925, p. 75].

> To inhale, it is only necessary that pressure should be, as far as possible, removed from the lungs and that air should be permitted to enter through the nose, or the mouth and the nose in a calm, quiet, unobstructed fashion [Douty, 1924, p. 16].

> Should I breathe through the nose? Certainly, in the open air, when the weather is cold. The nostrils are meant for warming the breath before it enters the lungs.
> Should I not breathe through the nose while singing? Sing a song and try. It is difficult to sniff in suddenly the huge breaths necessary for singing; the nostrils are too small. When you have time it matters little, but the singer seldom has time. Besides, it would appear odd to be closing the mouth whenever you take breath [Shakespeare, 1924, pp. 9-10].

Quantitative Factors

A number of factors related to the taking and husbanding of the breath are divided here under four headings. These concepts are so closely related, however, that overlapping, even within single sentences of a statement is common.

Breath economy. "The breath, when inhaled, should be carefully economized, in order, if necessary, to execute an entire phrase in such a manner as the musical punctuation may require" [Anfossi, 180-, p. 12]. "A good writer can say much in a few words, and in the same way a good singer requires little breath in order to sing a great deal" [Bach, 1880, p. 16]. "It is astonishing with how little air man may produce sounds, and that the sounds produced with little air, are the finest in piano or in forte, because too much air imparts to the tone a hoarseness, frequently a screeching sound, and both these qualities destroy the tone" [Guttmann, 1887, p. 197].

> Steadiness of tone depends upon a control of the breath which allows a minimum volume of air to pass out under sufficient tension to produce vocalization.
> It is not the quantity of breath inhaled that is significant, it is the amount controlled. Get, therefore, all the breath necessary, and keep it, but without rigidity [Fillebrown, 1911, pp. 26, 30; Duff concurs, 1919, p. 15].

Other valuable sources regarding this subject are Hiller [1780, p. 14], Corri [1811, p. 11], Fucito [1922, p. 117], and Dodds [1927, p. 5].

Breath pressure and support. "The first and most necessary Rule in singing, is to keep the voice steady" [Tenducci, 1785, Rule I]. "By a too great pressure of the breath, the form of the waves of sound most favourable to a good sound is disturbed" [Seiler, 1871, p. 110]. "It is also of the utmost importance that the voice emitted should be less in force than the force of the breath which supports it; this will render the singing more natural, even and spontaneous" [F. Lamperti, 1883, p. 13]. Later discussions contribute specific reasons for good breath support:

> Should the indifferent performer venture on a soft effect, the absense of breath-support would cause him to become inaudible; on his attempting to swell out such a note, the result would be throaty and unsatisfactory [Shakespeare, 1910, pp. 40-41].

Voices produced with overburdened breath pressure be-

come wooden, explosive, off-key, and lacking in
carrying power.... If students would use a bit of
logic they would realize that to force or push the
breath means to compel the throat to resist unneces-
sary pressure [Proschowsky, 1923, p. 33].

Shaw and Muckey preach control because voice is
sound waves and not the force of breath pressure:

The present definitions of the voice by teachers, critics
and others show that they cannot appreciate the nature
of the voice. Voice is variously defined as 'vocalized
breath,' 'vibrated breath,' 'vitalized breath'.... The
voice is air-waves, which like those of any other
sound, travel at the rate of 1,100 feet per second or
about 750 miles per hour. Breath is an air current,
and air-currents traveling at the rate of 750 miles
per hour would destroy everything in their path [Muckey,
1915, pp. 111-112].

The breath of the singer merely sets the cords vibrating which in turn develop sound-waves--voice [Shaw,
1914, p. 55 fn].

Two authors explain the use of support in ending the
sound:

When one finishes a sound without having exhausted
all the breath, it is necessary to use care to stop the
remaining breath very gently, and not fling it out with
a kind of expiration very disagreeable to hear [Lablache,
184-, p. 5].

According to Witherspoon, in the bel canto era

the pupil was taught to imagine he sang or sustained
a tone a tiny bit longer, perhaps the value of a grace-
note, than he actually sang or sustained it. That is,
in vocal parlance, ie 'held on to his breath support'
a 'nota mentale' or mental note longer than the tone
he actually sang, so that the breath effort or tension
ceased after the tone ceased. This prevents the 'grunt'
or gasp which occurs when the tone and breath support
cease at the same moment [1925, p. 64].

Breath renewal, frequency, and speed. Hiller states
that the student should be able to take in a breath in the im-

perceptible blinking of an eye [1780, p. 14]. D'Aubigny says
that only with a deep breath can artistic singing be accomplished, for many short breathes are trying to the singer
[1803, pp. 75-76]. "Take as much breath as you can, draw
it with a moderate quickness, with suspiration, as if sighing,
use it with economy" [Corri, 1810, p. 7]. "Should the scholar
feel his voice weak and prove to flatness, he must draw his
breath slowly and throw it out suddenly, that he may attack
the notes with strength" [Ferrari, 1818, p. 7].

Overcrowding is a concern of a number of authors.
The first rule is to avoid "a respiration either insufficient
or in excess," says Costa [1824, p. 14]. "It must be emphatically repeated that it is quite possible to overcrowd the
lungs.... [I]t is sure to lead, sooner or later, to forcing
and inequality of voice" [Browne and Behnke, 1883, pp. 148-
149]. Henderson [1920, pp. 58-59] and van Broekhaven [1908,
p. 44] also warn against overcrowding.

Giovanni Lamperti stresses that "at the close of each
exercise or phrase, a comfortable amount of air must remain
in the lungs, for it is a vicious and injurious habit to finish
a passage with exhausted lungs" [1905, p. 12].

Ten writers consider the half-breath important to discuss. The first is Bassini, who writes that the half-breath
is employed "when the singer has not time to take a long
one" [1857, p. 10]. Kofler, who favors nose breathing,
states that mouth breathing must accompany nose breathing
whenever the half-breath is needed [1897, pp. 55-56]. Henderson affirms that one or two half-breaths placed within a
long phrase are better than one sudden and violent effort
just before the phrase [1920, pp. 39-40].

The silent, unobserved breath. Fourteen writers believe that a well-taken breath is barely noticeable to the ear
and the eye. "The breath should be taken without any appearance of effort" [Cooke, 1828, Introduction]. Panofka
maintains that the breath must be taken "ohne Geräusch,
Schluchzen oder Seufzen"/ without noise, sobs (hiccups), or
sighs [1859, p. 7]. "You can improve your method of attack
by the use of much less and never audible breathing" [Wieck,
1875, p. 86]. Shakespeare and Mackenzie tell the story of
Lablache watching Rubini "for four minutes without being able
to see him inspire" [Mackenzie, 1891, p. 95 fn; Shakespeare's
version in 1910, p. 15]. Tetrazzini relates similar feelings
about herself:

People have said that they cannot see when I breathe.
Well, they certainly cannot say I am ever short of
breath even if I do try to breathe invisibly. When I
breathe I scarcely draw my diaphragm in at all, but
I feel the air fill my lungs and I feel my upper ribs
expand [1909, p. 14].

Taylor offers a reason why the breath should be inaudible. "It is of the utmost importance that the inspiration
in singing be absolutely noiseless. Any noise caused by the
taking of the breath is a sign of throat stiffness" [1914, p.
33].

ANALYSIS AND COMMENTS

Breathing is the initial action in the vocalization chain.
It is the motor or driving force that enables the production
of sound. Most authors not only feel compelled to discuss
this subject in depth, but in fact place it in a premier position in their books, directly after the statements of philosophy
and procedure. A complete survey of the statements made
on breathing within the 160 sources would more than fill a
volume. Fortunately, there is much overlapping of ideas,
since a number of concepts are agreed upon in breathing:

(1) Breath is a primary consideration in singing.

(2) A high rib-cage aids breathing in both inspiration
and expiration.

(3) A standing posture, with the body erect, the head
straight, the chest slightly forward and the shoulders
low and relaxed is acknowledged as conducive to
tonal freedom.

(4) Breathing through the nose is good for health reasons,
i. e., warming and filtering the air; breathing through
the mouth enables the great quantities of air required to be inspired more quickly and with less
effort than by nose breathing alone.

(5) The breath should be economized, not only to sing
longer phrases but also because wasted breath is
counterproductive to tone quality.

(6) Constant breath support is necessary for a steady
sound; undue pressure, however, results in excess
force which must be resisted by the throat.

(7) Overcrowding of the lungs is as bad as insufficient breath; this may be avoided with half-breaths.

(8) The correct action of inspiration is unlabored and should be accomplished without noise or gross body movements.

Some of the concepts surveyed here and in the works of Fields and Burgin arose during the time span of this study. The concept of pre-vocalic breath exercises is an extension of the physiology books which proliferated in the period from 1870 to 1900 and later in the eurythmic studies of such authors as Delsart, Hulbert, and Dalcroze (ca. 1895-1910). The concept loses popularity in more recent times. Thirty-five sources comment on pre-vocal training in this study, whereas only 13 and eight believe in it in the studies of Fields and Burgin, respectively.

Discussions of the action of ribs, diaphragm and associated muscles and their relative importance in the total coordination of breathing was not a concern of the voice teacher/writer until the age of scientific investigation (beginning with Garcia, ca. 1840, but more properly around the 1860's).

As in other areas, the psychological approach seems relatively unimportant or at least undiscussed in comparison to the technical approach. This, again, is largely a product of the philosophy; once the idea of natural, unaided action is expounded, little more can be said without venturing into technical controls.

IV

PHONATION

Definition. According to Fields, "phonation is
the act or process of generating vocal sound; it
is the inception of vocal tone at its point of production in the larynx. More explicitly, phonation
is the vibratory activity of the vocal cords, so
as to produce pulsations sufficiently rapid to cause
the sensation of tone" [1947, p. 98]. Also discussed in this chapter are the various structures
and mechanisms involved in controlling and mod-
ifying the raw spectrum of sound that emanates
from the glottal area.

THEORIES : GENERAL DESCRIPTIONS
AND PHYSIOLOGICAL FACTORS

The Importance of Correct Phonation

As far back as 1824, Costa warns his readers against
"an excessive contraction of the throat ... producing generally a disagreeable, guttural, dry or husky and indistinct
voice" [p. 14]. In the same decade, Cooke states that "the
voice should come with a pure and steady tone from the
chest, divested of all nasal or guttural sound" [1828, Intro-
duction]. More recently, van Broekhaven writes

the vocal tone is produced in the larynx, and is no
longer under the control of the singer's will when it
passes out of the larynx into the throat cavities, the
pharynx and the mouth. ... [N]o position of the pharynx, palate, uvula, tongue or lips will improve a tone
when it is poorly produced in the larynx [1905, p. 8].

Theories of Phonation

In the late seventeenth and early eighteenth centuries,

Table 4. SUMMARY OF CONCEPTS OF PHONATION

I. Theories of phonation	
General description and physiological factors	54
II. Methods of controlling phonation	
A. A psychological approach to phonation	
1. total coordination is required	5
2. mental concept of tone and pitch	13
B. The technical approach to phonation	
1. control of the oral cavity	
a) mouth opening is important	54
b) mouth opening is not important	1
2. lingual controls	
a) low tongue is advised	40
b) free tongue is advised	31
c) use of the lips	21
3. palatal controls	
a) palate should be raised	32
b) palate should be free	9
4. open throat concept	
a) control of throat advised	6
b) control of throat not advised	10
c) yawning as a device	12
d) jaw low and free	35
5. position of the larynx	
a) larynx should move	17
b) larynx should not move	6
c) larynx should remain low	7
6. the attack	
a) theories and descriptions of attack	27
b) the coup de glotte advised	17
c) the coup de glotte not advised	18
7. the vocal vibrato and the tremolo	19
TOTAL STATEMENTS	434

phonation was not discussed from a theoretical standpoint. However, as scientists such as Helmholtz and Merkel and scientifically-oriented voice teachers such as Manuel Garcia began to publish works on the anatomy and physiology of the instrument, many authors felt the need to embrace some concept. Unfortunately, the complete analysis of the action of the laryngeal mechanism, minute and rapid, defied investigators who lacked the aid of radiology, high-speed photography and other modern tools. Many theories arose. Even as recently as 1973, John Burgin writes in Teaching Singing, "There is yet no complete agreement as to how the voice is produced in the larynx."

In 1849, Panseron writes,

> Of all the theories that have been published on the
> subject of how the voice is produced, the following
> appears to be the most simple and rational. The air
> forced through the lungs at will, in breaking through
> the lips of the glottis, produces the sonorous undula-
> tions which are modified by the pharynx, the tongue,
> the lips, the internal nasal apertures, in short, by
> all the vocal apparatus. The production of the vocal
> sound and its different modifications would then be
> the result of the glottis being more or less open,
> according to the contraction or relaxation of the lips
> of the glottis, or vocal chords [p. 1].

He is, of the 100 authors surveyed, the first to express such a complete theory, a theory which he no doubt gleaned from various physiology and anatomy books of his time. Generally, however, the more famous teacher, Garcia, is given credit for introducing phonatory anatomy and physiology to singing books. Emma Seiler, in her book of 1871, quotes liberally from his paper, published by the London, Edinburgh, and Dublin Philosophical Magazine and Journal of Science, vol. X, 4th series, London, 1855, entitled "Observations with the Laryngoscope." Therein, Garcia writes,

> The inferior ligaments at the bottom of the larynx
> form exclusively the voice, whatever may be its regis-
> ter or its intensity; for they alone vibrate at the bottom
> of the larynx.... By the compressions and expansions
> of the air, or the successive and regular explosions
> which it produces in passing through the glottis, sound
> is produced [as quoted in Seiler, 1871, p. 48].

Other authors of singing books in the 1860's and 70's more or less repeat the findings of Garcia and nineteenth-century physiologists:

> All sound is the effect of vibration of something. In
> the voice it is the ... 'vocal cord' [Daniell, 1873, p.
> 18].

All physiologists agree that the inferior vocal cords are the principal source of the voice, that the difference in pitch depends upon the degree and mode in which the five pairs of muscles, which regulate the larynx, contract or dilate the glottis, and that the entire apparatus partakes at once of the nature of a reed and stringed instrument [Bassini, 1869, pp. 5-6].

Bassini is thus the first in this group to compare the action of the vocal bands to reed and string instruments. Many authors including Holmes, Browne and Behnke, and Lunn concur subsequently:

The economy of nature ... has given us a pair of membranous reeds, the so-called vocal cords, as the essential part of our vocal apparatus. But, compared with artificial reed instruments, the voice appears to exceed them as much in complexity as it does in beauty [Holmes, 1879, pp. 76-77].

The reed theory is the one most generally accepted by modern writers, and so far as the actual production of the original tones of the voice is concerned it is absolutely correct, because the vocal ligaments cut up the column of air passing between them into a quick and regular succession of puffs, just the same as reeds [Browne and Behnke, 1883, pp. 70-71].

Browne and Behnke also state that two other theories, the string and the flute-pipe theories, are plausible, within limits:

the vocal ligaments were compared 200 years ago by Ferrein to vibrating strings, and as the sounds of both are raised by tension there seem, at first sight, to be good grounds for this comparison. We have since learnt, what Ferrein did not know, that the tone of the vocal ligaments may be raised, like that of strings, by shortening, which fact goes a long way towards confirming this theory. Nevertheless, the comparison breaks down as soon as we examine it at all carefully, for it is found by experiments that the scale of changes produced by the tension of strings is totally different from that of the same process applied to the vocal ligaments [p. 70].

We have seen in the chapter on sound that the pitch

of tones produced by flute-pipes is mainly governed
by the length of the tube. Now the larynx, as a general rule, stands lower in the throat in the production
of low tones than in the production of high tones,
which, of course, means that the vocal tube is longer
in the production of low tones and shorter in the production of high tones. There would, consequently,
seem to be some justification in comparing the human
voice to a flute-pipe. But when we consider that it
requires an open tube of about six feet to produce the
low G of any ordinary bass voice, we see at once
that this comparison cannot for a moment be seriously
maintained [p. 70].

The voice is a reed instrument, embracing the principles of a string, and indirectly in small degree of a
pipe [Lunn, 1880, p. 8].

In most cases, these analogies are directly applicable to a
true vocal band theory, such as is stated by Behnke or Mackenzie:

The vocal ligaments, having met, are struck by the
air blown against them from below, and being elastic
they yield, allowing themselves to be forced upwards.
A little air is set free, and the pressure from below
is diminished, in consequence of which the vocal ligaments resume their former position, and even move a
little downward. The renewed pressure of the air
once more overcomes the resistence of the vocal ligaments, which again recede as soon as another escape
of air has taken place, and this process is repeated
in rapid succession. In this manner alone, is vocal
tone produced, whether it be called chest, falsetto,
head or by any other name [Behnke, 189-, p. 38].

Three factors must be taken into account in considering any vocal sound produced by the larynx: first,
the degree of tension of the cords; secondly, the
quantity of reed that is thrown into vibration (this
may vary as regards (a) length, and (b) breadth); and
thirdly, strength of blast. Stretching will of itself
raise the pitch, the strength of blast remaining the
same, and, conversely, increase of blowing-power
alone will heighten pitch, the tension remaining the
same [Mackenzie, 1891, p. 64].

Lunn, however, uses the same analogies of reed, string, and

pipe in his explanation of the false vocal band theory, variously called valvular or ventricular control. Miller credits Mackenzie with naming the false vocal bands "ventricular bands," and this may be so. But Mackenzie believes in a true vocal band mechanism. Nevertheless, it is probably Mackenzie's use of this term that leads such writers as Myer [1891, pp. 54-55] to claim Mackenzie for the ranks of those teachers who believe in a false vocal band theory.

The author generally acknowledged as the first to propose a ventricular band theory is Charles Lunn. He claims to have based his findings on Dr. Wyllie's analysis of a corpse's larynx:

> The ventricles that lie between the true and false cords supply the explanation of all voice production. ... [T]he upper part of the ventricle of Morgagni serves to increase the resistence of the true vocal cords whenever the latter have to maintain a relatively greater pressure [1880, p. 13].

Lunn is, therefore, espousing a double valve theory in which

> ... [T]he false cords alone may slightly separate, assuming a fixed position, restraining the escape of vocalized air, while the true cords of themselves, by their own elasticity, alternate between parallel lines and ovals. This ... is true production [1888, p. 26].

Two other authors who concur with this theory are Myer [1891, pp. 44-56] and van Broekhaven [1905, pp. 9-10].

This theory of false vocal band control is largely confined to the 30 years 1880 to 1910, but it had become popular enough during that period to warrant attack by a number of authors, including Miller and Proschowsky:

> Nearly every authority on the physiology of voice-production believes that the vocal tone is produced solely by the vibration of the vocal cords, and that the entire vocal tract situated above the vocal cords is concerned merely with augmenting the tone and determining its timbre and quality [Miller, 1910, p. 83].

> Many theories have existed regarding the purpose of the false vocal chords,--for instance: that falsetto was produced by the false vocal chords. Many other

statements have been made that were more fancies than facts. One theory as to vibrations taking on modulations of form according to the opening or expanding of these pockets, still remains unproven; and as these movements can never be definitely controlled and only exist in theory, my advice is not to attach any importance to the claim [Proschowsky, 1923, p. 16].

A few authors present theories uniquely their own. Francis Romer, in his Physiology of the Human Voice, introduces his first chapter with the statement:

> On the vocal instrument having two distinct points for producing its vibrations, one for forming its speaking voice and other its musical quality of tone--the speaking voice depending on modifications and contractions of the larynx and glottis, the musical voice being a vibrated column of air, depending upon the openness of the tube [1845, p. 5].

On page 13 of the same chapter, he adds to this theory, "It is my opinion that the first vibrations of the musical voice are produced by the smaller bronchial tubes."

The nineteenth century is not the sole era of exotic theories. Ernest G. White declares that the two major premises of his The Voice Beautiful in Speech and Song are:

> a) The vocal cords ... are not the seat of sound ... [and] in neither speech nor song do the vocal cords actually create the tone. b) To show that the whole compass of the human voice is divided between four sets of sinuses (or cavities) which are found on each side of the head [1927, pp. 5-6].

It is these sinuses that produce the sound, White claims.

Descriptions of the Anatomy and Physiology of the Larynx and Associated Phonatory Apparatus

After the decade ending 1879, more than half of the sources surveyed offered a description of the anatomy of the larynx, of the physiology of the larynx, or of both. Some also offered a synopsis of the major laws of acoustics affecting vocal tones. Those volumes that offer primarily anatomy include Lamperti [1883], Mackenzie [1891], Hulbert [1921], and Witherspoon [1925]. The Mackenzie Hygiene of the Vocal Organs is particularly excellent. Authors who discuss both anatomy and physiology in noteworthy form include Bassini [both 1857 and 1869], Browne [1887], Browne and Behnke [1883], Holmes [1879], Nathan [1836], and Seiler [1871]. Two sources, particularly fine regarding acoustics, are Voice, Song and Speech [1883] of Browne and Behnke and The Way to Sing [1923] of Proschowsky. Three of the most complete analyses of phonatory physiology are offered by Henderson [1906], Miller [1910], and Shakespeare [1910]. Parisotti devotes two pages of his work to terminology related to phonation [1911, pp. 5-6].

METHODS : THE PSYCHOLOGICAL APPROACH

Total Coordination Required

Many authors believe that phonation is best effected when attention is paid to the total coordination of the muscles of singing and a minimum of attention is directed to the throat. Clippinger warns that there must never be local controls in the throat [1910, p. 4]. Myer says, "Release everything above the chest" [1913, p. 9], and Taylor affirms that "no mechanical means has ever been found for directly controlling the operations of the vocal cords" [1917, p. 43]. The same concept is held for other local efforts:

> When the writer in early student days concentrated his attention upon the tongue, he found that this member became very stiff and unruly indeed. When, on the other hand, he relaxed mentally, and thought only of what he had to pronounce, his tongue reposed peacefully enough in its place at the bottom of his mouth [Ffrangçon-Davies, 1904, p. 83].

Mental Concept of Tone and Pitch

To many authors, the mental image of the correct tone and pitch is the primary condition.

> It is an absolute condition that the singer should have each note he wishes to produce beforehand in his mind as an intelligent conception [Bach, 1894, p. 149].

> First, he must form a definite mental conception of

every tone, and that same concept must include the vowel on which it is to be sung [Rogers, 1910, p. 100].

Mental concept precedes the action and governs it. Therefore, instead of producing tone by local effort, by conscious muscular action of any sort, correctly think the tone, correctly shape and color it mentally. Every vocal tone is a mental concept made audible [Fillebrown, 1911, p. 82].

We hear the tone mentally before we sing it, and we should hear it as distinctly as if it were sung by another [Clippinger, 1917, p. 6].

If you are to sing a certain pitch you must first hear it mentally; otherwise you are most likely to sing the wrong pitch [Downing, 1927, p. 16].

METHODS : THE TECHNICAL APPROACH

Control of the Oral Cavity

The mouth opening is important. Only a few authors speak specifically of the importance of the mouth opening:

Es ist wichtig, dass man beym singen den Mund gehörig öffne/ It is important that in singing the mouth should be properly open [Pfeiffer and Nägeli, 1830, p. 10].

In respect to the former [the mouth] it is certain that the slightest change or variation in the form of the mouth will cause an equivalent change and variation in the tone, and it will come forth harsh or sweet, full or thin, brilliant or heavy, according to the method which the pupil is taught to form this feature [Lanza, 1818, x].

The mouth is undoubtedly the most important cavity of our resonator, and the shape of it may be altered by the action of the lower jaw, the lips, the tongue and the soft palate [Browne and Behnke, 1883, p. 158].

Many authors speak indirectly of the importance of mouth opening by offering suggestions for correct formation.

Of the 100 authors, almost half comment on this concept.
It is especially important in the earliest years of this study,
where 10 of the first 13 writers speak of it.

> The Mouth should be moderately open, that the tones
> may come forth freely [Corfe, 18--, p. 4].

> Er verhüte dass sie den Mund nicht zu weit öffnen/
> Guard that you don't open the mouth too wide [Lasser,
> 1805, Preface].

> Open the mouth in an oblong form, as smiling [D.
> Corri, 1811, p. 11].

The concept of the smiling position is the oldest in
this study. In 1780, Hiller writes that a gentle smile is
"die anständigste beym Gesange, und die bequemste zur Hervor-
bringung eines guten Tons der Stimme"/ the most proper in
singing, and the most comfortable for bringing forward a good
tone in the voice [p. 6]. Other early writers also consider
this the best position:

> It is when the mouth is in a smiling form that the
> sweetest tones are produced [Nathan, 1836, p. 161].

> The mouth to be opened, a smiling position of it being
> most favourable to the production of a good tone [Cooke,
> 1828, Introduction].

> The mouth should be kept smiling, without distortion,
> and open sufficiently to admit the end of the forefinger
> [Lablache, 184-, p. 5].

This smiling position can be found in more recent writings:
"The mouth is to be opened as far as a gentle smile, so that
it may form an oval in a horizontal position" [Bach, 1898,
p. 28]. This concept is opposed, however, by six writers
of the twentieth century, beginning with Salvatore Marchesi.

> The 'smiling mouth' ... is absolutely contrary to the
> laws of acoustics, and consequently hinders the pro-
> duction of aesthetic, rounder sounds, homogeneous in
> their succession [1902, p. 15].

> The smiling mouth ... favoured by many professors
> past and present, is absured ... smiling causes the
> mouth to assume the position required for pronouncing

the Italian vowel E (pronounced ay) ... and gives a
too open tone to the voice, called by the Italians voce
sgangherata and by the French voix blanche [Mathilde
Marchesi, 1903, xii].

Fillebrown affirms that a smile draws back the corners of
the mouth and thus lessens the resonance of the sound [1911,
p. 10]. Downing allows a slight smile, because he believes
that it "will stretch the palate sidewise and will prevent
'nosey singing,'" but too broad a smile makes the tone thin
[1927, p. 5]. Stanley writes that it spreads the tone and
loses the timbre [1916, p. 11].

Another technique for regulating the mouth opening is
the use of one or two fingers placed between the teeth.

The mouth should be open so far that the end of the
forefinger may have free play between the teeth [Mason,
1847, p. 100].

The old Italian school says the singer should open the
mouth as far as to be able to place his forefinger between the teeth [Bach, 1898, p. 28].

Guard particularly against opening the mouth too little
or too much; an exact rule for all cannot be given,
but there should be distance enough between the teeth
to admit the end of one or two fingers [Oliver, 186-,
p. 4].

Other writers who present this technique are Lablache [184-,
p. 5] and Seiler [1871, p. 127].

Only one writer, Caruso, minimizes the importance
of mouth opening, and this only in comparison to throat opening:

It must not be imagined that to open the mouth wide
will do the same for the throat. If one is well versed
in the art, one can open the throat perfectly without
a perceptible opening of the mouth, merely by the
power of respiration [1909, pp. 52-53].

Lingual Controls

Low tongue is advised. The first writers within the

confines of this study to advance the idea of a low tongue are
Pfeiffer and Nägeli, who write

> Während ihr ein Ton aushaltet, muss die Zunge flach
> und still liegen, und vorne sanft an die zähne ange-
> stossen werden/ While sustaining a tone, the tongue
> must lie flat and quiet, and the front be pressed easily
> against the teeth [1830, p. 10].

The first to give a reason why a low position of the tongue
is necessary is Costa, when he speaks of the cause of the
nasal tone.

> This voice is formed by the lower part or root of the
> tongue rising in contact with the soft pallet [sic] or
> roof of the mouth, and thus forcing a part of the so-
> norous air to pass ... through the nasal cavities
> [1838, p. 26].

Lablache believes the true reason for the tongue to
lie low is "to leave the greatest possible space" [184-, p. 5].
Two explanations from later periods are offered by Bach and
Downing.

> We expressly say 'with the tongue lying perfectly still
> and flat,' [because] ... if the epiglottis, by the re-
> traction of the tongue, is firmly pressed down on the
> vocal cords ... it muffles the sound and makes the
> notes thick and dull. Besides, the tones lose resonance
> as the tongue is raised. On the other hand, with a
> flat position of the tongue, the epiglottis is lifted up,
> and the voice sounds clear and full, pure and brilliant
> [Bach, 1898, p. 35].

> Train the tongue to relax (I use the term 'relax' in
> the sense that every organ or muscle works elastically,
> and under full control but it does not collapse) on the
> floor of the mouth.... If the back of the tongue
> bunches up in the throat, it acts as an obstruction,
> making it impossible for the tone to pass freely into
> the mouth and head for resonance [Downing, 1927, pp.
> 5-6].

Other writers who comment on this idea include Sieber [1872,
p. 47] and Garcia [1894, p. 18], who think that the singer
may have to press the tongue down with a spoon if it proves
too unruly, Lablache [186-, p. 1], Daniell [1873, p. 21],
and G. B. Lamperti [1905, p. 10fn].

In the first decade of the twentieth century, a new concept is added to the low-tongue theory, namely the "lingual furrow."

> A furrow must be formed in the tongue, which is least prominent in the lowest tones, and in direct head tones may even disappear.... Still there are singers whose tongues lie very well without a furrow [Lehmann, 1906, p. 54].

> The correct position of the tongue is raised from the back, lying flat in the mouth, the flattened tip beneath the front teeth, with the sides slightly raised as to form a slight furrow in it. When the tongue is lying too low a lump under the chin beneath the jaw will form in singing and the tight muscles can be easily felt [Tetrazzini, 1909, p. 18; Duff concurs, 1919, p. 25].

One author opposes the low-tongue concept.

> To train the tongue to habitual flatness at the middle and base as in the pronouncing of ah, is an error; all vowels except ah require conditions other than flatness of tongue [Russell, A Plain Talk with American Singers, 1904, p. 12].

Free tongue is advised. Five of 31 statements approving the free tongue are included here as typical.

> The pharynx can also give a fake timbre, as the guttural, the nasal and the round, which are produced when its cavity is disturbed by swelling the root of the tongue, a habit, unfortunately too common among singers [Bassini, 1869, p. 7].

> The tongue must be kept limp and motionless, neither raised at the point nor swollen at the root [Garcia, 1894, p. 18].

> If you can absolutely relax the root of the tongue, and let the tip of the tongue be softly against the lower teeth, you will rarely have difficulty with it [Duff, 1919, p. 25].

> As the parts under the chin go to form the root of the tongue, any rigidity here would involve the body

of the tongue, and thus prevent the purity in the tone of the voice [Shakespeare, 1924, p. 14].

The tongue ... should remain free to function in whatever way may be required of it by the pitch of the tone and the vowel in unity [Rogers, 1925, p. 64].

Use of the lips. An area not surveyed in the books of Burgin or Fields is the importance and the use of the lips in forming the tone. This concept is relatively important to the period covered by this study, since 21 authors talk of the lips.

The proper position of the lips is likewise of the greatest importance. For, besides materially affecting the appearance, they essentially contribute to the clearness of the voice, and of the pronunciation [Anfossi, 1800, p. 13].

Parisotti states that the lower lip should be consciously dropped while singing [1911, p. 33].

Two authors warn that the lips can interfere with good tone production. Seiler, says that lips too thick and stiff sometimes injure the timbre of the tone [1871, p. 128], while Russell notes that "lip shaping for vowel making is one of the errors through which intelligible diction among singers has been so nearly destroyed" [1904, p. 12].

Palatal Controls

The palate should be raised. Novello [1856, p. 15] and Bassini [1857, p. 10] are the first in this study to suggest that the palate be raised in order to create the greatest volume possible in the oral cavity. Simultaneously, the larynx finds its lowest position to further increase the size of the cavity. Thorp and Nicholl concur [1899, p. 11]. Behnke states that the palate must be raised to shut off the nasal cavities [189-, p. 59]. Others who agree include Guttmann [1887, p. 80], Bach [1894, p. 74], and Lablache and Taylor, who write:

... the soft palate and uvula descending, the sound is no longer able to issue freely, but introducing itself into the passage G [Lablache refers to a lettered diagram where G is the posterior nasal passage] which communicates with the nose, it becomes, in consequence, nasal [Lablache, 1860, p. 1].

In theory, the mechanical prevention of nasal resonance is very simple. It is necessary only to raise
the soft palate in singing, and thus to cut off the ex-
pired breath from passing into the nasal cavities.
Most vocal scientists advise that the singer hold the
soft palate raised for every note [Taylor, 1917, p. 64].

Two statements were found that declare palate position
a function of pitch.

The soft palate rises with the ascending scale, the
arch between the pillars of the fauces becomes nar-
rower and higher, and the uvula diminishes in size
[Browne and Behnke, 1883, p. 166].

In the medium and low voice the soft palate is more
or less raised, depending upon the vowel or word to
be sung. But as higher pitches are reached, the palate lowers and moved forward, making more space
behind the palate for the flow of tone to continue more
freely into the head and giving freedom and a ringing
quality to the head tones which cannot be secured in
any other way [Downing, 1927, p. 4].

The palate should be free. The 32 authors who support
a raised palate are opposed by nine authors. The arguments
of this smaller group, however, are numerous. Taylor states
that any tone is made difficult to produce when the palate is
forceably held up [1917, p. 128]. Parisotti thinks that raising
the palate only serves to create a cul-de-sac above the pharynx
which offers "a circuitous course" out of the throat [1911,
p. 23]. Muckey and Miller believe that nasal resonance is
shut off:

If we cut off the upper pharynx and nasal cavities by
raising the soft palate there is not sufficient resonance
space left to properly reinforce the fundamental tone
and it remains weak [Muckey, 1915, pp. 64-65].

Drawn upward and backward against the pharyngeal
wall, it [the soft palate] shuts off the superior resonating chamber, destroying the four upper partials,
and leaving the fundamental weak [Miller, 1917, p.
194].

Clippinger believes that raising the palate serves no purpose
at all:

But whether the soft palate is high or low does not settle the matter. It is not at all necessary that breath should pass through the nasal cavities in order to make them act as resonators. In fact it is necessary that it should not. It is the air that is already in the cavities that vibrates. Neither is it necessary that the vibrations should be transmitted to the head cavities by way of the pharynx and over the soft palate. They may be transmitted through the bones of the head [1917, p. 16].

Myer believes that drawing up the palate causes the walls to become hard, "and the tone will be hard, metallic or white" [1891, p. 71].

Open Throat Concept

Control of the throat. Six authors advise some form of throat control. Ten authors oppose the concept. Two statements advocating throat control are followed by five statements opposing the concept.

A careful study of the production of singers who use an open throat, shows that the voice is produced from lowest to highest tones with scarcely any change in the position of the mouth and pharyngeal cavities. When the point in the ascending scale is reached where the disagreeable tone appears, instead of closing the throat so as to avoid that tone, they make an effort to open it still wider, and by so doing the quality is maintained. In short, a uniformly open throat produces a uniformly open and even tone throughout the scale. Such a use of the voice we call 'open production' [Thorp and Nicholl, 1896, p. 11].

To have the attack true and pure one must consciously try to open the throat not only in front, but from behind, for the throat is the door through which the voice must pass, and if it is not sufficinetly open it is useless to attempt to get out a full round tone [Caruso, as quoted by Marafioti, 1922, p. 157].

The second important fallacy for consideration is the instruction to open or close the throat [Shaw, 1914, p. 4; his first fallacy is the idea that one should consciously control the breath expiration].

The throat must be free from local effort to realize
pure tone quality [Russell, 1904, p. 11].

Singers should never be conscious of effort in the
throat; they should feel it all below the throat in the
muscles of the body.   The whole neighborhood of the
throat should be kept quiet [Henderson, 1920, p. 39].

Foremost, then, is dropping all throat consciousness,
all thought of the throat, all drawing of attention to it.
The larynx must be uncramped, unhindered to do its
work in free unconsciousness, which it will do if not
disturbed by tension in its neighborhood, or by mis-
directed thought [Fillebrown, 1911, pp. 75-76].

The proper office of the throat is simply that of a
passageway [Duff, 1919, p. 39].

Yawning as a throat-opening device.   Eleven authors
recommend that the student should either imagine the feeling
of a yawn or actually practice yawning to open the throat.
(Statements by Garcia on yawning appear in the books of 1894
and 1924, accounting for the tally of 12 statements in Table
4.)

The sensation of freedom in the throat should be 'as
before drinking' or 'as before yawning' [Shakespeare,
1924, p. 14].

Most of my readers have yawned once or twice in
their lives; if they will do it once more, in front of
their looking-glass, and watch the inside of the mouth
as they yawn, they will see and feel the exact position
in which the throat should be during good singing
[Crowest, 1900, p. 56].

The main singing effort (physical) is that of breath
control.   Now suddenly change the effort and open the
throat and back mouth (the fauces) wide, for a good
hearty yawn.   Notice the stretching of the soft palate
upward and sidewise; the uvula recedes, often quite
out of sight; the tongue flattens, and the back part
recedes, as it were, into the throat [Russell, 1912,
p. 15].

Whenever the tongue rises at its base, it drives back
the epiglottis on the column of ascending air, and

causes the voice to be emitted with a guttural choked
sound.   The best method of correcting this defect is
to keep the tongue flat as in yawning [Garcia, 1924,
p. 6].

The jaw low and free.   Passages dealing with the correct position of the jaw were found in 35 sources.   Six representative statements serve here as examples.   Costa's
"Eighth Fault" of a singer is "the intractability of the lower
jaw ... and, on the other hand, a too running movement of
the same jaw" [1824, p. 18].

The jaws should not remain perpendicularly one over
the other (as has been wrongly said) but in the position
which is most natural for the conformation of the pupil's mouth [Lablache, 184-, p. 5].

It is the sign of good singing when the tongue and jaw
act in complete independence.   In a free emission of
the voice, the mouth opens of itself and the jaw drops
as it were by its own weight....   Happily, when singing with the throat open, we cannot hold the jaw [Shake-
speare, 1924, pp. 14-15].

A rigid jaw is perhaps the singer's greatest enemy.
There is nothing which will handicap clear enunciation
or produce a more metallic tone quality, than a rigid
jaw.
    To relax the jaw, think of loosening the muscles at
the angle of the jaw below the ears, these being the
muscles that tighten the jaw.   Relax these muscles
and let the jaw hang.   However, the jaw cannot always
hang in a wide open position; but no matter what position the jaw is in, it can be relaxed by practicing in
this manner.
    Keep the upper and lower back jaw well separated.
This position allows more space in the mouth and
throat and enriches the tone quality [Downing, 1927,
p. 8].

The jaw must be dropped down, not back, or out [Stan-
ley, 1916, p. 21].

The free movement of the lower jaw is downwards and
backwards.
    During singing it should be unconstrained, balanced,
floating, as it were, and entirely independent of the
movements of the tongue [Shakespeare, 1910, p. 27].

Position of the Larynx

The larynx should move. Among the authors who believe that the larynx moves in singing, only two suggest that
this should be in some way a conscious effort on the part of
the singer. The other authors observe this as a natural function, and some warn against conscious control.

Anna Lankow believes the larynx should be depressed
and kept in this position whenever singing [1899, p. 18 and
1903, p. 18]. Browne and Behnke take a more conservative
viewpoint:

> With regard to the general position of the larynx the
> most contradictory opinions are entertained by different
> teachers. Some say that it should be kept rigidly fixed
> quite low in the throat. This is a mistaken idea, for
> it is impossible to hold the voice-box absolutely in
> the same position. But even continually to depress
> the larynx as far as possible is an unwise proceeding,
> involving an unnatural strain upon the vocal organ
> which must, in the long run, be injurious.
>   Other teachers maintain, on the contrary, that the
> larynx must have free play, and that its movements
> must not on any account be interfered with. ...
>   The proper thing is to avoid both extremes and to
> give the larynx just that amount of fixity which enables
> it to offer the necessary resistance to the pressure of
> the air from below, thus giving the muscles governing
> the pitch of the voice the best chance of acting with
> ease and certainty [1883, pp. 157-158].

Two authors acknowledge that thought regulates the
movement of the larynx, but indirectly through the desire to
alter pitch and intensity or to achieve an open feeling, and
not by local effort controls.

> Why should there be so much said about the larynx in
> singing? Nature never intended that man should man-
> age the position and movements of the larynx by a
> direct control effort, any more than she intended that
> he should always be a conscious local effort, approxi-
> mate the vocal cords when he desired to sing or speak.
>   It is true, the larynx does go up and it does go
> down in correct singing, and at times it is in a fixed
> firm position, not as the result of local control, but
> as the result of thought or effect. The correct move-

ments and position of the larynx in the properly man-
aged voice depend entirely upon the thought, upon the
effect which the singer may desire to produce [Myer,
1891, pp. 115-116].

The larynx must be allowed freedom to move, but it
must not be continually moving up to the top of the
throat, as it will act as an obstruction, as does the
high position of the tongue. To relax the larynx, think
the throat open and relax the jaw [Downing, 1927, pp.
8-9].

Other sources describe movements of the larynx without
mentioning any process of thought.

In the chest tones the position of the larynx is lowered
[Seiler, 1871, p. 127].

The action of the larynx being pressed down towards
the throat by the windpipe shortening and dilating,
produces the lowest notes; in forming the higher notes
of the scale, the larynx is then pressed upward to the
fullest extent which the elasticity of the windpipe will
allow [Bishenden, 1876, p. 15].

The depression of the larynx should not be the same
for every gradation of tone, but its position should
vary with the formation of the different vowels, each
of which requires it to be in a special position [Gutt-
mann, 1887, p. 93].

When singing in what is called chest-voice the voice-
box rises gradually with each higher note [Behnke,
189-, p. 69].

Two authors affirm that throat movement must be made,
but stress that this is done without conscious thought.

In order to sing evenly, smoothly and effectively it is
absolutely necessary that all thought of holding the
larynx up or down, or fixed in any position, be abandoned [Shaw, 1914, p. 81].

The larynx should never be held raised or pressed;
nothing must be done to impede the natural movements
which belong to the accomodating process of pitch and
vowel [Rogers, 1925, p. 63].

The larynx should not move. One author believes that the singer should ignore the larynx and it will not move. The rest believe that the singer must consciously seek to fix the larynx.

> Leave the larynx, as a whole, in a state of quiet repose, and the tone and word assume at once a histrionic, eloquent character [Ffrangçon-Davies, 1904, p. 84].

> Fix the larynx at the highest elevation for each fundamental note [Lunn, 1880, p. 24].

> The larynx, or upper part of the windpipe, plays a most important part in singing. Upon it depends all the beauty, and quality, and richness of the voice. The singer will do well to constantly think about the larynx, to watch it, to feel that it is well down below the mouth before commencing the first note of a song. ... Then the larynx must never be allowed to rise above the fixed point. It may be deepened, and must be, for the higher notes, but it must never ascend [Crowest, 1900, p. 57].

Russell also believes that the larynx must be constantly kept down [1912, p. 37].

The larynx should remain low. A few of the statements quoted above in regard to the larynx show that a number of authors believe the larynx must lie low in the throat at least some of the time. Two authors, Crowest and Russell, (directly above) believe that the larynx should be fixed in a low position. Other authors reach more moderate conclusions:

> When the larynx is held too high, the pharynx is unduly contracted, and the so-called 'throaty' tone results [G. B. Lamperti, 1905, p. 26].

> Only one muscular action has ever been defined by which the throat might be 'opened.' That is, the lowering of the larynx and the raising of the soft palate.... [T]he power of the voice is developed by singing with the larynx low in the throat [Taylor, 1917, p. 60].

In the attempt to get the tone forward, the larynx is

frequently pushed up. Remember that the tone can be forward while the larynx remains in its natural low position. Your throat will feel comfortable if you let it alone [Shaw, 1914, p. 187].

The training of a singer to lower the larynx for the production of a certain quality of tone has been successful to some extent, but at the risk of making the voice darker than normal.... However, those who understand the value and right use of the low larynx are at great advantage in their art.... In working for the ideal condition of the low larynx, I would prefer calling it a loose, low, open, comfortable throat. We must start with these conditions from our lowest tones.... The vowel-sound that is most effective in lowering the larynx is oo [Proschowsky, 1923, p. 97].

The Attack

Theories and descriptions of attack. "The attack of the tone is that starting point of its sounding, which is caused by the vibration of the breath against the vocal cords in the larynx" [Russell, 1912, p. 44]. Attack is an action that undergoes considerable analysis during the time span of this study. One concept generally associated with Garcia and his adherents, the coup de glotte, is given separate attention.

In the early years of this study, the main attention in attack was centered on precision of execution. Two habits that mitigate a clean attack are scooping and aspirating.

Dieser Fehler besteht in der Gewöhnung, einen Vorschlag von oben herunter, oder von unter hinauf, an den Anfang oder das Ende der Töne zu hängen/ This failure [unclean attack] comes about through the habit of entering the attack from above downward or from under upward at the beginning or the end of a tone [D'Aubigny, 1803, p. 117].

The point is, to attack the given sound, previously in mind, with precision and confidence.... The attack must be direct and instantaneous [Bassini, 1857, p. 5].

We must avoid commencing a sound, by preceding with a kind of preparation, which may be expressed by um [Lablache, 184-, p. 5].

Aspiration is recommended by two authors of the twentieth century, however:

Do not venture to sing without aspirating the word about to be sung, as though warming some object [Shakespeare, 1910, p. 54].

Van Broekhaven declares that the attack should be softened with the thought of an aspirate H [1908, p. 21].

Authors of the twentieth century tell how a clean attack should be accomplished.

One of the most important acts in singing is attack, or the beginning of the tone. First of all the singer must have a strong mental conception of where the tone is to be produced and how it must sound. Let the breath be directed to that point, as the attack is made with the breathing muscles. Never make the attack with the muscles of the throat and larynx. The throat should remain open during the attack. Should the attack not be made with the breath, then the throat and larynx will contract and the glottis will strike for the attack, a method which should never be used except for rare dramatic effects [Downing, 1927, p. 12].

The attack of the sound must come from the apoggio, or breath prop. In attacking the very highest note it is essential, and no singer can really get the high notes or vocal flexibility or strength of tone without the attack coming from this seat of respiration [Tetrazzini, 1909, p. 16].

The emission of the singer's breath and the attack of tone must take place simultaneously [Fucito, 1922, p. 128].

The coup de glotte. Few concepts in vocal pedagogy have aroused such heated discussion as the concept of the coup de glotte. Hardly a book in the period 1890-1927 ignores the idea. Even authors such as Fucito and Downing (see immediately above) who avoid directly naming the concept, obviously have taken opposing sides in the argument whether or not there is a need to regulate attack with the vocal ligaments. The concept is, therefore, more important than the figures in Table 4 would seem to indicate. An attempt will be made at the end of this chapter to clarify the problem. Various arguments in support of both sides are set down here in exemplification.

> We must make the pupil understand that the action of
> the glottis in setting the sound (the stroke of the glot-
> tis) is a normal, and not an extraordinary, accidental
> function of the vocal organism, which henceforth has
> to be subordinated to the will, instead of being an un-
> conscious act.... Of course, the bringing together
> and the tightening of the edges (lips) of the glottis must
> not be exaggerated by extraordinary compulsion on
> attacking the sound in singing, but must be accomplished
> in a smooth way as in speaking [S. Marchesi, 1902,
> p. 19].

Q. What follows after the preparation above noted?
   [stance and positions of the jaw and lips]
A. The actual articulation of 'stroke' of the glottis.
Q. What do you mean by the stroke of the glottis?
A. The neat articulation of the glottis that gives a
   precise and clean start to a sound.
Q. How do you acquire that articulation?
A. By imitation, which is quickest of all; but in the
   absence of a model, let it be remembered that
   by slightly coughing we become conscious of the
   existence and position of the glottis, and also of
   its shutting and opening action. The stroke of
   the glottis is somewhat similar to the cough,
   though differing essentially in that it needs only
   the delicate action of the lips and not the impulse
   of the air....
Q. How are sounds to be attacked?
A. With the stroke of the glottis just described [Gar-
   cia, 1894, pp. 13-14].

Immediately below the vocal cords there exists a valve;
the breath should be raised to that valve ready before
the sound is required, then when the valve is opened
the pressure of wind produces the sound or sequence
of sounds the singer or speaker wills [Santley, 1908,
p. 62].

The pupil should hermetically close the glottis so that
its extreme edges, called the Vocal Cords, may be
set vibrating by the air which bursts at the moment
of Expiration.
   The closing of the glottis is, then a natural and

spontaneous organic action.... The pupil need do no more than endeavor to keep the glottis contracted after its lips have been brought together [M. Marchesi, 1903, xii].

There is a moment of time when vibration commences, and that commencement is the true stroke of the glottis [Daniell, 1873, p. 66].

The stroke of the glottis is truly the basis of all correct teaching [Myer, 1886, p. 73].

Others who speak favorably of the stroke of the glottis, however they define it, include Lunn [1888, p. 21], Thorp and Nicholl [1896, pp. 29-30], Russell [1912, p. 49], Curtis [1914, pp. 141-147], Bach [1894, pp. 128-135], Miller [1910, pp. 132-134], and Botume [1897, p. 17].

The real opposition to the coup de glotte begins around the year 1900, or about six years after Garcia's Hints on Singing was published. Mathilde Marchesi, who may have been brought over to the side that favored the coup de glotte by her husband (see immediately above) in 1901 seems somewhat skeptical of the technique as interpreted by most teachers:

I would ... caution the pupil against a too violent attack (called 'coup de glotte') which many teachers council and which wearies the vocal cords [1901, p. 3].

The injurious 'stroke of the glottis' should under no consideration be employed in tone-attack; it ruins the voice, and ought, in spite of the apparent certainty attained in tone-production, to be wholly eschewed [Lamperti, 1905, p. 10 fn].

If you ever hear this stroke of glottis on the attack, you may know that the singer did not attack far enough back in the throat [Caruso, 1909, pp. 52-53].

Anna Lankow, a collaborator with Garcia before his death, admits that she cannot agree with Garcia on this point.

Above all things, I positively reject the glottis attack, which even Garcia approves. Not only does the tone thus begun cause an inartistic, hard and toneless click before the real singing tone is perceived, but the glottis attack also gives a kind of shock, each time, to the vocal cords, which weakens their otherwise artistic capabilities, and often causes diseases of the cords, such as nodes or knots of the same. An attacking ... with the stroke of the glottis is altogether and entirely precluded [1903, p. 19].

Others who reject the stroke of the glottis include Shaw [1914, p. 199], Duff [1919, p. 40], Hulbert [1921, p. 116], and Melba [1926, p. 16].

The Vocal Vibrato and the Tremolo

The dictionary defines vibrato as "a pulsating effect, less extreme than a tremolo, produced by rapid alternation of a given tone with a barely perceptible variation in pitch." Tremolo is defined as "a tremulous effect produced by the rapid reiteration of the same tone ... [and is the] same as vibrato." Two valuable articles on vibrato and tremolo are found in the Harvard Dictionary of Music (2nd ed.). The article on "Vibrato" (2) states that, in singing, there is some uncertainty as to what vibrato actually means, as well as some confusion of it with tremolo. According to some authorities, vocal vibrato is the quick reiteration (usually eight times per second) of the same pitch produced by a quickly intermittent stream of breath with fixed vocal chords. ... Excessive vibrato results in a real wobble, caused by a lack of control of the vocal apparatus, extreme fatigue, or even psychological factors. This unwelcome effect in singing is called "tremolo." The article on "Tremolo" (III) states that a singing tremolo "commonly means the excessive vibrato that leads to deviation of pitch." Some concepts of vibrato and tremolo from the sources of this study agree closely with these definitions. Others do not. A number of statements are offered as examples.

The vibrato is a rhythmic pulsation of the voice. It often appears in untrained voices, in others it appears during the process of cultivation. Some have thought it the perfection of sympathetic quality; others esteem it a fault.
The vibrato is caused by an undulating variation of pitch or power, often both. The voice does not hold steady and strictly to the pitch, and according to the amount of the variation a corresponding vibrato, or tremolo, is produced. ...
Three sources are ascribed for the vibrato; one is

a rapid, spasmodic vibration of the diaphragm, causing variation of breath pressure; another is the alternate tension and relaxation of the larynx and vocal cords; a third is that commonest of faults--throat stiffness [Fillebrown, 1911, p. 80].

The difference between vibrato and tremolo is, that one is voluntary and produced by the respiratory act, while the latter is caused by a lack of tonicity of the cords and their mechanism [Curtis, 1914, p. 161].

Vibrato is the first stage, tremolo the second and much more hopeless.... Referable in the same way to the overburdening of the vocal cords is the excessive straining of the throat muscles [Lehmann, 1906, p. 144].

Vibrato is local and specific, while tremolo is constitutional and general, a chronic affection in vocalism [Miller, 1917, p. 135].

Some singers--as well as teachers--do not seem to be able to distinguish between the objectionable tremolo and the artistic vibrato.... The vibrato ... is an artistic phase of tone obtained only by such voices having a natural facility to assume any muscular position with ease, without having to resort to a rigid tension of the muscles. The vibrato results therefore from an easy control of the muscular functions, while the tremolo is due to muscular weakness, or lack of training [van Broekhaven, 1908, p. 45].

I consider that a 'wobble' can be produced either (a) by breath-controlling muscles, or (b) by throat muscles or tongue; and the wobble (a) I call tremolo and (b) I term vibrato [Dodds, 1927, p. 63].

A number of authors discuss the ideas that both vibrato and tremolo are in some way a lack of control, and that the true difference is in degrees.

One hears from time to time of vocalists who talk of possessing a natural tremolo.... [A] natural tremolo (uncontrolled or unconsciously produced) is quite possible, though it is not at all natural but habitual, and should be classed with the 'natural breathiness,' with 'natural throatiness,' or a hundred other things that are often termed natural [Dodds, 1927, p. 63].

To render the voice firm is to make it capable of swelling without tremor, and with a perfect intonation on any note [Anfossi, 1800, p. 11].

The shaking voice is the result of over-straining the vocal chord. The pupil imitates it, and lo! the fashionable 'tremolo' [Daniell, 1873, p. 53].

Usually tremolo is the result of organic weakness, sickness, poor use of the breath, or stiffness of the vocal organs. If it is a fault of production, it can be corrected. Quick exercises are advisable for curing this defect [Wronski, 1921, p. 64].

Proschowsky's cure is to "use as little effort as possible" in expiration [1923, p. 73]. Tetrazzini also has a cure:

The tremolo is a sure sign that the vocal chords have been stretched beyond their natural limits, and there is only one thing can cure this. That is absolute rest for some time and then beginning the study of the voice, first singing with the mouth closed and relying on very gentle breath pressure for the production of the sound [1909, p. 37].

Anything which tends to tie up the vocal cords, to rob them of perfect ease will bring on vibrato [Henderson, 1906, p. 56].

As an effect the vibrato is occasionally useful. Its use often becomes a habit, to the serious damage of voices. Vibrato is nothing else than overtaxing the voice. The vocal machinery, breath and larynx, are used to full capacity and then it is attempted to add 'some more.' That 'some more' is forcing [Wronski, 1921, p. 52].

Dodds reverses the popular view of tremolo as a more harmful condition than vibrato:

Vibrato ... is a most terrible fault, and much more serious in its consequences than the tremolo.... It is in the first place almost a certainty that you habitually sing with too great a breath pressure, constantly endeavoring to press out more breath than is advisable .... The resultant resistance of the throat muscles

to this pressure is the primary cause of your trouble
.... try to sing without breath pressure entirely.
Then let your throat loose, leave it alone. Slacken
all effort [Dodds, 1927, p. 67].

ANALYSIS AND COMMENTS

A total of 434 statements were found related to concepts of phonation. The corresponding chapters in the books
of Fields and Burgin uncovered 463 and 558 statements, respectively. This would seem to indicate that the subject of phonation has received increasing attention through the years.
Another figure that would bear this theory out is that the
first two-thirds of this study (one hundred years) contains
less than 20 per cent of the statements on phonation. Of
this small percentage, the vast majority of statements concern
themselves with positions of the mouth, lips, tongue and jaw.
Discussions on the nature of phonation and on relative merits
of local control in the throat simply do not appear until the
"scientific age" of vocal pedagogy. These facts would tend
to prove that teachers of the eighteenth and early nineteenth
centuries followed the bel canto adage, "An Italian singer has
no throat," patently refusing to draw the pupil's attention to
this area. Only those parts of the phonatory apparatus above
the larynx, areas visible for the purpose of adjustment, were
considered.

In the period beginning approximately 1840, the source
of the vocal sound begins to be examined by many writers on
vocal pedagogy. Writers, realizing that phonation is the piv-
otal component between the motor element (breathing) and
the quality-regulating element (resonance), feel a need to explain the subjects of phonation at length. Since science had
not yet developed tools sensitive enough to thoroughly examine
the phonatory process, a number of conflicting theories evolve.
Three popular analogies arise and are embraced by many
writers, namely the reed, string, and pipe theories. To a
certain extent this is unfortunate, since the voice is too unique
and complex a structure to be successfully compared with
other musical instruments.

The concepts discussed by the writers of the period
prior to the 1840's, i.e., high palate, low tongue, jaw low
and free, and the device of yawning continue to find acceptance
throughout this study. One idea that was formerly a cliche
of singing, the idea of fixing the smiling expression of the
face, falls out of favor in the twentieth century.

Despite the many analyses of the anatomy and physiology of the phonatory apparatus, authors are loath to speak of the throat in the act of singing. This is reflected in the low number of statements made concerning such important concepts as "control of the throat advised/not advised," and "larynx should/should not move." Quite possibly, the many writers who say nothing agree with the "old masters" that discussions of the throat have no place in teaching the voice.

The second half of this study witnesses the rise of two well-discussed theories, namely false vocal band (or ventricular) phonation and the stroke of the glottis (coup de glotte). The books of Fields and Burgin do not hold any statements on the false vocal band theory. Discussions of the stroke of the glottis are largely confined to historical discussions of the controversy. These two concepts, therefore, are basically confined to a period of fifty years centering around the year 1890. The arguments of the adherents of the false vocal band theory are clearcut, and no attempt will be made here to comment on the validity of the theory.

The subject of the stroke of the glottis, however, merits analysis and comment. Basically, the argument against stroking the glottis directs itself against the use of the term "stroking." Such a term engenders thoughts of slapping the vocal cords together with a "kind of shock," as Anna Lankow puts it. Garcia was well aware of the harm that the name, coup de glotte, was producing on his theory. In 1894 he wrote a footnote to "The Attack of Vocal Sounds" in Hints on Singing:

> The meaning of the term 'stroke of the glottis,' which was invented by the author (French: coup de glotte), has been seriously misrepresented, and its misuse has done a great deal of harm. To the student it is meant to describe a physical act of which there should be merely a mental cognizance, not an actual physical sensation. The 'articulation' which gives 'the precise and clean start to a sound' is not felt in the throat (i.e., the larynx) of the singer. It is the sound itself, the attack of the note, beginning clean, clear, and true, upon the middle of that note, without preliminary movement or action of any sort beyond the natural act of singing [p. 13].

Garcia is simply seeking, therefore, the clean attack mentioned by D'Aubigny [1803] or Bassini [1857] (see "The Attack"), free of scooping or aspiration.

The nature of the human vocal apparatus is such that, at some point, the vocal cords have to become taut and have to assume approximation in order to generate sound. It is possible to stop the breath altogether with the cords, so that the primary expulsion of air will blow the cords open violently with an accompanying click. This is not what Garcia desires. However, he fails to note that another control must come into play if the vocal bands are not to be solely responsible for the onset of attack. Henderson notes this other regulating element, the breath:

> If the singer thinks of the tone apart from its motor, the air column, he will fall into one or two vices: either his vocal cords will come together before the air strikes them from below, or afterward. If they do the former, the air will forcibly open them and a little clucking sound will be caused.
> This is not quite accurately described by some of the authorities on singing as the audible stroke of the glottis. It is most unbeautiful and is the most vicious form of bad attack [1906, pp. 49-50].

The stroke of the glottis should, therefore, not be an attack that begins with the vocal bands completely closed. The confusion is easy to understand, however, when we read in the same volume that contains Garcia's footnote (above), "The stroke of the glottis is somewhat similar to the cough" [1894, p. 13].

V

RESONANCE

Definitions. "Resonance is caused when a sounding body communicates its vibrations to another
body; or when, in other words, the second body
is thrown into co-vibration with the first body"
[S. Marchesi, 1902, p. 27]. Thorp and Nicholl
agree with this definition and add, "the second
body in such cases is called a sympathetic resonator" [1896, p. 68]. Parisotti defines resonance
differently:

> The name of resonance stands for the quantity
> of multiplication of the sound by reflections,
> and the name of tone stands for the quality of
> the sound, brought about by the particular con-
> figuration or shape of the resonator [1911, p.
> 8].

Myer includes resonance as part of the total
sound-making process:

> A singing tone is a musical sound caused by
> the pressure of a column of air from the
> lungs upon the vocal chords, which are there-
> by set in vibration, and which in turn cause
> the air, which is pressing through the glottis,
> to vibrate. This vibratory column of air
> passing into the pharynx and mouth causes
> the air in the pharynx and mouth, the resonant
> cavity of the voice, to vibrate. The vibratory
> waves of the resonant cavity communicate vi-
> bration to the outer ear, conveying to the ear
> the sensation of a musical sound, either good
> or bad, right or wrong, considered as a sing-
> ing tone [1883, p. 33].

Table 5.   SUMMARY OF CONCEPTS OF RESONANCE

I.   Theories of resonance

A. General descriptions	39
B. Acoustical factors	21
C. Physiological factors	
1. head resonance	
a) head cavities are important	9
b) head cavities are not important	1
2. function of sinuses	
a) sinuses are used	4
b) sinuses are not used	1
3. nasal resonance	
a) cavities are consciously employed	18
b) cavities are not consciously employed	8
4. importance of mouth and throat cavities	8
5. importance of chest cavity	12
6. the entire body as a resonator	2

II.   Methods of controlling vocal resonance

A. A psychological approach	
1. expressional intent controls resonance	5
2. the possibility of direct control	
a) resonance is directly controllable	15
b) resonance is not directly controllable	2
B. The technical approach	
1. acquiring a vocal focus	
a) the voice should be consciously focused	21
b) the voice should not be consciously focused	10
2. the value of humming	
a) humming is a useful device	13
b) humming is not a useful device	4
TOTAL STATEMENTS	193

THEORIES : GENERAL DESCRIPTIONS

Importance of Resonance

"The sound of the human voice is very complex and rich in harmonics, for the mouth, and various cavities opening into the mouth, act as resonators" [Thorp and Nicholl,

1896, p. 36]. Many writers voice the opinion of Myer, that "reinforcement by resonance ... is an important point in the training and development of the voice" [1891, p. 78]. Marafioti explains why this is true:

> Resonance is the most important factor in voice production. It furnishes to the voice volume and quality, and emphasizes its loudness. To rely on resonance rather than on force is essential for producing a big and pleasing voice [1922, p. 51; Muckey concurs, 1915, Introduction].

Another author who links quality to resonance is Behnke, who writes, "The quality of tone depends on the form of the vibrations ... and to give it some special quality, is the work of the resonator" [189-, p. 56; Fillebrown repeats this statement almost verbatim, 1911, p. 45].

Regarding the relation of quantity of sound to resonance, Shakespeare writes, "Unless the spaces in the mouth and throat vibrated in sympathy, there would be little volume in the sound of the voice" [1924, p. 45]. Two singers, Anna Case and Ursula Greville, both agree that a small voice, properly placed, will carry farther than a large voice, improperly placed [in Martens, 1923, p. 58 and p. 128, respectively].

Two authors point out the fact that the vocal cords alone cannot put out the artistic tone:

> The vocal cords do not sing; they only produce a sound, which ascends to the mouth. In the mouth the sound is transformed into tone, which, with proper cavity formation and breath control, resonates in the mouth and cavities of the head [Downing, 1927, p. 12].

> The vocal cords alone cannot make music any more than can the lips of the cornet player apart from his instrument. The tone produced by the vibrations alone of the two very small bands must, in the nature of things, be very feeble [Fillebrown, 1911, p. 44].

Some authors state that resonance is not enough, it must be correctly produced resonance:

> Any interference with the resonance mechanism necessitated a much wider swing of the cords for the pro-

duction of the required volume. This very wide swing interfered with the proper origination of the partial tones and thus impaired the quality [Muckey, 1915, p. 23].

When voices are forced, the overtones become more prominent than the fundamental tones [Marafioti, 1922, p. 6].

A correct vocal tone is the result of a properly controlled column of breath, and a correct cavity formation or space, in which the tone resonates. Big tones ... are produced in large, resonating spaces, while small tones are produced in small resonating spaces [Downing, 1927, p. 1].

Muckey believes that "the full use of resonance is ... the most important factor in economizing the breath" [1915, p. 63].

Descriptions of the Resonating Cavities

Many authors consider the resonator as the third member of the vocalization system, following the motor (breath) and the vibrator (the vocal ligaments). Behnke defines the vocal resonator:

We now come to the last part of our instrument, namely, the resonator, which is formed of (1) the pockets of the larynx; (2) the tube above the pocket ligaments; (3) the upper part of the throat; (4) the mouth; and (5) the nose [189-, p. 56; a similar description may be found in Myer, 1891, p. 122].

Authors who offer detailed descriptions, often accompanied by drawings and diagrams, include Browne and Behnke [1904, pp. 61-65], Curtis [1914, pp. 70-71], Mackenzie [1886, pp. 232-233], and Miller [1910, pp. 93-94].

The Nature of the Resonating Cavities

Strictly speaking, many of the statements contained within this heading are also part of acoustics (more abstract concepts are discussed later in this chapter under the heading, "Acoustics"), but these quotations deal specifically with the acoustical nature of the cavities themselves.

The nature of the resonating cavities, like the nature of the phonatory apparatus, was not a concern of the early writers in singing. The analysis of the resonating process is also an outgrowth of the "scientific era." (see the first few pages of Chapter IV):

> The intimate relationship existing between voice culture and the science of acoustics was formerly slightly perceived. The teaching of singing, as an art, then rested altogether on an empirical basis, and the acoustics of singing had not received the attention of scientists.
> With the publication in 1863 of Helmholtz's great work a new era began, although singers and scientists yet continue to look upon each other with suspicion [Fillebrown, 1911, p. 43].

Taylor affirms that the "old masters" had methods of controlling resonance:

> The old Italian masters naturally knew nothing whatever of resonance, nor of any kind of acoustics. Yet the accepted theories of resonance in its relation to the voice are directly based on a set of empirical observations made by the old masters [1917, p. 54].

Unfortunately, Taylor does not become specific. Perhaps he considers the rules governing the mouth, lips, tongue and jaw (see Chapter IV, Phonation) also as rules of correcting faults of resonation.

As was found in the chapter on phonation, the first hundred years of this study witness very few statements regarding resonance. Bassini is the first writer to offer specific suggestions regarding the control of resonance:

> In order to [sic] the production of the sombre tone, the pharynx (which it will be remembered modifies the tone) must enlarge, admitting the greatest practicable volume, or bulk, of air; and the larynx must fall. In producing the clear tone, on the contrary, the pharynx must lengthen and narrow, thus increasing the intensity or force of the air column, while it diminishes its bulk, and the larynx must rise [1857, p. 8].

However, the nature of the apparatus, or physiologically why such movements must take place, are not the concern of

Bassini. Real discussions of this order only begin in vocal pedagogy books after Helmholtz's <u>Die Lehre von den Tonempfindungen</u>. A few representative examples are included here:

The intrinsic tone of the vocal chords is a compound sound. The voice, as we hear it, is a more or less imperfect reinforcement of the intrinsic tone. ...
While singing, place the hands on different parts of the head, neck, or body above the waist line, and the vibrations of these resonators will be felt. All these, whether upper partials of the intrinsic tone, are themselves producing sound which unites with and increases the compound tone [Thorp and Nicholl, 1896, p. 35].

There are two kinds of sympathetic resonators of the voice--the fixed and the adjustable. To the first belong all the fixed bones situated above the abdominal cavity. To the second belong the walls of the chest, the trachea, the larynx, the tongue, the lower jaw, the soft palate, the lips, the cheeks, and nostrils, together with all the muscles which vibrate during the production of tone. ... The voice, unlike other instruments, can be used so that its sympathetic resonators produce different degrees and qualities of sound [Thorp and Nicholl, 1896, pp. 70-71].

A musical instrument is enriched in tone, either by the sympathetic vibration of a sound-board, or by that of the air in an enclosed compartment. ... In the human voice, the pressure of the breath is the motive power which sets in vibration the vocal cords, and thus acts like the bow of the violin. ... The hard palate and the teeth may be considered as the sounding-board, from which the voice is reflected and by which it is increased in force and brilliancy [Shakespeare, 1910, pp. 29-30].

The human voice is endowed with two adjustable resonating chambers, one above the other at the back of the tongue; and it is these which, when set in sympathetic vibration, add fullness and richness to the tone of the voice during singing [Shakespeare, 1924, p. 45].

About the year 1880, Professor F. C. Donders, of Utrecht, Holland, noticed that each vowel, when whis-

> pered, causes the air in the mouth and throat to re-
> sound at a different pitch [Shakespeare, 1924, p. 51].

Drew notes the complexity of the sounds produced by the vocal
cords:

> It is this complexity which makes it possible, when
> singing a given note, to produce at will all the dif-
> ferent vowel sounds, and also to suggest different
> emotions with the same vowel sound. ... [T]he sound
> produced by the larynx is reinforced by the air cav-
> ities in the throat, mouth and nose. The sound given
> by the fork is nearly a simple one, i. e. , partials are
> almost entirely absent, whereas that produced by the
> larynx is usually rich in partials. If there happens
> to be in the mouth, nose or chest an air cavity which
> is 'tuned' to one of these partials, that particular par-
> tial is reinforced, but the partials which find no sym-
> pathetic resonator remain relatively insignificant. The
> very large variation in quality which can be produced
> by a single voice is due almost entirely to the flexi-
> bility of the tongue, lips, soft palate, and walls of
> the throat, for this enables the resonators to be changed
> in volume, shape, and size of opening in an immense
> number of ways [Drew, 1924, p. 21].

> It is well known that every resonance-cavity has what
> may be called an 'elective affinity' for one particular
> note, to the vibrations of which it responds sympathet-
> ically, like a lover's heart answering that of his be-
> loved [Mackenzie, 1891, pp. 43-44; this quotation is
> repeated in Miller, 1910, pp. 93-94].

THEORIES : ACOUSTICAL FACTORS

It was not until the 1870's that vocal pedagogy books
began to include paragraphs or chapters on acoustics. One
of the earliest works is Emma Seiler's The Voice in Singing
(1871). Here she speaks of the laws of acoustics and then
applies the laws directly to the singing voice. Between pages
85 and 96, she presents three of the four most commonly
discussed elements of acoustics relating to the voice: (1) the
concept of the fundamental and its overtones (especially partials), (2) the properties of a tone, and (3) the nature of wave
generation. The concept that she does not analyze, but which
is prevalent in many subsequent chapters on acoustics in other
sources is (4) the sympathetic vibration of cavities in resonation.

The Fundamental and Its Overtones

When we are once convinced of the existence of partial tones (Partialtöne), if we concentrate our attention, we can also distinguish them. The ear hears, then, not only that tone, the pitch of which is determined, as we have shown, by the duration of its vibrations, but a whole series of tones besides, which Helmholtz names 'the harmonic over-tones' of the tone, in opposition to that first tone (fundamental tone) which is the lowest among them all, generally the strongest also, and according to the pitch of which we decide the pitch of the tone. The series of these overtones is for each musical tone precisely the same; they are, namely, the tones of the so-called acoustical series....

The different timbre of tones thus depends upon the different forms of the vibrations, whence arise various relations of the fundamental tone to the overtones as they vary in strength [Seiler, 1871, pp. 96-97].

Seiler's explanation is derived from Helmholtz, who is quoted by Thorp and Nicholl [1896, pp. 63-64]. Others who devote space to the explanation of fundamental and partials include Mackenzie [1891, p. 43], Miller [1898, p. 3], Fillebrown [1911, pp. 45-46], and Proschowsky [1923, pp. 8-9]. Lunn offers an important thought that these other authors do not spell out:

The prime tone is the one which gives the name to the sound, but the quality is a compounded musical resultant. The different quality that is noted between one instrument and another arises from the special upper partials that blend with the fundamental [1880, p. 47].

The Properties of a Tone

Tone, in the musical sense, is the result of rapid periodic vibration. The pitch of tone depends upon the number of vibrations in a given period; the loudness of tone depends upon the amplitude of the vibrations; the quality of tone depends upon the form of the vibrations; and the form of the vibrations depends upon the resonator [Fillebrown, 1911, p. 45].

Regarding the quality of the tone by itself, Browne and Behnke write:

We therefore come to the conclusion that the quality
of a tone depends--
1. Upon the number of partials of which the tone
    consists.
2. Upon their relative position.
3. Upon their relative degree of loudness [1904, p.
    21].

Other authors who present these concepts include Proschowsky
[1923, p. 7], Miller [1910, p. 68], and Muckey [1915, pp.
45-50].

The Nature of Wave Generation

The vibrations of the sounding body are communicated
to the air, not by propelling individual particles of it
through space like a shot, but by setting up to-and-fro
motions which knock, so to speak, one particle against
its neighbour, after which it rebounds and finally returns to its original position; just as the excursions of
a pendulum get smaller by degrees, until at last they
cease entirely. The neighbouring particle imparts the
motion to another one, and also returns to its original
position, and so on. Alternate condensations and rare-
factions of the air are produced, travelling outwards
with its succeeding rarefaction being termed a sound
wave.... It must further be observed that the sound
waves do not only travel in one direction, but in every
direction all around [Browne and Behnke, 1904, pp.
15-16].

Helmholtz devises an image that is repeated by many
authors to demonstrate the action of sound waves:

Imagine a stone thrown into perfectly smooth water.
Around the point of the surface struck by the stone
there is instantly formed a little ring, which, moving
outwards equally in all directions, spreads to an ever-
enlarging circle. Corresponding to this ring, sound
goes out in the air from an agitated point, and enlarges
in all directions as far as the limits of the atmosphere
permit. What goes on in the air is essentially the
same that takes place on the surface of the water; the
chief difference only is that sound spreads out in the
spacious sea of air like a sphere, while the waves on
the surface of the water extend only like a circle....

[T]he condensation of the sound-wave corresponds to the crest, while the rarefaction of the sound-wave corresponds to the sinus of the water-wave [as repeated by Emma Seiler, 1871, pp. 87-88].

Other authors who use this image include Mackenzie [1891, pp. 39-40] and Lunn [1904, p. 22]. Authors who discuss wave generation at length include Curtis [1914, pp. 78-79] and Proschowsky [1923, pp. 6-7].

Sympathetic Vibration of Cavities

Mackenzie's quotation of the "elective affinity" of cavities has already been quoted under "Descriptions of the Resonating Cavities," above, as has the quotation of W. S. Drew on this subject. Miller offers one of the most lucid discussions of the relations of resonating cavities to the emission of beautiful tones:

Voice being, like instrumental tone, a commixture of fundamental and overtones, and the manner in which the composite conformation of collective waves strikes the ear being largely determined by the cavities of resonance, the control of these is of great importance to the singer. This control, should, by thorough training, be brought to such a degree of efficiency that it becomes subconscious and automatic, so that the resonance-cavities shape themselves instantly to the note that is being produced within the larynx and, vibrating in sympathy with it, sound the overtones. The reciprocal principle of elective affinity between fundamental and overtone, between the shape assumed by the larynx for pitch and the shape assumed by the resonance-cavities for quality, is illustrated by the exciting influence of a sounding instrument upon a silent one tuned to the same pitch which ... sounds in sympathy with the one that is being played on.... This is the result of sympathetic vibration. Thus, although vocal tone originates within the larynx, it sets the resonance-cavities into sympathetic vibration, and these produce the harmonics that give the fundamental tone its timbre [Miller, 1910, pp. 94-95].

Other authors who discuss cavity tuning or affinity are Bach [1898, pp. 73-83] and Browne and Behnke [1904, pp. 25-26].

THEORIES : PHYSIOLOGICAL FACTORS

In many sources the statements regarding resonance throughout the body are collective or generalized. Such statements have been here avoided because there is little application possible. Instead, statements regarding specific areas of resonance have been selected as examples of thought on the subject. Also, during this period, a number of authors discuss what is often called "head," "middle," and "chest" voices or resonances. Although resonance plays an important part in such concepts, these are basically concepts of registration and will be analyzed in Chapter VI under "Theories: Vocal Registers."

Head Cavities

The overwhelming majority of sources that comment on head cavities declare them essential for resonance. Three positive quotations are followed by the only negative statement disclosed.

The true value of the nasal and head cavities are as reinforcing agents in the production of tone [Fillebrown, 1911, p. 2].

The resonance cavities here referred to, which influence or modify the color, character, and power of the tone, are the ventricles of the larynx, the pharynx, or lower throat, the upper throat, the nasal cavities and the mouth [Myer, 1891, p. 122].

I find in my practice that generally the origin of illness and failure of the voice in singing or speaking come from some irritation and defect in these hollow spaces. By hollow spaces I mean principally the laryngeal, oral, nasal and its accessory cavities, the nares, and in addition the frontal and sphenoidal sinuses, the antra, also we may say the ventricular and bronchi, trachea and all pulmonary cavities [Miller, 1898, p. 6].

The sources of resonance of tone ... are the chest, the throat, the pharynx, the nasal cavities, and the mouth.... I purposely omit mentioning the head cavities.... I don't see how they can possibly be counted among the resounding cavities, for their communication with the sonorous current can only take place through almost capillary and tortuous tubes [Parisotti, 1911, pp. 50-51].

Sinuses

Few authors consider the sinuses worthy of mention in connection with cavities of resonance. Two statements favoring use of the sinuses precede one that opposes the concept:

> On either side of the nasal passages are hollow spaces known as sinuses, in the bones of the face, which communicate with the nasal cavity. These spaces naturally vary in size with different persons, and they have much to do with vocal resonance. There is also a posterior or sphenoidal, and two anterior or frontal sinuses, which act as resonators, but are not as important as the lateral or maxillary sinuses called the antra [Curtis, 1914, p. 73].

> In neither speech nor song do the vocal cords actually create the tone; ... the whole compass of the human voice is divided between four sets of sinuses (or cavities) which are found on each side of the head [White, 1927, p. 5].

Referring to the sphenoidal and front sinuses, Hallock writes:

> It is sometimes urged that these cavities together with the antra, aid in resonance, but it is practically impossible, since at best their openings are small, and they are usually closed entirely, as is the cavity of the inner ear [1896, p. 5].

Nasal Cavities

The most controversial topics dealing with head resonance are related to the nasal cavities. Most arguments center on two questions: should the nasal cavities be consciously employed, and if the nasal cavities do resonate (either naturally or by conscious control) how is this effected. The decade in which many authors favor nasal resonance in this study is 1910-1920, where eight of the 18 sources used give favorable statements.

The nasal cavities should be used. This dictum is supported by the following statements.

Wenn der Ton des Stimmes schön lauten soll, so muss

eine gewisse Quantität der Luft die sie anklingen macht,
durch die Nase gehn/ If you want the singing tone to
sound beautifully, a certain quantity of air which you
have made sound must go through the nose [D'Aubigny,
1803, p. 114].

The sound waves from the vocal chords fill the pharynx
and mouth. Part of the waves in the pharynx pass
upwards behind the uvula into the nasal chambers,
while the waves in the mouth act freely upon the hard
and soft palates, thus communicating the vibrations
to the nasal chambers which are above.... M and
N are the letters used in the development of this
resonance [Thorp and Nicholl, 1896, p. 38].

The singer must have some nasal quality, otherwise
the voice sounds colorless and expressionless. We
must sing toward the nose (not necessarily through
the nose) [Lehmann, as quoted by Brower, 1920, p.
46].

Thorp and Nicholl (see immediately above) mention
conductivity of waves in the mouth through the soft and hard
palates. Other authors speak of such transmission, including
Miller and Clippinger:

Of what use is the nasal passage as a cavity of resonance if, in order to prevent nasal quality of tone,
the passage during voice emission is shut off by the
action of the soft palate [raised], or by the combined
action of the soft palate, uvula and tongue? The
answer is, first, that it is not always to be closed
off, because there are times when a slightly nasal
timbre in voice is desirable; secondly, that even when
the nasal cavity is shut off, the hard palate being not
only the roof of the mouth, but also the floor of the
nose, its vibrations are communicated to the nasal
cavity, but not directly enough to give a disagreeable
nasal quality to the voice [Miller, 1910, pp. 97-98].

Whether the palate is high or low does not settle the
matter. It is not at all necessary that breath should
pass through the nasal cavities in order to make them
act as resonators. In fact it is necessary that it
should not. It is the air that is already in the cavities that vibrates. Neither is it necessary that the
vibrations should be transmitted to the head cavities

by way of the pharynx and over the soft palate.   They
may be transmitted through the bones of the head
[Clippinger, 1917, p. 16].

Many writers who favor some use of the nasal cavities
feel a need to defend their theories from authors who declare
that nasal resonance is automatically "nasal twang" or nasality (some of these attacks will be quoted under the next heading).

> Singing nasal or toward the nose (not to be confounded
> with 'nasal twang,' which is produced by a high larynx
> and by pinching the tongue on a͞) cannot be enough
> studied and utilized.   On account of its tonal effect,
> its noble timbre, it should be amply employed on all
> kinds of voices.   By it is effected the connection of
> tones with each other, from the lowest chest to the
> highest head voice....   This is all that singers mean
> when they speak of 'nasal singing'--really only singing
> toward the nose [Lehmann, 1906, p. 78; since this is
> part of the premise of her book, Lehmann devotes
> pp. 76-83 to the subject].

> Nasal tones are caused by a raised or stiffened tongue,
> a sagging palate, a stiffened jaw, or by other rigid-
> ities that prevent free tone emission and which at the
> same time--note this--prevent true nasal resonance
> [Fillebrown, 1911, pp. 52-53].

> It is certain that a perfectly free channel, down the
> nostrils will never produce the so-called 'nasal tone.'
> This tone is produced by partly closing the nasal pas-
> sage [White, 1918, p. 13].

> The right use of the nasal cavities produces what is
> called 'Nasal Resonance,' the wrong use 'Nasal Tone.'
> In both of these the air is made to vibrate and so add
> resonance to the voice....   What, then, are the right
> and wrong due to?   In a word to the action of the
> soft palate [Dodds thinks that a high palate equals
> resonance and a low palate equals a nasal tone; 1927,
> p. 16].

Henderson believes that the nasal cavities resonate,
but that this action should be unconscious:

> The proper way to employ the nasal cavities is to let
> them entirely alone.   In speaking one does not think

about them and they attend to their business. In singing one should think of them only as much as is necessary to avoid closing them. They should be left open so that they may freely communicate with the rear arch of the mouth, and thus the resonating cavities not only of the nose but also of the head will without any thought on the part of the singer perform their natural offices and bring out the natural timbre of the tones [1906, p. 83].

The nasal cavities should not be used.   Opposing the above comments are the following three.

The nasal sound is ... because the breath is forced into the cavities of the nose [Lablache, 184-, p. 5].

If we raise the soft palate, shutting the nose off from the throat, then the tone passes through the mouth, and assuming that its exit takes place in a normal manner, it will be a pure vocal tone.   If we lower the soft palate, thereby shutting the mouth off from the throat, then the tone passes through the nose, which gives a nasal quality [Browne and Behnke, 1904, p. 164].

As an objection to my opinion [that the soft palate should always be raised], it might be asserted that the vibrations of the air are continued to the nasal cavity through the soft palate; if this be possible at all, it can be but to a very insignificant extent.   Rather than this, it might be assumed that the vibration of the bony palate, partaking of the resonance in the mouth, are imparted to the air contained in the nasal cavities....   I therefore feel entitled to say that the passage of breath through the nose weakens rather than strengthens the resonance [Bach, 1880, p. 70].

Importance of the Mouth and Throat Cavities

The mouth and pharynx are usually mentioned in passing by authors, in an introductory sentence on the resonating cavities of the head.   Little information beyond this is offered. Some of the few statements uncovered are included.

We have now to deal with that important resonance chamber, the mouth.   It is a large, spacious cavity, the roof being formed by the hard palate.   The parts

composing its floor are soft, and only partially fixed
by their connection with the lower jaw. The anterior
border of the mouth is bounded by the lips. A number
of muscles, some entirely situated within, and others
entering them, enable the lips to assume different
shapes and to open and shut in a variety of ways and
degrees. The posterior border of the mouth, as we
have seen is bounded by the soft palate and its pillars.
The interior of the cavity of the mouth can be enlarged
by the depression of the lower jaw, and modified in
its form by advancing the latter, and also altered in
a great variety of ways, both in form and width, by
the activity of the tongue.

The position and shape of the lips and mouth have
also the greatest influence upon the timbre of the
voice. The mouth is another important resonator, the
pitch of which necessarily varies with the changes
which take place in its dimensions [Curtis, 1914, p.
72, p. 75].

In every case, for the highest tones of the voice the
widest possible opening of the mouth is necessary,
and even when, in the formation of the vowels, the
lips have to be brought nearer to each other, yet the
teeth within must be kept apart, that the cavity of the
mouth may remain large enough [Seiler, 1871, p. 126].

Even the smallest dimensions of the mouth strikingly
alter the formation of the tone [Henderson, 1906,
p. 88].

The upper throat is the cavity which is bounded by
the base of the tongue, the arch of the soft palate,
the pillars of the fauces and the tonsils, and the back
wall of the throat. The cavity exerts a wonderful influence on the tone [Myer, 1891, p. 122].

Importance of the Chest Cavity

As with the mouth and throat cavities, the chest is
given passing mention in a number of sources after approximately 1870, while specific statements are infrequent. Positive statements from four authors are followed by five negative
remarks.

There must be resonance in the chest as well as in
the mouth and head [Downing, 1927, p. 9].

Insufficient chest-resonance produced a flat tone without carry-power; the voice seems to hang in the air [G. B. Lamperti, 1905, p. 26].

Excepting the chest and trachea the resonance-cavities of the voice are located above the larynx. To the chest as a resonator the low tones of the voice owe much of their great volume. Indeed, the chest is such a superb and powerful resonating box that, if it resonated also for the high tones, these, with their inherent capacity for penetration, probably would become disagreeably acute. Therefore, nature, wise in this as in many other things, has decreased chest vibration as the voice ascends the scale [Miller, 1910, p. 95].

David C. Taylor refers to chest resonance in three separate sections of his The Psychology of Singing. He acknowledges the chest as an important resonator, but, he says,

When it comes to telling the student how to learn to govern the chest resonance, the teacher has practically nothing to offer. No direct means has ever been found for causing the air in the thorax to vibrate [1917, p. 61].

Intelligible instruction in the use and management of chest resonance is hardly to be expected [1917, p. 62].

Taylor believes that the sensations of vibration from the chest are the only guide to its use:

A feeling of trembling in the upper chest is usually held to indicate that the chest cavity is working properly as a resonator. This sensation is therefore the chief reliance of most teachers in 'placing' the lower tones, especially for low voices [1917, p. 80].

Witherspoon declares that the chest is "an indirect resonator, because it is in opposite direction to the soundwaves, which ascend" [1925, p. 72]. Muckey does not believe that such resonance is useful at all. "Any vibrations that may occur in the air in the chest are useless for reinforcement, since the cavity is closed, and a closed cavity cannot reinforce a tone" [1915, p. 62].

The Entire Body as a Resonator

The sources of this study reveal only two statements specifically regarding the entire body as a resonator. Taylor states that this is a common assumption among vocal scientists:

> The acoustic principle of sounding-board resonance, in its application to the voice, is discussed by several vocal scientists. It is usually treated under two heads: first, the entire body is looked upon as a sounding board, capable of reinforcing the tones of the voice, under certain conditions. Secondly, the tones of the chest and of the head are thought to be thrown into vibration, in sympathy with the vibrations of the air in the chest--and nasal cavities respectively [1917, p. 65].

The other source is Thorp and Nicholl, who write that "the sound waves pass into the air-chambers both above and below the larynx, thus transmitting the tone to the resonators which surround these chambers" [1896, p. 36]. Included in their list of resonating bodies are the ribs and the diaphragm.

METHODS : THE PSYCHOLOGICAL APPROACH

Expressional Intent Controls Resonance

The concept that resonance is basically controlled through expressional intent finds few adherents. The studies of Fields and Burgin uncover six and 14 statements, respectively.

> The timbre of the human voice is almost entirely under the control of the will, on account of the great and varied alteration that the muscular boundaries of the resonance chambers can induce in their capacity, and must therefore owe much of its character to the taste of the speaker or singer [Holmes, 1879, p. 155].

> Nature attaches to each sentiment distinctive characteristics, a timbre, an accent, a modulation of the voice [Garcia, 1872, p. 139].

Yeatman Griffith believes that only in the ideal case can expressional intent guide the resonance, but that any fault

in tone production will limit the singer's ability to produce
the desired resonance [Brower, 1920, pp. 254-255]. David
Ffrangçon-Davies, the outspoken champion of natural singing,
declares that any control of resonance other than mental
imagery is "placing." "The process of 'placing' voices results too often in their being put on the shelf, where they
are indeed useless" [1904, p. 16 fn]. He further states
that if students "spoke the words with correct atmosphere,
this placing would not be necessary" [1904, p. 15].

The Possibility of Direct Control

Sixteen authors express opinions on the possibility of
direct control of resonance (Tetrazzini has statements in
both her 1909 and her 1923 books, accounting for the total
of 17 statements in Table 5). Fourteen favor this concept
and two stand in opposition. This prevalence of positive
statements is not the case later in the twentieth century, if
we look to the studies of Fields and Burgin for statistics.
In these works, in fact, opponents of direct control of resonance slightly outweigh supporters (8 to 5 and 9 to 7, respectively). A clue to the many positive statements may be
found in the publishing dates of the books which contain them.
Twelve of the statements are found in the period 1904 to
1923, which closely parallels the dates of the majority of
positive statements made concerning conscious employment
of the nasal cavities. Statements on direct control and on
conscious focusing of the voice are also very closely linked.

> The most important thing in the culture of the voice
> is the timbre of the tone, for here it is in our power
> to form out of a sharp, hard and disagreeable voice,
> a voice sweet and pleasing.
> A good tone in singing is formed,
> 1. By controlling and correctly dividing the air
>   or breath as it is expired;
> 2. By a correct direction of the vibrating column
>   of air [Seiler, 1871, pp. 109-110].

Taylor states that the old Italian masters advocated resonance
control when they instructed the student to sing the tone forward [1916, p. 99]. Stanley updates the maxim:

> To sing on the timbre one must learn to pronounce
> forward.... To obtain this condition the pronunciation
> must be forward and kept, what I call, the right shape
> --narrow, not spread [1916, p. 5].

By thinking of the face or the throat and, so to speak, apparently fixing it there, you can modify the disposition of the various parts in question and so influence the quality of the tone produced. This mysterious placing of the voice means therefore, in reality, nothing more than finding out in each individual instance the best position of the vocal organs for getting the best results [Tetrazzini, 1923, p. 60].

It is obvious that all statements made to the effect that the voice should be focused can be also considered as representing views in support of the possibility of direct control. The specific concepts of focus will be discussed in the next section.

Taylor and Rogers oppose the control of resonance:

To imagine the directing of air vibration, as we direct a stream of water out of a hose, is absurd [Taylor, 1917, p. 126].

Your sway over the vocal parts is indirect.... the true medium of action is your sense of sound [Rogers, 1925, pp. 61-62].

METHODS : THE TECHNICAL APPROACH

Acquiring Vocal Focus

John Burgin has written, "The term 'vocal focus' is in that category of expressions which are similarly confusing and contradictory." He goes on to say, "'Focus' is often considered synonymous with 'placement.' Placement has two meanings: (1) to 'place' or to localize the tone in a particular part of the human anatomy, and (2) to 'find,' to enhance, or to achieve a good vocal coordination. Focus is also used to describe a tone with 'point,' or 'ring'; in this context, the term finds its most favorable reception and empirical use" [Teaching Singing, 1973, pp. 92-93]. It is obvious from the number of opposing comments that even a few authors who welcome some form of direct control of resonance do not believe in the concept of focus (however they understand it).

The question of tone placing, then, revolves itself into this: Is it possible by taking thought about the various resonators to bring out the best qualities of a singing voice? The experience of nearly three centuries of

study and experiment by singers and teachers of singing
has resulted in a consensus of opinions that it is. In
spite of this there are still some who do not believe
in any consideration of the resonating cavities [Hender-
son, 1906, p. 81].

Placing or 'focusing the voice' I have found to be
chiefly a matter of control and use of the resonator,
consisting of chest, pharynx, mouth, and the nasal
and head cavities.
    Now 'voice placing' depends primarily on correct
vowel placing, which in turn depends on proper adjustment of the resonators, which again depends chiefly
on the positions and motions of articulation. The
interdependence of tone quality and pronunciation is
therefore obvious [Fillebrown, 1911, pp. 51-52].

The Medium sounds are produced by directing the
breath against the teeth. The Head sounds are made
by directing the breath entirely toward the front sinuses
[Lablache, 184-, p. 5].

    Lunn bases his arguments for forward production on
the writing of Emma Seiler. He gives five reasons why forward production is necessary, among them, that cords are
aligned at a right angle to the air pressure in this situation,
and another that the mouth cavities are better magnified [1880,
p. 71]. Bach relies on the authority of the old Italian masters, who allegedly said,

    'Bisogna cantare sul fior della labra--'One must form
    the tone at the edge of the lips,' by which they meant
    that the tone should never be formed in the back, but
    always in the front of the mouth [1894, p. 130; this
    statement tends to bear out the argument of Henderson,
    above].

Shakespeare offers specific adjustments of the tongue, jaw
and larynx "on which the art of placing the voice depends"
[1910, pp. 19-21]. G. B. Lamperti tells which areas must
be focused upon for various registers:

    The point of resonance for the medium voice is the
    hard palate; for the head-tones, the top of the head,
    in front. Should the latter vibrate in the forehead,
    the high tones will lack metallic resonance [1905, p. 26].

Lilli Lehmann offers diagrams and lengthy discussions on the

exact locations of every tone. She states that these directives
are meant to give the reader the correct mental images for
forming good placement [1906, pp. 60-102].

Edmund J. Myer believes that focus is a necessary
element in creating resonance but that many students have
an incorrect idea of the action of focusing:

> There is one important point that singers as a rule
> lose sight of, or do not seem to understand. That
> point is, that the air current, or the direction of the
> air current, is one thing; and the muscular effort, is
> altogether another thing. If in the production of tone
> the muscular effort follows the direction of the air
> current, then the conditions cannot possibly be right,
> then the tone or the voice will be pushed.
> The pushed voice, the most common of all wrong
> conditions, is largely due to the fact that singers
> are made to think that they must place the voice for-
> ward, they must send it out. ... In their desire to
> send the air current forward and out, every muscular
> effort is made in the same direction. ... [T]he pupil
> must be taught to think the air current in one direc-
> tion, and the muscular effort or resistance in the
> opposite direction [1891, pp. 107-109].

Louis Arthur Russell and David C. Taylor also explain why
the concept of focusing can lead the student into false ideas
of sound generation:

> Singers ... wonder at last why their voices have so
> soon worn out. The answer is readily found; they
> have tried to discount nature ... and endeavored to
> make their vocal apparatus do certain things by mus-
> cular effort, which things should have been allowed,
> not forced, to operate. ...
> No tone should be 'reached' for, 'pushed into place,'
> or forced in any way. ... We gain intensity through
> the body's effort, not through local effort at throat
> or mouth [Russell, A Plain Talk with American Sing-
> ers, 1904, pp. 5, 12].

The 'forward emission' theory assumes the existence
of a current of air, issuing from the vocal cords as
a tone. In other words, the tone is supposed to con-
sist of a stream of air, which can be voluntarily directed in the mouth, and aimed at some precise point
in the roof of the mouth. This is an utter mistake
[Taylor, 1917, p. 126].

Other authors who agree that the idea of focusing can be misleading include Muckey [1915, p. 116], and Rogers [1925, p. 65]. Fillebrown applies the same warning to those who teach the so-called register images: "Head tones, chest tones, closed tones, open tones, etc., as confined to special parts of the range of the voice, are distracting distinctions arising from false education" [1911, p. 5].

Proschowsky and Clippinger agree that the terms "voice placing" or "singing forward" should be used merely to represent the good tone:

> The term, singing forward, so frequently used, is a most misleading one.... Usually the term for placing the voice forward stands equivalent to good singing; but no more than that. The head-resonance that makes the voice perfect is a result of proper balance, but not of placing the voice [Proschowsky, 1923, p. 22].

> Now voice placing means just one thing, not half a dozen. It means learning to produce beautiful tone.... The injunction to place the voice invariably leaves in the mind of the student the idea that he must direct the tone to some particular point ... whereas the truth is that when the tone is properly produced there is no thought of trying to put it anywhere; it seems to sing itself [Clippinger, 1917, p. 3].

Shaw dislikes the term "voice placing" because he thinks it gives the singer an idea of a static state.

> The sensations which accompany the correct voice placing are invariably the result of moving breath. The static effect of tone placing usually causes an involuntary halting of the breath activity [1914, pp. 107-108].

The Value of Humming

Humming has been endowed with many supposed powers by teachers and singers. Thirteen statements in favor of humming are opposed by four negative statements. Nellie Melba uses humming to get the feel of resonance in the nose [1926, p. 17]. Marguerite D'Alvarez, another singer who uses humming, says, "When I begin to study in the morning, I give the voice what I call a massage.... This massage consists of humming exercises with closed lips. Humming is the sunshine of the voice" [as quoted by Brower, 1920, p. 144].

A number of authors employ humming as a corrective device for different faults:

An excellent exercise for promoting the ability to carry downward the larynx, is to practice the singing of the chest-tones with the mouth closed, as this can be effected easily only with depressed larynx and raised palate [Guttmann, 1887, p. 67].

Soft humming can never lead to the forming of the habit of nasal singing. It will even break a person of the habit of singing nasal. Let the throat be completely relaxed, especially ... in front of the larynx and upward [Kofler, 1897, p. 155].

By far the most reliable and safe system is that of beginning the study of natural production, full development of resonance, and forward direction of the voices, independently from any vowel association, by correct humming.
The correct humming, which requires the closing of the lips, takes place if we keep the nostrils properly dilated and depressed, the soft palate fully and naturally dropped, the tongue well forward and scooped without contraction of any sort, the lower teeth slightly behind the upper ones. The sound thus produced will be felt strongly in the low labro-dental space and very slightly within the nostrils [Parisotti, 1911, p. 86].

In the treatment of relaxed cords and of congested cords a good piece of advice to give a pupil is this: until you can do a pure Hum with the mouth closed and without effort, do not attempt to talk, simply whisper and make the attack upon the lips even while doing this [Curtis, 1914, pp. 155-156].

When first I heard her speak, I noticed the escape of the breath forward through the mouth, so I explained to her that sound is made in the head, not in the throat; then, having made her hum, she was able in less than thirty minutes to speak in quite a natural manner, and she has never experienced difficulty since [White, 1918, p. 13].

Lamperti, Proschowsky, and Wronski each oppose humming for different reasons:

The pupil is also warned to avoid humming as, wanting
in the support of the chest; there is nothing which more
fatigues the throat, or renders more uncertain the tone
[F. Lamperti, 1883, p. 19].

By humming, we understand singing with the mouth
closed, the voice being produced only through the
nasal cavity. Observe a skull and notice what little
opportunity there is of making the skull reverberate
or resound through the nasal cavity compared with the
back part of the skull which is supported by the verte-
brae. Observe that with the mouth closed, articulation of vowels is impossible. Notice that the sound
obtained while humming, is idential to that of a consonant. Observe that consonants are very inferior in
resonance to vowels, consequently a vowel partly or
almost entirely placed in the position of that taken by
the humming voice, could only lose in resonance and
never gain.... The effort of the singer to produce
volume in the nasal cavity, which is dull by nature,
could only eventually teach him to force. Consequently,
all humming, if done for the purpose of placing the
voice perfectly, is contradictory to the laws of singing
laid down by nature [Proschowsky, 1923, pp. 81-82].

To sing with the mouth closed is bad. To place the
voice in a position which is not of natural and normal
phonation is absurd, no matter what the impression
acquired through this original process may be. Humming occasionally may help to free the throaty voice,
but it is dangerous and may be said to be substituting
one evil for another [Wronski, 1921, p. 60].

ANALYSIS AND COMMENTS

In comparison to breathing and phonation, the other
two basic elements of the vocalization system, resonance receives considerably less comment. There would seem to be
two major reasons for this fact. First, as was seen in the
chapter on phonation, there are very few statements made
before the so-called "scientific era" of vocal pedagogy, and
these are concepts stemming from actions which are empirically observable. Secondly, even within the age inaugurated
by Helmholtz's Die Lehre von den Tonempfindungen (1863),
authors begin to understand the application of laws of acoustics
to the resonating cavities of the human body, but see little

possibility of "improving on nature" with direct controls. Most authors who grant that the areas below the larynx and the area of the sinuses act as resonators, do so only in passing, as if unsure of their own statements. Those who mention chest resonance do so because they have observed the vibrations of this cavity during the act of singing. Few are bold enough to actually state how this closed cavity contributes to vocal tone quality or quantity. As we have seen, Taylor states that "no direct means has ever been found for causing the air in the thorax to vibrate" [1917, p. 61].

The mouth and throat cavities receive little attention, especially in view of their relative importance in the cavity system. This study discloses eight statements; the Fields study counts eleven. Burgin has documented 45 statements. This higher figure indicates that in the last three decades intensive investigation has been placed on the oral-pharyngeal cavity system, using techniques unavailable to vocal scientists and pedagogues of earlier eras.

The subject of nasal resonance receives the most attention of any cavity area, and approximately the same amount of attention in all three studies. Already in the mid-nineteenth century, vocal scientists recognized that the posterior opening of the nasal cavities could be regulated by action of the soft palate and the fauces. Consequently, many positive and negative agencies are attributed to this one directly controllable action. Those who wish the soft palate raised claim that a lowered palate allows air into the nasal passages, causing "nasal twang" or nasality. Those who wish the soft palate to be left hanging "naturally" declare that nasality is caused by stiff jaw, stiff tongue, etc. Many conflicting opinions arise.

The concept of focusing or placing the voice is also a question of direct control over resonance. Many believe this concept is both possible and beneficial. The major objection to voice placing is that students confuse the current of sound waves with the current of air, and consequently over-exert their system in an upward direction in an effort to forceably push the air stream forward.

Humming is considered beneficial for a variety of reasons, some having nothing to do with resonance. The arguments against humming in this study do not direct themselves against the positive statements made by other authors, but instead seem to be isolated musings, based on questionable logic.

VI

RANGE

Definition. When speaking of vocal range, we
mean "the full extent of pitch, from highest to
lowest tones. " (Webster's) Another term, used
interchangeably with range, is compass.

THEORIES : COMPASS

Average Compass of Voices

Most authors agree that artistic singers should have
a range of at least two octaves at their disposal. Occasionally, larger compasses are considered normal:

Eine gute und schön gebildete Stimme muss in unsern
Zeiten wenigstens dem Umfang von zwei Oktaven über-
flügeln/ A good and refined voice must in our times
surpass at least a compass of two octaves [D'Aubigny,
1803, p. 88].

Each singer has ordinarily an extension of two octaves,
some more, some less [Costa, 1838, p. 18; he mentions that a few singers have four octaves].

The average compass of the singing voice is from two
to two and a half octaves; a range of three octaves is
exceptional, whilst one of four is almost phenomenal
[Mackenzie, 1891, pp. 50-51].

The compass of from two, two-and-a-half, to three
octaves, producable by the vocal chords, is now seldom heard, the extreme notes being impossible on
account of imperfect production [Thorp and Nicholl,
1896, p. 6].

A number of authors provide Grand Scale diagrams
which superimpose the vocal ranges of the various types of

Table 6. SUMMARY OF CONCEPTS OF RANGE

I. Theories of vocal range

A. Compass
  1. average compass of voice   28
  2. expanding the natural compass   13
B. Theory of registers
  1. general descriptions   63
  2. number of registers in the voice
    a) voice has none   10
    b) voice has one   7
    c) voice has two   8
    d) male voices have two; female voices have three   12
    e) voice has three   32
    f) voice has four   5
    g) voice has five   19
  3. the falsetto   28

II. Methods of cultivating range

A. A psychological approach
  1. mental causes affect registers   2
  2. using the level of the speaking voice   4
  3. the "high" and "low" fallacy   4
B. The technical approach
  1. sectional treatment
    a) practice with entire range   4
    b) practice with middle range   17
  2. directional treatment
    a) downward practice   14
    b) approaching high tones   11
  3. various technical devices
    a) importance of scale work   25
    b) blending the registers   37
    TOTAL STATEMENTS   343

voices. Lablache, for example, provides a scale from F_2 to C_6, giving each voice about a two-octave range, and positioning neighboring voice types either a major or a minor third apart [1860, p. 3]. Another diagram of this nature is provided by Curtis [1914, p. 168], and the total range of all the voices in this diagram is from E_2 to E_6. Holmes also believes that the total vocal range is four octaves [1879, pp. 132-137].

Of course the naming of the various voice types predates this study. Generally, authors divide the male and
female voice types into three categories each. A typical
example is Bassini's Art of Singing [1857, pp. 7-8], where
he uses the terms "soprano, mezzo-soprano, contralto," and
"tenor, baritone, and bass." Bassini describes the timbre
of each voice type and divides the range of each according
to chest, medium, and head registers. Lanza adds a high
soprano to this traditional classification [1818, pp. 66-69].
The oldest source in this study to describe vocal range classification is Corrette [1782, p. 19]. He calls the voices
"la Basse contre, la Basse-taille [the cutting bass], la Taille,
la Haut-contre, le Bas dessus, le Dessus."

Increasing the Vocal Compass

Thirteen authors comment on increasing the vocal compass. Generally, they believe that this is to be done carefully, if at all. A number of authors bemoan the fact that
"modern" singers are obliged to sing older compositions in
what is in effect transposed keys, since concert pitch continued to rise from the late eighteenth century into the nineteenth century. Seiler states that this seeking after constantly
brighter tones may result in "forcing the registers beyond
their natural bonds" [1871, p. 70]. She also remarks that
tenors, who formerly sang their upper tones in falsetto, are
required by custom in her time to sing the upper tones in
full voice. A number of statements are here presented in
chronological order to show the evolution of expression on
this subject. Hiller states that the compass should not be
forced, but built over a period of weeks or even years [1780,
p. 8].

Never force the Voice, in order to extend its Compass
in the Voce di Petto upwards; but rather to cultivate
the Voce di Testa in what is called falsetto [Tenducci,
1785, Rule IX].

I believe the organs of the throat are so constructed
that the voice rarely acquires compass at one extrem-
ity, without losing or impairing the tone at the other.
I do not however mean to say, that high notes are
never acquired without sacrificing of low, or that immense increase of power is not to be obtained by well-
conducted practice [Bacon, 1824, p. 96].

When Signora Grassini first appeared at the King's

Theatre as a contralto singer--although her compass was limited to only seven notes, her beautiful intonation blended with sweet richness of tone and elegance of style, commanded great delight. After a few years absence on the Continent, where she had extended her compass above two octaves--she appeared in this country as Prima Donna, but they who remembered her voice when she was in England before, found it comparatively thin and feeble--thus by indiscriminately forcing her compass, her voice lost its richness and with it public admiration. It is thus evident that quality of voice should be regarded before compass [Nathan, 1836, p. 140].

Sing in a comfortable compass. Even the illustrious prima donna of the woods, the nightingale, does not sing higher than one octave [Bach, 1880, pp. 39-40].

A belief still prevails among pupils and teachers ... that it is possible to alter the compass of the voice at will, to make it ascend or descend in the scale, according to one's desire. This belief is the ruin of many a voice which, with proper training might have achieved fine results [Guttmann, 1887, pp. 184-185].

From time to time attempts have been made to raise barytone voices to tenor voices. In some cases a certain amount of success has followed, artistic as well as financial, especially where the voices were marvelous in quality. But to the sincere and honest critic the question was always open as to the voice being a 'made' tenor or a 'natural' tenor. In all cases the lives of such voices have been short and uncertain [Proschowsky, 1923, pp. 85-86].

Holmes is one of the very few who do not mention any danger in extending the range of the voice:

The extension of the vocal compass may be obtained by specially practicing the voice at the extremes of its natural scale. If a gain in the lowest notes is desired it is necessary to produce an extra-ordinary relaxation of the vocal cords [1879, p. 178; Holmes observes that adduction in the upper extreme makes extension 'an almost insuperable obstacle'].

THEORIES : VOCAL REGISTERS

No aspect of vocal pedagogy has undergone such close scrutiny or has evolved into so many conflicting theories as has the subject of vocal registers. So much has been written during the time period of this study that a number of closely-related subdivisions are necessary in analyzing the subject. As much as possible, the authors have been allowed to speak for themselves without interpretation.

The Complexity of the Subject of Vocal Registers

A very Babel of confusion exists on this important subject, and we are not only perplexed by a multiplicity of terms, but also by the various and often contradictory meanings attached to them [Behnke, 189-, p. 86].

In most works on the art of singing one meets with the greatest vagueness with regard to the so-called registers of the voice, and to the terms applied to them. One author says there are two registers, another gives three, others four; and lastly, even five registers are given. There are chest, stroh-bass (Garcia), middle, falsetto and head voice [Bach, 1898, p. 51].

Probably no other topic of Vocal Science has been studied so earnestly as the registers of the voice. Yet on no other topic is there such wide diversity of opinion among theorists and investigators [Taylor, 1917, pp. 34-35].

The subject of vocal registers is a difficult one--difficult to understand and, when understood, difficult to make intelligible to others. In fact, it is so difficult that some people get rid of it by calmly asserting that there are no registers. This is unfortunate, because the blending of the registers, the smoothing out of the voice where one register passes over into another, the elimination of the 'break' between them, is one of the greatest problems which the teacher of voice-production is obliged to solve. Like so many other branches in the art of voice-production, the subject is complicated by initial misunderstandings. Numerous people suppose, for example, that the vocal registers are synonymous with the different kinds of voices, and speak of the alto, soprano, bass or tenor register as if register stood for quality, which it does not. Another complication results from the fact that certain phenomenal voices, chiefly tenor, literally rise superior to the law of vocal registers [Miller, 1910, p. 103].

Perspectives of the History of Register Investigation

Mancini, writing as far back as 1774, says that in certain rare instances there is only one register--the chest--used throughout the whole compass of the voice [Curtis, 1914, p. 109].

Very little is definitely known regarding the manner in which the subject of registers was treated by the old Italian masters. Suffice it to say here that the old masters did not refer the registers to changes in the laryngeal action. They were treated simply as different qualities of tone, each quality best adapted to be sung only in a portion of the voice's compass.

In the early decades of the nineteenth century of registers of the voice received much attention from vocal theorists, especially in Paris. Garcia's first published work, Mémoire sur la Voix humaine, was presented to the Academy of Science in 1840. This mémoire gives the results of observations which Garcia made on his own pupils; it deals mainly with the position of the larynx during the singing of tones in the various registers. Garcia describes how the larynx is raised and lowered in the throat, according to the register in which the tones are produced. He also notes the position of the tongue and the soft palate.

Widespread interest was awakened by the account of Garcia's laryngoscopic investigations of the registers, published in 1855. The attention of the great majority of vocalists was at once drawn to the subject, and the actions of the vocal cords in the different registers were studied by many prominent physicians and voice specialists [Taylor, 1917, pp. 34-35].

Mackenzie also gives Garcia credit for spurring interest in the adjustments of the vocal mechanism throughout its compass [1891, p. 53].

Definitions of "Register"

The first author to attempt a definition of this term

in this study is Manuel Garcia. He writes:

> Par le mot registre, nous entendons une serie de sons
> consecutifs et homogènes allant du grave a l'aigu,
> produits par le développement du même principe
> mécanique, et dont la nature essentiellement d'une
> autre série de sons également consecutifs et homogènes,
> produits par une autre principe mécanique/ By the
> word register, we understand a series of consecutive
> and homogeneous sounds running from low to high,
> produced by the same mechanical principle, and dif-
> fering essentially from another series of equally con-
> secutive and homogeneous sounds produced by another
> mechanism [1849, p. 4].

This definition, minus the phrase "running from low to high,"
is repeated in the famous Hints on Singing of 1894 [p. 8],
and has proven itself by far the most popular definition of
"register." It is repeated, more or less verbatim, by Bach
[1898, p. 67], Behnke [189-, p. 86], Curtis [1914, p. 109],
Fillebrown [1911, p. 38], and Miller [1910, pp. 111-112].
Lilli Lehmann adds a statement about the physical mechanism:

> What is a vocal register? Only a vocal position. A
> series of tones sung in a certain way, which are pro-
> duced by a certain position of the vocal organs--larynx,
> tongue, and palate [1906, p. 107].

Tetrazzini repeats Lehmann verbatim [1909, p. 20], while
Duff adds the vocal cords to the list of vocal organs [1919,
p. 51].

Since definition is the essential key to the understanding of an author's concept, a number of other definitions of
"register" are included. Some align closely with Garcia's
quotation and others approach the concept from fundamentally
different viewpoints.

> Register refers to the compass of the voice [Shryock,
> 1856, p. 18].

> It is of the first importance in this somewhat intricate
> matter to define terms. This is the more necessary
> as the word 'register' has been used in two different
> senses, one in which it signifies the pitch of a given
> note, whilst in the other a particular mode of produc-
> tion is meant.... By a register I mean the series of

tones of like quality producible by a particular adjustment of the vocal cords [Mackenzie, 1891, pp. 53-54].

A tone can be produced twice from the same vocal
cord by strong breath and weak stretch, and by weak
breath and strong stretch, in this way the several
registers of the human voice originate.
Every compass of voice in individuals of moderately
good voice is composed of two or three rows of registers of tones, partly following or lying over each other,
which allow various sounds to be heard, and which
are caused by various vibrating mechanisms of the
vocal cords. By a register of tones we understand
a continuous longer or shorter row (scale) of tones,
which are produced by an instrument by one and the
same vibrating mechanism, whereby the general timbre
of the tones may not be changed [Guttmann, 1887, p.
70].

According to Lunn, there are two registers, and these
correspond to light and dramatic colors or resonances. "The
dramatic register is obtained by letting the larynx fall, thinking lower down, and thinking, not making, the sound oo"
[1904, p. 47]. Two other authors who believe that the vocal
registers are determined by points of resonance are G. B.
Lamperti [1905, p. 10], and Randegger, who writes:

The distinctive character assumed by the voice, according to the particular action of the vocal organs and
the particular cavity employed as its 'resonance chamber,' constitutes what is commonly called 'register.'
The registers, like their corresponding resonance
chambers, are three in number, viz. :--
(1) The chest register--reflecting the voice in the
lower or upper parts of the chest.
(2) The medium register--reflecting the voice in
the lower or upper parts of the mouth.
(3) The head register--reflecting the voice in the
upper part of the head [1912, p. 8].

Descriptions of the Mechanism of Registration

In some of the descriptions quoted below, the term
falsetto is used and its generating mechanism is mentioned.
A more detailed analysis of falsetto will occur later in this
chapter.

When preparing to emit a sound the two sides of the glottis, which are separated for breathing, shut the passage, and if the sound be a deep chest note, they become slightly tense. The whole length and breadth of the lips (comprising the anterior prolongation, or process of the arytenoid cartilage and the vocal cord) are engaged in the vibrations. As the sounds rise in the register the tension of the lips increases, and the thickness diminishes. Meanwhile the contact of the inner surfaces of the arytenoids will progress and extend to the end of the vocal processes, thereby shortening the vibratory length of the lips. The medium or falsetto is the result of similar actions, save that the lips come into contact, not through their depth but merely at their edges. In both registers the glottis has its length diminished from the back, by the arytenoids, which advance their contact till their adhesion is complete. As soon as this takes place, the falsetto ceases, and the glottis, consisting of the vocal cords alone, produces the head register. The resistance opposed to the air by the large surfaces generates the chest register, and the feebler opposition presented by the edges produces the falsetto [Garcia, 1894, p. 8; Behnke concurs, 189-, p. 86, as does Shakespeare, 1910, p. 32].

Bassini observes also that changes in the length and thickness of the vocal bands produce the phenomenon of registration [1869, p. 8]. Van Broekhaven incorporates the register mechanism into his ventricular band theory:

The production of tone in these registers [chest, medium and falsetto] is conditioned by the size of the ventricles, or portices of the larynx. As different individuals have more or less extensive pockets, it follows that, according to the size of these pockets, the singer's registers and vocal range are the result of his capacity to expand or enlarge the inner larynx spaces ... and his power to manage the dimensions of the trachea, or windpipe, below the larynx [1905, p. 9; van Broekhaven provides diagrams of the shape of the ventricles in the three registers, pp. 5, 7, 11].

Salvatore Marchesi includes resonance in his explanation of the nature of registers:

The Vibrator (the glottis) in its normal state is sus-

ceptible to numerable degrees of tension and contraction. It can also lengthen and shorten its orifice,
and, in fact, there are two pairs of muscles called
the 'ring-shield muscles' and the 'shield-pyramid
muscles,' which by stretching or slackening, pressing
together or drawing back the vocal cords, govern the
pitch of the sounds produced by their vibrations. This
process of altering the pitch of the sounds is also produced in connection with the shortening or lengthening
of the resonance-tube, by raising or lowering the larynx. But in all this, no modification can be detailed
in the physical structure or physiological activity of
the glottis as a vibrator that could account for the
different timbre of the sound in a change of register....
    Now, if what we call Register consists in a series
of homogeneous sounds which are essentially different
in timbre from those of the succeeding higher or lower
register, it follows that the vocal apparatus must contain as many distinct special resonance-chambers as
there are registers. These various cooperative Resonators, built of different organic texture (hard or
soft), impart, by reason of their physical properties,
a characteristic, distinct color to each series of sounds
contained within the limits of each register [1902, p.
26].

Stanley and Shakespeare remark that registers overlap
one another and Shakespeare finds an application for this fact:

Registers so cover each other that several notes can
be sung in both, and there should be no obvious change
in going from one to the other if you are singing in
the timbre [Stanley, 1916, p. 13].

The true artist prefers to strengthen the lower notes
of each register and these he is able to intensify....
The bad singer ... is compelled to rely on the highest
notes of the registers, with the result that his singing
is characterized by a sense of strain and effort [Shake-
speare, 1910, p. 40].

Guttmann also discusses this point (see "Definitions
of 'Register'," above).

Registration as a Natural Function

Although many authors become involved in the attempt

to describe the physiology of the registration phenomenon, very few suggest that this process is in any way to be directed by local efforts.

> The student must be taught not to worry about registers and they will 'do' themselves [Stanley, 1916, p. 13].

> Many teachers and singers have now reached what they consider a demonstrated conclusion that registers are not a natural feature of the voice, yet a large contingent still adhere to the doctrine 'register,' depending for their justification upon the unreliable evidence furnished by the laryngoscope, not realizing that there will be found in the little lens as many different conditions as the observers have eyes to see. Garcia himself, the inventor of the laryngoscope, soon modified his first claims as to its value in vocal culture [Fillebrown, 1911, p. 2].

> I have no faith in the thought that the voice should be trained in its several parts in different ways; that each vowel fits some part of the voice and no other, and that the voice should be treated accordingly. To me this is merely business cant, or crass ignorance of a self-evident truth, viz., there is no part of the voice that is not likely to be called upon to sing every possible vowel sound in the language.... When the proper conditions are under control of the will ... registers will be but a name to the singers, or at most a mark of emotional color. A properly controlled voice calls for no worry about its registers [Russell, 1912, pp. 48-49].

> What may be termed 'registers' unquestionably exist in the operation of the normal voice, and depend entirely upon pitch and character of expression. The register used should not be preconsidered in production, but should occur automatically in the natural response to the character of the idea to be expressed .... To compel the phenomena is to interfere with workings of nature [Shaw, 1914, p. 106].

Taylor [1917, pp. 55-56] and Fillebrown [1911, p. 39] both agree that the most detailed knowledge of the vocal cords cannot help control their operation.

If each register is considered an entity and trained in

its own special quality, the difference between the registers will become more pronounced and the act of passing from one to the other will be accomplished by more effort [Curtis, 1914, p. 169].

Rogers defends the study of registers even though she supports a "natural" control:

It may be objected that if these registers are inherent in the voice, and will therefore assert themselves naturally and merge imperceptibly into one another, what need is there to learn about them? The answer is, first, that without a conscious recognition of natural law, as manifested in the voice, or anything else, the tendency is almost invariably to ... resist it in one way or another.
Secondly, that the excessive tension which has become almost second nature with nine people out of ten prevents the natural law from prevailing, or even making itself known [1895, p. 92].

Register Breaks

"The term 'break' is generally used to indicate the point at which a new register with sudden change appears" [Fillebrown, 1911, p. 38]. Shakespeare offers an indirect definition:

Have we not realised, on singing up the scale, or when swelling a note from soft to loud, that the voice is accompanied by various physical sensations in the chest, in the mouth, or towards the back of the head? This, together with the fact that most of our voices have weak spots at which the note can be sung in different ways, may account for the vocal range having been mapped out into what are termed registers [1924, p. 36].

Lankow remarks that males and females experience their primary break in the same pitch area, i. e. , middle C to F#4. "Whereas the most marked break in the female voice is met with its lowest range, we find that the break of the male voice is to be located in its highest range" [1901, p. 5].

Heinrich offers voice placing, Parisotti proposes free-

dom of local control, and G. B. Lamperti recommends breath
control as solutions to the control of register breaks:

> Correct voice placing gives the student the ability to
> sing the entire range of a given range in such a man-
> ner that the passing from one register (so called) to
> another shall not be observable, shall take place with-
> out exposing the much and justly feared 'break' so
> that the entire range of the voice is sung with the
> ease, resonance, and beauty of tone belonging to the
> natural, easy, resonant and beautiful tones of that
> voice [Heinrich, 1910, p. 21].

> There is only one remedy for the breaks, and that is
> to give them the widest berth by allowing the organs,
> both of production and of development of the voice,
> absolute freedom and independence in the performance
> of their respective natural tasks [Parisotti, 1911, p.
> 59].

> There is no doubt that the greater part of the difficul-
> ties encountered at a change of register, as well as
> the uneven tones within one and the same register,
> may be traced to faulty breathing. At the change of
> register, especially, the breathing must be calm and
> easy. When it is so, and the body is in a normal
> position, with the mouth and pharynx opened, no one
> will experience difficulty at the change of register [G.
> B. Lamperti, 1905, p. 23; Henderson quotes Lamperti
> verbatim, 1906, p. 90].

The Origin of the Term "Register"

> In Italian the stops of the organ are called the regis-
> ters (i registri). It is probably due to this fact, that
> as the various parts of the human voice are charac-
> terized by a different quality of tone, viz. , grand,
> silvery, or flute-like, these different sections have
> been termed the 'registers of the voice' [Shakespeare,
> 1910, p. 32].

Taylor agrees that organ stops provided an analogous mechanism for comparison [1917, pp. 55-56], as does Salvatore Marchesi. Marchesi echoes Garcia's famous definition of registers, writing:

> In the invention of the grand instrument, it was intended

to designate a series of homogeneous sounds completely differing in their timbre (color) from the others produced by the same agency [1902, p. 26].

Bach believes that this analogy is unfortunate:

I think the term 'register' not well applied to the human voice, this term being borrowed from the mechanism of the organ, which has no resemblance to that of the human voice, and which certainly came into existence at a considerably later period. While an organ requires many sets of pipes for the production of sounds of different pitch and of different timbres, the human apparatus has but a single pipe, which, however, can produce a greater variety of effects than all the organ pipes in the world [1898, p. 68].

Head, Medium, and Chest Registers

The terms "head," "medium," and "chest" are the most popular appellations for the different register mechanisms. These terms are a carry-over from earlier eras. It is known that these terms date back at least as far as Ceroni [1566-1625; cf. Duey, Bel Canto in Its Golden Age, 1951, p. 112]. According to Lablache,

The sounds of the Chest-register should be produced by sending forth the breath freely, and in such a manner as not to strike against any point of the mouth on its passage.... The Medium sounds are produced by directing the breath against the upper teeth. The Head sounds are made by directing the breath entirely toward the frontal sinuses [1860, p. 5].

In 1917, Clippinger writes that "all voices should have a head register" [p. 11], meaning the singer should not carry his heavier "chest" mechanism up to the limits of his compass. Such use of these terms as are demonstrated by Lablache and Clippinger are common throughout the study. More examples will be found in quotations within the next section, "Number of Registers in the Voice." Beginning in the "scientific era," some authors explain that these names refer to local sensations. Some authors condemn the use of these terms outright as potentially misleading.

The vocal registers are determined by the different points of resonance of the tones.... There are three vocal registers, varying according to the individuality of the voice, namely the Chest-, Medium [sic], and Head-Register [G. B. Lamperti, 1905, p. 10].

In Voice Building and Tone Placing, Curtis writes that Mackenzie "says that there are essentially two registers--one the chest ... and the other the head" [1914, p. 112]. While it is true that Mackenzie acknowledges two mechanisms, it is also true that he refers to these mechanisms as "the so-called 'chest' and 'head' registers, or what may be called the lower and upper stories of the voice" [1891, p. 54]. Mackenzie does not believe in the use of these terms and writes,

> It cannot be too clearly understood at the outset that the voice is generated solely in the larynx. It is necessary to insist on this elementary fact with some emphasis, as much confusion has been caused by fanciful expressions like 'head-voice' and 'chest voice.' Philosophers are never tired of warning us not to mistake names for things, but it is an error to which we are all liable....
> The originators of the terms 'head-voice,' &c., no doubt applied them with subjective accuracy, i.e., the name expressed the fact as they conceived it. But just as 'the evil that men do lives after them,' misleading terminology continues to work havoc in the minds of learners long after its incorrectness has been recognized by teachers, who, however, adhere to it from a mistaken notion of its practical usefulness.... The larynx is the organ of voice just as the eye is the organ of sight, or the ear of hearing. Everyone would laugh at a man who should pretend to smell with his lips or see with his fingers; yet such claims are not one whit more absurd than those of singers who profess to fetch their voice from the back of their head, the roof of the mouth, the bottom of the chest, or anywhere else that their misinterpreted sensations lead them to fancy. As a basso profundo is sometimes figuratively said to 'sing out of his boots,' we may perhaps be grateful that there is no voce di piede among the acknowledged registers [1891, pp. 27-28].

Curtis agrees with this reasoning [1914, p. 112], as do Henderson [1906, p. 91], Randegger [1912, p. 8], and Muckey [1915, p. 120]. Henderson explains further that

This expression, 'head voice,' simply means that the

notes in its range seem to cause vibrations in the skull or some part of it, whereas the physical feeling of vibration in the medium register is in the pharynx and in the lowest tones in the upper part of the chest [1906, p. 94].

Bach provides an amusing anecdote to bear out the fact that the head voice is not produced in the head:

When giving a concert and lecture in London this season, I made a lady, now well known as an artist, sing notes in the so-called head-register. She maintained that she formed the high notes in the head, and her master in Milan had stated to her that, with head-tones, the air must pass through the nose so as to resonate from the cavity of the skull and the ear; besides that the pressure must be felt between the nose and the eyes. 'If you really form your head-notes in this manner,' I observed, 'air must escape through your nose.' On placing a glass closely to her nose, it remained clear and undimmed; besides, I caused her to close the nose whilst she was forming head-notes, and there was no difference observable in sonorousness and power. 'Do you see now, Madamoiselle, what is imagination?' I said [1880, p. 72].

Number of Registers in the Voice

The upshot of the many theories of registration is that authors must find a number of registers to agree with their observations of the laryngeal area. Most opinions fall into one of the seven possibilities listed below.

No registers. A few authors state unequivocally that there are no such things as registers. Other authors suggest that the singer pretend that there are no registers. Yet another class of authors take these first two views to task.

Do registers exist by nature? No. It may be said that they are created through long years of speaking in the vocal range that is easiest to the person, or in one adopted by imitation, which becomes a fixed habit [Lehmann, 1906, p. 107; Yeatman Griffith concurs, as quoted by Brower, 1920, p. 255].

What changes are taking place in the larynx itself we

are entirely unconscious of, and we need never know anything at all about them.... Of course, what we are actually feeling is resonance rather than registers [Dodds, 1927, pp. 48-49].

To some authors "no registers" means one mechanism:

In the chapter on 'Pitch' it is seen that a range of three octaves may be produced without any change in the action of the mechanism.... The only difference in the action of the mechanism for the production of high and low tones is in the degree of contraction of these two muscles [thyro-arytenoid and crico-thyroid]. There is, therefore, in correct voice production no change in action of the mechanism, and hence no 'registers.' ... 'Registers' mean wrong production, or production with interference [Muckey, 1915, p. 123].

There are no registers in the singing voice, when it is correctly produced. According to natural laws the voice is made up of only one register--its entire range [Marafioti, 1922, p. 51].

Daniell and Miller oppose the "no register" concepts:

Pupil: Then this contraction [of the vocal cords] may be continued indefinitely, until the very highest tones are reached, may it not?
Teacher: No: there is the error of the advocates of 'no register.' ... It is a fact, that the female voice will change in character about the middle F, G; but the teacher's work should be to so equalize the tone, that no perceptible change can be discovered [Daniell, 1873, p. 19].

The subject of vocal registers is a difficult one--difficult to understand and, when understood, difficult to make intelligible to others. In fact, it is so difficult that some people get rid of it by calmly asserting that there are no registers. This is unfortunate, because the blending of the registers, the smoothing out of the voice where one register passes over into another, the elimination of the 'break' between them, is one of the greatest problems which the teacher of voice-production is obliged to solve [Miller, 1910, p. 103].

One register. The theory that the voice should be

treated as if there is but one register is a relatively recent one. All statements to this fact occur after 1905.

One mechanism may be cultivated throughout the entire compass of the voice [Botume, 1910, p. 8].

We are convinced that one mechanism may be cultivated throughout the entire compass of the voice, that the vocal cords may be made to assume a position in which they are to all extents and purposes parallel throughout their whole extent [Curtis, 1914, p. 115].

Two other authors who believe in a one register technique are Fucito [1922, p. 145], and Duff, who recognizes that there are changes, but that "one should not be able to distinguish when one passes from one so-called register to another" [1919, p. 47].

Two registers. The theory that embraces a two-register system is almost entirely confined to the period of time before the twentieth century. More recent authors tend to align themselves with either the one-register or the three-register philosophies. Lasser creates a two-register system when he equates the falsetto with the head voice:

Der Lehrer bemühe sich, bey Untersuchung der Stimme seiner Schüler jene Stelle zu entdecken, wo die Brust-stimme zu Ende ist, und das Falsett, oder die soge-nannte Kopfstimme eintritt/ The teacher should endeavor to find, by investigation of the student's voice, where the chest-voice ends and the falsetto, or so-called head-voice begins [1805, Preface].

Bach, Lanza and Clifton also believe in a two register mechanism:

If we are to speak of registers at all there are but two--chest and falsetto registers [Bach, 1898, p. 69].

There are two different sorts of voices in both male and female--the one is called Voce di Testa (voice of the head), and the other Voce di Petto (voice of the chest); the latter is the best and every means should be tried by the singer to attain it [Lanza, 1818, p. 76].

The Scale of the female as well as the male voice,

combines two qualities; the female or Soprano scale
(from low to high) changes from a deep or rough, to
a higher or clearer tone, about e-g and which improves
in strength and clearness as it rises. This last voice
may be called the feminine; the other the masculine
voice. The male or Tenor scale (with adults) changes
from its natural to a feint or falsetto about e-g. The
lower tones are the masculine; the upper or falsetto
the feminine voice, which should be used as seldom
as possible [Clifton, 1846, p. 2].

Men have two; women have three registers. One theory
which enjoyed greater acceptance during the nineteenth century
but has not been totally abandoned in the twentieth century,
is that men have two registers available to them for artistic
singing and women have three. D'Aubigny states that both
men and women possess chest and head voices, but that women, children, and castrati have also a usable falsetto [1803,
p. 97]. Lablache agrees with D'Aubigny's statement, and
adds that this highest voice comes into use for the women
around the pitch E_5 [186-, p. 4]. Novello, who also believes
in this theory, points out that the different qualities of chest
and head "are much more perceptible in male than in female
voices" [1856, p. 4]. Other authors who express a belief
in this theory include Everest [1861, p. 28], F. Lamperti [1864,
p. 2], Crowest [1900, pp. 30-46], and Stanley [1916, p. 14].

Three registers. Three-register theories are the most
popular, and this is true throughout the study. About 1800,
Corfe describes the voce di petto, the voce di testa, and the
falsetto [p. 5], and these have been traditional divisions of
the vocal range well before his time. Ferrari calls the three
registers "Grave, Medium, and Acute," the first two being
called "voce di petto and voce di testa, chest and head voice,
although both are generated in the throat by the impulsion of
the lungs." The falsetto he terms "an acute artificial voice
which seldom unites with the chest voice" [1818, p. 2].
Other early writers who describe three-register systems
include Furtado [18--, p. 5] and Marx [1826, p. 109].

The most important statement in defense of a three-
register system is found in Garcia's oft-quoted volume, Hints
on Singing. This statement, which is repeated below, is a
simplification of his five-register theory of 1861 (see "Five
registers," below).

Q. Is the voice of the same nature throughout its
    range?

A. Every voice is formed of three distinct portions, or registers, namely, chest, medium, and head. The chest holds the lowest place, the medium the middle, the head the highest. These names are incorrect, but accepted [1894, p. 7].

Other authors who agree with Garcia include Botume [1897, p. 19], Mathilde Marchesi [1903, IV], van Broekhaven [1905, pp. 5-6], Parisotti [1911, pp. 61-62], and Dodds [1927, p. 49].

Four registers. Five authors are found to have believed in a four-register system, although these systems are not necessarily synonymous. Nathan discusses the chest, throat, and falsetto voices, and adds a fourth which he calls the feigned. "This voice," he writes, "is little appreciated, consequently rarely cultivated" [1836, p. 117]. Nathan, however, calls the falsetto also a kind of feigned voice. Costa names his four registers "chest, mezzo falso, falsetto or head voice, and flautino or extremely upper notes." He goes on to say, "Tenors and contraltos have generally three registers--chest, mezzo-falso, and falsetto. Sopranos have three and sometimes four registers,--the three last named and the flautino. The mezzo-falso is that which forms one register to the other, and partakes the character of both" [1838, p. 18].

Anna Lankow outlines the traditional chest, medium, and head voices, since she is an adherent of Garcia's teachings. However, she maintains that five of her sopranos have "a quality of tone which I call the fourth or flageolot register" [1903, p. 10]. This register encompasses D_6 to G_6 (above "high C"). A collaborator of Lankow's, F. E. Miller, also remarks on this highest register [1898, p. 11].

Salvatore Marchesi talks not of registers but of "resonance-walls" [1902, p. 28]. The fourth "wall," is the male falsetto.

Five registers. Curtis recounts the fact that Garcia, writing in 1861 (Physiologigues sur la voix humaine, Paris, p. 25),
divided the voice into three registers, chest, falsetto, and head--all three of them common to both sexes.... He further divided the chest into an upper and lower, and the head into an upper and lower register, thus making five distinct mechanisms. Madame Seiler followed Garcia in his divisions of the registers [1914, p. 111].

The Garcia monograph of 1861 was not available for this study, but Emma Seiler's work of 1871 does indeed outline five registers. She declares, however, that her information is the result of her own observations with the laryngoscope. On pages 65-66 she provides a summary of her findings of "five different actions of the vocal organ":

1. The first series of tones of the chest register, in which the whole glottis is moved by large, loose vibrations, and the arytenoid cartilages with the vocal ligaments are in action.
2. The second series of the chest register, when the vocal ligaments alone act, and are likewise moved by large, loose vibrations.
3. The first series of the falsetto register, where again the whole glottis, consisting of the arytenoid cartilages and vocal ligaments, is in action, the very fine interior edges of the ligaments, however, being alone in vibrating motion.
4. The second series of the falsetto register, the tones of which are generated by the vibrations of the edges alone of the vocal ligaments.
5. The head register, in the same manner and by the same vibrations, and with a partial closing of the vocal ligaments.

Myer concurs with this theory [1883, p. 20]. Behnke prefers to call the five registers "lower thick," "upper thick," "lower thin," "upper thin," and "small" [189-, p. 115]. Rogers dubs the registers "lower chest," "upper chest," "throat," "mouth," and "head" [1895, p. 91]. While Botume's names are "deep chest," "mid-chest," "neck," "mouth," and "head" [1897, pp. 19-20].

It should be noticed that most five-register theories occur a few years after Garcia's initial presentation. Few five-register theories exist after Garcia modified his theories to a simple three-register system.

As many registers as notes. One final category which cannot properly be considered a theory, but which is mentioned in passing by a few authors is that "there are as many registers as there are notes" [Wronski, 1921, p. 31]. Another author who mentions that some believe this is Tetrazzini [1923, p. 64].

The Falsetto

During the first 110 years of this study, the term
"falsetto" appears frequently.   It is safe to say that most
authors regard the falsetto as part of the register phenomenon.
Beyond this, the reader must look to each author for his
particular definition of this term.   A few examples are included to demonstrate the complexity of this problem of defining the term "falsetto. "

> The 'falsetto,' so called, is generally confused by
> definitions.   Some people call the high sounds pro-
> duced by blocking the length of the vocal cords 'fal-
> setto,' or as it is called, 'a natural falsetto;' this
> production being termed in Italy, when applied only
> to high sounds, 'Voce Mezzci. '   The ordinary choir
> falsetto is not produced by longitudinal influence, but
> by latitude or depth in extent of vibration (harmonics
> of the rim).   This is why such voices sound 'woody;'
> the vocal cords being so asunder that they only catch
> the air in passing, but do not afford from their width
> any perceptible resistence [Lunn, 1880, p. 10].

Lunn changes his opinion in later works:

> Falsetto ... is, as its name implies, a false produc-
> tion; it is created by the false cords being squeezed
> together, the true cords being open [1888, p. 55].

> Falsetto is a whistle through the false cord, the true
> cords not acting.   It is utterly unemotional and is
> rarely used by an artist....   It requires no study
> [1904, p. 46].

> The word falsetto, I am aware, is often applied to
> the peculiar tones in men which are produced in imi-
> tation of women's tones--or in a more general sense,
> perhaps, to the highest regions of the voice [Bassini,
> 1857, p. 6].

> In the 'head' voice, or falsetto, only a part of the cord
> vibrates, and the sound is reinforced by the upper
> resonators, mouth, bony cavities of the skull &c....
> The two cords are forced against each other at their
> hinder part with such force as to stop each other's
> movement.   While the notes of the chest register issue
> from the natural aperture of the larynx, the head notes

come through an artificially diminished orifice, the
chink becoming gradually smaller till there is nothing
left to vibrate, when the limit of the voice is reached
[Mackenzie, 1891, pp. 55-56].

Falsetto is making use of the smallest possible column
of air, and directing it only through, or rather around,
the frontal sinus via the infundibulum.... [T]he biggest
possible tone can be developed from it when the student has learned how to make a crescendo and how
gradually to bring the other sinuses into combined
use with the frontal [White, 1918, p. 51].

Even greater confusion is created by those authors
who use the term "falsetto" without definition. This was
especially the case with authors who wrote prior to the last
two decades of the nineteenth century (as we have seen in
numerous other instances throughout this study). A survey
of the representative statements already included in this chapter demonstrates the complexity inherent in the term "falsetto":

Tenducci states that a falsetto sound can be applied to
the head voice;

Garcia writes that falsetto is another name for the
medium register;

Van Broekhaven believes the medium and the falsetto
are two different mechanisms;

Lasser states that the falsetto is the head voice;

Corfe distinguishes the head voice from the falsetto;

Ferrari calls the falsetto an "acute artificial," and
unlike the chest and head registers; and

Nathan distinguishes falsetto from the feigned voice,
but later states that falsetto is a type of feigned voice.

The value of falsetto is obviously a highly debatable
point, since a general definition cannot be established. Statements for and against are presented in chronological order,
since opinions vary too greatly to be readily classified.

The counter-tenor is the highest male adult voice,
and is usually the voce di testa, or falsette. A good
falsette will extend to E in alt., the range below being
uncertain [Bacon, 1824, p. 89].

The tenor who wishes to preserve his voice and not to scream in the upper tones, who desires always to have a piano at command and to possess the necessary shading and lightness as well as elegance and flexibility, should cultivate the falsetto, and endeavor to bring it down as far as possible into the chest register [Wieck, 1875, p. 102].

It is generally regarded as something to be avoided, but I doubt whether it is wise to give it up. It is certainly most necessary to possess the ability to produce it. In former times the falsetto tone was regarded as much a part of the voice as any other, and you observe that the action is perfectly natural [Daniell, 1873, p. 35].

The falsetto or middle register is the chief one of women; it sounds better, fuller and nicer than a man's falsetto (and it is more consistent with the feminine disposition) [Guttmann, 1887, p. 72].

'Falsetto tones' are principally used by male altos. These tones lack resonance and richness, and are usually separated from the so-called 'chest voice' by a strongly marked break [Thorp and Nicholl, 1896, p. 42].

When blended ... it furnishes the student with an ideal instrument [Clippinger, 1910, p. 7].

It is an unmanly little whining trick, for which there is not the least justification, and to which no self-respecting and thoroughly capable vocalist should ever lower himself [Parisotti, 1911, p. 70].

The voice is naturally divided into three registers--the chest, medium and head. In a man's voice of lower quality this last is known as 'falsetto,' but in the case of a tenor he may use a tone which in sound is almost falsetto, but is really a mezza voce, or half voice. This latter legitimately belongs to a man's compass; a falsetto does not [Caruso, 1909, p. 54].

Clippinger states that using the falsetto is not artful singing, but it is certainly natural [1917, p. 25].

METHODS : THE PSYCHOLOGICAL APPROACH

Mental Causes Affect Registers

With all the discussion throughout the time span of this study about the nature, function and control of registers, it is surprising to note that only two persons state that all this discussion may adversely affect singers. Interestingly, they are both singers themselves.

> This striking contrast of the different vocal ranges has given them the name of 'register.' These are everywhere accepted as a matter of course, and for years have been a terror in the teaching of singing, that has done more than anything else to create a dreadful bewilderment among singers and teachers.... As long as the word 'register' is kept in use, the registers will not disappear [Lehmann, 1906, pp. 111-112].

Ursula Greville considers registers largely a part of the imagination. She is quoted by Martens as having said,

> I prefer the word range to 'register' or 'registers,' so often used, because 'registers' are really only arbitrary divisions of a naturally continuing range. Provided her tone placing has been developed as it ought to have been, this difficulty should not exist [1923, p. 142].

Using the Level of the Speaking Voice

According to Miller, "the easy singing range of each individual voice, usually is about identical with the pitch of its possessor's speaking voice" [1910, p. 140]. Miller and Shaw agree that "voices should be tonally trained in the musical scale, from the natural conversational tones of the speaking voice--generally from the highest easy-speaking tone--downward, and then from the lowest tone upward, taking care that the extension exercises should be graduated" [Shaw, 1914, p. 157].

Buzzi-Peccia makes an observation about using Italian teaching methods which directly relate to the speaking voice.

It would be wrong to say that the Italian method can

be taught to American pupils in the same way in which it is taught to an Italian student, not because of the difference in musical aptitude or capacity, but on account of the vast difference in the languages they speak.

The Italian language is spoken by every Italian in the nasal cavity, without the least preoccupation or thought of direction and without any effort to support the voice in that place.... The articulation of the consonants is performed by the lips and tongue in such a way that the sound is helped to go in front, leaving the lower part of the mouth (the jaw) entirely free and relaxed, which is one of the greatest advantages a singer can have [1925, p. 19].

The "High" and "Low" Fallacy

Only four authors acknowledge the fact that "high" notes are an image, and that such a concept as "high" does not apply to the formation of pitches. The fourth fault in Costa's list of singer's errors is "the extreme force with which the sopranos usually treat the high notes comparatively to the middle and lower voices" [1824, p. 14].

In taking the octave or higher, retain the same general position, and your tone will be pure. Distortion of tone results when the singer thinks only of reaching a certain note, regardless of the way in which it is obtained. The manner of getting it is of the first importance [Daniell, 1873, p. 22].

Ernest White quotes another singing teacher, John Kennedy, as having said, "height and depth do not enter into the composition of sound." White adds, "We agree, they do not" [1918, p. 48]. White also states that children are taught about higher class levels, higher military ranks, higher numbers; to tell a child to sing higher will be to ask him to do the reverse of what his body effort should be when singing.

METHODS : THE TECHNICAL APPROACH

Sectional Treatment

Practice with the entire range. Relatively few writers discuss practice with the entire range of the voice. Galli-

Curci says that "you cannot develop well-rounded, beautiful high tones without actually practicing them" [as quoted by Martens, 1923, p. 106]. Rogers quotes Lehmann as having written, "Never neglect to practice every morning proper singing exercises through the whole compass of the voice" [1925, p. 81]. While it is true that Lehmann recommends using the full range of the voice, she warns that this is not for beginners and never to be done at the expense of vocal strain [1924, pp. 186-188]. Taylor suggests that the entire range be practiced only after a considerable period of study [1914, p. 47].

Practice with the middle range. A much larger group (17 authors) favor practicing with the middle range. "The easy singing range of every singer's voice is located in the middle of his own vocal compass, and embraces about an octave" [van Broekhaven, 1908, p. 17]. Anfossi, Panofka, and Lunn state that practice in the middle voice can develop the extremes:

He [the singer] ought likewise to avoid carrying it [the scale] beyond its natural extent, as nothing is more prejudicial--whereas by practicing the middle notes the chest is strengthened and the voice expands in depth and elevation, and acquires mellowness and force [Anfossi, ca. 1800, p. 13].

Die tiefen oder hohen Töne einer Stimme deren Ansatz anfänglich nicht mit Leichtigkeit und vollkommener Klangstärke geschehen kann, dürfen keiner speziellen Uebungen unterworfen werden; sie werden sich nach und nach von selbst das Studium derjenigen deren Ansatz leicht ist, entwickeln/ The higher or lower tones which cannot be delivered in the beginning with ease and perfect sonority, must not undergo special exercise; they will little by little be developed, merely by the study of the tones that are easy to deliver [Panofka, 1859, p. 10].

It [the middle] is practiced most to develop muscle, economise air, and extend compass [Lunn, 1904, p. 31].

The balance of statements regarding use of the middle compass also express similar opinions. Other authors who value this concept include Ferrari [1818, p. 3], Wieck [1875, p. 86], Bach [1894, p. 166], Henderson [1906, p. 71], Lehmann [1906, p. 186], and Proschowsky [1923, p. 93].

Directional Treatment

In practice that involves more than one pitch, many authors express a preference for downward practice. Authors also consider special actions whenever a vocalise or song requires movement up to higher pitches.

Downward practice is advised. A number of authors believe that the correct method for blending the registers is to carry down the "lighter" mechanism.

You must also make use of the voice in the middle register [as well as the chest], and strengthen the good head-tones by skillfully lowering them; you must equalize the registers of the voice by a correct and varied use of the head tones, and by diligent practice of solfeggio [Wieck, 1895, p. 86].

Carry the color and quality of the head tones down into the medium voice and the medium down into the chest voice [Myer, 1913, p. 57].

The best method of 'blending the registers'--of smoothing out the breaks--is to bring a higher register several tones down into the one below and thus bridge over the passage from one adjustment to another [Miller, 1910, p. 131].

Others who speak of this concept include Bassini [1865, p. 7], Curtis [1914, p. 170], Duff [1919, p. 55], and Garcia [1924, p. 9].

Garcia [1924, p. 9], Duff [1919, p. 55], and Behnke believe that upward practice should definitely be avoided in register blending.

Never 'extend' lower registers upwards, but strengthen the upper registers, and carry them downwards, thus equalizing the voices from top to bottom, and enabling your pupils to sing without strain [Behnke, 189-, p. 104].

Downward practice concept opposed. Witherspoon calls the popular downward concept "a ruinous fad." He also writes,

The use of descending scales as the principle exercises, so that the head voice will be developed ...

in time weakens the fundamental of the tone and does
not develop the lower tones. Common sense would
dictate the use of both ascending and descending scales
for the attainment of an even scale [1925, p. 51].

One fatal method of teaching ... is to find the so-
called light upper voice which is all on the throat--
not necessarily throaty--and bring it down, spreading
it at the very bottom to keep the lightness.... This
production becomes a light coloratura type, flexible
and apparently effortless, but in the end it always
ruins the voice.
     The singer can only swell to a certain strength or
the note would crack and it is easier to sing softly,
as the throat is held closed all the time.... The few
that survive have flexibility and softness at the expense
of power, top ring, depth and meaning, and real beauty
and magnificence [Stanley, 1916, p. 7].

Approaching the high notes. A number of suggestions
are offered throughout the study for easing and securing the
high notes of the singer's compass. The first two concepts
are closely related. These are that the singer should maintain the same position as for lower tones, and that the singer
should have the upper notes in mind when singing the preceding lower tones so that his position will be pre-set before-
hand.

In taking the octave or higher, retain the same position, and your tone will be pure. Distortion of tone
results when the singer thinks only of reaching a
certain note, regardless of the way in which it is
obtained. The manner of getting it is of the first
importance [Daniell, 1823, p. 22].

If the lower tones are produced correctly, and an
even poise is maintained in ascending the scale the
higher tones will benefit by the support of the lower
ones--especially by keeping the throat well open
[Fucito, 1922, p. 150].

Other authors who favor this concept are Tetrazzini
[1909, p. 16], and Shakespeare [1924, p. 66].

In a musical figure I must place the lowest note in
such a way that I can easily reach the highest [Leh-
mann, 1906, p. 51].

Marafioti quotes from Caruso's The Art of Singing [1909, p. 55]:

> In the matter of taking high notes one should remember that their purity and ease of production depend very much on the way the preceding notes leading up to them are sung [Marafioti, 1922, p. 158].

Shakespeare and Stanley discuss psychological aspects of approaching high notes:

> Avoid thinking of the high notes as they are approached, for any sense of fear produces rigidity; remember that through silent breathing and open throat, high notes become as easy as low ones [Shakespeare, 1924, p. 66].

> In a tenor voice the top notes of the lower register-- E flat, E and even F--are the open tone.... When one changes from the open tone to the upper register, the only difference in feeling is that the note is floating up in the head for the one, and opened up--not out-- for the other [Stanley, 1916, p. 2].

Tetrazzini and Miller specify physical actions in approaching and making high notes:

> The true high note requires increased tension with the development of breath-power and control [Miller, 1917, p. 133].

> The attack of the sound must come from the apoggio, or breath prop. In attacking the very highest notes it is essential, and no singer can really get the high notes or vocal flexibility or strength of tone without the attack coming from the seat of respiration [Tetrazzini, 1909, p. 16].

Shakespeare advises practice for insuring secure high notes:

> Through the singing of solfeggi, the master endeavors to make the pupil gradually attain the higher notes. By this means, with practice, he acquires as wide a compass of notes as possible. He must observe that the higher the notes are, the more softly they must be produced in order to avoid shrieking [1924, p. 77;

this is a paraphrase from Pietro Tosi's <u>Opinions of Singers</u>].

Various Technical Devices

<u>Importance of scale work</u>.   The importance of scale work cannot be determined merely by counting the number of statements made on the subject during the time span of this study.   Examination of the many exercises or vocalises in the books surveyed, not to mention the multitude of books in this period that contain only exercises, reveals implicity that exercises are a fundamental technique for improving range and the transition from one vocal mechanism (register) to another.   The 25 statements gleaned from this study's sources merely verbalize a commonly-agreed-upon concept.

According to Tenducci, one of the prime requisites of a good singer is "to sing the scale, or Gamut ... which must be sung in the same breath" [1785, pp. 2-3].

> The objects proposed to be thus accomplished by the practice of the scale then are the production of the purest and the best tone, uniformity of voicing and the power of sustaining, swelling, and diminishing. These are the very foundation of good singing--the foundations of the great style and of execution, not less than expression.   No attempt should ever be made to go beyond the scale till they are acquired and fixed as matters of habit.   The process is slow--very slow; but it is that which alone is sure [Bacon, 1824, pp. 91-92].

> The scale is the greatest test of voice production. No opera singer, no concert singer, who cannot sing a perfect scale can be said to be a technician or to have achieved results in her art [Tetrazzini, 1909, p. 28].

> For many ills of the voice and tone production, I use long, slow scales.   They are an infallible cure [Lehmann, as quoted by Brower, 1920, p. 46].

<u>Blending the registers</u>.   Downward practice has already been observed to be beneficial in blending registers and although these statements are not repeated here, they are included in the total count of statements regarding this subject. Early writers, however, offer other solutions:

In singing the scala filata, namely, that scale which
is composed of long notes, great care should be taken
to combine these qualities of chest and falsetto in
singing those notes where two registers meet.   In
order to produce this connection, it is advisable not
to carry the chest voice to its highest pitch, but rather
to make use of the falsetto instead.   This is called
uniting the registers [Anfossi, 180-, p. 11].

Anfossi states further that notes should be equalized by dwelling on them, and modulating the voice, beginning pianissimo,
proceeding gradually to forte, then diminishing to pianissimo
again [also p. 11].   Cooke suggests a similar method:

There is in almost every voice one note between the
natural (or lower) and feigned (or upper) voices, the
production of which is infinitely less certain than that
of any other.... The best mode of blending ... to be
that of endeavoring to strengthen the note alluded to
in the feigned and so to soften it in the natural voice,
to accomplish which, the pupil should commence gently
with that note in the feigned tone and gradually swell
it into the natural voice [1828, p. 8].

Nathan also believes in the use of the feigned voice:

There is a break, more or less, in the voices of both
sexes, but more particular in that of the male, between the voce di petto and falsetto ... by the Italians
called Il Ponticello, 'The little bridge. ' Blending
cannot be accomplished without the aid of the feigned
voice, which may be justly considered the only medium
or vehicle by which the falsetto can be carried into
the voce di petto [1836, p. 144].

I recommend the student to vocalize and solfa the
scales in major and minor keys, likewise scales of
semi-tones [Ferrari, 1818, p. 4].

The best means of uniting the two kinds of sounds, is
to begin by making a single sound pass from the chest-
register to the head-register and vice-versa [Lablache,
184-, p. 6].

Downward practice is not the only technique of the
more modern teachers, although it is the most predominant
one.

The lowest notes of a register, in most voices, have not so much power as the highest notes of the preceding register. To equalize and blend the chest with the medium register, the pupil must slightly close the two last notes of the former in ascending, and open them in descending [M. Marchesi, 1903, xv; Marchesi's blending exercises run up and down; an exercise will ascend and the next exercise will descend in mirror fashion].

Bach suggests that soft singing will equalize the registers [1894, xiv], and Lankow observes that a mechanism which she calls voix mixte correctly effects blending [1901, p. 6]. Tetrazzini also states that mixing is the correct technique in blending:

The note of each register should partake sufficiently of the quality of the next register above or below it in order not to make the transition noticeable when the voice ascends or descends the scale. This blending of the registers is obtained by the intelligence of the singer in mixing the different tone qualities of the registers, using as aids the various formations of the lips, mouth and throat and the ever present apoggio without which no perfect scale can be sung [1909, p. 28].

Proschowsky believes that knowledge of tone-coloring through vowel selection aids blending:

The training of the one-register scale has best resulted from a knowledge of vowel combinations. The vowels have a definite effect upon the larynx position as well as upon the adjustment of the vocal lips. With this knowledge the vocal chords can be trained to produce with ease the one-register scale with normal uniform tone quality throughout the range on all vowels, the top voice being rounded, but not covered [1923, pp. 28-29].

Every tone in the ascending scale should be 'slightly' graded in volume so as to cause the different qualities to merge imperceptibly into each other.... In this way there is no note in the scale where any radical change is felt or where there is any difficulty to be overcome, for the larynx and tongue-bone will move in the exact ratio required for grading the tone as you conceive it, provided you do not interfere.

Equalizing the registers of the voices should, therefore, be interpreted grading the scale [Rogers, 1925,
p. 66].

W. J. Henderson, in his The Art of the Singer, offers
his own survey of other authors' techniques of attaining blend
throughout the range. This valuable 11-page survey contains
the thoughts of G. B. Lamperti, Meyer, Paul Marcel, Albert
Bach, and Clara Rogers [1906, pp. 99-109].

Lamperti recommends for practice in equalizing the
registers the use of the four notes of the chords of
C major and D flat major. He advises his pupil to
sing the chord ascending in one breath with careful
attention to legato, and then, after taking a breath,
to sing it down again. This exercise introduces the
low E and F, on which the passage from the low to
the medium is likely to occur. A similar exercise
is recommended, going up as far as G above the clef,
for crossing the bridge between the medium and head
registers [Henderson, 1906, p. 103].

ANALYSIS AND COMMENTS

Analysis of the primary sources of this study has revealed 343 statements relative to the subject of range. The
corresponding chapters in the studies of Fields and Burgin
disclose 228 and 257, respectively. This appreciable dis-
parity in figures is directly attributable (see "Theories: Vocal Registers," pp.   ff. , above) to the fact that teachers
of the early years of this study (1777 to ca. 1860) inherited
a large vocabulary of range-related terms. Authors of the
bel canto era had already used such terms as "head," "medium," "throat," and "chest" voices or registers, "falsetto"
and "feigned" voice, and the term "register" itself. Unfortunately, no standardized definitions accompanied these terms,
and this is understandable since these are subjective words.
As a number of authors in this study have remarked, the
teachers of the bel canto era no doubt observed a more or
less self-regulating range mechanism at work within the
singer's vocal apparatus. Teachers learned to associate
various vibratory sensations in the local areas of the chest,
neck and head with different pitch levels in the singer's compass. With sensation as the only means for analyzing this
phenomenon, the rise of a multiplicity of subjectively derived
theories is understandable.

What is a bit more difficult to understand is that the so-called "scientific era" of vocal pedagogy had not significantly simplified the understanding of the registration mechanism. Garcia is generally credited with the invention of the laryngoscope, a mirror on a long stem, for observing the actions of the laryngeal area during phonation (1855). Here at last seemed to be an objective means for studying the very source of vocalization. Teachers, singers, and vocal scientists alike availed themselves of this simple tool in the attempt to explain the nature of phonation and of registration. Unfortunately, as a number of authors in this study have observed, the action of the laryngeal area was still to undergo subjective interpretation. From our vantage point, it is easy to understand that the laryngoscope is an insufficient tool for a thorough understanding of the so-called registration mechanism. Hence, we find the writers of the nineteenth and early twentieth centuries still using subjectively-derived terms of former centuries for the defense of every imaginable theory. Many authors, no doubt, never used a laryngoscope, but relied on Garcia's findings to advance a theory for their own books. We find a majority of five-register theories between 1861, when Garcia first presented the theory, and 1894, when he modified his theory to a simpler three-register system. Thereafter, we find the majority of authors also favoring a three-register system.

Any summarization of register theory must be very generalized. It is probably safe to say that, while many feel impelled to speak of the nature of registration, few authors believe in local control of the muscles of the throat for governing pitch changes. Conscious controls are generally confined to the changeover points between registers. Here, many authors favor practicing downward scales in an effort to bridge with a lighter mechanism. In the most recent volumes, we find the concept of vowel color selection as an aid to blending the registers.

Four points seem to enjoy general agreement in this chapter: (1) Artistic singers should have a range of at least two octaves. (2) The natural vocal compass should not be overextended. This applies especially to singers who wish to extend their voices upward into the next higher voice classification. (3) The middle range of the voice is the best area in which to practice. And (4) scale work is essential for a variety of artistic objectives, including smoothness of execution throughout the vocal range, and breath support discipline.

VII

VOCAL DYNAMICS

Definition. Dynamics is the effect of degrees of
loudness or softness in the performance of music.
Victor Alexander Fields, in Training the Singing
Voice, notes that the concept of dynamics has
three senses related to music. These are physical force, power or energy; the acoustical mea-
surement of relative intensity or force in producing a sound; the musical, which relates the variation of volume, quantity or power of musical
sounds. Fields also points out that, "Like most
vocal and acoustical terms, dynamics has both
subjective and objective connotations. Hence it
is broken down into loudness and intensity" [p.
166].

In all, 110 statements were gathered for seven basic
categories related to vocal dynamics.

THEORIES

There are no abstract theories of vocal dynamics to
be found in the literature consulted. John Burgin makes a
valuable observation regarding the relative paucity of statements regarding dynamics:

The theories for attaining a wide range of dynamics
are discussed to a lesser degree than other phases of
singing. The reason for this may be that intensity,
softness, and loudness are so closely allied to the
breath, to phonation, and to resonance [Teaching Singing, pp. 120-121].

Rather than theories, seven authors offer ideas about the
nature and importance of vocal dynamics. Each of these
statements was published after the year 1849. No explana-

Table 7.   SUMMARY OF CONCEPTS OF VOCAL DYNAMICS

I.	Theories of vocal dynamics Nature and importance	7
II.	Methods of controlling vocal dynamics	
A.	A psychological approach The importance of mental imagery	3
B.	The technical approach	
1.	physical action in dynamic change	8
2.	resonance and vocal dynamics	6
3.	breathing and vocal dynamics	5
4.	loud versus soft singing in practice	
	a) loud tones should be used	14
	b) loud tones should not be used	15
5.	the messa di voce as a device	52
	TOTAL STATEMENTS	110

tion can be offered regarding the absence of earlier statements other than the observation that toward the mid nineteenth century, subtle dynamic shadings became increasingly prevalent in solo vocal works.   Prior to this period, many works only indicated generalized sections of piano or forte and long passages on one note that called for the device of messa di voce.

In 1858, Ferdinand Sieber offered a definition for vocal dynamics:

> What is the meaning of the word Dynamics?   It is the doctrine of the degrees of force, of the increase and the decrease of the accentuation, etc., of notes or tones, and groups of tones--of shading, in a word, in all its degrees.   It is clear that this is of the very highest importance in execution [p. 143].

Panseron observes that, "that which gives the human voice a marked advantage over all other mechanisms is its facility of dynamical emphasis and employing those various effects" [1849, p. 2].   Shakespeare expands on the thought, including the mechanism:

> The voice, nature's instrument, is unique in its capacity of diminishing the sound of a long note from loud to soft, and swelling from soft to loud, by chang-

ing its mechanism [Shakespeare has previously described the alterations in length, mass and tension capable of the vocal bands] from the long and broad vibration, to the others of shortened length and reduced breadth, and vice versa, the listener being unable to detect any such change [1924, p. 12].

Lablache explains the importance of dynamics:

In order to phrase well, it is not enough to comprehend and unfold the musical meaning; it is still necessary to give each phrase, to each member, a suitable coloring. Light and shade constitute the principal element of expression; and the artist who does not know how to put a variety of color into his singing will always be commonplace and cold.... Too much application, then, cannot be bestowed upon the facility of producing at will, forte and piano, and of passing gradually from one to another [1872, p. 143].

Our earliest source [Panseron], points out that dynamic changes should be a voluntary part of the art:

To produce good notes, to keep them pure, equal, and in tune as long as the respiration allows, indicates a good singer, modifications in intensity are more easily obtained than equality of tone [1849, p. 2].

METHODS : THE PSYCHOLOGICAL APPROACH

Using Mental Imagery

Only three statements were found related to the psychological aspect of dynamic change. All three are of such generalized nature that other authors may have assumed such knowledge on the part of the reader.

In order to control a crescendo and a diminuendo it is all-important that the singer's ear be sufficiently trained in keeping exact vowel form and tone-color fixed in his memory or he will soon mistake crescendo for an increase in darkness and a diminuendo for, perhaps, an exaggerated thinning out of the voice [Proschowsky, 1923, p. 48].

Lunn believes that "variableness ... is in response

to will" [1888, p. 27], while the unconscious will is the subject of Shakespeare's concept: "Let every note be produced in unconscious freedom, and the power of crescendo and diminuendo, the messa di voce, are at command through the registers unconsciously changing whenever necessary" [1910, p. 40].

METHODS : THE TECHNICAL APPROACH

Physical Action

If the roles of breath and breath pressure are given a separate heading, the number of statements related to the physical action of dynamic change become quite small. Even such a remark as, "If we want the sound louder, we ... strengthen the point of resistence" [Lunn, 1904, p. 16] may be coupled with breath control. Two of the eight statements offer clearcut explanations of physical acts during dynamic change:

> In messa di voce singing the high notes requires [sic] the mouth to be more fully opened at the forte, the tone otherwise sounding compressed and squeezed owing to the increased force of the breath. On the other hand, the lessened current of air in the piano, in order not to be too much dispersed ... demands a more closed position of the mouth [Bach, 1898, p. 43].

> I do not believe that a knowledge of the vibratory surfaces of the vocal chords and the changes that are involved in producing a crescendo or diminuendo would necessarily be of value to a student seeking to cultivate pianissimo. But it may not be unproductive of good results if we present the matter in as simple a picture as possible.... First, consider the glottis vibrating while producing a tone of normal size. If the tone increases in size, the longitude of the vocal lips also increases and in consequence the corresponding amplitude of the vibrations. A diminuendo ... is dependent upon the reverse movement [Proschowsky, 1923, p. 47].

Resonance and Vocal Dynamics

"Resonance is the important factor in both volume and

quality" [Muckey, 1915, p. 56]. "Resonance is caused when a sounding body communicates its vibrations to another body; or when, in other words, the second body is thrown into co-vibrations with the first body ... [and] the loudness of the resulting sound is increased because a larger body of air is set vibrating" [Behnke and Browne, 1904, pp. 24-25]. In forming the messa di voce, Clippinger says,

> The aim should be to make the diminuendo perfectly symmetrical and retain the resonance to the end. Resonance is the life of the tone--the carrying power. Without it the tone is dead. The softest pianissimo must be resonant no less than the forte [1910, p. 34].

Fillebrown explains that

> We are now prepared to realize the error of the common notion that loudness of tone is due entirely to increase of breath pressure on the vocal cords. Simple experiments with the tuning-fork have shown that while the volume of sound it gives forth is due in part to the amplitude of its vibration, its loudness is chiefly due to the character of the resonance provided for it [1911, p. 49].

Breathing and Vocal Dynamics

Guttmann and Shakespeare concur that, "as to the influence of the air pressure upon the quality of the loud voice, it is certain that by a stronger pressure of air the sound of the voice will become stronger, but it will also become higher. If, by a stronger pressure of air against the vocal cords, you wish to prevent the heightening of the sound, a consequent remission in the contraction of the vocal cords is necessary" [quotation is that of Guttmann, 1882, p. 64. Shakespeare's statement, in his own syntax, is in 1924, p. 4]. "In diminishing the tone, the opening of the throat remains the same. Only the quantity of breath given forth is diminished. That is done by the diaphragm muscle" [Tetrazzini, 1909, pp. 12-13]. Shakespeare explains that without breath support, soft effects cause the singer to become inaudible, swells become throaty and upper tones resemble shouting [1910, p. 40]. Proschowsky relates the ear to breath control in dynamic change:

> If a tone produced in normal size is to be increased

in volume and the intensity of the breath is being
increased by muscular pressure instead of being instinctively or automatically controlled and guided
through the sense of hearing, the crescendo would be
forced or overbalanced, and a diminuendo would be
impossible or would be dull or breathy, as the overburdening of the crescendo would react on the diminuendo
and continually have to be counteracted [1923, p. 48].

Loud Practice Should Be Used

A number of teachers believe in loud or "full voice"
practice. "Light attack and piano singing generally fail"
[Lankow, 1899, p. 8]. "Commence practice with moderate
power and without restraint. At first it is not desirable to
practice too softly as the tendency is towards too much restraint, resulting in pinched tone" [Shaw, 1914, p. 190].
Stanley thinks that

a very common, but absolutely fatal, error into which
many professors of singing fall is to teach a pupil to
start softly, telling him he will develop or build on
the soft voice. This is absolutely wrong, as a beginner is bound to use a throat control for his soft voice
to start with. Soft singing on the timbre is the last
and hardest thing of all to learn [1916, p. 6].

Marchesi points out that the concept "loud" should be clearly
understood. "In order to develop the power, extent, and
equality of the voice, and to succeed in blending the registers, the scales should be practiced with full voice, but without forcing it, and avoid shouting" [1903, xvi].

Practice is one area in which singers feel secure
enough to comment. One singer-teacher and two singers,
who are interviewed in Brower's Vocal Mastery, 1917, speak
of loud practice.

All scales and exercises should be sung with full voice,
but without forcing. By practicing with half-voice,
the tension of the glottis will never develop, neither
will the tones attain the requisite power [Marchesi,
1903, p. 9].

I do not, as a rule, use full voice when at work.
But this admission, if followed, might prove injurious

to the young singer. In the earlier stages of study, one should use full voice, for half voice might result in very faulty tone production [Florence Easton in Brower, 1917, p. 132].

Singing pianissimo in the beginning is another fallacy. This is one of the most difficult accomplishments and should be reserved for a later period of development [Oscar Saenger in Brower, 1917, p. 261].

Loud Practice Should Not Be Used

Almost an equal number of teachers and singers are opposed to those who favor loud practice. Kofler says, "Soft vocalizing has always been considered the most important and beneficial practice for the beginner and the finished artist alike" [1897, p. 155]. Shakespeare thinks that "through piano singing, loud singing first becomes beautiful" [1924, p. 82]. Wieck advises that "the lady singer ought to commence quite piano, at first in the one-lined octave, and to sing up and down ... without any expenditure of breath" [1875, pp. 118-119]. Curtis agrees, adding, "There should be, as yet, no attempt to produce intensity of tone" [1914, p. 174]. From the point of view of Bach [1894, p. 166], the reason for soft singing is that it keeps the singer from pushing, and Behnke elaborates: "The practice of always singing loudly is greatly to be deprecated, leading as it does to undue strain, to coarseness of the voice, and to utter inability to modulate it into softness and purity of tone" [189-, p. 131].

While the others consider soft singing from the point of view of breath support and throat hold, Clippinger views it as a valuable asset in register blending. "In preparing the head voice the student must begin with a tone that is entirely free from resistence and build from that. In a large majority of voices it means practicing with a light, soft tone. A voice that cannot sing softly is not rightly produced" [1917, p. 17].

The Messa di Voce

If the bel canto period saw the birth and rise of the messa di voce, the nineteenth and early twentieth centuries saw it flourish as both a dynamic embellishment in performance and a teaching device in practice. No fewer than 52

writers and singers have commented on its usage. Five
early books present the device among other exercises, but
since they offer no statement as to its nature or usefulness,
these instances are not included in the count.

Many authors, especially those of the early period,
offer a definition of the messa di voce. Variances in syntax
aside, they all agree. Tenducci and Lanza are typical sources.

> Rule VI. To sing a messa di voce: that is, by swell-
> ing the voice, beginning Pianissimo and encreasing
> [sic] gradually to Forte, in the first part of the Time;
> and so diminishing gradually to the end of each Note
> [Tenducci, 1785, p. 2].

> Q. How should the voice be exercised upon the differ-
> ent syllables:
> A. Each syllable should be begun in as soft a tone
> as possible, and the breath retained to increase
> it when required.
> Q. Must not the sound be increased by almost imper-
> ceptible degrees till it reaches the full power of
> the voice?
> A. Yes; and it must in the same manner diminish,
> till it becomes as soft as when it began; this
> method in Italian is called 'messa di voce' [Lanza,
> 1818, p. 75].

Ferrari [1818, p. 5] describes the same action, but
calls it "filar la voce, filar i suoni. " In the mid-nineteenth
century, messa di voce is termed "swell" by a few writers
of works in English.   Two of these are Bassini [1857, p. 17]
and Everest [1861, p. 28].   Another is Lablache, who outlines the usefulness of messa di voce.   "The practice of
scales with the swell is the most useful exercise which can
be performed for good singing. By this means, one corrects
the faults of the voice, gives firmness to it, increases its
power, and acquires the flexibility which is indispensible for
colouring the melody" [184-, p. 20].

In regard to specific application, Bach [1880, p. 30]
considers it the means of acquiring breath control.   Fucito
agrees [1922, p. 195], while Rogers [1893, p. 116] uses the
term, "breath pressure. " Oliver assures the reader that the
messa di voce "is the only means of acquiring that command
of the voice, is necessary to sustain it the required length
of time, with the proper degree of firmness, equality and

variety of strength" [186-, p. 6]. Anfossi states that it is
useful to eliminate tremolo [1800, p. 11], while Dodds says
that it can eliminate vibrato [1927, pp. 36-39]. Van Broekhaven values it as a register blending device [1908, p. 51].

While no one condemns outright the messa di voce as
a practice device, a number of authors set restrictions on
its employment.

> What the Italians term messa di voce ... ought not to
> be frequently used. I knew one very excellent teacher
> of public singing, who on the contrary desired his
> scholars to begin with any given quantity of tone, and
> to preserve the same quality evenly throughout. His
> reason was, that by this practice the scholar would
> acquire the power of producing any desired quantity
> at pleasure, and there appears to be some force in
> the remark. Others make the scholar sing the notes
> fortissimo, forte, and piano successively, in order
> to confer the power of producing any given quantity
> of tone [Bacon, 1824, p. 90 fn].

Crowest agrees that scales should be sung in three dynamic
shades [1900, p. 67]. Bach warns that "singing messa di
voce on high notes ... ruins young voices" [1894, p. 108].
Mathilde Marchesi, who, we have seen, favors loud practice,
advises that the device be used only when the singer "has
acquired a certain degree of suppleness and flexibility" [1903,
p. 39]. Curtis [1914, p. 174] believes that the messa di
voce produces strain and forcing in beginners, and Manuel
Garcia corroborates this: "The use of the 'messa di voce'
requires a singer to be expert in the control of the breath
and of timbres. At this elementary stage it would cause only
fatigue" [1894, p. 14]. Lamperti calls it "the ultimate exercise, not for beginners" [1864, p. 6] and states that "not
until the voice has gained decided agility and facility, should
the pupil begin to practice tones, together with the Messa di
voce" [1905, pp. 20-21]. Henderson, however, notes this
quotation in his publication of 1906 and makes the observation,

> Why agility, which means the ability to sing runs and
> florid passages, should be acquired before the messa
> di voce is begun is a question which I find myself
> quite unable to answer. The ability to sing a good
> messa di voce depends entirely on the control of the
> breath and the consequent steadiness and gradation of
> tone ... control of the breath is the first thing the

student has to learn.... the next step ought logically
to be toward the messa di voce [p. 110].

ANALYSIS AND COMMENTS

If the statements regarding loud and soft practice and
messa di voce were eliminated from this chapter, only 29
quotations would remain. It should not be thought, however,
that these authors do not consider dynamics an integral part
of teaching the voice. Rather, it is a basic ingredient of
all music, vocal or instrumental and is therefore not germane
expecially to the subject of vocal pedagogy. Those aspects
of dynamics which concern voice practice, namely loud and
soft singing and the messa di voce, are discussed at length.
The basic arguments of the first subject seem to center on
the concepts that loud singing is good if not overdone, and
that soft singing is necessary to master the art, but beginners
will find difficulty in control due to the demands of coordinating breath support and laryngeal adjustment. The messa di
voce is generally regarded as the device for determining and
for developing good breath support and economy in practice.
Other remedies are reported to be obtainable by its application. As with all popular concepts, its application is subject
to provisos.

VIII

EAR TRAINING

Definition. Ear training requires a specialized
interpretation in reference to the subject of singing.   Victor Alexander Fields, in Training the
Singing Voice, writes, "Ear training in singing
may be defined as the process of becoming pro-
ficient and skillful in recognizing, retaining or
reproducing vocal tones by means of practice
in experiencing their auditory sensations.   In
other words, it is the means of receiving and
retaining mental impressions of vocal tones and
tonal relations through the medium of the sense
of hearing" [p. 176].   This study has assembled
131 statements on the subject of vocal ear training.   The parallel chapters in the books of Burgin and Fields contain 155 and 157 statements,
respectively.   Those two subject areas more
frequently discussed in the works of both Burgin
and Fields are "sensation as a reliable guide"
and "critical listening to vocal models. "

THEORIES : GENERAL CONSIDERATIONS

The Nature of Ear Training

It is fitting to begin this chapter with four statements
made by David C. Taylor, for he is a champion of ear training, both as the major secret of the old Italian School and
as the alternative method to those based on physics and
anatomy/physiology.   "Nature's provision for the guidance of
the singer's vocal organ is the singer's own ear" [1916, p.
6].   "It is seen that under normal conditions the voice instinctively obeys the commands of the ear" [1917, xii].   "We
have here the only law of vocal management:--The vocal
organs adjust themselves instinctively and automatically to
produce the tones demanded by the mental ear" [1914, p. 2].

Table 8.   SUMMARY OF CONCEPTS OF EAR TRAINING

I.	Theories of ear training General considerations--the nature and importance of ear training	38
II.	Methods of ear training	
A.	A psychological approach	
1.	tonal imagery a factor	15
2.	self-listening as a vocal aid	
	a) self-listening is recommended	17
	b) self-listening is not recommended	5
3.	sensation as a guide to vocal action	
	a) sensation is reliable	11
	b) sensation is not reliable	3
B.	The technical approach	
1.	critical listening to vocal models	13
2.	imitation as a factor	
	a) imitation is recommended	25
	b) imitation is not recommended	4
	TOTAL STATEMENTS	131

"Provided the mind has the right conception of artistic tone ... correct tone production is acquired by the practice of singing under the sole guidance of the ear" [1914, p. 4].

Observations on the nature of ear training date back at least to the beginning of this study.   In 1780, J. A. Hiller asserts that the ear doesn't make the tone, but does govern it [p. 5].   Later, Mackenzie explains, "The difference in most cases between singers and those who have 'no voice' is really a defect of ear on the part of the latter, who are naturally unable to imitate sounds, that is, reproduce gradations of pitch, which, as a matter of fact, they either do not hear at all, or only imperfectly" [1891, p. 50].   According to Miller, the ear is "the true diagnostician" [1917, p. 11].

The weak points of this servomechanistic theory of singing are also noted by two authors.   "Those who, whilst singing, trust for guidance to the ear only, should be reminded that the ear, perceiving the sound after its production, is merely able to judge of its effect, but cannot possibly influence its cause" [Randegger, 1912, p. 4].   W. Warren Shaw [1914, pp. 172-174], quotes at length the writing of a Dr. G. Hudson, in the April 1908 issue of the Laryngoscope, to convey to the singer the dualistic nature of hearing:

> The faculty of hearing in so far as it relates to the faculty of speech may be divided into two classes, subjective and objective hearing.
>
> By the former is meant the hearing of one's own speech at the time of its production by the natural organs, and by the latter is meant the hearing of the speech of others and the reproduction of one's own speech, as in the phonograph.
>
> That there should be a difference in these two classes of hearing is apparent when we consider their physiology. In subjective hearing the sound waves are received not only through the external auditory canal by air conduction, and through the external bones of the head, but also and in large measure directly from the organs of speech through the Eustachian tube, and through what may be called internal bone conduction.
>
> In objective hearing the sound waves are conducted through the external auditory canal, through the bones of the head, and to some extent also through the Eustachian tube, but the direct effect of the actual vibrations in the laryngeal, oral, and nasal cavities so manifest in subjective hearing is entirely lacking.
>
> In addition to these physical differences between subjective and objective hearing, there is a less tangible, but no less actual psychical difference. A man hears the speech of others with a more or less critical ear, while to his own speech he turns a tolerant and even approving ear.
>
> Hearing in its finality is a mental process, and, like all mental processes, it is susceptible to training. ... We hear in great measure what we have learned to hear, and what we desire or will to hear, and it is of prime importance that we learn to hear ourselves aright, because the inability to do this leads to grave defects of voice and speech.

The Importance of Ear Training

Shakespeare shows that the importance of ear training was a concept dating back to the early bel canto period when he quotes De Bacily's Curious Remarks on the Art of Singing Well: 'Hearing is a special gift.... It is this endowment alone which leads to accurate singing. In order to become a

good singer, three very different gifts of nature are requisite: viz. voice, ability, and ear or intelligence' [1924,
p. 73]. Teducci, in 1785, states that "without a perfect
intonation, it is needless to attempt singing" [p. 2]. Corfe's
wording is almost identical [18--, p. 3]. Other early writers who consider a good ear a "prime requisite for a singer"
are Anfossi, D'Aubigny, and Nathan. Artists of the twentieth
century who agree include Lehmann, Nordica and Wronski.

"The nicest attention must be given to the accuracy
of the intonation as well as to the quality of the tone....
The consent between the ear which regulates and the throat
which forms the tone should be so complete, that they should
act by a mechanical impulse as it were" [Bacon, 1824, p.
91]. "I cannot say that I think a musical ear is given to so
few persons as is generally supposed, but the fact that the
ear is not trained sufficiently early, or carefully, to appreciate and to differentiate musical sounds" [Browne, 1887, p.
33]. "The real and only power that rules the art of singing
is the perception of sound" [Rogers, 1910, p. 51].

A number of authors within a thirty-year period present
the case of the deaf speaker to illustrate the importance of
the ear in governing sound production. Among them are
Holmes [1879, p. 171], Bach [1894, p. 74], and Rogers
[1910, p. 36], who is here quoted:

It is sound perception, reacting on sound conception,
which controls and coordinates that mechanism of muscles and ligaments.... If any proof be needed to
bear out the above statement, we have only to hear
the speaking voice of a deaf-mute who has been taught
'visible speech' to realize how utterly unmusical is
voice-production based only on an understanding of
the mechanism of sound.

METHODS : THE PSYCHOLOGICAL APPROACH

Tonal Imagery

"For the production of vocal tones of any kind, the
mental ear is the guide of the voice. The desired tone is
first conceived in the mind, the vocal organs then adjust
themselves for the formation of the tone" [Taylor, 1916, p.
8]. "The vocal organs adjust themselves to perform the
tone preconceived by the mind. The ear discovers whether

the tone produced corresponds to the one preimagined by the mind; and that is all" [Buzzi-Peccia, 1925, p. 13]. "In developing the voice the most important part of the teacher's work is that of forming the pupil's taste in tone quality.... [T]he tone is the thing, and ... how it sounds is his primary concern" [Clippinger, 1910, p. 7].

Self-Listening as a Vocal Aid

The subject of self-listening raises the questions of how to approach the inherent subjectivity and also how to deal with the phenomenon of proprioceptive hearing which makes the singer hear a different voice than is heard by his audience. Seventeen writers believe that self-listening is an important concept.

Ferrari is the isolated source in the early nineteenth century. He writes that, "the ear being the supreme judge, it must listen with the utmost attention to discover truth and correct error" [1838, p. 5]. Years later, Downing writes, "In your own work listen to every tone you sing; train your ear to recognize and tolerate only the very best tone quality possible to produce, either in singing or speaking; each one will help the other" [1927, p. 16]. "The ear is the court of last resort, and the ear, which is another name for tone concept, or musical taste, must at all times decide whether the tone is good or bad. A musical tone is something to hear, hence how it sounds is more important than how it feels" [Clippinger, 1910, p. 4]. Taylor writes:

> How readily the voice responds to the demands of the ear is easily seen. Strike a note on the piano, and then sing a tone on this note. Your ear hears the note and your mind bids your vocal organs to produce it. This the voice does instantly.... So also in producing tones of any particular quality, the vocal organs adjust themselves in the same instinctive manner. Certain adjustments of the vocal cords and resonance cavities are required. But we need know nothing of this [1914, p. 2].

Many singers credit self-listening as the guide to their tonal successes. These include Lehmann, Tetrazzini and Galli-Curci. Three others record typical thoughts:

> Listen to yourself; your ear will tell you what kind of tones you are making [Caruso in Brower, 1920, p. 6].

> When singing a role, I am always listening--watching--
> to be conscious of just what I am doing.... I can
> tell just how I am singing a tone or phrase by the
> feeling or sensation. Of course I cannot hear the
> full effect; no singer ever can actually hear the effect
> of his work, except on the records [De Luca in Brower,
> 1920, p. 65].

> The singer of course hears himself, and with study
> learns to hear himself better. In fact I believe the
> lack of this part of vocal training is one of the greatest
> faults of the day, and that the singer should depend
> more upon hearing the sound he makes than upon feel-
> ing the sound. In other words, train the ear, the
> court of ultimate resort, and the only judge--and for-
> get sensation as much as possible, for the latter leads
> to a million confusions [Witherspoon in Brower, 1920,
> p. 247].

Shakespeare explains that listening provides the natural
equivalent of a servomechanism which guides the placement
of each sound:

> The violinist shortens his strings by fingering nearer
> the bridge.... It is not so with the singer. He can-
> not tune his cords by anything he can see or feel;
> having no direct control over them, he can only judge
> of the tuning after he has heard the sound of his voice
> [1924, p. 11].

Thorp believes that practice with a critical listener
can overcome the problem of self-hearing:

> At first do not trust your ear to guide you in vowel
> sounds. Sing 'o' as in 'old,' and ask someone what
> vowel you have sung. In most instances it will be
> taken for some other vowel sound. In this way learn
> to hear your vowel sounds as others hear them. Until
> you can do this, do not practice alone [1899, p. 31].

A fence-straddler on this issue is W. J. Henderson,
who admits that listening is necessary but advises the singer
not to expect to hear what others hear. In relating how the
student knows his attack is correct, Henderson explains,
"There are two ways of ascertaining. One is by one's own
sensations and the other is by the report of a competent
hearer. It is in the latter capacity that the trained teacher

is essential.... One cannot hear his own voice as others
hear it, and the teacher is the guide whose experienced ear
detects vocal error" [1906, p. 55].

Five writers were found to oppose self-listening. Basically, the argument against self-listening centers around the
inability to hear ourselves as others do. "The singer cannot
properly and must not listen to himself or herself sing.
Firstly: because chiefly the back resonance on ring is heard
by the singer and not the front ring; since the back ring is
inside and all for one's own ears, but the front ring floats
away from the singer. Secondly: because if one listens he
expresses what he thinks he hears, creating, usually, a
concerted appreciation of his own voice" [Stanley, 1916, p.
16]. "The great difficulty in teaching as well as in learning,
is due to the very fact that the singer cannot hear his own
voice. His judgement, therefore, is not a direct one--it is
the reflection of the effect of his voice on other people. On
this ... vicarious experience, the singer has to depend almost entirely" [Buzzi-Peccia, 1925, p. 85]. "You can feel
if you are right, but you cannot hear. Your ear is no use
whatever as a guide to the remedying of production faults in
your own voice" [Dodds, 1927, p. 10].

Sensation as a Guide

Strictly speaking, hearing must be considered a sensation since sensation is the immediate reaction to external
stimulation of a sense organ; conscious feeling or sense impression. Some writers in fact include hearing when they
speak of sensation (see Henderson, 1906, p. 55 above).
Many writers, however, use the term in the more limited
connotation of appraising the stimuli of sound production by
feeling, divorced of the sense of hearing. Taylor further
divides the meaning of sensation into two categories. "Direct
sensations of tone are the sensations actually felt by the
singer as a result of the exercise of the vocal organs. Sympathetic sensations of tone are the muscular sensations experienced in imagination by the hearer as a result of the
listening to tones of voices other than his own" [1908, p. 161].

"An agreeable sensation is our first basis of musical
expression" [Lunn, 1904, p. 13]. "I do not actually hear
my voice, except in a general way; but we learn to know the
sensations produced in muscles of throat, head, face, lips
and other parts of the anatomy, which vibrate in a certain

manner to correct tone production. We learn the feeling of
the tone. Therefore everyone, no matter how advanced, requires advice as to the results" [Farrar in Brower, 1920,
p. 16].

Lilli Lehmann is the great proponent of the efficacy
of sensation. She has many things to say of the use of sensation in How to Sing, including a rationale:

> Since in singing we sense none of the various activities
> of the cartilage, muscles, ligaments, and tendons
> that belong to the vocal apparatus, feel them only in
> their cooperation, and can judge of the correctness of
> their workings only through the ear, it would be ab-
> surd to think of them while singing. We are compelled,
> in spite of scientific knowledge, to direct our attention
> while practicing to the sensations of the voice, which
> are the only one we can become aware of--sensations
> which are confined to the very palpable functions of
> the organs of breathing, the position of the nose, of
> the larynx, of the palate, of the diaphragmatic attacks
> and finally, to the sensation of the resonance of the
> head cavities. The perfect tone results from the com-
> bined operations of all these functions, the sensations
> of which I undertake to explain, and the control of
> which the ear alone can undertake [1924, pp. 90-91].

Perhaps it is the method of complete control by sensation espoused by such teachers as Lehmann that led Russell,
in The Singer's Body and Breath Under Artistic Control, to
write:

> There is ... a real study in sensations. Many items
> of voice-culture depend upon acutely perceiving and
> accurately locating sensations. The student (and, of
> course, the teacher) must be aware of any tendency
> toward morbid or hysterical conditions.... He should
> seek for reasons for all theories and not depend upon
> a momentary 'I-think-I-feel-it-there' location of a
> sensation for a basis of practice [1904, p. 15].

Only three authors were found who believe that sensation is not always a reliable guide. Each of these, however,
admits in another section of his book that sensation is useful
under certain circumstance:

> It is well to understand in the beginning that physical

sensations are not an unfailing guide to good voice production. The most important physical sensation is that of the absense of all effort. The sensations in the front of the roof of the mouth and in the nasal cavities are so common in the production of the upper part of the voice, both male and female, are indicative of the right placing, or focus of the tone, and there is no objection to the use of these suggestions, but they are by no means considered the final test [Clippinger, 1910, p. 4].

There are few things so difficult to express in language as mere physical sensation, and the more subtle the sensation, the more difficult is its description.... The ability to locate physical sensation is not always present among students, or, in fact, professional singers, consequently it is not always safe to follow advice which is the result of how or where someone feels a sensation in singing. In some mental and physical conditions the various parts of the body are so closely in nervous sympathy, that the locating of certain subtle sensations is as difficult as it is to locate the aching tooth which causes "all the teeth to grumble" [Russell, The Singer's Body ..., 1904, pp. 14-15].

Describing to the student the sensations which ought to be felt, does not help in the least.
Nothing else can bring about the sensations of correct singing, but correct singing itself.
Further, no amount of attention paid to muscular sensations will inform us exactly what muscles are contracted in any complex action [Taylor, 1908, pp. 114, 115, 171].

METHODS : THE TECHNICAL APPROACH

Critical Listening to Vocal Models

"An immense fund of information about the vocal action is obtained by attentive listening to voices, and in no other way" [Taylor, 1917, x]. Three authors recommend that the teacher may use him or herself as a model under certain circumstances. In Panofka's Gesang-ABC of 1859, exercise #1 instructs the teacher to sing each phrase and the pupil to imitate him. Lamperti states that, "only when the pupil feels uncertain should the teacher sing to her,.... He should also show her the proper posture of the mouth, and breathe with her, though without singing" [1905, p. 11]. Shaw writes:

> A strong factor of the old Italian School was undoubt-edly the practical demonstrations of the Maestri. In this way they made their meaning clear. Pupils were not asked to imitate the master, but by hearing the master produce the tone they more readily acquired the mode [1914, p. 163].

Shaw also quotes Mancini to show that the teacher may imitate the pupil as a model for the pupil's objective listening. "The easiest way and the one by which I had good results, is to give the student the evidence of his error, and to this end the teacher himself must faithfully reproduce the defect of the student" [1914, p. 110].

> Giuseppi Campanari and Albert Bach advance the idea that the great artists provide the great models. "My advice to the voice students of America is to hear great singers" [Campanari in Cooke, 1921, p. 75].

> A note sung to a pupil is more instructive than the best explanation, and in many respects listening and imitating does most for the learner. I remember Dr. Filippi of Milan giving to the thousands of singers congregating in that city the sound piece of advice to go, and, as a real lesson, listen to Signora Adelina Patti, who was just then singing in the Scala Theatre [Bach, 1898, p. 21].

> Four singers and two teachers take advantage of the then recent invention, the phonograph in their advice to the student. Tetrazzini is one singer especially sanguine about its advantages in training the ear:

> The student can take a particular aria and hear it by Caruso again and again until he is familiar with every detail of his rendering--can note his breathing, his phrasing, and every other detail in a manner which would be quite impossible by any other means [1923, p. 112].

The other writers who recommend the phonograph are Bispham, Botume, Muckey, Saenger, and Witherspoon. One author cau-tions his readers not to imitate an artist's timbre:

A phonograph record of a great artist will be of value
to a student in developing his artistic point of view,
his musical sense, his grasp of rhythm, his pronunciation of foreign tongues, but will prove disasterous
should the student attempt to imitate the singer's tone,
deformed by and subordinated to mechanical necessities
[Wronski, 1921, p. 7].

Imitation as a Factor

"Imitation or Cultivation by means of the ear is also
an important agency in training voices" [Kofler, 1897, p. 22].
"The mystery surrounding the old Italian method is dispelled
so soon as the possibility is recognized of teaching singing
by imitation" [Taylor, 1905, p. 11]. "Imitation, which in
many other arts becomes plagiary, in singing is most desirable; for singing, more than any other art, rests on tradition"
[Crowest, 1900, p. 85].

In at least seven cases, authors tie imitation with
listening to vocal models. For example, Bacon [1824, p.
77] exhorts English singers to attend the performances of
Italian singers in their theatres and to imitate the purity of
their vowels. "By no means the worst lesson which you can
have will be gained by imitation of some acknowledged first-
rate singer, whose voice is of the same kind as your own....
[P]rocure copies of his songs.... [H]ear how those works
are rendered.... [A]nd while the impression made upon you
is still fresh, go home and imitate them as closely as you
can" [Crowest, 1900, p. 70]. Miller holds that care should
be given to imitate only perfect models [1917, p. 13], and
Russell believes, "The accuracy of the model plays an important part in the result of the copy. If the model be bad,
the copy will likewise be bad" [1904, A Plain Talk with
American Singers, p. 8].

Shryock's approval of imitation arises from his observation that, "children first learn to sing, not as they learn
to read, but as they learn to talk. The art of speech is
universally acquired by imitation" [1856, p. 1].

In 1883, Behnke and Browne wrote, "Singing cannot
be learned exclusively by imitation, any more than painting
by copying the works of masters, however great" [p. 2].
Salvatore Marchesi also believes in the limited effect of
imitation, but does not reject it in this case, when he writes,

"Singing cannot be learned exclusively by imitation, any more than can painting by copying the works of the masters of art" [1902, p. 48].

Few authors of this period are opposed to imitation, and the reasons they offer are not particularly convincing. Daniell takes the point of view that it is not safe to imitate even professional singers: "The uneducated singers have declined because they have listened to professional singers of lesser calibre" [1873, p. 10]. Buzzi-Peccia offers a number of reasons why the vocal model and its imitation are unreliable:

> Imitation is a very poor form of art.... As a matter of fact, the vocal masters who produced the greatest celebrities were not singers themselves.... Moreover were the exact imitation of vocal emission desired, it would not prove practicable. What kind of example could a tenor, even with a Caruso voice, give to a coloratura soprano, a basso to a tenor and vice-versa [1925, p. 37]?

ANALYSIS AND COMMENTS

There is a basic unanimity among the authors of this period concerning the importance of ear training. The techniques of educating and employing the sensations of aural and proprioceptive hearing are widely agreed upon, and those who demur do so only to suggest restrictions. The number of authors who recommend self-listening is more than three times those who do not. Those who disagree with the value of self-listening argue that it is impossible to hear oneself accurately, but that the singer can either develop a means of listening through the help of an objective party or can rely on the aid of his teacher in eary study until his own sensational judgments are developed. Also, more than three times the number of authors do than do not agree that sensation is a reliable guide to vocal action, and, once again, those who express doubts admit that sensations have at least limited value in tone production. The authors who recommend imitation number more than five times those who do not. Moreover, the disagreements regarding the skillful perception and interpretation of sensory stimuli in ear training do not align themselves with the opposing camps of science and tradition. Authors from all pedagogic viewpoints recognize the values of self-listening, sensational guidance, vocal models and imitation.

IX

DICTION

Definition. The need to capture the concept of
diction by means of an accurate definition was
apparently never felt by the writers of the period
1777 to 1927. Even the respected English Diction
for Singers and Speakers by Louis Arthur Russell
presents no phrase or sentence concerning the
meaning of diction. Victor Alexander Fields, perhaps feeling this need when writing Training the
Singing Voice (1947), offers definitions of not only
diction, but of its elements, articulation, enunciation, and pronunciation, tailored specifically to
the vocal specialist:

"In defining diction, it must be borne in mind
that language is a synthesis of differentiated
vocal and non-vocal sound patterns into larger
syllabic and verbal groupings that can be standardized as to meaning. Thus language becomes
a means of symbolization and communication of ideas
and diction is the process of manufacturing these
symbols out of vocal raw materials. [Webster's]
The diction of singing therefore, may be defined
as the clear and accurate formation, production
and projection of the elementary sounds of language, and the combining of these sounds into
fluent sequential patterns that are suited to the
tonal expression of the words and music of a
song.

"Articulation is a formative or moulding process,
involving organic mechanisms of the vocal tract
that incipiently shape the phonetic patterns of the
language.

"Enunciation is a projective, dynamic or energiz-
ing process whereby vocal sonancy or audibility
is applied to the vowels and consonants articulate
for purposes of communication to a listener.

Table 9.   SUMMARY OF CONCEPTS OF DICTION

I.   Theories of diction

A. General considerations	53
B. Vocal factors in the singer's diction	
1. vowel as a vocal vehicle	16
2. vowel characteristics	44
3. importance of consonants	27

II.   Methods of cultivating diction

A. A psychological approach	
1. importance of mental imagery	8
2. speaking as a device	14
3. whispering as a device	8
4. chanting as a device	1
B. The technical approach	
1. value of sol-fa training	28
2. vowel techniques	
a) importance of ah vowel	49
b) lingual and labial controls	6
c) other physical controls	2
d) Italian vowels	10
3. vowel alteration	
a) high pitched vowels are altered	7
b) high pitched vowels are not altered	2
4. consonant techniques	
a) physical controls	7
b) consonants as tone-interrupters	7
c) interrupters of rhythm	2
d) exaggeration as a device	4
5. phonetic knowledge is advisable	1
TOTAL STATEMENTS	296

> Pronunciation is an integrative or combining pro-
> cess whereby vowel and consonant sounds are
> united into larger rhythmic groupings called syl-
> lables, words and phrases [p. 190].

Altogether, 296 statements were gathered for this
chapter.   This chapter differs with its counterparts in Fields'
and Burgin's works in that a section on "the value of using
Italian vowels" is also included.

CONCEPTS : GENERAL CONSIDERATIONS

In the eighteenth and early nineteenth centuries, generalizations about the importance of good diction abound. It is difficult to find the writer who does not give diction at least an acknowledgment:

"Gut gesprochen, ist halb gesungen"/ Good speaking is half the singing [Hiller, 1780, p. 25]. "Rule V--To articulate perfectly each syllable" [Corfe, 18--, p. 4]. "Wer gut spricht, hat für den Gesang einen grossen Vortheil erlangt"/ He who speaks well has acquired a great advantage for singing [D'Aubigny von Engelbrunner, 1803, p. 142]. To be successful in singing, "vorher muss aber der Schüler mit der richtigen Aussprache der Buchstaben, Sylben, und Worten bekannt werden"/ first the student must be acquainted with the correct pronunciation of the letters, syllables and words [Lasser, 1805, p. 30].

Yet the particulars of creating good diction are not to be found. As late as 1836, Isaac Nathan complains that one singer, "when executing the delightful air in Sheridan's opera of the Duenna 'Had I a heart for falsehood framed,' he usually pronounced it 'Had I a har-rat,' which gave great offense to the critics" [p. 163], and says no more to the reader. The assumption is that the student needed only to pronounce carefully and problems of diction were solved. This is, in fact, voiced by Lablache, who states, "Pronunciation, in singing, is subjected to the same rules as in speech. Good pronunciation consists in giving to each letter or to each syllable, the sound which belongs to it" [184-, p. 87].

It is not until the investigations of Helmholtz and his subsequent publication of Die Lehre von der Tonempfindungen als physiologische Grundlage für die Theorie der Musik (1863) that writers such as Seiler and Garcia begin to explain the how as well as the why of good diction.

If the singer has not carefully analysed and completely mastered the mechanism which produces vowels and consonants, the words, besides being indistinct and incorrectly delivered, create obstacles which impede the smooth and harmonious flow of voice and the facile formation of timbres [Garcia, 1894, p. 49].

In the twentieth century, writers talk of diction in terms of physical and acoustical laws. Speaking about vowel

formation, Shakespeare says, "The human voice is endowed
with two adjustable resonating chambers, one above the other
at the back of the tongue; and it is these which, when set in
sympathetic vibration, add fullness and richness to the tone
of the voice during singing" [1924, p. 45]. In the minutely
detailed analysis of cavity coupling and formant theories, the
writers of the time period of this study cannot touch those
of the later twentieth century. This study can only show the
foundations from which these analyses have evolved.

Diction, however, did not become the sole property of
the scientists. As the areas of resonation and phonation
came under increasing scrutiny, and as complex systems of
physical adjustments were evolved, those writers who pro-
claimed a psychological approach turned to diction and ear
training as a counter-methodology.

"In acquiring a clear enunciation the ear is a safe
guide, and indeed the only safe guide. No one need be told
how to sing distinctly, any more than how to speak distinctly" [Taylor, 1914, p. 26]. "Pure pronunciation, once achieved
ensures right tone production, and consequently right tone"
[Ffrangçon-Davies, 1904, p. 86].

Ffrangçon-Davies is the most outspoken anti-technical
writer of his time. Taylor is also opposed to local efforts,
but he warns against any theory such as that of Ffrangçon-
Davies that suggests correct diction as a vocal panacea:

Vocal teachers always recognize the importance of a
clear delivery of the text in singing. Correct enunciation is therefore considered in all methods. A few
teachers believe that a clear pronunciation helps greatly to establish the correct tone-production. But this
theory calls for only passing comment. One has but
to turn to the vaudeville stage to see its falsity. For
singers of that class, the words are the utmost importance, while tone production is usually the very
worst [1917, pp. 88-89].

In speaking of vaudeville singers, Tetrazzini says that
"one of the compensations of the 'white voice' singer is the
fact that she usually possesses a perfect diction" [1909, p.
31]. Madame Tetrazzini represents the neutral faction that
considers diction important for the sake of diction, but not
as a developer of tonal quality.

Two writers of the twenties express their disappoint-

ment with the diction of professional singers.   Dodds states
that poor diction must be considered the rule, since at every
recital he attends in which the texts are provided, there is
a flurry of sound at the turn of the page [1927, p. 11].
Wronski remarks wryly, "The term 'pronunciation' admirably
sums up the physiology of the act.   Many singers practice
retronunciation" [1921, p. 36].

Vowels Are the Vocal Vehicle

In the period covered by this study it was found that the
concept of the vowel as the carrying agent of tone is largely
implicit.   Authors demonstrate the function of the various
vowels without feeling the need to remark on this fundamental
aspect.   Notwithstanding, 16 authors were found to have something to say.   "What is actually sung is only vowels," writes
Bach, "Consonants ... are but momentary accessories"
[1894, p. 52].   Clippinger notes that, "vowels are formed
without interference of any organs of speech, hence the entire
range of vowel sounds may be produced in succession without
interrupting the flow of the tone" [1910, p. 13].

Too much of this uninterrupted flow is a fault discussed
by Douty:

> While the singer is trained to breathe, to use his
> resonance and not stiffen, yet his exercises are usu-
> ally upon vowel sounds alone, or even upon two or
> three selected vowels, ignoring the others.   He seldom
> understands thoroughly the value of a consonant, nor
> is the difference made clear to him.   As a result his
> tone is a thing of beauty, directly emotional in its
> appeal, and thrilling in its effect upon an audience.
> Dramatically he is usually quite at sea, and all too
> often his words are unintelligible.   This is the reason
> why the actor seldom cares for singing, and why the
> singer does not appreciate the art of the actor [1924,
> p. 12].

Vocal Characteristics

Maria Anfossi is the earliest in this study to discuss
the nature of vowels.   She describes to the English public
the "five Italian vowels" and their proper pronunciation [ca.
1800, p. 44].   In 1846, Clifton demonstrates that the first

vowel in a diphthong must be the one that is prolonged in singing [p. 3].

In the decade beginning 1870 the examination of vowels becomes a major issue in vocal pedagogy works. Helmholtz's name begins to appear as often as those of Mancini and Tosi. The minutely detailed descriptions of each vowel and its corresponding physical adjustments are beyond the scope of this study. Those who seek such information would do best to consult the works of Bach, Heinrich, Kofler, Miller, Proschowsky and Stockhausen. A few representative remarks are selected to demonstrate approaches to the character of vowels:

> Q. How many vowels are there?
> A. Though grammarians admit generally nine (in Italian), the number is, in fact unlimited.
> Q. How is this?
> A. The mouth being formed of elastic and movable organs, has an unlimited power of modifying its shape and capacity, and each change is a mould whereby a particular vowel is formed [Garcia, 1894, p. 45].

The length of the cavity of the mouth is the greatest in sounding oo, the least in e, intermediate in a. The Swiss form the o and u like the a in father, broadest at the back of the mouth, and the e broadest toward the front [Seiler, 1871, p. 122; she gives similar descriptions for all vowels].

For the U (oo in pool) the vocal tube is arranged to give its lowest tone of resonance.... For O (o in note) the lips retract and enlarge the opening, so that the pitch of the cavity is considerably raised. For A (a in father) the oral aperture is still further increased in size, and for A (a in bath) the mouth is wide open [Holmes, 1879, pp. 140-142].

The researches of Helmholtz, Koenig, Willis, Wheatstone, Appunn, Bell and others have shown that each vowel sound has its own pitch.... In the natural resonance of the vowels ee is highest in the head, ah is midway in the scale, and oo is lowest in the resonance [Fillebrown, 1911, p. 20].

Julius Stockhausen describes in detail the physical ad-

justments of vowel formation (pp. 6-12). He devises as well
a vowel chart, based on tongue and lip positions [1884, p.
6]:

middle tongue, middle lip

```
              A
            ä    au
          ae  e    ǒ
          E   ue     O
           i   ui    ù
high tongue    I          U   low tongue
lip spread                    lip rounded
```

Kofler offers the reader a system that classifies the
vowels into long and short: AA, Â, EE, AW, Ō and ă, ĕ,
ĭ, ŏ, ŭ, ŏŏ respectively [1897, pp. 131-138]. Myer shows
by chart the relative positions of vowels from E, forward
and high to U (oo) low and back in the oral cavity [1897, p.
99]. Miller's Vocal Atlas presents diagrams which locate
each vowel in side views of the laryngeal, pharyngeal, oral
and nasal cavities. Rogers orders the vowels according to
registers [1895, pp. 108-110]:

```
oo = lower chest
 o = upper chest
ah = lower middle
 a = upper middle
 i = high
```

An early description of the cavity coupling system of
the mouth is provided by Shakespeare. He writes, "There
are two main resonating chambers in the mouth. Each vowel
requires an appropriate adjustment of these chambers, in
forming which the tongue is, of course, the chief factor....
Thus the richness of every vowel depends on the freedom in
the shape of the tone spaces" [1924, p. 46].

Definitions of Consonants

Consonants are the expositors of thought, vowels the
expositors of emotion [Bach, 1894, p. 152].

Consonants are the skeletons of words. Applied to
song, they have three distinct functions:

1. To convey the sense of words.

> 2. To beat time and mark the rhythm by their percussions.
> 3. Through their varied degrees of energy they declare the state of activity of the sentiment, just as the vowels manifest its nature [Garcia, 1894, p. 47].

Consonants are 'the cement of words' [Heinrich, 1910, p. 42].

The consonants are modifications of the sonorous current brought about by obstruction and release in rapid succession of that current during its progress towards the opening of the mouth [Parisotti, 1911, p. 112].

Using Consonants

> The art of pronouncing the consonants with precision, brevity, force and grace, in every variety of slowness or rapidity of execution ... is an attainment confined to performers of extraordinary qualifications and consequently reflects the highest merit [Costa, 1824, p. 40].

Henderson points out that bad attack "occurs almost entirely on words beginning with vowels. Consonantal beginnings make it nearly impossible, or at any rate cover it up" [1906, p. 50], while Dodds cautions that "we usually put in beginning and middle consonants" but fail to observe many final ones [1927, pp. 77-78]. "Four powerful tuned consonants are of great importance in lending fullness to the voice," says Shakespeare. They are L, M, N, and R, while the consonants s, p, k, t, and ch are sound interrupters [1924, p. 48, p. 55].

Avoiding early training with consonants. Cattaneo is quoted by Lunn [1904, p. 9], as having written: "Q. Is the study of consonants with vowels of use? A. No." Henderson agrees:

> In general let the consonants alone in the early stages of your practice, with one exception--the letter L. It is recommended by most of the old masters as aiding in setting the mouth, lips, tongue, etc. in the natural position for the production of a good tone [1906, p. 53].

METHODS : THE PSYCHOLOGICAL APPROACH

Importance of Mental Imagery

Those authors that choose to influence the reader through mental imagery do not discuss the subject per se, but rather employ it in direct manner. "The secret of treating the vowel sounds is this: pronounce beautifully and you will be able to sing the sounds without difficulty, except in one or two cases" [Henderson, 1906, p. 160]. "In pronunciation the words should seem to be formed by the upper lip and to come out through it.... The words will thus be formed outside the mouth and be readily heard" [Fillebrown, 1911, p. 19]. Quoting David Ffrangçon-Davies, Henderson writes, "Right breathing can only be judged by right tone" and that "right tone can only be judged by the summum bonum of the singer, viz. , pronunciation--pure, truthful pronunciation, in every part of the voice, high or low" [1906, p. 159]. Shakespeare compares the voice to the violin and states, "English singing is a prolonged tuning of vowel sounds, thirteen in number, of an equal number of tuned consonants, and of, besides, a clear articulation of nine other consonants which have no tune" [1924, p. 46]. From these statements it can be seen that those who would influence diction by imagery, rely on the powers of the physical ear and the ear of the mind.

Speaking as a Device

From the earliest sources, speaking as a device to improve singing diction has been applauded. "In Italy all the vocal students receive lessons of declamation from some master of elocution. This is another cause of their superiority, for however weak the voice may be ... the sense of the author will be clearly understood" [Furtado, 18--, p. 9].

Crowest and Tetrazzini agree that the student must "study correctness and propriety of emphasis quite apart from singing" [Crowest, 1900, p. 22]. Witherspoon suggests, "When correct action does not ensue, try simply 'pronouncing' the words instead of singing them" [1925, p. 107].

Whispering as a Device

According to the research of this study and that of

Burgin and Fields, whispering as an aid to improve diction
or to save the voice is a concept that came into vogue and
then was discarded largely within the period 1847-1924.
Burgin uncovers one statement and Fields two, while this
study has accounted for eight, a significantly larger number.
No negative statement could be found to account for the aban-
donment of this device.

"One can exercise by whispering, an easy means which
spares the voice" [Garcia, 1847, p. 17].   Drew suggests an
exercise wherein the vowels are whispered to give correct
vowel placement [1924, p. 49].   To eliminate "the glide of
the glottis," Behnke gives the exercise [189-, p. 112]:

Up!	U, U, U	Ah
(spoken)	(whispered)	(sung)

A fine sense of forward placement is gained through
the use of the whisper, not the whisper which is too
far forward and carries with it the whistling noise
(sufflated) which we do not want, but the quiet whisper with as little of lip and tip tongue hiss as possible.... The whisper may be made fuller (darker)
by filling into the back mouth somewhat [Russell, 1912,
p. 47].

A unique thought is that whispering may be used for
breath control and to "prepare us for the tuning of the 'Ah'
later on" [Shakespeare, 1924, pp. 8-9].

Chanting as a Device

An examination of the 160 source books revealed only
one statement concerning chanting as a device for good diction, the 1894 edition of Hints on Singing of Garcia.   He
calls the practice "intoning" [p. 49].

METHODS : THE TECHNICAL APPROACH

The Value of Sol-Fa Training

Throughout the eighteenth and nineteenth centuries authors regarded the use of solmization with vocal exercises
as virtually obligatory.   It was one of the firm traditions of
the bel canto era.   Twenty-eight statements were collected
from the sources of this period.   In other sources such as

those of Shryock (1856) and Bassini (ca. 1869) no statement is put forth, but sol-fa syllables are found under the vocalises. In the twentieth century, however, solmization seems to have suffered the same fate as the device of whispering. The Fields study counts only nine statements, while the more modern work of Burgin finds none. In truth, the great majority of statements found for this study occur before 1890, and thereafter the decline is sharp.

In 1785, Tenducci advises his reader "to exercise the Voice in solfeggio every Day, with the monosyllables Do, Re, Mi, &c" [Rule VII]. Anfossi's Trattato Teorico has neither words nor syllables beneath the exercises but they are called "Solfeggios" nevertheless [ca. 1800, p. 19]. D'Aubigny von Engelbrunner regards the term "Solfeggio" also in the broadened sense of vocalises with syllables:

> Das Solfeggio ist ein Kompendium solcher Stellen, die der Sänger zwar mit der Zeit, hier und dort, in verschiedenen Musikalien finden und ausheben dürfte um sich daran zu üben/ Solfeggio is a compendium of such figures, that the singer certainly with time, here and there, in various music books will find and ought to take out in order to practice [1803, p. 131].

Cooke assures the reader that, "a steady perseverance in Solfaing will insure improvement" [1861, p. 8]; Everest assures the reader that sol-faing will help "to acquire the proper sound of the vowels" [1861, p. 3]. Lamperti declares that "the surest foundation for a good pronunciation" is "the study of Solfeggio, the importance of which cannot be overrated" [ca. 1883, p. 20]. Wieck [1875, p. 86] recommends solfeggio as the means of equalizing the registers downward from the head voice.

One of the last proponents of solfeggio was Bishenden. He writes:

> The exercise of the solfeggi is of use in giving the singer the power of combining together syllables with modulated sounds, and in prolonging the accented vowel in each syllable, thus giving a clear articulation of words and the act of modulation; it is also of much service in singing from one interval to another with accurate pitch and precision [1875, p. 22].

A statement made by Charles Lunn in The Philosophy

of Voice indicates the state of eclipse into which sol-fa train-ing had fallen by 1904. He recommends the use of exercis-ing with "ah" and denigrates sol-fa, writing, "solfeggi were introduced because a number of teachers arose who could not train a level tone, and so ... they fled to the use of words" [p. 24].

Vowel Techniques

The importance of the "ah" vowel. The ah has found favor with many teachers of singing because it is neutral, that is, it requires a minimum of tongue and lip movement or tension in its formation. While the Fields and Burgin studies indicate continued usage (11 and 26 statements, respec-tively), this concept held its greatest favor before 1920. At this time a number of negative statements appear. From the 41 positive statements, 12 have been selected:

> The vowel a (ah) is and remains for ever the king of vowels [Bach, 1894, Preface].

> Take as much breath as you can, draw it with a moder-ate quickness, with suspiration, as if sighing, use it with economy, and at the same instant sound the letter A as pronounced by the Italian or Scotch, thus ah [Corri, 1811, p. 11].

> Instead of the syllables [solfas], some may prefer the use of the vowel A, as in Ah or Father [Everest, 1861, p. 3].

> 'Ah,' when properly sung, with the tongue low and for-ward at the base, gives the broadest position of the upper part of the pharynx [Thorp, 1899, p. 33].

> The vowel to be used in study is ah, without the as-pirate, as this is the acoustical equivalent to an open unmoulded mouth plus voiced air [Lunn, 1904, p. 22].

Four authors discuss the securing of the correct posi-tion for ah. One is Daniell, whose statement is found in the next section under la. The other three are also worth quota-tion:

> To get a pure tone, flatten the tongue and raise the veil of the palate, and to ascertain the exact quality

of voice, sustain a rather long note on the word 'ah,'
keep the tone steady, and the mouth moderately open
[Bishenden, 1875, p. 17].

The Italian A is represented as an arch with heighth
[sic], breadth, and depth. The tongue is the base,
the roof of the mouth the arch, and the fullness or
freedom of the mouth backward, including the pharynx
is the depth [Myer, 1886, p. 49].

The vowel a lifts the epiglottis, it must always be
kept in mind, always be placed and pronounced anew--
even when other vowels are to be articulated [Lehmann,
1924, p. 20].

A number of authors believe that prefixing an "l" to
the sound of ah improves its ability to create the free tone
condition. Lamperti mentions la but does not use ah [1905,
pp. 9-10]. Daniell recommends ah but states that la is better because "for that the tongue must be flat in the mouth,
the tip resting firmly against the teeth" [1873, p. 22]. "A
forward position of the tongue is a proof of its freedom,
hence all the exercises such as ah and lah for producing its
forward action if rightly studied, must result in the desired
freedom" [Shakespeare, 1908, p. 23].

Pasquale Amato reminds the reader that the correct
vowel sound must be understood by the syllable ah:

I was drilled at first upon the vowel 'ah.' I hear
American authorities refer to 'ah' as in father. That
seems to me too flat a sound, one lacking in real
resonance. The vowel used in Italy ... is a slightly
broader vowel, such as may be found halfway between
the vowel 'ah' as in father, and the 'aw' as in law
[Cooke, 1921, p. 41].

Those who are opposed to the use of ah, particularly
to the exclusion of other vowels number Botume, Duff, Galli-
Curci, and Julia Claussen (the last two quoted in Brower and
Cooke, respectively) in their group. Quotations of the five
most outspoken opponents have been chosen. The first statement extends Pasquale Amato's observation (see above) to an
admonition:

The vowel ah is the most difficult to sing perfectly,
on account of the many degrees of tone color possible

in its delivery.   The free Italian ah is really natural
only to the Italian [Shaw, 1914, pp. 188-189].

> The vowel 'ah' is frequently chosen as the best one
> for vocalising, because in its pronunciation it is easy
> to put the mouth in a good position; and voices are
> trained on it exclusively, with the result that no other
> vowel, or vowel shade, is perfectly produced [Behnke,
> 189-, p. 134].

Regarding control of the coup de glotte, "we find by
prefixing a labial consonant M, P, or B, that the shock is
reduced to a minimum; ... hence, Ma or Maw should be the
word to use in practice, and almost never Ah, and never E"
[Curtis, 1914, pp. 142-143].   Lehmann states that the pure
ah "is the root of all evil" and that three manifestations of
the vowel must be mastered for complete control; with ē for
tone-height, with ā for strength and brightness, and with ōō
for tone-depth and flexibility [1924, p. 61].   Taylor observes
that although the use of ah is traditional "for acquiring the
command of the 'open throat,' no convincing reason has ever
been given for this belief" [1917, pp. 85-86].

Lingual and labial controls.   Those authors who give
special attention to each vowel and consonant often provide
diagrams or photographs to show the placement of lips and
tongue in each instance.   Three such authors are Proschowsky
in The Way to Sing (1923, pp. 60-640), Miller in The Vocal
Atlas (1912, pp. 5-10), and Fillebrown in Resonance in Singing and Speaking (1911, pp. 20-22).   In addition, many other
statements related to the tongue can be found above in Chapter IV (under "Methods : The Technical Approach").

> In the formation of vowels and consonants the utmost
> flexibility of the lips and tongue is necessary....   The
> velocity and ease with which both lips and tongue move
> depend upon the breath pressure balancing the elasticity
> of the vibrating organ [Thorp, 1899, p. 56].

> Our bright vowels are dependent upon a broader form
> of the inner mouth and at the back, a higher standing
> tongue.
>   We often say that the tongue is an organ impossible
> to control.   Many a teacher, in an effort to cover up
> his own ignorance, teaches his pupils not to think
> about the tongue.   This may suffice in some cases,
> but rarely [Proschowsky, 1923, p. 54].

In the formation of tones the lips are not to be for-
gotten, as their position has not a little influence on
vocal sounds. Only general rules can be laid down
for this detail. The one fundamental law of good tone
production, that there should be no holding or tightness,
no forcing, but a feeling of comfortable relaxation,
stands good here.... Some teachers and some singers
believe that the secret of good tone lies in pushing
forward the lips [Henderson, 1906, p. 86].

Among the many errors of teaching which have so long
stood in the way of singers' advancement in art is
the thought that correct vowel making is a matter of lip
shaping.... [Vowels are] made in the mouth behind the
lips, and practically by the mid and back tongue, the lips
having nothing to do with the vowel color, although
some vowels find their focus at the lips. Every shade
of vowel color can be readily made and should always
be made without interference of the lips [Russell, 1912,
p. 32].

Other physical controls. Two statements were found
that related the area below the oral cavity to vowel formation. Proschowsky, in discussing the vowels oo and o, calls
them elongated. "Elongation of the vocal tube means that
the larynx lowers and that the lips protrude, the most important of which, however, is the lowering of the larynx"
[1923, p. 57]. "Vowels should always be attacked by the
stroke of the glottis" [Garcia, 1924, p. 42].

The value of using Italian vowels. Ten authors recommend the use of Italian vowels in exercises because of their
purity. Perhaps the most articulate defense of Italian vowels
is offered by Shakespeare [1910, p. 43]:

Our own language as ordinarily spoken does not demand
that we rest on the vowel sounds. Italian, on the
contrary, may be said to be a language consisting
mainly of sustained vowel sounds and of consonants
from which all awkward combinations have been eliminated. By sustaining the vowels and simplifying the
consonants a language has been formed which is in
itself an education in the freedom of action of the
tongue and throat.

This statement and the observation that Italian vowels are
free from diphthongs form the basic thoughts of Bacon [1824,

p. 14], Vaccai [1848, Preface], Mathilde Marchesi [1901, p. 69], Proschowsky [1923, p. 67], and others.

Alteration of High Pitched Vowels

Today the relationship between the frequencies of vowel formants and the formation of particular vowel postures on relative pitches is well understood. With certain vowels such as i the frequency of the first formant (300 cps) may be lower than the fundamental of the pitch sung. Therefore a closely related vowel with a higher first formant may need to be substituted. Before such scientific investigations, the ears of a few of our authors led them to favor alteration of high pitched vowels. The earliest statement uncovered is that of Manuel Garcia, who says, in regard to the attack of high notes, "the alteration of the vowel in certain syllables is a convenient resource" [1847, pp. 45-46]. An adherent of Garcia's (and a pupil of Wieck and Helmholtz), Emma Seiler, expands:

> The female voice ... has only a few tones more than an octave, upon which every one of the vowels can be distinctly sung.... As unfortunately our Song composers do not always keep this fact in view, as the old Italians did, and since words with the most unfavorable vowels often underlie the notes, it as often becomes necessary to mingle with the unfavorable vowel something of the sound (Klang) of the vowel properly belonging to the note; as, for example in the word 'ring' upon f, to sing the i with a mixture of the sound (Klang) of a [1871, p. 103].

Thus Seiler is suggesting a substitution toward the vowel with the highest first formant (700 cps). Myer suggests changing the vowel to its covered or closed equivalent when singing from lower to upper chest resonance. He gives ample illustrations, one being, "When I^2 is carried open too high, it becomes hard and white and sounds more like E^2 [let] than I^2" [1891, pp. 174-180, specific illustration from p. 178]. Rogers states simply, "In determining the vowel for a specific word the pitch of the prime tone is the leading factor" [1925, p. 42].

Costa urges the student to attempt to maintain the same sound on higher pitches. He cautions against "the progressive approaching of the lips and teeth during the sound of the same vowel from which results not only an alteration in the purity of the voice, but in that of the vowel itself" [1824, p. 16].

Henderson is opposed to conscious vowel modification. "It is quite possible to sing all the pure vowels without modification throughout the range of the voice" [1906, pp. 153-156]. He admits that many teach this modification, but the finest teachers such as Lamperti teach pure vowels. In point of fact, Lamperti recognizes an occasional need for alteration:

> We take no singer to task for changing the position of
> such words [those with i in German and with ü in
> French], or for substituting others with more euphoni-
> ous vowels--provided that he possess the technical
> ability to vocalize the above-named vowels on high
> tones [1905, pp. 29-30].

Consonant techniques

Physical controls. Referring to the passage from the superior surface of the vocal bands to the outer lips, Clippinger states that, "consonants are produced by the partial or complete closing of this channel by interference of the lips, tongue, teeth and soft palate" [1910, p. 13]. Myer recognizes that the consonant is the opposite of the vowel, i. e. , the result of a complete or partial obstruction and/or explosion. "There are three points of obstruction: 1. The contact of the base or back of the tongue and the soft palate. 2. The contact of the tip of the tongue and of the roof of the mouth. 3. The contact of the lips or of the lower lip and the teeth" [1891, p. 183]. Lilli Lehmann offers a unique thought as to the action of closing the nasal passages to create consonantal interruption:

> The tediousness of singing without proper separation
> of the syllables is not appreciated till it has been
> learned how to divide the consonants. The nasal
> close of itself brings a new color into the singing,
> which must be taken into account.... By the nasal
> close, also, an interrupted connection is assured be-
> tween the consonant and the tone, even if the latter
> has to cease, apparently, for an instant [1924, p. 185].

Just one passage will be offered to demonstrate the

pages of specific directions for mastering correct formation
of each consonant. The books of Bach, Kofler, Lehmann,
Miller, Proschowsky and Stockhausen all give information on
jaw, lip and tongue manipulation.

> The consonants m, p, and b require the closing of
> the lips and the shutting off of that part of the tone
> which is coming through the mouth, so that only the
> tone which passes behind the soft palate and through
> the upper pharynx and nasal cavities can be heard
> [Muckey, 1915, p. 75].

Consonants as tone interrupters. "Consonants are
more or less complete interrupters of the tone" [Muckey,
1915, p. 90]. "Q. What are the elements of words? A.
Vowels and consonants. The vowels are moulded by the
shapes which the vocal tube assumes while traversed by
breath or by sounds, the consonants result from the obstacles
opposed to the issuing sounds or breath by the organs of the
mouth" [Garcia, 1894, p. 45]. "It is the consonant, the
articulating elements, which destroy the continuity of the tone
and make it difficult to sing legato" [Clippinger, 1910, p. 13].
"Consonants must not be allowed to interrupt the continuity
of the pitch produced by the vocal cords. This is necessary
to preserve legato" [Clippinger, 1917, p. 77].

Myer minimizes the interrupting effect of consonants
correctly produced. "When true conditions prevail and the
action of the voice is simply suspended, not relaxed, then
the articulation of consonantal sounds will be so short and
distinct that often to the listener the voice will not seem to
have stopped at all" [1891, p. 186]. Rogers attacks those
who minimize the importance of consonants:

> Consonants have too long been regarded as a disturb-
> ing factor in singing--as an obstruction to a free un-
> trammeled emission of tone.... This complaint that
> consonants upset everything has been tacitly accepted
> by singers in general and also admitted by some
> teachers. Such a conclusion is, however, quite wrong
> .... [T]he proper articulation of consonants can aid
> materially in effecting a clear and incisive emission
> of tone [1925, p. 25].

Consonants as markers of rhythm. Garcia states that
one of the three distinct functions of consonants is "to beat
time and mark the rhythm by their percussion" [1894, p. 47].

Proschowsky also states that consonants beat time and that they "give the rhythm decision" [1923, p. 89].

Exaggeration of consonants. "In song, the vowels are necessarily dwelt upon at greater length than in speech, and, therefore, to counterbalance, as it were, this longer sustaining of the vowels, the articulation of the consonants should be slightly exaggerated and more marked than in speaking" [Randegger, 1912, p. 175]. "If we let our consonants fall or become weak, our text becomes insipid ... and the result is a lack of distinctness" [Proschowsky, 1923, p. 65]. "The rolling of the R, the hissing of the S ought not to be extravagant; but it is necessary above all, to apply one's self to giving to each of the vowels the sound which is proper to it" [Lablache, 184-, p. 87].

Phonetic Knowledge Advisable

In 1886 the International Phonetic Association standardized the International Phonetic Alphabet (IPA). It is surprising that the teachers and singers of the latter period of this study did not recognize the potential value of such a tool in training the singing voice. Only one author, Herbert Wilbur Greene, obliquely mentions that in training the student, "teach him that every work that is correctly sung is phonetically spelled" [1920, p. 77].

ANALYSIS AND COMMENTS

Concepts of diction as part of artful singing have appeared before the limit of this study, but up to the mid-nineteenth century statements were only of the most generalized nature, without benefit of much scientific support. In the late 1860's and the 1870's, investigations by Helmholtz and others demonstrated that pronunciation, articulation and enunciation were subject to tangible laws of physics. The class of voice teachers who followed such empirical investigations attempted to incorporate these physical laws into a teaching methodology. To some of these teachers the precision of science must have seemed a valuable alternative to the nebulous theories of traditional methods. Others may have seen local adjustments of the jaw, lips and tongue as a shortcut to good tone production.

Toward the mid 1880's we find a reaction on the part

of those traditionalists who looked with dismay on this zealous application of science to art.   This class of voice instructor also uses diction as a means to good singing, but by means of psychology.

The methods of speaking and chanting are found to gain favor in this period and to continue into the later twentieth century.   Solfeggio, long a dominant tradition, all but dies out if we can use the sources of this study as any criteria.   The practice of vocalizing on the vowel ah does not die out, but loses its absolute supremacy to the methods of lah or a variety of sounds.

Although investigations and applications of the laws of diction had already reached relative sophistication by the year 1927, so much has been discovered since that date (e. g. , Gunnar Fant's Acoustic Theory of Speech Production, 1960) that this chapter should not be considered a truly valuable compendium of ideas, but rather a survey of the state of thought concerning diction at the time.   It is however quite possible that much more precise and articulate material is available in books of the early twentieth century that are specifically devoted to diction or phonetics.   Therefore a preliminary list of works is here presented for the reader who might wish to continue his investigation of the subject.

Baldwin, Adele.   Laeis-Baldwin system of practical phonetics for singers and speakers.   New York: Phonetic Publishing Co. , 1923.

Brennen, C. J.   Words in singing; a practical guide to the study of phonetics and its application to song.   London: Vincent Music Co. , 1905.   [PU]

Ellis, Alexander J.   Pronunciation for singers, with especial reference to the English, German, Italian and French languages.   London: J. Curwen & Sons, 1877.

Hawn, Henry Gaines.   Diction for singers and composers. New York: Publication Department of the Hawn School, 1911?

Henschel, George.   Articulation in singing; a manual for student and teacher with practical examples and exercises. Cincinnati: John Church Co. , 1926?

Jones, Dora Duty.   Lyric diction for singers, actors and

public speakers; with a preface by Madame Melba.   New York: Harper & Brothers, 1913.

Maghee, Frances D. Rhythmic phonetic training for voice and speech. Boston: Stratford Co. , 1922.

Rogers, Clara Kathleen. English diction for singers and speakers. Boston: the author, 1912.

Russell, Louis Arthur. English diction for singers and speakers. Boston: Oliver Ditson Co. , 1905?

X

INTERPRETATION

<u>Definition.</u> <u>Interpretation</u>, as regards singing, may be defined as "the representation of a musical composition according to one's conception of the author's idea" (<u>Oxford English Dictionary</u> [OED]). The singer, therefore, is the medium by which the intent of the composer (as apprehended by the singer) is interpreted for the benefit of the audience. The singer's unique and particular contribution, beyond the technical skills of voice management and musicianship, falls into the abstract realm of expression and taste. <u>Expression</u> is generally defined as "the aspect (of the countenance), intonation (of the voice) as indicating a state of feeling," or, regarding music in particular, "the manner of performance (with respect, e.g. to degrees of loudness and softness) suited to bring out the feeling of a musical passage" (OED). <u>Taste</u> is defined as "the sense of what is appropriate, harmonious, or beautiful, especially discernment and appreciation of the beautiful in nature or art" (OED).

Some concepts not specifically linked to interpretation, such as the study of foreign languages, are placed in this chapter for the sake of expediency. A total of 239 statements were gathered and are divided by category in this chapter's table.

CONCEPTS : GENERAL THEORIES

Nature and Importance of Interpretation

The recognition of the importance of interpretation has existed since the earliest voice primers. Tenducci's Rule

Table 10.   SUMMARY OF CONCEPTS OF INTERPRETATION

I. Theories of interpretation--General considerations	
1. the nature and importance of interpretation	20
2. individuality in interpretation	19
II. Methods of achieving interpretational skills	
A. Psychological approach	
1. emotional emphasis	21
2. personality emphasis	22
B. Technical approach	
1. mastery of the text	
a) text comes before tone	18
b) speaking the song	6
2. criteria of song selection	21
3. foreign language study	
a) foreign language study is essential	20
b) foreign language study is not essential	0
4. techniques used in interpretation	
a) memorization	11
b) note connection: legato and staccato	29
c) tone color	15
d) phrasing	7
e) unclassified	1
5. visual factors in performance	29
TOTAL STATEMENTS	239

XVI states that "in pronouncing the words, care must be taken to accord with the sentiment that was intended by the poet" [1785].   About 125 years later, Henderson acknowledges the fundamental nature of interpretation at greater length.

> This is the secret of ultimate perfection of style.   One may have a perfect attack, a beautiful legato, a ravishing portamento, a noble messa di voce and an elastic fluency of delivery, yet sing ineffectively.   If the singer bestows all his thought on the perfection of each phrase as an individual entity he will never sing eloquently, though here and there he may rise to heights of extraordinary beauty....   The singer must grasp his aria or his recitative in its entirety....   Only in this way can he arrive at a proper conception of the delivery of his music, for only thus can he determine the distribution of vocal effects [1906, p. 254].

Clippinger considers that "the imagination is the most important factor in interpretation" [1917, p. 79] and also "that intelligence must be taken for granted" [1917, p. 78].

Carlo Bassini rejects the intellectual approach, writing, "The singer's mind should always be rather on the sentiment he is uttering than on the execution. The singer should <u>feel</u> for the time all he is expressing, and <u>be</u> all that he represents" [1857, p. 18].

The term "expression" enters into a number of discussions concerning interpretation. "From expression we receive a sentimental appeal to our feelings," writes Isaac Nathan. "It strikes the imagination, affects the mind, and commands the passion" [1836, p. 195]. Garcia relies on a quotation to present his belief: "'The great law of the arts,' Mr. Cousin has said, 'is expression; every work which does not express an idea means nothing.' The artist would seek vainly to have an effect on the souls of his listeners, if he did not appear himself to be vitally affected by the emotion which he would communicate to others" [1847, p. 138].

Lablache also relies on the words of another to instruct his readers. "'Expression,' says J. J. Rousseau, 'is a facility, by which the musician feels deeply, and brings forth, with energy, all the ideas which he ought to bring forth, and all the feelings which he ought to express'" [184-, p. 19].

Finally, one author, W. J. Henderson, makes a special effort to point out to his readers that "style is general; interpretation is particular. Style is the character of a period or a school or a master. Interpretation is the disclosure of an individuality. Style may embrace all the songs of a single composer, though it seldom does; but interpretation can only apply to one at a time" [1906, p. 207].

Individuality in Interpretation

Those authors who speak of interpretation in terms of individuality all agree that the singer has a right and an obligation to contribute something personal to the songs he or she sings.

How can there be such a thing as 'traditional' interpretation? The singer either has her own individual conception of the poem and projects its music accordingly, or she has not. Clinging to tradition often means an artistic tragedy for the artist. The artist should be allowed to follow her own instinct in interpreting [Sophie Braslau in Martens, 1923, p. 25].

"Taste and genius," according to Ferrari, "are inborn qualities; therefore an attempt to give rules for their acquirement would be presumption" [1818, p. 22]. Nathan believes that "the power of expression is the great secret of Genius: it is a secret because it is rarely to be acquired, unless there be a natural talent for it" [1836, p. 195].

Santley defends individuality by writing, "The interpretation depends greatly on the idiosyncrasies of its interpreters; if they are experienced artists, though the mode of carrying out the interpretation be in each case different, the result will be clear, forcible and logical" [1908, p. 67].

Clara Kathleen Rogers states simply, "Art is properly the expression of the individual" [1895, p. 170].

METHODS : THE PSYCHOLOGICAL APPROACH

Emotional Emphasis

The most common opinion shared by those authors discussing emotionality in interpretation is that one must feel in order to make others feel.

"One understands ... that the artist produces on us only the emotions analogous to those which he feels himself" [Garcia, 1847, p. 130].

"The singer should feel for the time all he is expressing, and be all that he represents" [Bassini, 1857, p. 18].

Rogers considers "the mind as an obstruction to the spontaneous utterance of the emotions. The mind should neither direct the powers, nor take cognizance of it during the act of singing.... The mind, then, is manifestly an intruder between real emotion, and its organ of expression, the body" [1895, pp. 28-29].

Anna Case prefers to regard the singer's contribution as spiritual:

There are certain ideals which every singer desiring

> to achieve success should bear in mind, one of the
> most important ... is the emphasis to be laid on the
> spiritual factor in song interpretation.... The more
> spiritual, the more ideal quality in interpretation al-
> ways represents the finest and highest. And this
> quality the artist must develop out of herself [Martens,
> 1923, p. 121].

Russell points out that "emotional expression is relative and not a matter of excessive force" so that "small
voices can express as intense emotion as large voices,
though of course not with the same degree of physical force"
[1904, Some Psychic Reflections for Singers, p. 8].

One author warns against abandoning all technical controls to emotionality. "The advice commonly given to singers
and actors to feel the emotions they express, is not quite
right.... Were he really to feel, to experience these emotions, not only would he be unable to sing or to recite, but
his voice would be spasmodic in action, tremulous and irri-
tated from nervous excitement" [Kofler, 1889, p. 28].

Personality Emphasis

Twenty-two statements were found relating to artistic
personality. Max Heinrich offers a description of the phenomenon:

> How then, does 'artistic personality' of an artist mani-
> fest itself? And wherein lies the decided difference
> between merely a good singer, one who uses his voice
> well according to the principles of the art of singing,
> enunciates well, phrases correctly, and yet does not
> touch the heart, and the really great singer, who,
> often the possessor of a voice not to be compared
> intrinsically in beauty with the former, nevertheless
> arouses the senses of the auditor to the highest pitch
> of enthusiasm, wonder and admiration, while the
> other leaves him cold and indifferent? The solution
> of this question rests in the different 'personalities'
> of these two singers and nothing else [1910, p. 50]!

"Whatever characteristics the singer's style may disclose, his singing will be convincing only as it emanates
from his real personality" [Fucito, 1922, p. 207]. "Personal
magnetism, the ability to hold an audience, is also to a great
extent a gift of the imagination" [Taylor, 1914, p. 18].

METHODS : THE TECHNICAL APPROACH

Mastery of the Text

Text comes before the tone. Of the 18 authors who
commented on this subject, only one was opposed to it. This
author, Anfossi, interestingly, is also the earliest writer in
the group. She suggests that "before the pupil attempts to
sing any song he must first try the air without words, as if
it were a solfeggio, or a vocalizzo. After he has learned
the tune, he must read the words, taking care to pronounce
them distinctly and with proper accent" [ca. 1800, p. 64].

Clippinger counsels the student to "study the poem
until it creates the mood. Read it, not once, but many
times" [1917, p. 86]. Lehmann thinks it is best to get "an
entire picture" of the text before first singing it [1924, p.
204]. "It is necessary for the singer to read the text many
times until the finest gradations in the underlying thought
become clear" [Proschowsky, 1923, pp. 89-90].

Speaking the song. It seems that this technique is
enjoying more popularity in the late twentieth century than it
did in the period to 1927 because the works of Fields and
Burgin contain significantly more entries than were uncovered
for this study (74 and 32 respectively, as compared with six).
What is more, all six statements were gleaned from sources
published after 1893.

The first to comment is Garcia, who says, "The pupil
must read the words of the piece again and again till each
finest shadow of meaning has been mastered. He must next
recite them with perfect simplicity and self-abandonment.
The accent of truth apparent in the voice when speaking naturally is the basis of expression in singing" [1894, p. 59].

Proschowsky recommends that "the text be recited
with simplicity and self-control" [1923, p. 90], while Clippinger, referring to the text, writes, "Read it aloud. Determine its natural accent. The singing phrase grows out of
the spoken phrase" [1917, p. 87].

Criteria of Song Selection

Using the classics. According to Bacon, when giving
the student his first songs "it is above all things important

that his first studies and earliest ideas be drawn from classical authorities" [1824, p. 36].

Start simple. "The simplest songs should be chosen
at the beginning; and the natural capabilities of the singer
and the degree of training undergone should at all times be
well considered" [Randegger, 1912, p. 176].

David Taylor has the most to say on the subject:

In the choice of songs for daily practice the student
must be guided first of all by personal taste. Only
those songs should be chosen which the student likes,
and enjoys singing. Another important point is that
each new song should be slightly more difficult than
the one preceding it. Simple songs with flowing melodies are in every way the best for purposes of voice
culture. Training both in the management of the voice
and in expressive singing is best secured through the
study of songs of the simple melodious type [1914,
p. 25].

Vocal limitations. Anna Case, Frieda Hempel, and
Salvatore Fucito warn that the prime consideration for song
selection must be that it lie "within the vocal limits" of the
singer [Fucito, 1922, p. 213].

Selection of songs and arias. Since the heyday of concert singing occured before the 1920's, it is curious that all
the statements about song and aria selection for recitals
occur in the last seven years of this study. To be certain,
opera singers continued to derive important second incomes
on concert tours through that period into the present time,
but why nothing is said before 1920 is a mystery or a coincidence of the sources selected.

Fucito suggests that songs must be ordered on the
program so that a contrast is provided, to avoid monotony
of dynamics, mood, style, etc. [1922, p. 212]. Nordica
agrees, especially regarding the placement of sad songs
[1923, p. 123].

Regarding the place of the aria in concert, Sophie
Braslau, is quoted as saying, "I do not think the opera aria
belongs on the concert program" [Martens, 1923, p. 28].
Louise Homer, on the other hand, feels the audiences desire
the arias that brought the artist his or her initial acclaim

[Martens, 1923, pp. 168-170]. Both these artists talk at good
length about interpretation and the mechanics of giving a concert recital.

Choosing material according to the audience. Both
sides are represented in statements from the twenties:

> The making of the recital program must depend upon
> the public. Take a metropolis, for instance, where
> people have the privilege of oratorio and opera, and
> audiences generally prefer a complete program of
> songs in different languages. In towns not so situated,
> the program had better comprise opera and oratorio
> numbers, and, especially songs in the vernacular
> [Nordica, 1923, p. 123].

> My experience has led me to use two types of concert
> programs, one for large cities like New York, the
> other for tours through the country in general. The
> metropolitan type of concert program, of course, must
> appeal to a highly trained and eclectic taste; the coun-
> try-wide type of program should appeal more to audi-
> ences who are deprived of the 'big town' opportunities,
> but who love music instinctively, and react to a clear
> melodic line and direct emotional expression [Anna
> Case in Martens, 1923, p. 47].

> I never classify audiences and try to make up programs
> for people of certain sections or parts of the country.
> The people who form the audience in Coffeeville, Kan-
> sas, do not want to feel that the artist who sings
> Moussorgsky in New York will pick out something
> gentler, sweeter or more obvious, thinking, 'they
> would understand it better.' Audiences do not want
> to be sung down to [Sophie Braslau in Martens, 1923,
> p. 28].

Foreign Language Study

During the period covered by this study, the dominance
of French, German, and classical repertoire made it impera-
tive for the American and English singers to learn at least
one foreign tongue. Unlike Fields' and Burgin's findings
(seven and six, respectively) there is not one statement declaring foreign language study unessential. While many American and English texts suggest the mastery of all three lan-

guages, the Germans suggest only Italian, and the Italians
declare that everyone ought to learn their language.

According to Nordica, "German, French and Italian is
a necessity" [1923, p. 89]. Caruso and Shaw agree [1909,
p. 71, and 1914, p. 24]. More specifically, Clara Butt believes "it is necessary for the student who would sing in a
foreign language to study in the country in which the language
is spoken" [as quoted in Cooke, 1921, p. 63].

A singer, Andreas Dippel [Cooke, 1921, p. 114], and
an essayist, Andreas Costa, stress the use of Italian in early
voice training for the reason that "using Italian helps ob-
viate mechanical problems of singing because of its purity"
[Costa, 1838, p. 31]. Myer admonishes the singer to "study
the Italian language in song; but he should first master his
mother tongue" [1886, p. 10].

Techniques Used in Interpretation

Memorization. It is known that memorization of recital materials was not de rigueur in the early part of the
nineteenth century. Hence, there is little surprise that only
one statement was uncovered before 1914 concerning memorization, and this that the singer should "at least memorize
the turn of the page" when singing publically [Anfossi, ca.
1800, p. 77].

Twentieth century sources, however, disclose ten statements concerning the subject, not all geared to performance.
W. S. Drew and Lillian Nordica agree that "to sing without
notes, if possible, is always preferable" [Nordica, 1923, p.
122]. According to Curtis, "All work of learning and mem-
orizing music should be mental. When the mind is concen-
trated upon learning the melody, rhythm, and construction of
a composition the voice should not be used" [1914, p. 207].
"In studying a song the first thing to do is to memorize it,
so that the mind will not be taxed with trying to recall the
words and the melody" [Taylor, 1914, p. 26].

One singer, Frieda Hempel, sees no harm in using a
written reminder:

> Shall the singer carry her music in a song recital,
> is a much discussed question. Many come on with
> nothing in hand. What then happens? The hands are

clasped in supplication, as though praying for help.
This attitude becomes somewhat harrowing when held
for a whole program. For myself I prefer to hold
in hand a small book containing the words of my songs,
for it seems to be more graceful.... I never refer
to this little book ... but I shall always carry it, no
matter what the critics may say [Brower, 1920, p.
209].

Legato and portamento. Some of the early sources
use the terms "legato" and "portamento" interchangeably.
To be certain, there is a fine shade of meaning between
"smooth and connected, with no breaks between the successive
notes" (legato) and "a gliding or passing continuously from
one pitch to another" (portamento) [both Oxford]. The difference, as understood today, is that in the portamento the passage between neighboring notes be more than a major second
and that the gliding between these notes be consciously per-
ceivable.

Tenducci avoids both terms, writing, "That in singing,
the tones of the voice must be united, except in the case of
staccato notes" [1785, Rule XVIII].

Three early writers examine the portamento:

This word has been wrested from its pristine and legitimate signification, which is--the department of
the voice, its purity and freedom from any corruption
of the genuine tone, by the nose, mouth, lips or the
throat [Bacon, 1824, p. 64].

The true carrying of the voice; which the Italians call
Portamento, occurs principally between two sounds
pitched at the distance of at least one third, and in
a rather slow movement [Lablache, 184-, p. 24].

Portamento di voce is the perfection of vocal music,
it consists in the swell and dying of the voice, the
sliding and blending of one note into another with
delicacy and expression [Corri, 1811, pp. 14-15].

Lamperti offers the theory that the "portamento signifies the gentle carrying-over (not dragging over) of one
tone to another. In doing so, the second tone is barely aud-
ibly anticipated at the end of the first" [1905, p. 21]. Both
of his accompanying examples glide upward the distance of
a sixth.

Two twentieth-century writers declare the importance of legato singing while a third warns of its overzealous application:

> Legato is the highest technical expression of vocal art.... Nothing lifts a singer to a higher level than a perfect presentation of this most fugitive attribute of the singer's art. Unconsciously, stopping one word to begin the next, making a cadence at the close of each phrase ... releasing the vitality to take a necessary breath--are but a few of the ways in which the perfection of the legato are violated [Greene, 1920, p. 63, p. 58].

> The word 'legare' meaning, in Italian, to join, gave rise to the term 'legato style,' and signifies a high class of singing, the attainment of which advances the singer to the front rank of his art. He must be able to pass from one note to another in such unconscious freedom, that no jolt or smearing between the different sounds can be felt or heard. There should be no 'seeking for,' or 'feeling for,' the note.... Notes sung legato have been said to resemble pearls on a string, the string being the breath.... The practice of scales, quick passages, and vocalises, is an infallible means of acquiring this legato [Shakespeare, 1924, pp. 54-55].

> Many singers in an attempt to create a fine legato overdo the blending of these sound-formations (vowels and consonants) and the result is a lack of distinctness [Proschowsky, 1923, p. 65].

Clara Kathleen Rogers adds a unique thought to the importance of developing a legato line in singing: "The legato is a great breath-conserver" [1925, p. 49].

Staccato. The opposite technique (and effect) to legato is staccato, involving distinct breaks between successive tones.

H. S. Kirkland offers a theory for the use of staccato. "Departure from the legato is not to be made merely for the sake of departure, nor for the sake of singing a passage in another mode, but to emphasize the emotion being expressed at the moment" [1916, p. 126]. Of its application, Kirkland writes, "One may disconnect the tone so slightly, and whenever possible so nearly fill the gaps with the articulation of consonants, that the staccato is crisp, distinct articulation, rather than of a detached style of singing" [1916, p. 127].

Pasquale Amato advises that the acquisition of staccato "is really a very difficult thing--difficult when it is right; that is on the pitch" [Cooke, 1921, p. 42].

Frantz Proschowsky devotes more than a page of one work to discussion of staccato in interpretation. He gives two essentials to its production, "perfect free breath-form" and "that the tone shall not be placed" [1923, p. 101].

Tone color. The concept of tone coloring extends back before the limits of this study. At the turn of the nineteenth century, Maria Anfossi offered a definition by declaring, "coloring is the general conformity of the tone of voice to the prevailing character of the composition. For instance, if it be a cheerful or martial cast, in those and other cases of similar energetic character, the singer should give all the brilliancy he can to his voice" [ca. 1800, p. 66]. In this century, Kirkland explains, "by the term color is meant whatever effect the position and condition of the parts above the larynx may have on tone generated in that organ" [1916, p. 68]. Also, quoting Garcia, he writes, "The timbres are one of the chief features of a true sentiment" [1916, p. 70].

Another concept is that "tone color ... is absolutely pure voweling" [Heinrich, 1910, p. 40].

In discussing the importance of tone coloring, Bacon offers this idea:

> It is not by degrees of loudness and softness only, but by the quality or kind of tone, that certain pas- sages are well and distinctly marked. This idea has been carried so far by some, that they suppose the voice in singing to imitate the tones of passion in speech, and there is undoubtedly some analogy [1824, p. 30].

Lablache counsels that "in order to phrase well, it is not enough to comprehend and unfold the musical meaning; it is still necessary to give to each phrase ... a suitable colouring. Light and shade constitute the principal element of expression" [184-, p. 27].

Anfossi and three other writers of the period touch

upon the use of timbre, but each in a generalized sense.
Perhaps Garcia best epitomizes the general opinion:

> Q. Is the great variety of timbres of any practical
>   use?
> A. They are the physiognomy of the voice. They
>   tell the involuntary emotions which affect us, and
>   assume a more clear or covered tint, a timbre
>   more brilliant or more obscure, according to
>   the nature of those feelings [1894, p. 45].

Phrasing. "Phrasing is simply musical punctuation,
which frequently coincides with that of the words" [Lamperti,
1905, p. 31]. "The art of phrasing occupies the highest
point in the science of singing" [Garcia, 1847, p. 49]. "It
is necessary, in order to make the musical sense intelligible"
[Bassini, 1857, p. 15]. "All the rules of phrasing, like the
rules of composition, grow out of what sounds well" [Clip-
pinger, 1917, p. 71].

Gaining familiarity with the style of a period. Henderson suggests that the singer add to the careful examination
of text and melody, a "thorough and intelligent reading of
such contemporary writers as may be obtainable. If one
reads the contemporaries of the famous singers of the eighteenth century he will not be in the dark as to the salient
traits of their style" [1906, p. 183].

Visual Factors in Performance

Instructions regarding the visual aspects of performance
predate this study by many years (see the works of Tosi and
Mancini). Tenducci is reflecting the general opinion of his
time when he sets down the maxim, "Scholars should appear
at the Harpsichord and to their Friends with a calm and
cheerful Countenance" [1785, Rule XII]. Corfe approaches
instruction from the negative side, writing, "the singer should
always stand in a graceful posture, avoiding all grimaces,
knitting the brows and distortions of the head and body"
[18--, p. 3]. Costa also cautions against "violent gestures"
[1824, p. 14].

Bishenden's viewpoint on visual communication is that
"vocalists should endeavor to attract the attention of the audience to the works being sung, and not to themselves" [1876,
p. 27]. As time passes, the advice becomes more specific:

The dramatic artist depends largely for her expression
on the changing lines of the mouth, chin and jaw, and
in any lines spoken which denote command or will,
you will see the actor's jaw setting and becoming
rigid with the rest of the facial mask.

Now, a singer can never allow the facial expression
to alter the position of the jaw or mouth.   Facial expression for the singer must concern itself chiefly
with the eyes and forehead.

The mouth must remain the same, and the jaw
must ever be relaxed, whether the song is one of
deep intensity or a merry scale of laughter [Tetraz-
zini, 1909, p. 29].

The artist on the operatic stage or the speaker on the
platform, without facial expression begotten of muscular activity, may lessen by half his power over the
audience.   To train the facial muscles is a complicated
task.   To do this, stand before a mirror and make
all the faces ever thought of by a schoolboy to amuse
his schoolmates.   Raise each corner of the lip, wrinkle
the nose, quilt the forehead, grin, laugh.   The grimaces will not enter into a performance, but their
effect upon it will be markedly beneficial [Fillebrown,
1911, p. 15].

Frossard asserts simply that, "ce sont les yeux qui
parlent"/ it is the eyes that speak [1914, p. 213].

Marten's The Art of the Prima Donna and Concert
Singer contains arguments for and against the use of gestures
in concert recital.   Emma Calvé explains,

I have been criticized for using gestures in my concert
singing.   Such criticism seems pedantic to me.   Every
song, especially every dramatic song, presents a
story or mood....   If the words of a song suggest or
describe action, they call for gesture in most cases
[1923, p. 41].

The singer Wronski devotes one-third of his book to a
presentation of the basic visual cues of emotionality by means
of word and photograph [1921, Part Two: Mimicry].

Amelita Galli-Curci does not agree, stating the "gestures seem quite out of place on the concert stage" [1923,
p. 114].

ANALYSIS AND COMMENTS

The 150-year span covered in this study witnessed a full swing of the pendulum from the dominance of the melodic line (e. g. , the works of Mozart) to the dominance of the text line (e. g. , the works of Wolf). In the eighteenth and much of the nineteenth centuries, writers basically confined their discussion of interpretation to general considerations, to note-connection and to the most elementary of visual factors. Interestingly, it is not the earliest era that is most devoid of interpretative commentary. Between the years 1876 and 1886, not one statement was found that merited inclusion in this chapter.

As the da capo aria with its elaborate fioritura gradually died out and the Lied emerged, a new emphasis was placed on the word. The poetry of the Sturm und Drang and the Romantic eras allowed, moreover required a new subtlety from the interpretive powers of both composer and performer. Pure vocal powers no longer stood as the sole determinate of artful singing; therefore, in the late nineteenth and the twentieth centuries we find an increasing incidence of quotations discussing interpretation.

During this time, the development of the Lied form created a popular idiom, the solo recital. Thought had to be given concerning the order of presentation in the performance. Memorization came into fashion and freed the hands and arms for those who wished to use them for gesturing.

The musicians and writers about music of the twentieth century are more conscious of history than those of any preceding era. This is well reflected in W. J. Henderson's remark that the styles and the writers of a period should be examined when performing its music. At the later end of the period of this study, two popular works were published that were devoted entirely to interpretation. They are Harry Plunket Greene's Interpretation in Song (London: Macmillan, 1924) and Yvette Guilbert's How to Sing a Song; The Art of Dramatic and Lyric Interpretation (New York: Macmillan, 1918). Because of the generalized nature of both works, neither was included in this study.

After 1927, a large number of works appear, the most celebrated being those of Pierre Bernac, Van Ambrose Christy, William Cox-Ife, Boris Goldovsky, George Griffith,

and Gerald Moore.   Attitudes of more removed performance
practice are well researched and presented in works such as
Arnold Dolmetsch's The Interpretation of Music of the XVII
and XVIII Centuries Revealed in Contemporary Evidence
(revised edition, 1946).

XI

OUTCOMES OF THIS STUDY

In the course of the research for this project, a bibliography of 608 separately-bound documents was assembled. Information taken from primary and secondary sources, one periodical article and the bibliography of the article entitled "Gesangspädagogik" in Die Musik in Geschichte und Gegenwart revealed 68 other documents which are not held by any of the seven libraries consulted (See Appendix One).

The exigencies of limited time and space required the researcher to reduce this study to the writings of 100 authors which were published during the time limits of the study (1777-1927).   To better understand the relationship of each of these authors to the teaching of voice and the reasons which may have impelled his or her writings, biographical information on each author was sought out.   Information, often meager, was found concerning 86 of these authors.

- 35 Primarily singing teachers
- 22 Primarily singers
- 13 Primarily writers on music
- 10 Primarily instrumentalists, conductors, or composers
- 5 Primarily scientists or physicians
- 1 Singing coach

Five of these career areas are prefixed by the word "primarily" because a number of authors in this study served in more than one branch of music.   Pertinent biographical information is included in the annotated alphabetical bibliography.

Some Historical Observations Concerning Vocal Pedagogy Texts Published Between 1777-1927

Before venturing into this discussion, it must first be stated that this section of the study is both subjective and

generalized. It is based on the partial data selected for the
body of this work, and, therefore, extrapolative. Also, no
attempt will be made to document various observations. Yet,
it is felt that a number of facts set down in Chapters II
through X have indicated states and trends in the history of
voice instruction between 1777 and 1927 to a degree that
attention is merited.

In approximately the first five decades of this study,
we find that many of those who wrote on singing were engaged
in other musical activities, i. e. , they were only part-time
voice teachers. Michel Corrette was both an organist and
a composer. Domenico Corri, Andrea Costa, Mme. Duval,
Nina D'Aubigny von Engelbrunner and Francesco Lanza were
also composers. T. S. Cooke and Ambrosio Minoja devoted
much of their time to conducting. Financially speaking, the
period between 1777 and 1827 was a perilous age for musicians,
and the ones who could also teach piano or voice were no
doubt better off. By the same token, however, it is true
that most voice teachers could not earn sufficient living by
this means alone. It is most likely that the ambitious singer
would choose to study with a person who had a direct connection with the performing community, despite the fact that such
a person might have had no voice training himself or no experience as a professional singer. Some of these part-time
voice teachers further capitalized on their second income by
having books printed with one to ten pages of traditional
"rules" followed by a set of graded exercises which invariably
led the student from a single reiterated pitch to the complicated fiorituri of the era. A number of these volumes indicate the location of the teacher's studio and his fee. While
many of these writers may have been accomplished voice
teachers, their ideas were certainly not novel. Time and
again, Tosi and Mancini are quoted, with or without citation.
Borrowings from other sources have been noted as well, but
this was not in that era akin to unethical action. There is
an attitude implicit in these books that voice instruction as
a profession had already reached its zenith in the former
bel canto period, and therefore a teacher need do little more
in his publication than repeat the time-honored rules. Such
unanimity of opinion is the reason there is no slandering
among authors of this period.

A few books of this age stand out from among the
others by reason of their thoroughness. These include the
writings of Anfossi, Bacon, D'Aubigny, Nathan and Novello.
Here the reader finds lengthy discussions on breath control,

posture, positions of the lips, tongue and jaw, diction, interpretation, song selection and many other related subjects.
These books are, however, no less a product of this empirical age. Speaking of this class of teachers, Fields, in
Training the Singing Voice, writes:

> First there are the empiricists, who derive their
> teaching methods largely from trial and error obser-
> vations. Their techniques are based on symptomatic
> judgements of the student's performance during the
> vocal lesson period. Underlying causes are guessed
> at or else ignored, the main objectives being the at-
> tainment of desirable results, by whatever means.
> Local effort and voluntary controls of the vocal ap-
> paratus are common instructional procedures and the
> chief criterion for evaluating any vocal technique is
> that the voice must sound better for having used that
> technique [1947, p. 243].

In short, the period 1777 to about 1860 was a pragmat-
ic age in regard to teaching the voice. Theoretical abstrac-
tions held little place in these writers' methodologies. Even
the concepts of head, middle, and chest register were not
concerned with the location of sound generation, but rather
with tangible sensations which might help guide the student
to a pleasing resonance quality.

In the early years of this study, we find a predomi-
nance of texts in French, German and Italian. Of the nine
English volumes surveyed for this project that were published
before 1830, only four were written by native Englishmen.
The remaining five were written by transplanted Italians.
The English language became the most important language
for vocal pedagogy texts around the sixth decade of the nineteenth century. Many important foreign treatises were translated. Another reason for the increase in number of publications in English is that voice teaching in public schools became common in both England and the United States. Johann
Heinrich Pestalozzi's name is found in many books of the
1810-1860 era. Pestalozzi was a Swiss educational reformer
who, in the first decade of the nineteenth century, developed
a progressive instructional methodology for the public school
teaching. This methodology was analyzed and expanded upon
by Pfeiffer and Nägeli (1810). From Switzerland, the concept spread quickly to England and the United States, where
a host of music primers using these methods appeared. Usually the word "voice" or "singing" was displayed prominently

on the cover. Actual voice instruction, however, was usually
limited to one or two pages, wherein the most famous maxims
of earlier eras were encapsuled. Most often, the remainder
of the books contained rules of basic musicianship in progressive order, and finally a few songs. Early examples used
in this study are the works of Corri (1820), Cooke (1828),
Mason (1836), and Day (1839). In many cases, books of this
period with "singing" or "voice" on the cover contain no instruction at all on voice training. When such volumes were
discovered, they were eliminated from the bibliography, although the researcher will find them placed alongside actual
teaching methodologies in the catalogues of both the New York
Public Library and the Library of Congress.

Another group of books excluded from this study are
those containing exercises and vocalises with no verbal directions. In this group are a number of well-known works by
authors surveyed in this study, including Panofka, Panseron,
and Sieber. In the period of this study, particularly before
1900, more than a hundred such books appear. Analysis of
the graded (progressive) order of the exercises and the structure of the individual exercises might yield implicit information on the teaching methods of the first half of this study.
Although the author did not have time or space to thoroughly
examine this source of information, a number of these books
were perused to better understand the total class of published
information in this era. It seems that the graded exercise
book of the 1777-1877 era served as a practical, wordless
methodology. If a student had successfully mastered the
first lesson of the exercise book, he was allowed to progress
to the next. Even a cursory examination of some of these
works reveals to the reader that the exercises are arranged
in order of increasing compass (extending range), increasing
length of phrase (breath control development), decreasing note
values (agility), and increasingly larger skips and leaps (register control). Later, phrase marks are added (legato), and
the messa di voce is presented (breath and dynamic control).
Finally, the essential fiorituri of the time are taught by example (runs, turns, shakes, trills, etc.). In truth, this
system has never been abandoned. The vocalises of Viardot,
Concone and Vaccai hold important places in the teaching
methodologies of many present-day teachers of voice. In the
later years of this study, we find three writers incorporating
vocalises into the explanations of their methods. These
writers are Mathilde Marchesi (1903), Alberto Randegger
(1912), and Nellie Melba (1926). The seeming anachronistic
nature of their books is understandable when the reader rea-

lizes that all of them were trained as singers in a conservative, traditional manner, and they were doing no more than
duplicating the style of training they themselves received.

Strict lines of demarcation are impossible in regard to
philosophical approaches toward training the singing voice;
the rise of one approach does not preclude the survival of
another. The so-called empirical methods endure even today,
although they have been expanded upon as far back as 1840.
That year may be regarded as the starting point of the so-
called "scientific era" of voice training, for it was then that
Manuel Garcia first presented his theories on register formation. It is also about this time that Dr. Louis Mandl and
other physicians published dissertations on the anatomy and
physiology of the vocal apparatus. Also in 1840, Madelaine
published a work entitled Physiologie du chant; Bronson's
Abstract of Elocution and Music, in Accordance with the
Principles of Physiology and the Laws of Life, etc. (1842)
was closely followed by Romer's The Physiology of the Human
Voice (1845). In 1855, Garcia's invention of the laryngoscope
allowed direct observations of the laryngeal area. In 1863,
Helmholtz published Die Lehre von den Tonempfindungen, an
invaluable treatise on the nature and propagation of sound
waves, and their perception by the human ear as sensation.

In 1861, the number of "empirical" publications roughly
equaled the number of "scientific" works. In that year Emma
Seiler issued her Altes und Neues über die Ausbildung des
Gesangorganes, a work that includes much of Garcia's findings
from the previous two decades. In the revised and enlarged
translation, entitled The Voice in Singing (1871), Seiler added
much information on Helmholtz's publication. The influence
of her work resulted in a number of imitations.

By the year 1891, almost every new major work included sections on anatomy and physiology and various theories
of breath, phonatory, and resonatory controls. The most
important works of the period, it seems, were penned by
physicians and scientists. These include the publications of
Browne (ca. 1877, ca. 1890), Holmes (1879, 1880), and
Mackenzie (1886). The inclusion of minute descriptions and
diagrams of the anatomy and physiology of the vocal apparatus
was apparently considered obligatory in this period. In the
space of a few years, improvements in scientific investigatory
procedures revealed a great new wealth of information on the
nature and function of the voice. Writers enthusiastically
included any and all bits of information in a well-meaning

attempt to give the teacher and pupil new insights into the workings of this basically unobservable and subjectively controlled mechanism. Emphasis was no longer placed on a series of progressively ordered exercises to develop the voice. Some volumes, in fact, contain no exercises. Toward the end of the nineteenth century, a scientific understanding of the vocal mechanism came to be considered the primary requisite for improving the voice. Unfortunately, too many authors dutifully included descriptions and diagrams without establishing a sufficient relationship of theorization to practical application. In other words, they seem to have had no idea how to apply this new-found information.

As the "scientific method" reached seemingly universal acceptance, a number of works began to appear which sharply criticize the inherent weakness of this approach. The year 1896 marked the beginning of a third class of authors which we now collectively term the "natural school." In that year two books were published that incorporate the word "natural" into their titles: Arlberg's Eine näturliche und vernünftige Tonbildungslehre für Sänger und Sängerinnen, and Thorp and Nicholl's A Text Book on the Natural Use of the Voice. Another 1896 book that warns the student against complete faith in science is Botume's Modern Singing Methods, Their Use and Abuse. According to Fields,

> The third or natural method group takes a middle
> path, disclaiming any detailed knowledge of vocal phys-
> iology, but seeking to eliminate local effort, so that
> natural vocal reflexes take their course. 'Train the
> mind, train the ear, but let the vocal organs alone'
> is the slogan of this last group [1947, p. 243].

The most reactionary members of this group include Ffrang-çon-Davies (1906), Heinrich (1910), Kirkland (1916), and Shaw (1914).

The tremendous upheavals in political, scientific and cultural thinking in the years around the turn of the twentieth century are paralleled in the multitude of unique approaches to the teaching of singing. No longer do we find the general agreement as to the basic tenets of singing that existed a hundred years earlier. Since vocal pedagogy is a profession without entrance qualifications, almost anyone can publish a book that claims to be "The Most Extraordinary, Comprehensive and Original Work Ever Written on the Singing Voice" (and Tilla Haydon did). Despite the numerous singular approaches, we find in the final four decades of this study a few classes into which some authors fall. One is the group that nostalgically sought to capture the "lost" teaching methods of the "old Italian school." Authors in this group include Botume (1890), Parisotti (1911), Shakespeare (1899, 1924), Shaw (1914), and Taylor (1916). Another group of authors, recognizing the multitude of methodologies prevalent in their time, offered the reader surveys of important contemporary and past treatises. Such authors include Henderson (1906), Klein (1923), Myer (1883), and Taylor (1908).

Singers were the first authors of books on singing, so it is no surprise that a number of singers write hints on their techniques in this era also. The relative number of contributors, however, is unusually large. Between the years 1900 and 1927, we find works by Sims Reeves (1900), Louise Pauline Viardot (1906), Lilli Lehmann (1906), Luisa Tetrazzini (1909 and 1923), Enrico Caruso (1909), Clara Rogers (1910 and 1925), Harry Plunket Greene (1912), Thaddeus Wronski (1921), Blanche Marchesi (1923), Lillian Nordica (1923), Herbert Witherspoon (1925), and Nellie Melba (1926). Also popular in the 1920's were the three volumes of short interviews with numerous singers, compiled by Brower (1920), Cooke (1921), and Martens (1923).

Closing Remarks on the Data Acquired in This Survey

In writing Training the Singing Voice, Fields was compelled to formulate operational definitions for 177 terms related to vocal pedagogy because the voice training profession at that time had no standard definitions. The problem is just as great if not greater in the period of 1777-1927. Much of the information offered by authors would be of considerably greater value if they had taken the trouble to define their terms. Special frustration was felt by this researcher when confronted with the many conflicting discussions regarding the undefined terms "compass," "diction," "vibrato," "tremolo," and the "head, middle, and chest" registers. It is also felt that much of the mutual vituperation hurled between adherents of the "scientific" and "natural" schools could have been avoided if a standardized vocabulary for teaching singing had been established.

Comparison with the survey studies of Duey, Fields, and Burgin yield additional insights into the data compiled for this study. First, that the common sense and "local

effort" rules of the bel canto empiricists find favor throughout the nineteenth and twentieth centuries up to the present
time. Such concepts as prerequisites of vocal study, "breathing is a primary factor," "correct chest position aids singing," "breath economy," "the importance of scale work," and
the regulation of the mouth opening, lips, tongue and jaw
have never lost favor. Secondly, that although a surprising
number of concepts have survived unchanged from the bel
canto period, not a few have also been added, altered or
have died out. The most important concepts to be rejected
were solfeggio training, the training of the voice at a very
young age, extensive pre-vocal exercises, and heavy emphasis
on the "messa di voce." Concepts which become more important late in the study are the use of songs for vocal development and the use of simultaneous mouth and nose breathing. Throughout the study, an evolution in determinators
for the classification of voice types is seen, from considerations of range alone to those of timbre, temperament, volume
and the use of the middle range.

Psychological considerations such as interpretational
controls regulating breathing or expressional intent regulating
resonance become important for the first time in the last
three decades of this study. The small number of statements
related to psychological concepts in comparison to identical
concepts in the studies of Fields and Burgin is reflective of
the fact that only during a small portion of the time period
of this study were these ideas discussed.

Concepts which arose after about 1850 include the complex
theories of phonation, resonation, and registration, the use
of vowel coloring for register blending, increased emphasis
on text interpretation, the memorization of recital materials,
chanting as a device for improving singing diction, and the
use of the phonograph for ear training purposes.

IN CONCLUSION, this study has revealed to the researcher that excellence in voice training, like excellence in
artistic singing, has never been confined to one age. The
writer who complains that the singers of his age represent
a new nadir in artistic excellence, or that the teaching skills
of the bel canto era will never be equalled belongs to that
class of men whom W. S. Gilbert epitomizes as "the idiot
who praises, with enthusiastic tone/ All centuries but this,
and every country but his own." Furthermore, those writers
who aver that the great singers have invariably been "nat-

urals'' who need no voice instruction would do well to research the pupils of the authors surveyed in this study.

The great singers of the years 1777 to 1927 based
their art on traditional principles passed from one generation
to the next. We have seen that the writers of the scientific
era did not seek to undo the traditional precepts of the empirical school but rather to strengthen these precepts through
an understanding of their basis in scientific law. Despite
the apparent surface differences in the various philosophical
approaches to teaching the singing voice, a generally agreed-
upon set of concepts created a concrete foundation upon which
every age may rely for the training of the artistic singing
voice.

GUIDE TO THE BIBLIOGRAPHIES

In order to effectively coordinate the numerous materials related to this study, six bibliographies were deemed necessary. The first, "Guide to the References," appears at the front of the book. It is in a sense the working bibliography of the study. Titles omitted for the sake of space in the body of the work are there joined to the names and dates found within brackets following each quotation.

Annotated Bibliography. Every separately bound work of possible direct relation to those areas of vocal pedagogy surveyed that is contained in at least one of the catalogs of the seven libraries researched is herein listed. Only those authors and books here given annotations were actually used in the body of this study. Directly after the publication data for certain entries, a symbol is contained within brackets, e. g. [PU]. These symbols indicate that the work is available in one of the following libraries:

BPL   Boston Public Library
IU   Indiana University School of Music Library,
        Bloomington, Ind.
NYPL   New York Public Library, Lincoln Center
PU   Princeton University Library, Princeton, N. J.
RU   Rutgers University Library, New Brunswick, N. J.
WCC   Westminster Choir College, Princeton, N. J.

Any entry without such a symbol is available at the Library of Congress, Washington, D. C. Only if the work is not held by the Library of Congress will there occur a bracketed symbol. In most cases, if the work is available at the New York Public Library, that library is given preference in notation because of the large number of volumes contained there and its relative accessability.

Chronological Bibliography. This bibliography was assembled to give the chronological order of appearance of each work contained in the annotated alphabetical bibliography. Asterisks precede each entry that was used for analysis and quotation in the main body of the study.

<u>Bibliography of Secondary Sources.</u>   The books con-
tained in this list fall into four categories: (a) books that
list and analyze the vocal pedagogy sources of other periods,
namely those of John C. Burgin, Philip A. Duey, and Victor
A. Fields; (b) an 1898 bibliography of works on singing, namely
that of J. Standford Brown; (c) two sources that lie outside
of the subject and time limitations of the study, namely the
works of Helmholtz and Tosi; and (d) numerous reference
materials that provide information on the authors and singers
quoted in the study.

<u>Appendix One.</u>   This bibliography gives a list of
sources known to have existed but which were not available
in any of the libraries consulted.

<u>Appendix Two.</u>   A list is presented of periodicals of
the 1777-1927 era in which valuable sources of comment on vocal
pedagogy exist.

ANNOTATED BIBLIOGRAPHY

Abt, Franz. Practical singing tutor. Braunschweig: H. Litolff, ca. 1876. Also, a rev. ed. : New York: G. Schirmer, 1893. [NYPL]

Adams, Frederic Augustus. The singer's manual for teachers pupils, and private students. New York: J. Wiley, 1849. [NYPL]

Adams, H. Travers. Physical development in relation to perfect voice production. London: W. Reeves, 1909.

_____. The "central point" in beautiful voice production. London: W. Reeves, 1926.

Adler-Selva, Johannes. Wie steuern wir dem weiteren Verfall der Gesangkunst? Eine Aufklärungsschrift für Lehrer, Sänger, und Schüler, sowie für das musikalische Publikum. Berlin: n. p. , 1927. [NYPL]

Aiken, William Arthur. The voice; an introduction to practical phonology ... with diagrams. London: Longmans, Green & Co. , 1910.
This is a new edition of The voice: its physiology and cultivation.

_____. The voice: its physiology and cultivation. London: Macmillan and Co. ; New York: Macmillan Co. , 1900.

Albert, Alfred G. Moderne Berliner Gesangspädagogen; eine Kritik ihrer Theorie und Praxis. Berlin: Kommissionsverlag von R. Rühle-Zechlin, 1908.

Aldrich, Perley Dunn. Vocal economy and expressiveness. New York: The Vocalist, ca. 1895.

Anfossi, Maria. Trattato teorico practico sull'arte del canto/ A theoretical and practical treatise on the art of singing. London: the author, 18--. [NYPL]
Anfossi taught singing in London at the end of the eighteenth century. She states that her treatise contains "... all the important rules of singing to be acquired by reading ... [and] exercises, which, though adapted to every kind of voice, are not so numerous as to perplex or discourage beginners" [Preface]. The treatise is among the most descriptive of its

time. Italian text is on the left page, its English equivalent on the right.

Arger, Mary Jane. Initiation à l'art du chant. Paris: E. Flammarion, ca. 1924.

Arlberg, Fritz. Eine natürliche und vernünftige Tonbildungslehre für Sänger und Sängerinnen, nach dem Schwedischen des Fritz Arlberg, von Axel Sandberg. Cologne: Druck der Kölner Verlags-anstalt & Druckerei, 1896.

_____. Theoretische und praktische Tonbildungslehre. Copenhagen: W. Hansen, 1899.

The art of improving the voice and ear; and of increasing their musical powers, on philosophical principles. London: Printed for S. Prowett, 1825.

Arthur, Alfred. 70 lessons in voice training for medium voice. Cleveland, OH: J. H. Rogers, 1889. [NYPL]

_____. 79 short studies for alto or bass; a practical course in voice training with technical rules. Cleveland, OH: J. H. Rogers, 1889.

Audubert, Jules. L'Art du chant. Paris: Brandus et Cie, 1876.

Averkamp, Antoon. Vit mijn practijk; Wenken en raadgevingen by het Onderswijs en de studie van den solozang. Groningen: J. B. Wolters, 1916.

Bach, Albert Bernhard. Musical education and vocal culture. 4th ed. London: W. Blackwood & Sons, 1884. 5th ed. London: Paul Trench, Trubner & Co. , 1898.
    Bach (real name Bak) (1844-1912) was a Hungarian singer, teacher, lecturer and writer. He studied at the Vienna Conservatory and in Italy, and sang opera in Italy, Hungary, Russia, Germany, and England between 1871 and 1885. A Loewe specialist, Bach edited three volumes of Loewe's ballads. He later taught voice and lectured in the British Isles.
    An expansion of the author's The principles of singing, with primary emphases on breathing, registers and register equalization, and vocal hygiene.

_____. On musical education. Edinburgh: W. Blackwood & Sons, 1880. [NYPL]
    A compilation of three lectures delivered in England and Scotland in 1880. "Lecture First. On the cultivation of the voice. " "Lecture Second. How can the musical education of the middle classes be improved?" "Lecture Third. Fully proves that there are no notes produced in the head" [from the subtitles]. The first lecture discusses fundamental precepts of voice study and what is necessary for one to be a good voice teacher.

_____. The principles of singing; A practical guide for vocalists
and teachers, with vocal exercises. 2nd ed. Edinburgh: W.
Blackwood & Sons, 1894.
Bach's major work on singing touches upon all aspects of
the art from a scientific viewpoint. Helmholtz's principles are
well covered.

Bacon, Richard Mackenzie. Elements of vocal science; being a
philosophical enquiry into some of the principles of singing.
London: Baldwin, Cradock & Joy, 1824. (Reprinted: Champaign, Il: Pro Musica Press, 1966.)
Bacon (1776-1844) was an English writer on music, music
critic, and founder and editor of The Quarterly Musical Magazine and Review, the first musical periodical in England.
The contents of this work were originally published as letters in this Quarterly (during the years 1818-1824). This is
one of the earliest pedagogical works written by a native
Englishman. It contains learned discussions on music in general, the state of singing in England, the nature of various
singing styles (oratorio, theatrical, church, etc.), and the
manner of execution of each.

Bagioli, Antonio. New method for singing; with an accompaniment
for the piano or harp. New York: Sold for the author by O.
Torp, ca. 1833. [NYPL] Also, 2nd ed.: New York: the
author, 18--.

Baker, Benjamin Franklin, and Southard, L. H. A complete method
for the formation & cultivation of the voice; a complete and
practical method of vocalization, consisting of every variety
of scale exercises and solfeggios, progressively arranged,
and adapted to the wants of beginners and advanced pupils in
the art of singing. Boston: E. H. Wade, ca. 1852. Another
ed.: New York: S. T. Gordon & Son, ca. 1856. [NYPL]

Baratoux, Jean. De la voix; étude scientifique de la formation et
son émission, ses maladies ... avec 146 illustrations. Paris:
A. Gutheil, 1923. English ed. The voice; a scientific study
of its formation and its ailments. Paris: A. Gutheil, 1925.

Barlow, James Smith. The balance of act in singing. Athens,
Tenn.: Athenian Print, 1896.

Barnett, John. School for the voice; or, The principles of singing,
being a short treatise, theoretical and practical, on the culture
& development of the voice. London: Hutchings & Romer,
1844. Another ed.: London: Addison & Hodson, 1845.

Barnette, Annie M. Talks about singing; or, How to practice.
Chicago: Chicago Music Co., ca. 1886.

Barth, Adolf Franz. Über der Bildung der menschlichen Stimme
und ihres Klanges beim Singer und Sprecher vom physiologisch-

physikalischen Standpunkt betrachet. Leipzig: J. A. Barth, 1904. [NYPL]

Bassini, Carlo. Bassini's art of singing: an analytical physiological and practical system for the cultivation of the voice. Edited by R. Storrs Willis. Boston: O. Ditson & Co., ca. 1857. [NYPL]
    Bassini (1812-1870) was an Italian singer and teacher; a pupil of Crescentini and of Zingarelli. He taught singing in later life in New York.
    Bassini's art of singing arose from a series of favorably received articles published in The Musical World, a journal of music published in New York. According to Bassini, his system " ... is founded on nature, as displayed in the anatomy of the vocal organs, and on art, as tested in long application of theory" [Preface]. The presentation is thorough for its era and provides exercises in graded order, divided according to specific vocal tasks and skills. Bassini indicates by letter above the pitches whether a note should be sung with chest, middle, or head register.

_____. Bassini's education of the young voice; a scientific and practical system of voice culture for young persons of both sexes. New York: F. J. Huntington, ca. 1865. [NYPL]
    Represents a major transition in Bassini's approach to teaching. Discussion of rules are minimized while the proportion of the book devoted to graded exercises is expanded. Yet, he asserts, "My new system of Voice Culture, [is] founded on scientific and physiological principles ... " [Preface].

_____. Bassini's new method for soprano and mezzo-soprano: being a thorough course of singing and cultivation of the voice. Boston: G. D. Russel & Co., ca. 1869. [NYPL]
    Follows the structure of Bassini's education of the young voice, with exercises tailored more carefully to the needs of the female voice.

Baxter, James. Technics for voice. Friendship, N.Y.: Crandall, 1871. [BPL]

Bedford, Hernet. An essay on modern unaccompanied song. London: Oxford University Press, 1923.

Behnke, Emil. The mechanism of the human voice, with a new chapter on voice failure by Mrs. Emil Behnke. Edited by Mrs. Emil Behnke. 12th ed. London: J. Curwen & Sons, 189-.
    Behnke (1836-1892) was a London authority on voice-training, a teacher and a writer on voice production for speakers and singers. His title page credits him as "Teacher of Voice Production at The Tonic Sol-fa College, London."
    A milestone in the scientific approach to the study of the voice. Anatomy is presented in fine detail, with singing con-

sidered as a function of the mechanism. Behnke relies heavily
on quotations from contemporary sources to support his views.

_____   see also Browne, Lennox

Behnke, Kate Emil. Singers' difficulties, how to overcome them.
London: Cassell and Company, 1926.

Belari, Emilio. An open letter to singers and vocal teachers concerning the modern or natural voice method. New York: n. p. , 1898.

_____ . The secrets of the voice in singing, explained according
to the laws of acoustics and physiology. New York: J. K.
Lees, 1883. [NYPL]

Benedict, Frank Johnson. A scientific system of voice culture without exercises; vocal myths and superstitions eliminated by
methodical application of correct physical, psychological and
musical principles, with complete and definite directions of a
practical nature. Cincinnati: John Church Co. , 1919. [NYPL]

Benelli, Antonio Peregrino. Regien für den figurirten Gesang; oder
Gründlicher Unterricht in den Lehrsätzen der Musik, by Anton
Benelli. Dresden: auf Kosten des Verfassers, 18--. [NYPL]

Benjamin, William Augustus. The singing voice ... [with an] introduction by David Bispham. Los Angeles: G. Schirmer music
stores, ca. 1921. [NYPL]

Bennett, Thomas. An introduction to the art of singing. New York:
Hewitt & Jaques, n. d. [NYPL]

Bishenden, Charles James. How to sing; containing ... useful information ... instructions and vocal exercises.... London:
H. White & Son, 1876. [NYPL]
    Bishenden (1848-) was an English bass singer. His name
is found in some contemporary sources as an example of
good singing.
    Of limited value, with general remarks on the study of the
voice, some basic precepts and a few exercises. It is liberally padded with personal anecdotes.

_____ . The voice and how to use it; describing the mechanism
of the vocal organs, how to strengthen the lungs, etc. London: the author, 1875. [NYPL]
    Both The voice and how to use it and How to sing are
typical examples of "textbooks" written by professional singers.
Scientific analysis of the vocal mechanism is avoided. The
bulk of the book is given to basic ideas of practice, common-
sense rules of production, preventions for health, and home-
remedy cures.

Blackman, Dwight A.   Mind vs. practice, no. two, presenting the
   psycho-vowel method of voice, building; a strictly psychological method which gives rapid control of a full musical
   voice.   New York: D. A. Blackman, 1924.   [NYPL]

Bonnier, Pierre.   La Voix professionnelle; leçons pratiques de
   physiologie, appliquée aux carrières vocales.   Paris: Larousse,
   1908.

_____.   La Voix, sa culture physiologique; theorie nouvelle de
   la phonation; conferences faites au Conservatoire de musique
   de Paris.   2nd rev. ed. , Paris: F. Alcan, 1909.

Booth, Josiah.   Everybody's guide to music, with illustrated chapters on singing and cultivation of the voice.   New York: Harper & Brothers, 1894.

Borese, Victor.   Emission esthétique et santé vocales résument tout
   l'art du chant; etude sure la voix.   Paris: Fischbacher, 192-.
   [NYPL]

Botume, John Franklin.   Modern singing methods, their use and
   abuse.   Boston: O. Ditson Co. , 1896.
       Teachings of the "Old Italian School" are compared with
   the latest scientific methods.   Much space is given to registers
   and the use of sensation to control registration.   There is an
   appendix of vocal pedagogy books and ideas from Tosi's Opin-
   ioni, 1723 to 1871, divided according to subject area.

_____.   Respiration for advanced singers.   Boston: O. Ditson,
   ca. 1897.   [NYPL]
       A very involved system of six different methods of breathing
   is presented, with examples as to how each finds its application in performance.

_____.   Voice production today.   Boston: the author, 1916.
       This little pamphlet contains a brief and elementary sketch
   of the singing methods and styles in use at the time of its
   publication.   Special emphasis is given to breathing and diction.
   (A number of entries in this bibliography closely correspond
   to Voice production today in that their purpose is most probably
   to secure voice students for the author/publisher.)

Bozzelli, Giuseppe.   Brevi considerazioni sull'arte del canto; lettera
   all'illustre maestro comm. Francesco Florimo.   Menaggio:
   A. Mastai, 1880.

Bradbury, William Batchelder.   The singing bird; or, Progressive
   music reader.   New York: n. p. , 1852.   [PU]

Bradley, Eugene Willis.   Science of voice placement simplifield for
   universal home study; standard method of voice production.
   New York: n. p. , ca. 1924.

Brand, Thomas Henry. Brand's system of voice building, introducing the position method. Madison, Wis.: Brand & Kopple, 1896.

Breare, William Hammond. Vocal analyses: sensitising breath-emotional evolution. London: Simpkin, Marshall, Hamilton, Kent & Co., 1924.

_____. Vocal faults and their remedies. London: G. P. Putnam's Sons, 1907.

_____. Vocalism, its structure and culture from an English standpoint. London: G. P. Putnam's Sons, 1904.

Broad, A. Richards. How to attain the singing voice; or, Singing shorn of its mysteries; a popular handbook for those desirous of winning success as singers in public and private life. 2nd ed. London: W. Reeves, 1924.

Broekhaven, John Andrew van. Some unfamiliar facts concerning the functions of the larynx in singing. New York: H. W. Gray Co., 1908. This is a reprint from the June 1908 issue of the New Music Review.
    Broekhaven (1852-) was a teacher and theorist. He was born in Holland and emigrated to the United States, where, among other positions, he held the professorship of Harmony and Counterpoint at the Cincinnati College of Music.
    Missing; no copy available for analysis.

_____. The tone producing functions of the vocal organs; A new theory with practical illustrations. Published in the New York Musical Courier, May 10th, 17th and 24th, 1905. New York: n.p., 1905. [NYPL]
    A brief theoretical treatise dealing primarily with phonation, registration, and the nature of the function of the larynx.

_____. The true method of tone production. New York: H. W. Gray Co., 1908.
    Broekhaven asserts, "What I offer in this work is entirely original in subject and treatment ... [being] hitherto overlooked, and therefore neglected by vocal teachers" [Preface]. An elaborate offense is mounted against the traditional theory that vocal sound is caused by vibration of the vocal cords. A theory of air current control by means of the ventricles of Morgagni and the false vocal cords is substituted.

Bronson, C. P. Abstract of elocution and music, in accordance with the principles of physiology and the laws of life, for the development of body and mind. Auburn: H. Oliphant, book and job printer, 1842.

Brouillet, Georges Antoine. Artistic tone production through natural breathing; the Brouillet-method; a reliable and expedient method

of teaching tone production and harmonics with the human voice.
Boston: F. E. Bacon & Co. , 1909.

_____ .   Science in vocal tone production.   Boston: Boston Text
Book Co. , 1916.

_____ .   Science of tone production.   Boston: n. p. , 1913.   Rev.
ed. :   Boston: n. p. , 1914.

Brower, Harriette Moore.   Vocal mastery; talks with master singers
and teachers.   New York: Frederick A. Stokes Co. , 1920.
    Brower (dates not known) interviews 25 noted singers of
her time.   In the strictest sense, Vocal mastery is not a
voice training book, although " ... every effort has been put
forth to induce artists to speak from an educational standpoint"
[Foreword].

Browne, Lennox.   Medical hints on the production and management
of the singing voice.   4th ed.   London: Chappell & Co. , 1877.
[NYPL]
    Browne (dates not known) was senior surgeon to the Central
Throat and Ear Hospital, and surgeon and aural surgeon to
the Royal Society of Musicians.
    The book investigates the physical aspect of singing, based
on empirical observations, other sources, and on the latest
scientific research.   Much space is devoted to hygiene.

_____ , and Behnke, Emil.   Voice, song and speech; a practical
guide for singers and speakers, from the combined view of
surgeon and voice trainer, 16th ed.   London: S. Low, Marston
& Co. , 1904.   22nd ed. :   New York: G. P. Putnam's Sons,
190-.   [NYPL]
    Perhaps the most widely circulated and oft-quoted vocal
work of the nineteenth century.   It has been described by
David C. Taylor, in his The psychology of singing as "The
most influential published work in popularizing the doctrine of
breath-control ... " (p. 24).   In fact, Browne and Behnke
present a doctrine of total body control through a system of
local efforts, declared compatible with the laws of physics
and acoustics.   The book's success can be partially attributed
to a dual-authority appeal:
    "Each of the Authors of the following pages has already
contributed something towards the store of literature on the
Human Voice.   These contributions have had a large circula-
tion and have so far been successful, but they have been necessarily one-sided and therefore incomplete; for while the surgeon
was unable to touch on matters musical, the teacher found
himself in a similar difficulty on many points of hygiene and
health" [Preface].   Much of the material is drawn verbatim
from each man's former works.

Bruns, Paul.   Carusos Technik in deutscher Erklärung.   Charlottenburg: O. George, ca. 1922.

_____ . Die Registerfrage in neurer Forschung. Berlin-Gross Lichterfelde: C. F. Vieweg, 1906.

Bryant, Harriet Crane. The voice instrument...; being an explanation and discussion of the human voice instrument and a manual of exercises for proper development of muscles necessarily employed, if voice production is to become ultimately free, full, resonant and sustained. Hamilton, NY: Printed by the Hamilton Republican, ca. 1913.

Burritt, William Nelson. A process of vocal study. Rev. ed. Chicago: F. Summy Co., 1922.

Busse, F. Der Singemeister. Leipzig: Friedlein & Hirsch, 18--. [NYPL]

Buzzi-Peccia, Arturo. How to succeed in singing; a practical guide for singers desiring to enter the profession. Philadelphia: Theo. Presser Co., 1925.
    Buzzi-Peccia (1854-1943) was a voice teacher of Italian origin. He emigrated to the United States in 1898 and taught mostly in New York. Alma Gluck was one of his pupils.
    Surveys many aspects of singing and the rigors of a professional career. The book is loosely structured, but contains many keen observations, presented with a sense of humor.

Calicchio, Isaia. The secret of how to become a great singer. Jersey City: Press of L. L. Van Benschoten, ca. 1915.

Cappiani, Luisa. Practical hints and helps for perfection in singing. New York: L. Feist, 1908. [NYPL]

Carozzi, Giuseppe Napoleone. Guida ant'igenica di ginnastica vocale. Milan: n. p., 1890. [NYPL]

Caruso, Enrico. How to sing; some practical hints. London: John Church Co., 1913. (Reprinted Brooklyn, N.Y.: Opera Box, 1973; also released as The art of singing.)
    Caruso (1873-1921) was the most celebrated Italian tenor of his time.
    As a teaching work, Caruso's book is generalized and incomplete. Fundamental rules are interspersed with personal reminiscences. "Pet superstitions of singers" is a chapter unique to vocal literature.

_____ see also Tetrazzini, Luisa; Fucito, Salvatore

Casella, Fabrizio. Compendia dell'opera sulle teorica per l'arte del canto. Rome: Tip. de C. Puccinella, 1848.

Cassius, Olga. Die Erziehung der Stimme und Atmung durch Artikulation der Konsonanten und Biegung der Vokale. Charlottenburg: G. Plothow, 1913.

Castex, André. Hygiène de la voix parlée et chantée. Paris: n. p. , 1894. [NYPL]

Cazalet, William Wahab. The voice; or, The art of singing. London: Addison, Hollier & Lucas, 1861. [NYPL]

Celentano, Luigi. Intorno all'arte del cantare in Italia nel secolo decimonono. Naples: Stabilimento Tip. Ghio, 1867.

Chater, Thomas. Scientific voice, artistic singing & effective speaking. London: Bell, 1890. [BPL]

Cheney, Albert Baker. The tone-line: principles of voice development. Boston: the author, 1896.

Chevé, Nanine Paris. Science et art de l'intonation; théorie et pratique, système des points d'appui. Paris: n. p. , 1868.

_____ and Chevé Emile J. M. An elementary course of vocal music upon the Chevé method, compiled from the work of Emile and Nanine Chevé. 3rd ed. [Philadelphia?]: n. p. , ca. 1900. [NYPL]

Clifton, Arthur. Clifton's vocal instruction (New vocal instructer) [sic]. Philadelphia: George Willig, ca. 1820. 3rd ed. , 1846. [NYPL]
Typical of mid-nineteenth-century American and English vocal books. Four pages are used for basic singing tenets, followed by graded exercises.

_____ see also Corri, Philip Antony

Clippinger, David Alva. The head voice and other problems; practical talks on singing. Boston: O. Ditson Co. , 1917.
Clippinger [1860-1930] was an American choral conductor, singer and teacher. He studied voice in London with Shakespeare and later settled in Chicago.
Improvement of the voice by ear training is called for, while sophisticated techniques and local effort methods are rejected.

_____ . Systematic voice training. Chicago: Gamble Hinged Music Co. , ca. 1910. [NYPL]
Precursor to the important Clippinger class-method of voice culture, 1932. Areas most stressed are correct tonal conception, breath control and freedom of the throat.

Coletti, Filippo. La scuola di canto in Italia; pensieri dell'artista cav. Filippo Coletti. Rome: Tip. del Senato, 1886.

Cooke, Clifton. Practical singing. London: K. Paul, Trench, Trubner and Co. , Ltd. , 1916.

_____ see also Heller, Gordon

Cooke, James Francis. Great singers on the art of singing; educational conferences with foremost artists ... a series of personal talks with the most renowned opera, concert and oratorio singers of the time, especially planned for voice students. Philadelphia: Theo. Presser Co. , 1921.

Cooke (1875-?) was a semi-professional singer and an eminent writer on music. He studied in the United States and Germany. He served as editor of The Etude from 1908 to 1949.

Twenty-seven artists speak on a variety of subjects related to singing and a singing career. The introduction is a miniature voice-training text in itself.

Cooke, Thomas Simpson. Singing simplified in a series of solfeggi and exercises progressively arranged with an accompaniment for the pianoforte. New York: William Hall & Son, 1828. [PU] Later released as Cooke's vocal method, containing, in addition to the original work, numerous exercises, solfeggios etc. , on portamento, sustension and flexibility of the voice. Rev. ed. , New York: S. T. Gordon, 186-.

The author (1782-1848) was an Irish conductor and later singer who moved to London and taught at the Royal Academy of Music.

An early example of the popular singing book that saw wide use in homes and schools of America and England. See, Clifton, Arthur.

Corfe, Joseph. A treatise on singing; explaining in the most simple manner, all the rules for learning to sing by note, without the assistance of an instrument. London: the author, 18--.

Corfe (1740-1820) was a chorister at Salisbury Cathedral and from 1792 until 1804 served as organist and master of the choristers at Salisbury Cathedral.

Exercises comprise the majority of this work. Corfe freely admits his dependence on Tosi for his basic rules.

Corrette, Michel. Le Parfait Maître a chanter; méthode pour apprendre facilmente la musique vocale et instrumentale, ou tous les principes devélopés nettement et distinctement. Rev. ed. Paris: the author, 1782.

Corrette (1709?-1795) was a French organist and composer who from 1738 served as organist at the Jesuit College in Paris.

Representative of the French singing book of the time, that teaches the basic rules and symbols of music, but relates to singing only in its presentation of voice types, basic rules for diction and a description of the use of solfeggio for exercise work.

Corri, Domenico. The singers preceptor, or Corri's treatise on vocal music. London: Chappell & Co. , 1810.

Corri (1746-1825) was an Italian dramatic composer, singer and teacher. He studied for five years with Porpora in Naples, until the master's death. In 1771, he was offered the position of Conductor of the Opera at Edinburgh. He later settled in London, teaching voice and composing.

Corri's offering to vocal literature is one of the best of its era, thorough and lucid. The subtitle reads, "This treatise is expressly calculated to teach the art of singing and consists of establishing proper rules, (the result of fifty years' experiences) accommodated to the capacity of every student whether amateur or professor, theatrical or choral; also to assist those who sing by ear only and so arranged as to enable the pupil to improve by the exercise of these rules, in the absence of a master." A question and answer format is used.

Corri, Philip Antony. New vocal instructor by Arthur Clifton. Philadelphia: Published and sold at G. Willig's Musical Magazine, ca. 1820. See Clifton, Arthur.

Costa, Andrea. Analytical considerations on the art of singing; containing an account of the various styles of singing prevalent in ... Europe ... sacred, popular, and theatrical. London: Sherwood, Gilbert, & Piper, 1838.

Andrea Costa was a composer, author and teacher. Born in Brescia, Italy, he settled in London around 1824.

The rules of singing discussed in the 1824 book [see next entry] are expanded upon. Much of the book is devoted to non-teaching areas: histories of six famous singers, generalizations of the singing timbres of various nationalities, etc.

_____. Considerations on the art of singing in general ... to which are added some opinions on the elemental instruction of the art. London: G. Schulze, 1824. [NYPL]

In this work, defects of the voice are divided into three categories: voice, production, method. The remainder of the treatise offers remedies.

Crivelli, Domenico Francesco Maria. The art of singing, adapted with alterations and new solfeggios for the cultivation of the bass voice. London: n.p., 18--.

Croker, Norris. Handbook for singers. 4th ed. London: Augener, ca. 1900. (1st ed., 1895).

Crowest, Frederick James. Advice to singers. 10th ed. London: F. Warne and Co., 1914. (1st ed.: 1900).

Crowest (1850-) was a singer, organist, and composer, but was chiefly known as an author of books of musical biography and anecdote. For some years he had success as a tenor, singing under the name Arthur Vitton.

Crowest states, "I give hints, not rules" [p. 11]. Commonsense precepts on practice, phonation, ear training and interpretation abound, although they are presented in disconnected fashion.

Curry, Samuel Silas. Mind and voice: principles and methods in vocal training. Boston: Expression Company, ca. 1910.

Curtis, Henry Holbrook. Thirty years' experience with singers. Edited by Music and Musician [magazine]. New York: n. p., 1918.

    Curtis (1856-1920) was an American physician, specializing in the throat. He was friend and consultant to many singers at the Metropolitan Opera Company.

    Not designed as a vocal pedagogy book, Curtis recalls his personal and professional involvement with singers. Pages 13-63 contain pictures of the singers.

_____. Voice building and tone placing, showing a new method of relieving injured vocal cords by tone exercises. 3rd ed. New York: D. Appleton and Co., 1914.

    Dr. Curtis applies an analysis of anatomy and physiology to rules of singing in an objective manner. With traditionally debatable subjects, such as registers, he presents a wide variety of opinions via quotations from more than 150 years of sources. Mos emphasis is placed on phonation and resonation.

Damoreau, Laure Cinthie Montalant. Méthode de chant, composée ses classes due conservatoire. Paris: A. Meissonnier, Heugel et Cie, ca. 1850. [NYPL]

Danby, John. La guida alla musica vocale, containing various progressive examples and duets calculated for the use of beginners. London: the author, 1787?

Daniell, William Henry. The voice and how to use it. Boston: J. R. Osgood and Co., 1873. Another ed., New York: S. R. Wells & Co., 1876.

    Daniell (1834-) was a self-taught American music teacher and writer. In 1878 he became lecturer and professor of singing at the New England Conservatory of Music in Boston.

    The use of the falsetto is encouraged. Daniell suggests that the subject of registers be ignored, that correct coordination provides an automatic mechanism for range adjustment.

Dannenburg, Richard. Handbuch der Gesangkunst. 5th ed. Berlin: Max Hesses Verlag, ca. 1920. [NYPL]

D'Aubigny von Engelbrunner, Nina. Briefe an Natalie über den Gesang, als Beförderung der häuslichen Glückseligkeit usw. Leipzig: Voss und Comp., 1803.

    D'Aubigny was the elder of two German sisters, noted as composers of the late eighteenth century.

    Historical, theoretical and practical viewpoints of the art of singing are presented at length in a series of "letters." Thereafter, eight tables of useful exercises are added.

Davis, Charles Henry Stanley. The voice as a musical instrument; with medical hints as to its proper training and culture. Boston: O. Ditson & Co., ca. 1879.

Day, H. W. The vocal school; or, Pestalozzian method of instruction in the elements of vocal music. Boston: Otis, Broaders & Co., 1839. [NYPL]
    The Pestalozzian system of progressive question and answer was devised to let students guide themselves to solutions in any learning situation. Day's book presents fundamentals of music, using the voice as the basic instrument.

Debay, Auguste. Hygiène et gymnastique des organes de la voix parlée et chantée; analyse des divers moyens gymnastiques et médicaux propres à developper la voix et à combattre ses alterationes. Paris: E. Dentu, 1861.

De La Marca, Raffaello. Important advice to singing students. N. P. : n. p., ca. 1919.

Delprat, Charles. L'Art du chant et l'école actuelle. Paris: Librairie Internationale, 1870. [NYPL]

De Rialp, Francis Charles Maria. The legitimate school of singing. New York: the author, 1894.

Dingley, Charles. The intellectual and practical singing book: embracing the elements of vocal music. New York: N. B. Holmes, 1834. [NYPL]

Dodds, George. Practical hints for singers. London: The Epworth Press, ca. 1927. [NYPL]
    Lack of information makes it impossible to be sure that George Dodds and George Robert Dodds [see next entry] are one and the same person. Information on the title page of Practical hints for singers tells us that this writer is also the author of the article on "Singing" in the 1926 edition of Encyclopaedia Britannica.
    Emphasis is placed on economy of effort, causes and cures of throaty singing, and vibrato versus tremolo, within a generally comprehensive text.

Dodds, George Robert, and Lickley, James Dunlop. The control of the breath, an elementary manual for singers and speakers. London: Oxford University Press, H. Milford, 1925. Another edition: 1938.
    George Robert Dodds was an associate teacher at the Royal College of Music. Lickley was a physician and lecturer on applied anatomy at the University of Durham College of Medicine.
    "This little volume is an endeavor to present a description of the mechanism of respiration, and an explanation of its action in such a manner that the student of singing, elocution,

or physical culture may have a basis upon which existing systems or authorities can be examined and judged" [Preface]. The anatomy and physiology of the larynx is also presented.

Dodge, Jenny Busk. The care of the voice; advice to young singers. Cincinnati: J. Church Co. , 1895.

Döring, Karl Heinrich. Aphorismen vom Felde der Kunst des Gesanges. Dresden: M. A. Hoffmann, 1860.

Douty, Nicholas. What the vocal student should know, an introduction to the art of singing. Philadelphia: Theo. Presser Co. , ca. 1924.
     Pre-vocal breathing exercises are stressed. During singing, natural breathing is advocated.

Dow, Sabrina H. Artistic singing. Boston: Lee and Shepard, 1883.

Dowd, Daniel L. Science and vocal culture. New York: n. p. , 1887. [NYPL]

Downing, William Bell. Vocal pedagogy for student, singer and teacher. New York: C. Fischer, 1927.
     Downing (dates unknown) was for 20 years professor of voice at the University of Kansas.
     A brief and concise text; each facet of the art is separately listed and headlined for ease of location. Extensive lists of songs are provided, arranged in order of difficulty, by voice classification, by occasion, by country, for duet, trio, etc.

Drew, William Sidney. Voice training; the relation of theory and practice. London: H. Milford, Oxford University Press, 1924.
     Stress is placed on phonation and diction. Drew advocates vowel modification. He provides practical exercises to induce freedom.

Duca, Giovanni. Conseils sur l'étude du chant. Translated by M. J. Boyer. Paris: Bonoldi Frères, 1851. [NYPL]

Duff, Sarah Robinson. Simple truths used by great singers. Boston: Oliver Ditson Company, 1919.
     Duff (dates unknown) taught singing in New York for 25 years prior to the publication of Simple truths used by great singers. She was the teacher of Mary Garden.
     "Complete relaxation of the body is your first principle" [p. 10]. Conservative principles are stated, with relaxation the guiding objective.

Duhamel, Raoul. Technique rationnelle du chant. Paris: Librairie Fischbacher, 1925. [NYPL]

Dunn, Sinclair. The solo singer. 3rd ed. London: J. Curwen & Sons, 189-. [NYPL]

_____ . The solo singer and vade mecum. 7th ed. London:
J. Curwen & Sons, 189-. [NYPL]

Duprez, Gilbert Louis. Sur la voix et l'art du chant. Paris:
Tresse, 1882.

Durieu. Nouvelle Méthod de musique vocale; concernant les principes de cet art, démonstré par des leçons, et accompagné
d'exemples qui en applanissent toutes les difficultés. Paris:
chez l'auteur, 1793.

Duschnitz, Marco. Theorie Tonerzeugung und der Gesangkunst auf
physiologischen und mathematischen Grundsätzen dargestellt;
eine Gesangschule für die naturgemässe Behandlung und künst-
liche Entwicklung der menschlichen Stimme. Leipzig: J.
Schuberth & Co. , ca. 1870.
    In the Philadelphia edition of J. Schuberth & Co. , ca. 1870
[NYPL], the text appears in both German and English. The
English title reads: Theorie of the production of vocal sounds
and the art of singing based on physiological and mathematical
principles.

Duval. Méthode agréable et utile pour apprendre facilement à
chanter juste, avec goût et précision. Paris: chez l'auteur,
ca. 1800. [NYPL]
    Mlle. Duval was a French eighteenth-century singer and
composer. She is known to have written a four-act opera-
ballet, Les Génies.
    No rules of singing are provided, but exercises are given,
with hints on their execution. The important ornaments and
embellishments are presented.

Duval, John H. The secrets of Svengali on singing, singers, teachers and critics. New York: J. T. White & Co. , 1922.

Dyer. Vocal preceptor. New York: n. p. , 1828.
    The author is most probably Samuel Dyer, an American
sacred music composer. In 1820 he published a valuable collection of 244 pieces, entitled Sacred Music.
    Beyond an outline of vocal compasses, no rules of singing
are provided. Solfeggio is used in a graded series of exercises.

Ebers, Karl Friedrich. Vollständige Singschule. Mainz: B.
Schott, ca. 1798.

Edgerley, Webster. Lessons in voice culture; the perfect method;
designed for the reader, the orator, the actor, the teacher,
the pupil, the elocutionist, and as the foundation of the singing
voice. By Edmund Shaftesbury [pseud.]. Washington, D. C. :
Martyn College Press, 1891.

Edwards, Henry. How to develop the voice for song. N. p. : the
author, ca. 1921.

Eirel, Franz. Die Stimmfähigkeit des Menschen und ihre Ausbildung für Kunst und Leben. Vienna: Mechitharistenbuchdruckerei, 1854.

Eitz, Carl Andreas. Bausteine zum Schulgesangunterrichte im Sinne der Tonwortmethode...; mit 4 Tafeln. Leipzig: Breitkopf & Härtel, 1911.

_____. Der Gesangunterricht als Grundlage der musikalischen Bildung. Leipzig: J. Klinkhardt, 1914.

_____. Das Tonwort, Bausteine zur musikalischen Volksbildung. Leipzig: Breitkopf & Härtel, 1928.

Emerson, Charles Wesley. Psycho-vox; or, The Emerson system of voice culture. Millis, Mass.: Emerson College Pub. Dept., 1915. [NYPL]

Emerson, Luther Orlando. Emerson's vocal method for contralto, baritone and bass voice. Boston: O. Ditson Co., ca. 1890. [NYPL]

Engel, S. Camillo. A few hints on the foundation of the voice in song and speech. New York: Knickerbocker Press, ca. 1892.

_____. The spirit of the art of singing; a compendium of the principles underlying my teaching. Los Angeles: n.p., 19--.

Everest, Cornelius. Everest's vocal instructor. Boston: O. Ditson & Co., ca. 1861.
"The object of the author in preparing this Vocal Instructor is to furnish a short and easy method, whereby the pupil may readily acquire a thorough knowledge of the rudiments of music, learn to read by note, and cultivate the voice" [Preface]. A few rules are presented, credit is given to Tosi and Mancini; graded exercises comprise the bulk of the work, while Concone's vocalises are recommended as adjunct material.

Fabio, Ermagora. Teorica del canto per servire al Musicale istituto eretto in Venezia dal Sigr. Giuseppe Camploy. Venice: Tip. Andreola, 1839.

Fauré, Jean Baptiste. Aux jeunes chanteurs, notes et conseils. Paris; Au Ménestrel: H. Heugel, 1890.

_____. La Voix et le chant; traité pratique. Paris: H. Heugel, 1886.

Federlein, Gottlieb Heinrich. Common sense in singing; an essay on the "practical school of vocal culture." New York: G. Schirmer, 1880.

_____. Gottlieb Federlein's practical school of voice culture. New York: Schuberth & Co., 1880. [BPL]

Fellowes, Townsend Harris. The art of singing...; a textbook for young singers. New York: Luckhardt & Belder, ca. 1916.

Ferrari, Giacomo Gotifredi. Breve trattato de canto Italiano. London: Schulze & Dean, 1818. [NYPL]
This book appeared same year, same publisher, in English translation: A concise treatise on Italian singing ... elucidated by rules, observations and examples.
Ferrari [1759-1842] was an Italian cembalist, teacher, writer and composer. He emigrated to London around 1810.
The book is particularly descriptive and thorough for its era. Its primary emphasis is placed on breathing, range, and diction.

_____. Giacimo [sic] G. Ferrari's celebrated instruction book for the voice, with accompaniment for the piano forte. New York: E. Riley & Co. , ca. 1838. [NYPL]
Much of the 1818 edition [see entry above] material is repeated here. The nature of registers and register blending receives special attention.

_____. Instruction book for the voice. Boston: Ditson, 184-. [BPL]

Feuchtinger, Eugene. Die Kunststimme. Ihre neueste Erklärung durch eine exacte, auf rein wissenschaftlichen Basis beruhende Methode. Regensburg: E. Feuchtinger, 1910.

_____. A manual for the study of the human voice. 5th ed. Chicago: Perfect Voice Institute, ca. 1925.

_____. The vocal organ--its mechanism. (Explaining a new discovery.) 4th ed. rev. and enl'd. Chicago: Perfect Voice Institute, ca. 1915.

Ffrangçon-Davies, David. The singing of the future ... preface by Sir Edward Elgar. London: J. Lane, Bodley Head, 1906. (Another ed. , 1920; A Reprint, Champaign, Ill. : Pro Musica Press, 1968.)
Ffrangçon-Davies [1860-1918] was an English baritone, a pupil of Randegger and Shakespeare. He flourished as a professional singer between 1890 and 1895. In 1903 he secured the position of teacher of singing at the Royal Academy of Music in London.
Champion of the psychological-natural school of singing, the author is left with little tangible to discuss, so he indulges in pages of purple prose. For example, 85 pages are devoted to answering the question, "What is singing?"

Field, Maria Antonia. Five years of study under Fernando Michelena. San Francisco: private printing, ca. 1922.

Fillebrown, Thomas. Resonance in singing and speaking. Boston: O. Ditson, 1911.

"It is attempted in this volume only to describe the value of each element in the production of the perfect tone and to demonstrate the principles which, if properly and faithfully applied, will develop the best that is possible in each individual voice ..." [Introduction]. Dr. Fillebrown considers resonance the most important factor in singing.

Fischer, Eugen. Neue Gesangschule, mit praktischen Beispielen auf den Grammophon, unter Mitwirkung von Elise Elizza. Leipzig: Breitkopf & Härtel, 1910.

Flatau, Theodor Simon. Das habituelle Tremoliren der Singstimme; neue Beitrage zur Lehre von den Stimmorganen der Sänger. 2nd ed. Berlin: A. Stahl, 1903.

Fles, Anna. Spreken en zingen. Tiel: D. Mys, 1923.

Fontana, Bartolommeo. The musical manual; containing both the theory and practice of instrumental and vocal music. London: Hamilton Adams and Co. , 1847.

Forchhammer, Jörgen. Theorie und Technik des Singens und in gemeinverständlicher Darstellung. Leipzig: Breitkopf & Härtel, 1921. [NYPL]

Foreman, Edward, comp. The Porpora tradition. N. p. : Pro Musica Press, 1968. Facsimiles of D. Corri's The singers' preceptor published in 1810, and the 2nd ed. I. Nathan's Musurgica vocale, published in 1836. [WCC]

Formes, Karl Johann. Karl Formes' method of singing for soprano and tenor. 2nd ed. [San Francisco]: n. p. , ca. 1885.

Fröhlich, Joseph. Systematischer Unterricht zum Erlernen und Behandeln der Singkunst, überhaupt, so wie des Gesanges in öffentlichen Schulen und der vorzüglichsten Orchester-instrumente. 2 vols. Würzburg: Gedruckt bey J. Corbeth, 1822-29.

Frossard, Henri Jean. La Science et l'art du chant; méthode complete de voix. Paris: C. Delagrave, 1914. This book, with additional material, was published as La Science et l'art de la voix; méthode complete de voix; méthode complete de voix à l'usage de tous ceux qui parlent ou chantent. Paris: Les Presses Universitaires de France, 1927.
     The pure science of voice production takes much more space than methodology. Hygiene is also stressed. Frossard agrees with Broekhaven in the theory of vocal sound production.

Fucito, Salvatore, and Beyer, B. J. Caruso and the art of singing, including Caruso's vocal exercises and his practical advice to students and teachers of singing ... with ten portraits and caricatures. New York: Frederick A. Stokes Co. , ca. 1922.

Fucito was Enrico Caruso's coach and accompanist from 1915 to 1921.

"I hope that I could pass on to all who are concerned with the art of singing Caruso's methods in breathing and producing tones, his vocal exercises and his views on vocal techniques, his ideals of singing as well as his practical advice to singers" [Preface]. Fucito's book is a better pedagogic work than Caruso's How to sing, especially in its presentation of exercises, yet more than half the book is a biography.

Furtado, Charles. General observations on the vocal art. London: Addison & Hollier, 18--. [NYPL]
Few rules are presented. A total system of education for the singer is suggested, including elocution, ballet and fencing.

Gaertner, Carl. The art of singing. For the pupils of his National Conservatory of Music. Philadelphia: the author, 1871. [NYPL] Another ed. , Boston: Osgood & Co. , 1871.

The Gamut; or, Rules of singing; being a concise introduction to practical music. Utica, N. Y. : Seward & Williams, 1815.

Ganter-Schwing, Joseph. The American method of tone production. Chicago: n. p. , ca. 1911.

Garaudé, Alexis de. Méthode complete de chant. Paris: Vaillant, 1825?. [NYPL] Italian ed. , Milan: Lucca, 183-. [NYPL]

_____. Nouvelle Méthode de chant et de vocalisation. Paris: chez l'auteur, 1809.

Garcia, Gustave. A guide to solo singing. London: Novello, ca. 1912. [PU]

Garcia, Manuel Patricio Rodriguez. A complete treatise on the art of singing. Eds. of 1847 & 1872 collated, edited and translated. New York: Da Capo Press, 1975. Also, Ecole de Garcia, traité complet de l'art du chant en deux parties. 9th ed. Paris: n. p. , 1893.
Garcia (1805-1906) was the most celebrated voice teacher of the nineteenth century. The son of the Rossini tenor, Manuel Popolo Vicente Garcia [real name Rodriguez], he studied with his father. He had a brief operatic career as a bass, singing with his family in the United States. He then turned to teaching. In 1855 he invented the laryngoscope; many consider him the father of scientific voice-teaching. However, there is reason to believe that much of his teaching is also a product of intercourse with pupils of Porpora. Among his pupils were Jenny Lind, Henriette Nissen, Mathilde Marchesi, Charles Santley and Henrietta Sontage.
This publication contains as Part One the Mémoire sur la voix humaine [see below] and adds to it the application of technique, especially in the interpretation of song.

_____ . Garcia's treatise on the art of singing; A compendious method of instruction, with examples and exercises for the cultivation of the voice. Edited by Albert Garcia. London: Leonard & Co. , 1924. [NYPL]
Much like the famous Vocal Wisdom issued under Lamperti's name, this volume, edited by the grandson of Garcia, contains many vocal hints in the form of the master's collected aphorisms.

_____ . Hints on singing. New York: Schuberth & Co. , 1894. [IU] Reprinted, Canoga Park, Calif. : Summit Pub. Co. , 1970.
A question and answer format leads the reader through a blending of scientific thought and traditional teaching methods. The much-debated coup de glotte is taught. The major embellishments are still included, demonstrating Garcia's traditional grounding.

_____ . Mémoire sur la voix humaine présenté à l'Académie des sciences en 1840. Paris: E. Suverger, 1849. [NYPL]
Describes Garcia's theories on register formation, on the nature of timbres and their application to each voice classification.

_____ see also Lankow, Anna

Garsó, Siga. Schule der speziellen Stimmbildung auf der Basis des losen Tones, mit praktischen Übungen. Berlin-Gross Lichterfelde: C. F. Vieweg, 1908.

Gautier, Marcel. Principes et techniques du chant. Paris: chez l'auteur, 1925.

Gelder, Marie Margaretha van. The foundation of artistic singing; practical rules for obtaining perfect breath control, true intonation, strength and beauty of tone. Atlanta, Ga. : Foote & Davies Co. , ca. 1916. [NYPL]

Gervinus, Victorie Schelver. Naturgemässe Ausbildung in Gesang und Clavierspiel mit besonderer Rücksicht auf Gemeinschaftlichen Unterricht nebst einer Harmonielehre und einer gewählten Sammlung von Lieder und Clavierstücken. Leipzig: Breitkopf & Härtel, 1892. [PU]

Gib, Charles. The art of vocal expression, a popular handbook for speakers, singers, teachers and elocutionists. London: W. Reeves, 1913.

_____ . Vocal science and art, being hints on the production of musical tone, the boy's voice, muscular relaxation, the art of deep breathing, elocution for ordination candidates. London: W. Reeves, 1911. [NYPL]

_____. Vocal success; or, Thinking and feeling in speech and song, including a chapter on ideal breathing for health. London: W. Reeves, 1922. [NYPL]

Gill, James. Golden rules for singers. Chicago: G. Gregory, 1899.

Girard, Mary Augusta Brown. Vocal art; how to tune a voice and make it a beautiful instrument; advice to singers by Mrs. M. A. B. Girard. Chicago: John F. Cuneo Co., 1909.

Glubka, Isidore F. A. Secrets of correct and beautiful singing. Chicago: the authoress, ca. 1926.

Goldschmidt, Bruno. Ein ärztlicher Ratgebar für Gesangstudierende. Berlin & Lichterfelde: B. Behr, 1914.

Goldschmidt, Hugo. Der Vokalismus des neuhochdeutschen Kunstgesanges und der Bühnensprache; eine sprach- und gesangphysiologische Studie. Leipzig: Breitkopf & Härtel, 1892.

Goodrich, Alfred John. How to sing: An explanatory treatise upon the resources and development of the human voice and the manner of producing various styles and effects; In three numbers. N.p.: n.p., ca. 1877.

Gordon y de Acosta, Antonio María de. Consideraciones sobre la voz humana. Havana: Empr. Militar, 1899.

Graben-Hoffmann, Gustav. Die Pflege der Singstimme und die Gründe von der Zerstörung und dem frühzeitigen Verlust derselben. Dresden: B. Wienecke, 1865.

Granier, Jules. Le Chant moderne; étude analytique. 2 vols. Paris: J. Hamelle, 1914-1920.

Grant, Herbert A. Vocal art as nature intended ... based on the principles of the old Italian singing masters. Boston: Vocal Art Music Co., 1903.

Greene, Harry Plunket. Interpretation in song. New York: Macmillan Co., 1912.

Greene, Herbert Wilbur. The singer's ladder. New York: C. Fischer, 1920.
 Using a psychological approach, blending natural endowments with diligent practice, Greene promises to lead the singer up his "ladder of technic" to success.

Grosheim, Georg Christoph. Über Plege und Anwendung der Stimme. Mainz: B. Schotts Söhne, 1830.

Guetta, Paolo. Il canto nel suo meccanismo; con 24 incisioni. Milan: U. Hoepli, 1902.

Guillemin, Auguste. Sur la génération de la voix et du timbre. Paris: Société d'Etudes Scientifiques, 1897.

Guttmann, Oscar [also Oskar]. Gymnastics of the voice; a system of correct breathing in singing and speaking. 2nd ed. New York: E. S. Werner, 1887. Also, 7th ed. , retitled: Gymnastics of the voice for song and speech; also a method for the cure of stuttering and stammering. New York: Edgar S. Werner & Company, 1927.
    "When, in 1860, the author made the attempt to write Gymnastics of the voice, he was almost alone in this field. So far as he knew, no one had published a method of vocal gymnastics for speakers and singers, based upon physiological laws" [Preface]. Singing is approached as an athletic art, employing a knowledge of anatomy and physiology as well as pre-vocal exercises.

_____. Key to the Guttman tables, illustrating gymnastic exercises for the development of breathing, voice and speech simultaneously. New York: the author, 1885.
    " ... I have observed, that directions for exercises, in the comprehension of which the eye takes a part, yield much quicker and surer results than such as are merely described in words" [p. 1]. Guttmann therefore attaches numerous symbols to selected lines of poetry to correct problems of breathing, phonation and diction.

Gutzmann, Hermann. Stimmbildung und Stimmpflege; gemeinverständliche Vorlesungen. 2nd ed. Wiesbaden: J. F. Bergmann, 1912.

Hacke, Heinrich. Lerne singen! Volkstümliche Sprech- und Singlehre zum Selbstunterricht. 2 vols. Berlin: Lorelei Verlag, 1905.

Hahn, Reynaldo. Du chant. Paris: P. Lafitte, 1920.

Hall, Flavil. Hall's Rudiments of music. Plain, concise and practical lessons for students in vocal music. Cincinnati: F. L. Rowe, ca. 1925.

Hallock, William, and Muckey, Floyd S. Rational scientific voice-production. New York: n. p. , 1896.

_____. Voice production and analysis. [Publication details not known.]

Hansen, Niels. Musikens første grundsaetninger anvendte paa syngekonsten i Sardeleshed. København: Trykt paa Glydendals forlag, 1777.

Haslem, W. E. Style in singing. New York: G. Schirmer, 1911.

Hastings, Thomas. Elements of vocal music, arranged as a brief text book for classes. New York: E. Collier & Co. , 1839. [NYPL]

_____. The musical reader; or, practical lessons for the voice. Utica, N. Y. : William Williams, 1819.

Häuptner, Thuiskon. Aussprache und Vortrag beim Gesange, mit Berücksichtigung der neuesten wissenschaftlicher Forschungen auf diesem Gebiete; ein Supplement zu des Verfassers "Ausbildung des Stimme. " Leipzig: E. Eulenburg, n. d. 2nd ed. , 1897.

Hauser, Franz. Gesanglehre für Lehrende und Lernende. Leipzig: Breitkopf & Härtel, 1866.

Hays, Edward A. The principles of vocal science. New York: Vocalist Pub. Co. , 1897. [NYPL]

Haywood, Frederick H. Universal song: some instruction in the culture of the human voice and the art of singing. Twenty lessons embracing the fundamental principals [sic] of automatic breathing and automatic breath control, together with the development of the vowel forms. New York: the author, 1917. [NYPL]

Heinrich, Max. Correct principles of classical singing, et cetera. Boston: Lothrop, Lee & Shepard Co. , 1910.
    Heinrich (1853-) was a German tenor (not baritone as is incorrectly stated in at least one biographical dictionary), writer and composer. He studied with Klitzsch at Zwickau. He taught at the Royal Academy of Music, London and later in Philadelphia and Chicago. He gave a series of successful concerts in New York between 1882-1888 and excelled in oratorio.
    Emphasis on diction and interpretation characterizes Heinrich's work. He is opposed to complex methods. Oratorio pieces make up the bulk of the examples.

Heinrich, Traugott. Studien über deutsche Gesangsaussprache; ein Beitrag zur Gewinnung einer deutschen Sangeskunst. Berlin: A. Duncker, 1905.

Heller, Gordon. The voice in song and speech. London: K. Paul Trench & Co. , 1917.

Helmore, Frederick. The Italian registers; voce di petto; voce di gola; voce di testa. London: J. Masters and Co. , 1887. [NYPL]

Henderson, William James. The art of the singer. Practical hints about vocal technics and style. New York: G. Scribner's Sons, 1906. Another ed. , 1920. [IU]

Henderson (1855-) was a music critic and writer. Self-taught in the art, he wrote criticism for both the New York Times and the New York Sun. He also wrote the librettos for Damrosch's The Scarlet Letter and Cyrano de Bergerac. With the craft of a professional writer and researcher, Henderson gives a straightforward presentation of rules and methods widely used in his time. He refers to the thoughts of many of the important writers in this field, dating back as far as d'Aubigny von Engelbrunner.

Henning, Karl Rafael. Die Unterscheidung der Gesangregister auf physiologisch Grundlage, mit besonderer Berücksichtigung der voix mixte. Leipzig: Gebrüder Hug, 1892.

Héritte-Viardot, Louise Pauline Marie. Die Natur in der Stimmbildung, für Redner und Sänger. Heidelberg: O. Pelters, 1906.

Herman, Reinhold Ludwig. An open door for singers; hints to vocalists. New York: G. Schirmer, 1912.

Herrmann, Georg. Die Stimmkrise; ein Läuterungs- und Heilmittel in der Bildung der menschlichen Stimme. Leipzig. F. Kistner & C. F. W. Siegel, 1926.

Herrmann, Heinrich. Die Bildung der Stimme. Berlin: Schuster & Loeffler, 1903.

Hess, Ludwig. Die Behandlung der Stimme vor, während und nach der Mutation mit physiologischer Begründung. Marburg: N. G. Elwert, 1927.

Hey, Julius. Deutscher Gesangs-Unterricht; Lehrbuch des sprachlichen und gesanglichen Vortrags. Mainz: B. Schott's Söhne, ca. 1888. [NYPL]

Hiebsch, Josef. Methodik des Gesangunterrichts. Vienna: A. Pichlers Witwe & Sohn, 1893.

Hild, Amélie. The art of singing. New York: Press of L. May, 1903.

_____. Our modern school of singing. Seattle: Lowman & Hanford Co. , cop. 1913.

Hiller, Johann Adam. Anweisung zum musikalisch-zierlichen Gesange, mit hinlänglichen Exempeln erläutert. Leipzig: J. F. Junius, 1780. 1st ed. : 1774. Another ed. , 1798. Hiller [real name Hüller] (1728-1804) was a German singer, composer and writer. He was a pupil of Homilius at Dresden. At Leipzig he served as both flautist and singer. In 1771 he founded a school of singing in Leipzig. From 1789 to 1801 he was music director at the Thomasschule. He is perhaps best remembered as the father of the Singspiel form.

Hiller issues a plea for the development of better voice training in Germany to rival that of the Italians. In the areas of range, diction and interpretation the work equals or surpasses any of the time. Hiller is one author who does not show respect to Mancini: "Es tut mir leid, das ich nicht viel zu meiner Absicht Brauchbares in diesem Buche gefunden habe. Practische Beyspiele fehlen fast ganz darinne" [v.].

_____. Kurze und erleichterte Anweisung zum Singen für schulen in Städten und Dörfern. Leipzig: Johann Friedrich Junius, 1792.

Hoche, Curt. Die Quintessenz des Kunstgesangunterrichts. Stuttgart: J. G. Cotta, 1912.

Hogdon, William A. The teachers' manual; a music primer and course of study with general suggestions to teachers. New York: Silver, Burdett and Company, 1896.

Holmes, William Gordon. The science of voice production and voice preservation. London: Chatto & Windus, 1880. [NYPL]
Holmes (1845-) was a physician to the Municipal Ear & Throat Infirmary, Edinburgh.
He writes of this edition: "It is an abridgement of my 'Treatise on vocal physiology and hygiene' for the use of those who do not require to study the subject in all its technical and theoretical bearings" [Preface].

_____. A treatise on vocal physiology and hygiene, with especial reference to the cultivation of the voice. London: J. & A. Churchill, 1879. [NYPL]
"The chief aim of this treatise is to furnish persons who make an artistic or professional use of the vocal organs with a concise, but complete account of those scientific relations of the voice, physical and medical, which are generally only alluded to cursorily or passed over altogether in works on elocution and singing ... " [Preface].

Höpflingen, Irma von, und Bergendorf, Maria. Renaissance der Gesangs- und Sprechkunst. Vienna: W. Braümuller, 1913.

Hopkins, Jerome. A method for teaching Orpheus singing classes on the famous system of Wilhelm and Hullah. New York: S. T. Gordon, ca. 1865. [NYPL]

Horspool, J. The alpha and omega of voice production. London: Albion House, 1911.

How to cultivate the voice; or, Singing made easy; explaining the pure Italian method for producing and cultivating the voice, management of the breath, etc. New York: G. Blackie & Co. , ca. 1875.

Howard, John. Expression in singing, including thirty-one exercises for voice culture. New York: n. p. , 1904.

_____. Papers illustrating the revoluntionary principles of the Howard method. Cincinnati: J. Church & Co. , ca. 1878.

_____. The physiology of artistic singing. Boston: J. Howard, 1886.

_____. Respiratory control for vocal purposes, inspiration--expiration. Albany, N. Y. : E. S. Werner, 1882.

Howe, James Hamilton. Voice culture and artistic singing, being a collection of rules and exercises for use in acquiring and developing pitch, breathing, execution. San Francisco: San Francisco College of Music, ca. 1901.

Hulbert, Henry Harper. Breathing for voice production. New York: Novelle, Ewer and Co. , 1903.
    Hulbert was house surgeon and clinical assistant, Throat Department, St. Thomas' Hospital, London. He was a lecturer in voice, hygiene and physical education to the University of London, Guildhall School of Music, etc.
    Basic rules of breathing are combined with many exercises in this work.

_____. Eurhythm: thought in action; the principles and practice of vocal and physical therapy designed for the use of teachers and students of vocal and physical education. London: Novello and Co. , 1921. [NYPL]
    A treatise on eurythmics, a fashionable concept at the time, with application to the study of singing.

Hurlbut, Harold. Voice fundamentals. New York: J. Fischer & Bro. , ca. 1916.

Iffert, August. Allgemeine Gesangschule. Leipzig: Breitkopf & Härtel, 1895. Another ed. , 1899.

Jacubert, Albert. Der Schüssel zum Naturgesetz des Singers. Berlin: Pass & Garlet, 1926.

James, Mary Ingles. Scientific tone production; a manual for teachers and students of singing and speaking. Boston: C. W. Thompson & Co. , 1903.

Joal, Joseph. On respiration in singing. Translated and edited by R. Norris Wolfenden. London: F. J. Rebman, 1895.

Killermann, Sebastian. Stimme und Sprache; ihre Entstehung, Ausbildung, und Behandlung. Regensburg: F. Pustet, 1910.

Kind, James. An introduction to the theory and practice of singing chiefly intended to facilitate the acquirement of singing at first sight, including 52 exercises, carefully selected and arranged for the practice of solfaing, on the plan of the late Mr. Webbe's "L'amico del principiante." London: the author, 1823.

Kingsbury, Frederick. The voice and the structure and management of the vocal organ. London: R. Cocks & Co., 18--. [NYPL]

Kirkland, Henry Stuart. Expression in singing; a practical study of means and ends. Boston: R. G. Badger, 1916.
   Kirkland is an adherent of the natural school, concentrating on development of interpretation and expression. "I have purposely avoided all discussion of the technical side, of that which is usually known as Method of Voice Production." [p. 16].

Kirkwood, Edith. A simple and practical method for obtaining correct voice production and for mastering the first principles of interpretation. [London: n.p., ca. 1914].

Kitchener, William. Observations on vocal music. London: Hurst, Robinson, and Co., 1821.

Klein, Herman. The bel canto with particular reference to the singing of Mozart. London: Oxford University Press, 1923. Also available in facsim.: Ann Arbor, Mich.: University Microfilms, 1976.
   Klein (1856-1934) was an English singing-teacher and critic. For a while, Manuel Garcia lived at Klein's parents' home in London. Klein studied with Garcia for four years and edited Hints on Singing. He taught for 13 years at the Guildhall School of Music. From 1881-1901, he served as critic for The Sunday Times. In 1903 he issued Thirty Years of Musical Life in London, a valuable chronicle.
   Much of The bel canto deals with Mozart's vocal music (which Klein considered the epitome of bel canto) and the techniques necessary to sing it. The rest is a reiteration of Garcia's favorite maxims.

Kofler, Leo. Die Kunst des Atmens als Grundlage der Tonerzeugung für Sänger, Schauspieler, Redner, Lehrer. Kassel: Bärenreiter Verlag, n.d. English translation: Art of breathing as the basis of tone production. New York: E. S. Werner, 1889. Also, 7th ed., 1897.
   Kofler (1837-1908) was an Austrian organist and singing-teacher. He studied at Stern's Conservatory in Berlin. In 1866 he emigrated to America and held various positions as an organist.
   All aspects of singing (not only breathing) are discussed. A scientific methodology is presented. Each major idea is clearly marked in the text.

_____. Take care of your voice; or, the golden rule of health.

New York: E. S. Werner, 1889. [BPL]
This is basically a vocal hygiene book, but indications of
things to be done to maintain the voice present an indirect
singing methodology.

Kohut, Adolph. Johannes Miksch, der grösste deutscher Singemeister
und sein Gesangssystem. Leipzig: C. Rühle, 1890.

Kuerzinger, Ignaz Franz Xaver. Getreuer Unterricht zum Singen
mit Manieren, und die Violin zu spielen. Augsburg: J. J.
Lotter und Sohn, 1793. [NYPL]

Kwartin, Bernard. Der moderne Gesangunterricht. Vienna: C.
Konegen [E. Stülpnagel], 1910. [NYPL]

_____. Prinzipien für Stimmbildung und Gesang. Leipzig: Uni-
versal-Edition, 1911. [NYPL]

Lablache, Louis. A complete method of singing for the bass voice
... with illustrative examples, exercises & progressive studies
in vocalization. Boston: O. Ditson, 184-.
Louis (or Luigi) Lablache (1794-1858) was generally considered the greatest bass singer of his time. He was a pupil
of Valesi at the Conservatorio della Pietà de' Turchini. He
made his debut at Teatro San Carlino, Naples 1818. He
created eight roles for Donizetti, including Don Pasquale, and
sang many Bellini roles as well. In London, he served for a
while as Queen Victoria's singing master. He retired in 1852
because of poor health.
This work is the best of the class of instruction-exercise
books of this period. The first ten pages are filled with the
general advice common at this time. Thereafter, the exercises
are arranged according to vocal difficulties with brief comments
interposed.

_____. Méthode complète de chant; vol. 1, sop. & ten., vol. 2,
bass & bar. Mayence: Les Fils de B. Schott, n. d. This
book appears in both English and Italian translations: Lablache's
complete method of singing, or, a rational analysis of the
principles to which the studies should be directed for developing
the voice and rending it flexible. Chicago: Root & Sons Co.,
n. d. Other eds., Boston: Wilkins, Carter & Co., n. d.; Boston: O. Ditson & Co., ca. 1860. Italian ed., Metodo complete di canto. Milan: G. Ricordi, 18--.
The two volumes of this edition closely resemble the contents and structure of the work for bass voice.

Labriet, Alfre Eduoard. La Chant scientifique. Nancy: the author,
1927.

Lacombe, A. La Science du mécanisme vocal et l'art du chant.
Paris: Enoch, 1876. [NYPL]

Lagourgue, Charles. The secret; vocal feelings and reactions. [Chicago: H. C. L. Pub. Co. , ca. 1924].

La Madeleine, Stéphen de. Théories complètes du chant. Paris: Amgot, 1852.

Lamperti, Francesco. L'arte del canto in ordine alle tradizioni classiche ed particolare esperienza. Milan: Ricordi, ca. 1883. [NYPL]
   Francesco Lamperti (1813-1892) was an Italian singing-teacher. He studied at the Milan Conservatory, where he later taught (1850-1875). Thereafter, he gave private lessons. His pupils included Albani, Artôt, Campanini, Cruvelli, Sembrich and Shakespeare.
   This is an expansion on Lamperti's first volume [see next entry], with more anatomy and physiology. The chapters on Italian dialetical variations are unique in the literature.

_____. Guida teorica-practica-elementare per lo studio del canto. Milan: T. di G. Ricordi, 1864. [NYPL] Also, A treatise on the art of singing ... trans. by his pupil J. C. Griffith. New York: E. Schuberth & Co. , 1871? [NYPL] Other English eds. : London: G. Ricordi & Co. , ca. 1877; New York: G. Schirmer, ca. 1890 [NYPL]; reprint of 1877 ed. , The art of singing. New York: G. Schirmer, 1916?
   The Guida is, as the title states, practical and elementary. A teacher-pupil format leads the reader through the fundamental precepts. Annotated, graded exercises follow. Special emphasis is put on breath pressure and support.

Lamperti, Giovanni Battista. The technics of bel canto. New York: G. Schirmer, 1905.
   Giovanni Battista Lamperti (1840-1910) was the son of Francesco Lamperti, and a student and exponent of his father's teachings which, he claims, "I can trace back to the Italian singing-masters Gasparo Pacchierotti (d. 1821), Giovanni Battista Velluti (d. 1861), and others" [Preface]. He taught chiefly in Milan, Paris and Dresden. Sembrich was one of his pupils.
   This is a small work (only 36 pages). Originally issued in German, it has proved one of the most popular turn-of-the-century works. This is perhaps due to its clarity, brevity and unity. Exercises are joined to the text as illustrations and as corrective devices. Some editions have an incorrect "Diagram of the Action of the Diaphragm" on page 6. Letter 'a' should read 'Inspiration,' and letter 'b' should read 'Expiration. ' This error was pointed out by W. J. Henderson in his The Art of the Singer (1906).

Langethal, Heinrich. Elementare Gesanglehre nach Grundsätzen der neueren Pädagogik. Leipzig: R. Forberg, 1877. [NYPL]

Lankow, Anna. Supplement to vocal art. New York: Breitkopf &

Härtel, 1901.
This supplement adds information on the male voice and on
the use of the upper range in all voices. The author calls
for a rediscovery and reusing of the voix mixte in the tenor's
upper range.

_____; Brömme, Adolph; and Garcia, Manuel. Kunstgesang
Schule ... mit praktischen Übungs-material. Vocal art, by
Anna Lankow. English translation by E. Buck. (New York:
F. Luckhardt, ca. 1899).
The English is printed on the left column, the German on
the right. Lankow teaches conscious control of registration.
She also claims to have discovered an ultra-high coloratura
register which she named "flageolot."

_____, and Garcia, Manuel. The science of the art of singing.
3rd ed. Translated into English by E. Buck. New York:
Breitkopf & Härtel, 1903. [BPL]
A straightforward compilation of scientific investigations
into phonation and resonation is applied to good singing. This
work represents a serious attempt to show how the laws of
physics have direct bearing on the voice.

Lankow, Edward. How to breathe right. New York: E. J. Clode,
ca. 1918.

Lanza, Francesco Giuseppe. Lanza's abridgement of his work on
the art of singing. Philadelphia: Blake, 183-. [BPL]
Francesco Giuseppe Lanza (d. 1862) was an Italian composer
and singing-teacher. He taught in Naples, then, beginning in
1793, in London.
Seven pages of rules are followed by 34 pages of exercises.
Much space is given to embellishments.

Lanza, Gesualdo. Lanza's elements of singing (in the Italian &
English styles). London: the author, 1813?
Gesualdo Lanza (1779-1859) was the son of Francesco Lanza.
He was a professor of singing in London and the author of a
dictionary of musicians (1827).
Sixteen of 96 pages are rules, the rest exercises. The
position of the mouth is considered very important to the tone.
Solfeggio is stressed. The book of the son closely resembles
that of the father. Since the book is printed at the author's
expense it may be surmised that he sold it to his pupils to
provide them with his basic rules and the exercises that would
be covered during lessons. Anfossi, Corrette, Duval and
King are others who published their own books during this
period.

Larkcom, Agnes J. The singer's art. London: Novello and Co.,
1920.

Larson, G. T. Everybody's self-culturing vocal method. St. Louis:
n. p., 1914. [NYPL]

Lasser, Johan Baptist. Vollständige Anleitung zur Singkunst so wohl für den Sopran, als auch für den Alt. Munich: Gedrückt mit Hübschmannschen Schriften, 1805.

    Lasser (1751-1805) was an Austrian singer and composer. He is variously listed as a tenor or a bass. He served as musical director at Brno, Linz and Graz. In 1791 he settled in Munich. He wrote about ten Singspiele.

    Most of Lasser's work is given to exercises, which he divides according to voice type. Breath study is basically confined to laws of dividing syllables.

Lawton, William Henry. The singing voice and its practical cultivation; exercises and studies for the controlling of the breath, facial muscles, and vibrations of the head, with historical and personal observations. New York: C. Francis Press, 1901. [NYPL]

Lefort, Jules. De l'émission de la voix. Paris: E. Heu, 1868.

Lehmann, Lilli. Meine Gesangkunst. Translated by Richard Aldrich. New York: Macmillan Co., 1912. Also, rev. and supplemented ed., translated by Clara Willenbücher; also released under title, How to Sing. New York: Macmillan Co., 1906. Also, 3rd ed., 1924.

    Lehmann (1848-1929) was a German dramatic soprano. She was taught by her mother, Marie, a leading soprano at Kassel. Lilli debuted in Prague in 1870. She sang in the premiere productions of the Ring des Nibelungen; Wagner himself coached her. Her pupils included Farrar and Fremstad.

    Meine Gesangkunst is one of the most notorious of vocal pedagogic works. This is due to Lehmann's singular theories on the use of sensations and of vowel placement to develop the timbre of the voice. The criticism is primarily leveled at her emphasis on local effort images based on her own sensations. Nevertheless, much of her teaching concurs with accepted thought on voice production.

Leipoldt, Friedrich. Stimme und Sexualität. Leipzig: Dörfling & Franke, 1926.

Lemaire, Theophile, and Lavoix, Henri. Le Chant, ses principes et son histoire. Paris: Heugel et fils, 1881.

Lepanto, J. M. Sprech- und Gesangsunterricht, ein Leitfaden der Tonsbildungslehre und Vortragskunst. Leipzig: Breitkopf & Härtel, 1910.

Leslie, Charles Eddy; Shaw, Clement B.; and Jacobs, F. D. The teacher's manual. Chicago: Chicago Music Co., ca. 1892.

Liévens, Léon. Méthode de voix labiale ideale, applicable aux chanteurs des deux sexes. 2nd ed. Paris: n.p., ca. 1925.

_____. La Vérité vocale sur la voix humaine, parlée, declamée, chantée. Yvetot, France: Imprimerie Commerciale, ca. 1925.

Litvinne, Félia. School of singing. Paris: Heugel, ca. 1924.

Loebmann, Hugo. Die "Gesangbildungslehre" nach Pestalozzischen Grundsätzen von Michael Traugott Pfeiffer und Hans Georg Nägeli in ihrem Zusammenhange mit der Aesthetik der Ge- schichte der Pädagogik und der Musik. Leipzig: Druck der Germania, 1908.

Ludden, W. School for the voice; being an analytical, theoretical and practical treatise upon the proper use and development of the vocal organs: together with a progressive course of études and exercises written expressly for the education of the voice in the art of singing. Boston: O. Ditson, 1871. [NYPL]

Lunn, Charles. The philosophy of voice: showing the right and wrong action of voice in speech and song. To which is added, The basis of musical expression. 4th ed. London: Baillière, Tindall & Cox, 1878. Other editions: 5th ed. enl'd., London: Baillière, Tindall & Cox, 1886; ed. retitled The philosophy of voice, showing the right and wrong action of voice in speech and song with laws of self-culture. 9th ed. New York: G. Schirmer, 1900.
    Lunn (1838-1906) was an English tenor who received good reviews during his brief career (1864-1867). He chose to teach full-time and became noted for it. He was a pupil of Sangiovanni, Cattaneo and Vizione.
    "Five-and-twenty years ago I said I would restore the old Italian school of voice-training, and prove its truth by scien- tific research and discovery. I have done it" [Preface]. Much of Lunn's writing is based on Garcia, especially the subject of attack. Lunn also teaches use of the false vocal cords in attack. This popular book was well named because it is more a philosophical enquiry into voice production than a methodology.

_____. The voice: its downfall, its training and its use. A manual for teachers, singers, and students. London: Rey- nolds and Co., 1904.
    This is a more carefully written book than its predecessors. Lunn uses many other authorities to corroborate his beliefs. The work is divided into three parts: structural, technical, artistic. The last section is quite abstract and therefore of little practical use.

_____. Vox populi: a sequel to The philosophy of the voice. London: W. Reeves, 1880.
    This is a reprint of articles that appeared in The Orchestra. "This without the former work is incomplete, as that is with- out this" [Introduction]. Lunn refers often to the work of a Dr. Wyllie to prove that vocal production is a product of ventricular

controls. He also advises forward focusing of tone. Lunn is guilty of pseudo-scientific explanations to give credence to his opinions.

Lyman, Rollo LaVerne. Self-instruction in voice training; one of a series of lectures in a systematic course. Chicago: La-Salle Extension University, 1916.

McCarty, Marie Louise. The natural singing voice. St. Louis: Press of C. P. Curran Printing Co. , ca. 1905.

Mackenzie, Sir Morell. The hygiene of the vocal organs. A practical handbook for singers and speakers. London: Macmillan & Co. , 1886. Other eds. : 4th ed. , 1887; 1890; New York: E. S. Werner & Co. , 1928 [NYPL]; De Hygiene der Stemorganen; een Handleiding voor Zangers en Redenaars, door Sir Morell Mackenzie. Haarlem: de erven F. Bohn, 1888. [NY-PL]
  Sir Morell Mackenzie was Physician to the Royal Society of Musicians and consulting physician to the Hospital for the Disease of the Throat, London.
  "I have no pretension to speak with authority as a musician or even as a physiologist. . . . Matters belonging to either of these provinces are dealt with only in their relation to the well-being and functional efficiency of the vocal organs. " [Preface]. Despite this statement, Mackenzie does include precepts on correct production as preventative medicine for the voice. Emphasis is placed on breathing and registration.

McKerrow, Janet. The vocal movements and some others; a study of parallels. London: K. Paul, Trench, Trubner, 1925.

Mackinley, Malcolm Sterling. The singing voice and its training. London: G. Routledge & Sons, 1910.

McLellan, Eleanor. Voice education. New York: Harper & Brothers, ca. 1920.

Madelaine, Etienne Jean Baptiste. Physiologie du chant. Paris: Deslogues, 1840. [NYPL]

Magrini, Gustavo. Il canto, arte e tecnica. 2nd ed. rev. and corrected. Milan: Hoepli, 1918. [NYPL]

Mahlendorff, Paul J. The science and art of adjustment between the production and reflecting vocal apparatus, alias the philosophy of the intercondylar foramen, involving the solution of the problem of the human voice. 2nd ed. London: Marriot & Williams, 1904.

Mainvielle-Fodor. Joséphine. Réflexions et conseils sur l'art du chant. Paris: Perrotin, 1857.

Manchester, Arthur L. Twelve lessons in the fundamentals of voice production. Boston: O. Ditson, ca. 1908.

Mancini, Giambattista. Practical reflections on the figurative art of singing. Translated by P. Buzzi. reprint. Boston: R. G. Badger, 1912. [NYPL]

Manuale dell'artista de canto, da teatro, da camera e del dilettanto, per C. B. Genoa: Tip. della Gioventù, 1878.

Marafioti, Pasqual Mario. Caruso's method of voice production; the scientific culture of the voice. New York: D. Appelton and Co. , 1922.
     The author states that the aim of the book is to create a vocal pedagogy reform " ... founded on scientific laws, freeing the field of singing from both the unprogressive and empirical, though correct, method of the old Italian school, on the one hand, and the devastating influence of the arbitrary methods of voice culture created by incompetent teachers, on the other" [Preface]. Marafioti fails in this aim. He uses the major part of the book to vilify all other teachers and their theories while offering little of substance in their place. Enrico Caruso and his method has little actual relation to the work.

_____ . The new vocal art. New York: Boni & Liveright, 1925.
     Capitalizing on the popularity of his first book, Marafioti launches into a more abstract and generalized discussion of the vocal art, stressing naturalness and relaxation as the keys to success. He increases his attacks on other authors.

Marcel, P. L'Art du chant en France. Paris: L. Grus, 1900.

Marchesi, Blanche. Singer's pilgrimage. London: G. Richards, 1923. [NYPL]

Marchesi, Mathilde. The Marchesi school; a theoretical and practical method of singing. New York: G. Schirmer, 1903? [NYPL]. Also, an unabridged reprod. of ed. orig. pub. in London by Enoch & Sons, retitled Theoretical and practical vocal method. New York: Dover Publications, ca. 1970.
     Mathilde (Graumann) Marchesi de Castrone (1821-1913) was a noted German singing-teacher. She studied in Vienna with Nicolai and in Paris with Garcia. She taught in London, Vienna, Paris and Cologne. Among her pupils were Nellie Melba, Emma Eames, Emma Calvé, and Frances Alda. Her daughter was the singer Blanche Marchesi.
     The Marchesi school is structured like books written a century earlier. About 18 pages are given to verbalization of technique, the rest to "elementary and progressive exercises. " Marchesi follows Garcia's methods closely. She lays emphasis on the nature and control of registers.

_____ . Ten singing lessons, preface by Madame Melba. New

York: Harper & Bros. , 1901.
    In Ten singing lessons, Madame Marchesi outlines a plan
for living for her pupils, all of whom were women. The style
is loquacious and contains many personal reminiscences. The
second half of the book is written as if Marchesi had transcribed herself teaching a few lessons. These particular lessons are group sessions.

Marchesi, Salvatore. A vademecum for singing-teachers and pupils.
    New York: G. Schirmer, 1902.
    Salvatore de Castrone, Marchese della Rajata (1822-1908)
was a Sicilian nobleman, exiled for participation in the Revolution of 1848. He was a baritone and studied under Raimondi,
Lamperti and Fontana. He made his debut in New York. In
London (1852) he studied with Garcia and married Mathilde
Graumann. He was also known as a composer, translator of
libretti and as author of a famous set of vocalises.
    Marchesi offers a practical book of singing ideas. His
guiding ideal was that "the teacher must present his explanations in a practical, rather than theoretical way, the important
point being to acquire the assurance that the pupil thoroughly
understands what the master means" [p. 6].

Markwort, Johann Christian. Gesang-, Ton- und Rede- vortraglehre
    Erster Hauptteil: über Stimm- und Gehörausbildung, nebst
    dazu geeigneten Ubungsbeispielen. Ein Lehrbuch zur systema-
    tisch praktischen Entwicklung sämmtlicher Anlagen und Fähig-
    keiten für Ton- und Redevortrag. Darmstadt: In commission
    bei C. W. Leske, 1827.

Martens, Frederick Herman. The art of the prima donna and con-
    cert singer. New York: D. Appleton and Co. , 1923.
    This volume belongs in the class of books by Harriet Brower
and James Francis Cooke, except that Martens lays more
emphasis on the extra-musical aspects of the professional's
life. Nevertheless, many excellent concepts are brought to
light. "The one great rule for achievement in any art is as
valid today as it has been in the past: learn from the greatest
exponents of the art.... Here the greatest artists of our age
have placed at the student's disposal the results of their actual
technical and artistic experience" [Introduction].

Martienssen-Lohmann, Franziska [Meyer-Estorf]. Das bewusste
    Singen; Grundlegen des Gesangstudiums. Leipzig: C. F.
    Kahnt, 1923.

_____. Die echte Gesangkunst dargestellt an Johannes Messchaert.
    Berlin: B. Behr (F. Federsen), 1920.

_____. Stimme und Gestaltung; die Grundprobleme des Lied-
    gesanges. Leipzig: C. F. Kahnt, ca. 1927.

Martini, Jean Paul Egide. Mélopée moderne; ou, L'Art du chant, réduit en principes composé. Paris: chez Naderman, ca. 1792.

Marx, Adolf Bernhard. Die Kunst des Gesanges, Theoretisch-Praktisch. Berlin: A. M. Schlesinger, 1826.
    Marx (1795-1866) was a German theorist. He was a pupil of Rürk and Zelter. He was also co-founder of the Berliner Allgemeine Musik Zeitung (1824-1830).
    Only part of this work is spent on voice-training per se. The first section outlines fundamentals of music, and the last talks about general health and the treatment of diseases. He also surveys church music of many denominations. In the voice-building chapters, Marx concentrates on breathing and registration.

Mason, Lowell. Manual of the Boston Academy of Music for instruction in the elements of vocal music on the system of Pestalozzi. 2nd ed. Boston: J. H. Wilkins & R. B. Carter, 1836. 3rd ed., 1839; 5th ed., 1847.
    Mason (1792-1872) was an American music educator and writer. A self-taught musician, he is famous for a collection of hymn tunes published in 1822. Most of his life was spent in the direction of music for church and public schools. Between 1829 and 1854 he was champion of the introduction of the principles of Pestalozzi to Boston public schools.
    The Manual conforms to the format of H. W. Day's The vocal school. Mason, however, based his work on the volume produced by Pfeiffer and Nägeli.

Massell, James. To sing or not to sing; practical suggestions and exercises for voice culture, hygiene of voice and body, dietetics for singers. (New York): the author, 1926? 2nd ed., ca. 1926. [NYPL]

Massimino, Federico. Nouvelle Méthode pour l'enseignement de la musique. Paris: Bernard-Latte, 183- or 184-.

Mastrigli, Leopoldo. La respirazione nel canto; la respirazione nasale e la respirazione buccale; la respirazione artistica ed il tipo adottato antichi maestri italiani. Rome: G. B. Paravia, 1899.

Maurel, Victor. Le Chant rénové par la science. Paris: A. Quinzard & Cie, 1892.

_____. Un Problème d'art. Paris: Tresse & Stock, 1893.

Medini, Frances Röena. The what and how of vocal culture. New York: E. S. Werner, 1873.

Melba, Nellie Mitchell [pseud.]. Melba method. London: Chappell & Co., 1926. [BPL]
    Nellie Melba [real name, Nellie Helen Porter Mitchell Armstrong] (1859-1931) was an Australian dramatic soprano. She

studied with Mathilde Marchesi in Paris, 1886. She made
her debut in Brussels in 1887. She performed throughout
Europe, Russia and the United States in a career that lasted
39 years.

Madame Melba outlines her fundamentals in the first 17
pages, then gives a detailed program of her daily exercises.
Part Two consists of vocalises for low and high voice.

Melchissédec, Léon. Le Chant, la déclamation lyrique, le mécanisme
et l'émission de la voix. Paris: Milsson, 1925.

Mengozzi, B. Méthode de chant du Conservatoire du musique contenant les principes du chant des exercises pour la voix.
Florence: Giglio, 1807. [NYPL]

Merkel, Karl Ludwig. Der Kehlkopf, oder Erkenntniss und Behandlung des menschlichen Stimmorgans im gesunden und erkrankten
Gestände. Leipzig: J. J. Weber, 1873.

Meyer, Julius Eduard. A treatise on the origin of a destructive
element in the female voice as viewed from the register standpoint, with illustrative diagrams and musical notes. New
York: Breitkopf & Härtel, 1895.

Meyer-Teeg, Arnold W. Concerning the psychological system of
voice-culture, and the exercises pertaining thereto. Washington,
DC: n. p. , 1894.

Michael, Isaak. Die Bildung der Gesangregister; für Musiker und
Arzte. Hamburg: L. Voss, 1887. Translated into English
by G. H. Cornell: The formation of the singing registers;
for musicians and physicians. New York: G. Schirmer, ca.
1888.

Miles, Charles Chester. Basic elements of speech, song, and
melody. Chicago: C. C. Miles, 1922.

Miles, Walter R. "Accuracy of the voice in simple pitch singing. "
in Psychological Monographs (Princeton, N. J. vol. 17, no.
3 (1914), pp. 13-66. [NYPL]

Miller, Frank Ebenezer. Vocal art-science and its application.
New York: G. Schirmer, 1917. 2nd ed. : New York: G.
Schirmer, ca. 1922.

Miller (1859-1932) was an American tenor of modest regard.
He pursued a career of medicine, specializing in laryngology,
and served as physician to the Manhattan Opera House.

This volume is set up like a college textbook. Laws of
physics and acoustics are followed by anatomy and physiology.
There is a history of vocal scientists and their contributions.
Two unique chapters deal with tuning fork tests made with
Helen Keller, and with the powers of dynamic pyramids.

_____ . "Vocal art-science from the standpoint of the use and abuse of the voice." [Reprint from Music Teachers' National Association Proceedings for 1912; Hartford, Conn. , 1912; Ser. 7, pp. 124-129].

Miller presents material that dates back as far as Observations on voice and voice fatigue [see below, with Wangemann as coauthor], which he later incorporated into Vocal art-science and its application.

_____ . Vocal atlas, designed for teachers and students of singing and speaking. New York: Morton, 1912. [PU]

The Vocal atlas consists of a number of cross-sections and diagrams of the body, some in the act of producing sound. "It visually portrays the different positions of the vocal organs in tone production--positions which in life are illusively fleeting" [Introduction]. Local adjustments are indicated for each vowel and consonant.

_____ . The voice; its production, care and preservation. 6th ed. New York: G. Schirmer, 1910.

The Voice is a beau example of the complete vocal pedagogy text, ca. 1910: "... nature, physiology, and psychology must be combined in any book that professes to offer a synthetic method of voice production" [p. 5].

_____ , and Wangemann, A. Theo. E. "Observations about the human voice." This essay, incorporated in The science of the art of singing by Anna Lankow, was orig. read before the Music Teachers' National Association, June 27, 1898.

The essay is an examination of the laws of resonance, considering it to be the most important controllable factor in production, using the "hollow spaces of the head."

_____ and _____ . Observations on voice and voice fatigue. New York: Blumenberg Press, 1898? [NYPL]

Miller, George Harold. Tone production; a treatise on singing. Mitchell, S. D. : the author, ca. 1916.

Miller, Olin W. Miller's thorough vocal instruction, issued semi-monthly, containing lessons in the theory of music and vocal culture. Vol. 1, no. 1. York, Pa.: O. W. Miller, ca. 1888.

Mills, Charles Francis Henry. Voice and vocal exercises; a textbook for the student of singing. London?: n. p., ca. 1909.

_____ . Voice and vocalism, including the subjects of illustrated, descriptive and applied vocal anatomy as a book of reference, and vocalism; treating of the subtle influence of singing. Mount Vernon, Iowa: The Hawkeye Press, 1909.

Mills, Thomas Wesley. An examination of some controverted points of the physiology of voice, especially the registers of the sing-

ing voice and the falsetto.   Cambridge, Eng. :   n. p. , 1883.
[PU]
  Mills (1847-1915) was a laryngologist.

_____.   Voice production in singing and speaking, based on sci-
entific principles.   4th ed.   Philadelphia: J. B. Lippincott
Co. , 1913.
  The author "had tried to keep in mind the real needs of
the practical voice-user, and to give him a sure foundation
for the principles that must underlie sound practice" [Preface].
Anatomy, breath control, and hygiene receive the emphasis in
this scientific presentation.

Minoja, Ambrosio.   Über den Gesang.   Leipzig: Breitkopf & Härtel,
1815.
  Minoja (1752-1825) was an Italian conductor and singing-
teacher.   He succeeded Lampugnani as cembalist at La Scala
(1789-1809).   From 1814 to 1824 he taught composition at the
Conservatory in Milan.   He also wrote celebrated solfeggio
books.
  Über den Gesang is almost certainly a translation of Lettere
sopra il canto, Milan, 1812, which did not exist in any of the
libraries consulted for this bibliography.   The translation is
an expansive survey of singing in the author's time and earlier.
The prerequisites of singing and the necessities of good diction
are stressed.

Moll, Adolf.   Singen und Sprechen; die näturliche Stimmbildung
nach Bau und Tätigkeit der Stimmwerkzeuge.   Leipzig: P.
Reclam, 1927?   [NYPL]

Monroe, Lewis Baxter.   Manual of physical and vocal training, for
use of school and for private instruction.   Philadelphia: Cow-
perthwait & Co. , 1869.

Muckey, Floyd S.   The natural method of voice production in speech
and song.   New York: C. Scribner's Sons, 1915.
  Muckey (1858-) was an American singing-teacher.
  The author claims to be the first to present a natural
method of voice production.   Other authors' opinions are dili-
gently attacked.   Muckey recommends voice classes as a more
advantageous learning experience than individual lessons.

_____   see also   Hallock, William

Mueller, Brunow.   Tonbildung oder Gesangunterricht.   Beitrage zur
Aufklärung über das Geheimnis der schöne Stimme.   Leipzig:
C. Merseburger, 1890.   [NYPL]

Mueller, R.   Theoretisch-praktische Anleitung zum Studium des
Gesanges.   Leipzig: C. F. W. Siegel, 1859?   [NYPL]

Muscat, Giuseppe.   Practical suggestions about voice culture and

the art of singing. Trenton, N. J. : Cresse & Roberts, printers, 1896.

Myer, Edmund John. Position and action in singing. A study of
the true conditions of tone; a solution of automatic (artistic)
breath-control. 8th ed. Boston Music Co. , 1911. 2nd ed. ,
New York: E. S. Werner, 1897. Orig. copyright assigned
in 1897.
   Myer (1846-) was an American singing-teacher and prolific
writer on singing. He taught in New York, with summer
classes at Chautauqua.
   Myer introduces the phrase "correct position and action"
as the secret of automatic control. "Through right position
and action of the body a natural and automatic adjustment of
all parts is secured" [p. 25].

_____ . The renaissance of the vocal art; a practical study of
vitality, vitalized energy, of the physical, mental and emotional
powers of the singer, through flexible, elastic bodily movements. Boston: Boston Music Co. , 1902.
   Myer asserts that singing can be returned to the heights of
the bel canto period if the old masters' empirical truths will
be proved out by scientific investigation.

_____ . Truths of importance to vocalists. New York: W. A.
Pond & Co. , 1883.
   Myer's earliest work surveys the general ideas and methods
of other authors popular at the time. The reason that good
"singers are rare even among professionals [is] that the art
of voice culture is, as a rule, empirical, and, not as it
should be, scientific" [p. 11].

_____ . The vocal instructor. Philadelphia: T. Presser, ca.
1913.
   "The main object of this work is to give to the vocal profession for the first time in print, the movements upon which
the whole system is based: the stunts, the singing movements,
the physical exercises, and the nerve callisthenics. These
movements develop the singer physically and vocally" [p. 3].
Bodily positioning and corresponding exercises promise to
create conditions that will assure beautiful tones.

_____ . Vocal reinforcement; a practical study of the reinforcement of the motive power or breathing muscles; of the resisting force or resistance in singing. . . . Boston: Boston Music
Co. , 1891.
   Myer divides this work into three parts for physical, intellectual and aesthetic development. "Reinforcement" is his
watchword for this volume; that is, the balancing of pressure
and resistance in the trunk during the singing act. False vocal
band control is emphasized.

_____ . The voice from a practical standpoint. New York: W.
A. Pond & Co. , 1886.

274 / Annotated Bibliography

The restoration of nature's gifts is the guiding objective of
Myer's second book. "Nature, as a rule, has endowed man
with a perfect vocal apparatus ..." [p. 18]. "A right system,
then, of voice teaching, must be a corrective study" [p. 23].

Nathan, Isaac. An essay on the history and theory of music; and
on the qualities, capabilities and management of the human
voice. London: Printed for G. and W. B. Whittaker, 1823.
The 2nd ed., enl'd. and rev., was retitled Musurgia vocalis;
an essay on the history and theory of music; etc. London:
Fentum, 1836.
Nathan (1790/2?-1864) was an English composer and tenor.
He studied voice under D. Corri. He sang briefly at Covent
Garden, but it is said that his voice proved too small for
opera. Lord Byron provided Nathan with texts for his Hebrew
Melodies. Ill fortune forced Nathan to emigrate to Australia
where he became known as the father of Australian music.
Musurgia vocalis is perhaps the most complete work of its
time, not only as a singing instructor, but as a history and
theory book.

Nava, Gaetano. Method of instruction for the baritone voice; containing a complete system of solfeggi, vocalises & exercises,
with general rules on the art of singing.... Edited by his
pupil, Charles Santley. London: Boosey & Co., 187-.

_____. Practical method of vocalization for bass or baritone.
Edited by Henry Blower. With a biographical sketch of the
author by Dr. Th. Baker. New York: G. Schirmer, 1899.

Nehrlich, Christian Gottfried. Die Gesangkunst physiologisch,
ästhetisch und pädagogisch dargestellt. 2nd ed. Leipzig:
B. G. Teubner, 1853.

_____. Gesang-Schule für gebildete Stände. Ein theoretisch
practisches Handbuch für Alle, welche höheren Gesang lieben.
Berlin: zu haben im Locale des Gesangconservatoriums, 1844.

_____. Der Kunstgesang physiologisch, pädagogisch und ästhetisch
dargestellt. Eine Gesang-Schule für gebildete Stände. 2nd
ed. Stuttgart: H. Lang, 1859.

Neidlinger, William Harold. A primer on voice and singing ... with
illustrations by Walter Bobbett. Chicago: Rand, McNally &
Co., 1903.

Neuner, Gustav Erwin. Gesanglehre für Alle (besonders für den
Vereins- und Hausgebrauch). Stuttgart: A. Klein, 1924.

Nöe, Oskar, and Moser, Hans Joachim. Technik der deutschen
Gesangkunst. Leipzig: G. J. Göschen, 1912. Another printing, New York: Atlantic Pub. Co., 1921?

Nordica, Lillian. Lillian Nordica's hints to singers, together with an account of Lillian Nordica's training for the opera, as told in the letters of the singer and her mother, Amanda Norton; transcribed by William Armstrong. New York: E. P. Dutton and Co. , ca. 1923.

Nordica [real name Norton] (1857-1914) was a distinguished American soprano. She studied with John O'Neal at the New England Conservatory and made her concert debut in Boston, 1876. In Milan, she studied roles with Antonio San Giovanni. She made her operatic debut in 1879 and sang until her death, during a farewell tour in 1914.

How much of this book is directly attributable to Nordica herself is given to question. It was supposedly transcribed by William Armstrong, and it was written and published after Nordica's death. Nevertheless, Nordica's name made the book a favorite.

"'Hints to singers' is not a technical book on singing, but a summary of many things which Madame Nordica, in the making of a great career, learned through experience" [Introduction]. The book deals as much with the attitudes and background necessary to attempt a professional career as it does with vocal technique.

North, Alfred Augustus. Voxometric revelation; the problems surrounding the production of the human voice finally discovered, the source and origin of the voice of mankind revealed for the first time, also a true and complete theory for the production and training of every character of voice, both in song and speech ... written and compiled by Justus Abner for the author, Alfred Augustus North. London: Authors' & Printers' Joint Pub. Co. , 1896.

Novello, Mary Sabilla. Voice and vocal art. London: J. A. Novello, 1856. [NYPL]

Novello (d. 1904) was an English writer and soprano, the daughter of Vincent Novello. She is known chiefly through her voice books.

Madame Novello designs her precepts and vocalises "to develope and assure the four following excellencies: Management of breath. Correct intonation. Extended compass. Beauty of tone" [Introduction].

Nozat, F. L'Art du faire une voix. 3rd ed. [Paris]: Institut Lyrique, 190-. [PU]

Oldenbarnevelt, Jeanne van. The art of breathing, its relation to sounds and words, its service to art and science. 4th ed. , enl'd. , London: n. p. , 1910. [PU]

Oliver, Edward Battle. The vocalist's companion, or exercises for developing, strengthening and equalizing the voice; designed as introduction to and to be used in connection with the celebrated solfeggio exercises of Panseron, Cruvelli, Lablache & others. Boston: O. Ditson, 187?

Oliver was an American writer on music. Rules are alternated with exercises to develop correct habits.

Orsin, Alessandro. Considerazioni generali sull'arte del canto. Rome: Tip. della Pace, 1876.

Osgood, George Lawrie. Guide in the art of singing based on the reliable tradition of the Italian school of vocalization and practical development of modern science. Boston: Ditson & Co., 1874. [BPL]

Palmer, Edward Davidson. The tenor voice and its training. London: n. p., 190-.

Panofka, Heinrich. Gesangs--A B C; vorbereitende Methode zu Erlernung des Ansatzes und der Feststellung der Stimme zum Gebrauch in Seminarien, Gesangschulen, Gymnasium und Instituten. Leipzig: J. Reiter-Beidermann, ca. 1859. French translation: Abécédaire vocal; méthode préparatoire de chant pour apprendre à émettre et a poser la voix, etc. 10th ed. Paris: P. Maquet, 188-.
Panofka (1807-1887) was a Polish singing-teacher who began his musical career as a violinist. He settled in Paris in 1834 and studied singing under Bordogni. He and Bordogni founded a singing academy in 1842. Between 1844 and 1852, he lived in London, teaching voice and also serving as assistant conductor at His Majesty's Theatre.
The majority of Panofka's work consists of 24 progressively more difficult exercises, marked for the places that require a stroke of the glottis, swell, breath, etc. With the first exercises, the teacher sings and the pupil imitates.
The French and German editions differ considerably; paragraphs are rearranged or deleted.

Panseron, Auguste-Mathieu. The A B C of music; or Easy solfeggi; to which is added a short and easy method of vocalization. Translated by W. J. Wetmore. New York: S. T. Gordon & Son, ca. 1865. [NYPL]
Panseron (1795-1859) was a French singing-teacher. He was taught music by his father, who orchestrated many operas for Grétry. At the Paris Conservatory, Panseron studied with Gossec, Levasseur and Berton, winning the Prix de Rome (1813). He began teaching voice in Paris in 1818 and also served as accompanist at the Opéra-Comique.
Only the most rudimentary rules are included in this work which is meant as a general music instruction book for beginning singers.

Paris. Conservatoire National de Musique et de Déclamation. Méthode de chant du Conservatoire de musique à Paris, en 3 parties contenant 1. Les Principes du chant et des exercices pour la voix; 2. Des solfèges tirés des meilleurs ouvrages anciens et modernes; 3. Au dans tous les mouvements et les différénts caractères. Leipzig: Breitkopf & Härtel, 18--.

Parisotti, Luigi. A treatise on speaking and singing, according to the principles of the old Italian school. New York: Boosey & Co. , 1911.

 Parisotti carefully explains those local effort controls that he believes belonged to the "old Italian school" era. Correct speaking is a fundamental prerequisite: "For my part, having obtained the most beautiful results from the application of that simple fundamental principle of the old Italian school, 'chi parla bene canta bene' ('who speaks well sings well'), I have made this the keynote of my studies, and their ultimate object" [Preface].

Parker, John S. The voice in speaking and singing. The principles at the foundation of proper voice production, arranged in ten lessons. Viroqua, Wis.: L. R. Gott, ca. 1895.

Parry, John. The vocalist, or, The rudiments of solfeggio. In eighty practical lessons, calculated to prepare students for more elaborate singing preceptors. London: Goulding & d'Almaine, ca. 1822.

 This volume is bound with that of Thomas Philipps.

Pastou, Etienne Jean Baptiste. École de la lyre harmonique. Cours de musique vocale, ou Recueil méthodique des leçons de ... Pastou. Paris: chez l'auteur, 1822. [NYPL]

Pattou, Ange Albert. The art of voice production established on a true scientific basis. Philadelphia?: n. p. , ca. 1909.

_____. The art of voice-production with special reference to the methods of correct breathing. New York: G. P. Putnam's Sons, 1882. [NYPL]

_____. The voice as an instrument. New York: Edward Schuberth and Co. , 1878.

Pellegrini-Celoni, Anna Maria. Grammatica, o siano regole de ben cantare. Rome: P. Piale, e G. C. Martorelli, 1810.

Perino, Marcello. Nouvelle Méthode de chant. Translated from the Italian by Auguste L. Blondeau. Paris: Ebrard, 1839. [NYPL]

Perkins, Theodore E. Physiological voice culture, the only system that will develop compass, resonance, power, execution, methodically arranged from the physiology of artistic singing; special studies for choir singers. Philadelphia: A. Sutherland, ca. 1913.

Persichini, Pietro. Anfangsgründe des Gesanges. ms. , 1815.

Pestalozzi, August. Bewegungsphysiologische Voraussetzungen zur technischen Beherrschung der Musikinstrumente und des Gesangs und der Weg, sie zu erreichen, mit besonderer Berücksichtigung der Klaviertechnik. Berlin: Trowitzsch & Sohn, 1927.

Pestalozzi, Heinrich. Kehlkopfgymnastik, der Weg zu einer schönen Stimme auf Grund einer neuen Entdeckung eines Trainings der Stimmuskulatur [Stimmkultur?] Leipzig: F. E. C. Leuckart, 1925.

Petit, Albert. La Fonction vocale et l'art du chant; émission, exécution, interprétation. Paris: n. p. , 1923.

Pfeiffer, Michael Traugott, and Nägeli, Hans Georg. Auszug aus der Gesangbildungslehre nach Pestalozzian Grundsätzen, von Pfeiffer und Nägeli. Zurich: H. G. Nägeli, 1830. [NYPL]
    Pfeiffer (1771-1850) was a music educator and writer. His father was an organist and Kantor. Johann [Hans] Georg Nägeli (1773-1836) was a Swiss publisher, writer and composer and the founder and president of the Swiss Association for the Cultivation of Music. He also served as a singing-teacher at a primary school, applying the Pestalozzian system.
    This second volume is a summary of the materials of the first [see next entry], specifically designed for the teacher of this method, his qualifications, how he should conduct lessons, etc.

_____, and _____. Gesangbildungslehre nach Pestalozzischen Grundsätzen pädagogisch begründet. Zurich: H. G. Nägeli, 1810. [NYPL]
    The Gesangbildungslehre is a progressive course methodology designed in the Pestalozzian tradition. Breathing and phonation are emphasized.

Pfordten, Hermann Ludwig. "Grundlagen der Gesangkunst" in Musikalische essays. Munich: C. H. Beck'sche Verlagsbuchhandlung, 1897-99.

Philipps, Thomas. Elementary principles and practices for singing, being a compendium of exercises, in solfeggi, simplified and explained, for improvement in syllabic articulation and delivering of words as well as tone of voice and execution, and calculated to assist the labours of both master and scholar. Dublin: I. Willis & Co. , 1830.

Pinks, Emil. Atem-, Sprech- und Singtechnik, Anleitungen und Winke ... mit Abbildungen und Zahlreichen Notenbeispielen. Leipzig: P. Pabst, 1910.

Povani, Guido. Five lessons in voice culture ... translated from the Italian by Josephine Manners. Jacksonville, Fla. : Lloyd Printing Co. , ca. 1918.

Powell, Alma Webster (Hall). Advanced school of vocal art ... with extracts from the works of Eugenio Pirani. Brooklyn, N. Y. : Powell and Pirani Musical Institute, 1905.

Powell, Ella May. Psychology and technique of speech and song. Gainesville, Ga: Resthaven Publ. , ca. 1922.

Pownall, Joseph. The singing voice and its development. Being a treatise on the production, management and improvement of the voice. London: F. P. Hart & Co. , ca. 1906. [NYPL]

Praetorius, Carl. The tone placed and developed. Chicago: Faulkner-Ryan Co. , 1907.

Pratt, Waldo Selden. Outline study-notes in elocution and singing. Hartford, Conn. : Hartford Seminary Press, 1892.

Preston, George A. Foundation facts in the development of the voice. Spokane, Wash. : the author, ca. 1918.

Price, Addison. Self-help in voice production. Springfield, Mass. : Mussett Pub. Co. , ca. 1916.

Proschowsky, Frantz. The singing school of Frantz Proschowsky. Philadelphia: T. Presser Co. , ca. 1927. [NYPL]
    This is also a complete survey of vocal fundamentals. The author's major idea is that to learn to sing is to learn to listen.

_____. The way to sing; a guide to vocalism, with thirty practical exercises. Boston: C. C. Birchard & Company, ca. 1923.
    "Nature alone has provided the true Method of singing" [Preface]. Proschowsky's method is aimed at making the singing act second nature. A well-designed sequence of chapters on all major areas of vocal study are followed by progressive exercises.

Pruckner, Caroline. Theorie und Praxis der Gesangkunst; Handbuch für angehende Sänger und Sängerinnen. Vienna: K. Czermak, 1872. [NYPL]

Pynchon, Edwin. The bête noir of the vocalist. Chicago: Clinic Pub. Co. , 1899. [NYPL]

Rand, Josephine. Practical method of singing, based upon natural and artistic principles, including a thorough course of training in the art of breathing and voice-building, together with a carefully prepared set of vocal exercises. Boston: O. Ditson, ca. 1886. [NYPL]

Randegger, Alberto. Singing. London: Novello, 1912.
    Randegger (1832-1911) was an Austrian composer, teacher and writer. In 1854 he settled in London where he became famous as a singing-teacher. In 1868 he was appointed professor of singing at the Royal Academy of Music. From 1879 to 1885 he conducted with the Carl Rosa company and between 1887 and 1898 at Drury Lane and Covent Garden.

Randegger follows the style of fifty years earlier, giving the large part of the book to exercise while interposing basic precepts. Dr. Louis Mandl's Mechanism of the voice, a work quoted in many vocal pedagogy books, is presented in translation at the back of this volume.

Ranske, Jutta Bell. Health, speech, and song; a practical guide to voice-production. London: S. Sonnenschein & Co., 1902. [NYPL]

_____. Voice and nerve control ... with seventeen diagrams. New York: Frederick A. Stokes Company, 1915.

Reeves, John Sims. Sims Reeves on "the art of singing." 2nd ed. London: Chappell & Co., Ltd., 1901. 1st ed., 1900.

Reichert, Franz. Die Lösung des Problems eines freien Tones auf Anatomisch-physiologischer Basis, ein Leitfaden für Arzte, Gesangpadagogen und Studierende. Leipzig: C. F. Kahnt, 1919.

Reinecke, Wilhelm. Die Kunst der idealen Tonbildung. Studie für Sanger, Schauspieler, Redner, Lehrer, Prediger. Leipzig: Dörffling & Franke, 1906. Another ed., enl'd, 1910.

_____. Die natürliche Entwicklung der Singstimme. Leipzig: Dörffling & Franke, 1910.

_____. Vom Sprechton zum Sington. Von der Menschstimme zur Vollstimme. Leipzig: Dörffling & Franke, 1912.

Rennie, James. The art of improving the voice and ear; and of increasing their musical powers. London: S. Prowett, 1826. [NYPL]

Reparlier. Principes de musique, les agréments du chant, et un essai sur la pronunciation, l'articulation et la prosodie de la langue françoise. Lille: P. S. Lalau, 1772.

Rockstro, William Smyth. Jenny Lind; a record and analysis of the "method" of the late Madame Jenny Lind-Goldschmidt ... together with a selection of cadenze, solfeggi, abellimenti, &c. in illustration of her vocal art. London: Novello & Co., 1894.
    This is a reprint of one section of Jenny Lind, the Artist, by H. S. Holland and W. S. Rockstro.

Rockwood, Caroline Washburn. Foundation stages of tone production with graded exercises and piano accompaniment ... for speakers, readers and singers. Ashville, N. C.: Hackney & Moale Co., 1902.

Röder, Karl. Vorbereitungen auf die Gesangstunde. Quedlinburg: C. F. Vieweg, 1902.

Röder, Marlin. Fundamental vocal exercises known as the Italian
method of singing. Boston: Oliver Ditson Co. , 1923.

Rodolphe, Jean Joseph. Solfège de Rodolphe ... containing elementary & progressive lessons ... to which is added a new analytical method with French and English text ... by Leopold
Meignen. Philadelphia: Fiot, Meignen & Co. , 1836.

Rogers, Clara Kathleen. My voice and I; or, The relation of the
singer to the song. Chicago: A. C. McClurg & Co. , 1910.
[NYPL]
    Rogers (1844-1931) was an English soprano and singing-
teacher, the daughter of composer John Barnett. She studied
singing with Goetz in Berlin and Sangiovanni in Milan. She
made her opera debut in Turin in 1863 and sang under the
stage name Clara Doria throughout her career. She came to
the United States in 1871, settled in Boston as a singing-
teacher, and from 1902 was a professor of singing at the New
England Conservatory.
    "The chief purpose of the following work is to draw atten-
tion to certain radical errors in the education of singers....
It is an attempt to throw light on the principles which underlie
the true art of singing" [Preface]. The author again stresses
the need for the psychological approach, and the evils of local
effort adjustments. The importance of ear training is heavily
accented.

_____. The philosophy of singing. London: Osgood, McIlvaine
& Co. , 1895. Other eds. , New York: Harper & Brothers,
ca. 1895, and 1903.
    An excellent example of the psychological approach to teach-
ing voice. "This treatise might properly be called 'The Philosophy of Life'" [Preface]. Madame Rogers' philosophy is
of the turn-of-the-century ladies' tea-party variety, digressive,
personalized and not suitable to direct application by the student.

_____. Your voice and you (what the singer should do), a prac-
tical application of psychology to singing. Boston: Oliver
Ditson Co. , ca. 1925. [NYPL]
    "All that this book contains is the result of experience
rather than of either anatomical study or laryngoscopic observation... [for] all that we really know is that certain things
which we do bring certain results" [Preface]. The attitudes
of Madame Rogers' first two works are rephrased. This
volume lays more stress on diction (her separately published
English diction was highly successful).

Röhrke, Karl. Tonbildung und Aussprache. Stettin, Germany:
Selbstverlag des Verfassers, 1901.

Romer, Francis. The physiology of the human voice; being a
treatise on the natural powers of the vocal organ, pointing
out the difference between the speaking and singing quality of
tone. London: Leader & Cock, 1845. [NYPL]

Ruff, Albert Edward. Vocal fundamentals for speech and song; a brief treatise on the vocal muscular system. Los Angeles: A. E. Ruff, ca. 1926.

Rush, J. The philosophy of the human voice. Philadelphia: J. Maxwell, 1827. Other eds. , all Philadelphia, 2nd enl'd ed. , Gregg & Elliott, 1833; 3rd enl'd ed. , J. Crussy, 1845; 5th enl'd ed. , J. B. Lippincott & Co. , 1859; 7th end. , rev. , J. B. Lippincott & Co. , 1879.

Russell, Louis Arthur. The body and breath under artistic control for song and fervent speech; a text book for private or class instruction. Newark, N. J. : Essex Pub. Co. , ca. 1904.
    Russell (1854-1925) was an American organist, pianist, and singing-teacher. He studied with William Shakespeare and George Henschel in London. He founded the Newark College of Music (1885) and organized the Newark Symphony Orchestra (1893).
    Russell also published a popular diction work, English diction for singers and speakers, ca. 1905.
    This pamphlet teaches that local control of the breath muscles leads to automatic breathing.

_____. The commonplaces of vocal art; a plain statement of the philosophy of singing. Boston: Oliver Ditson Co. , 1907. Another ed. , 1912.
    Much of the contents of Russell's pamphlets is gathered and expanded upon in this popular work. Russell believes that close examination of the physical actions of singing is needed to achieve freedom, however, he advises an avoidance of any local effort in the throat.

_____. A plain talk with American singers. Newark, N. J. : Essex Pub. Co. , ca. 1904.
    Advice on the selection of a teacher and principles of practice are the highlights of this pamphlet.

_____. Some psychic reflections for singers. Newark, N. J. : Essex Pub. Co. , ca. 1904.
    The third pamphlet in this series contains generalized comments on a mental approach to voice study, that is correct attitude, perseverance, common sense, etc.

Russell, William. Elements of musical articulation ... with illustrations on vocal music by Lowell Mason. Boston: Wilkins, Carter & Co. , 1845. [NYPL]

Rutz, Ottmar. Neue Entdeckungen von der menschlichen Stimme. Munich: C. H. Beck, 1908. [NYPL]
    Rutz (1881-1952) was a German writer on voice. He was the son of Josef and Klara Rutz, both singing-teachers in Munich. His writings are a reflection of their practice.
    Rutz presents a theory that there are four types of singing

temperaments and that each requires a different technique as regards throat and facial positions and especially manipulation of the breathing muscles.

_____. Sprache, Gesang, und Körperhaltung. Munich: C. H. Beck, 1911. [PU]
This volume is an expansion of the first one. Here three of the four temperaments, warm lyric, warm dramatique and cold lyric are linked to nationalities: Italian, German and French respectively. Cold dramatique is not unique to any one national background.

Santley, Charles. The art of singing and vocal declamation. New York: Macmillan Co., 1908. [NYPL]
Sir Charles (1834-1922) was a noted English baritone. He studied with Nava in Milan, then with Garcia in London. He made his debut in 1857. During his career, he sang throughout the British Isles, Australia, and the United States and was knighted in 1907.
Too much space is devoted to reminiscences and not enough to technical discussion to call this a valuable pedagogic work. Almost as much of the book is spent on dramatic conception, acting and various theatres as is spent on the voice itself.

Schaul, Johann Baptist. Über Tonkunst, die berümtesten Tonkünstler und ihre Werke; in Briefen zur Bildung des Geschmacks in der Musik. Karlsruhe: G. Braun, 1818.

Scheel, Josef G. Lösung des Stimmproblems? Berlin-Lichterfelde: C. F. Vieweg, 1927.

Scheidemantel, Karl. Stimmbildung. Leipzig: Breitkopf & Härtel, ca. 1908. Another ed., 1913; 7th ed., 1920. English translation, Voice-culture. 2nd rev. ed. Leipzig: Breitkopf & Härtel, 1910. [PU]

Schilling, William Paul. Unique voice training studies. New York: the author, ca. 1923. [NYPL]

_____. The upper soprano tones, and how every soprano may acquire them to high C and above, without strain or effort. New York: W. P. Schilling, ca. 1910. [NYPL]

_____. The upper tenor tones, and how every tenor may acquire them without strain or effort. 2 parts. New York: W. P. Schilling, ca. 1910. Another ed., 1912. [NYPL]

Schmauk, Theodore Emanuel. The voice in speech and song. New York: J. B. Alden, 1890. [NYPL]

Schmid-Kayser, Hans. Der Kunstgesang auf Grundlage der deutschen Sprache. Berlin-Lichterfelde: C. F. Vieweg, 1922. [NYPL]

Schmidt, Maria Heinrich. Gesang und Oper. 7 vols. in 1. Magdeburg: Heinrichshof'sche Musikalien-handlung, 1861-67.

Scholes, Percy Alfred. Crotchets; a few short musical notes. London: John Lane, 1924. This book contains 54 essays reprinted from The Observer.

Schubert, Johann Friedrich. Neue Singe-schule, oder gründliche und vollständige Anweisung zur Singkunst, in drey Abtheilungen mit hinlänglichen Uebungsstücken. Leipzig: Breitkopf & Härtel, 1804.

Schwartz, Rudolf. Die natürliche Gesangtechnik, systematischer Lehrgang der den Erfordernissen der Natur und den Gesetzen der Schönheit entsprechenden Kunstgemassen Gesangtechnik auf psychologisch-physiologischer Grundlage. Leipzig: C. F. Kahnt, ca. 1922.

Schwarz, Wilhelm. Die Musik als Gefühlssprache im Verhältniss zur Stimm- und Gesangbildung. Leipzig: C. F. Kahnt, 1860.

_____. System der Gesangkunst nach physiologischen Gesetzen; ein theoretisch-praktisches Lehrbuch. Hannover: Helwing'sche Hofbuchhandlung, 1859.

Sconcia, John A. An introduction to the art of singing. Upon a new and improved method. New York: the author, ca. 1839. [NYPL]

Scott, Charles Kennedy. Word and tone; an English method of vocal technique for solo singers and choralists. London: J. M. Dent & Sons, 1933.

Scripture, Edward Wheeler. Anwendung der graphischen Methode auf Sprache und Gesang ... mit 72 Figuren im Text. Leipzig: J. A. Barth, 1927. [NYPL]

Scudo, Paul. "L'Art du chant in Italie," in Critique et litterature musicales. Paris: Amyst, 1850.

Sedie, Enrico delle. Arte e fisologia del canto. Milan: G. Ricordi, 1876. English translation entitled A complete method of singing; a theoretical and practical treatise on the art of singing. New York: G. Schirmer, 1894. [BPL]

Segond, L. A. Hygiène du chanteur; influence du chant sur l'économie animale. Causes principales de l'affaiblisement de la voix et du développment de certaines maladies chez les chanteurs; moyens de prévenir ces maladies. Paris: Lahe, 1846.

Seiler, Emma. Altes und Neues über die Ausbildung des Gesangorganes mit besonderer Rücksicht auf die Frauenstimme. Leipzig: L. Voss, 1861. Translated into English by W. H. Fur-

ness and retitled The voice in singing.   Philadelphia: J. B.
Lippincott & Co. , 1868.   Other eds. : 1870, 1871, 1879, 1909.
    Seiler (1821?-) was a German singing-teacher and writer.
She was a pupil of Friedrich Wieck and of Helmholtz.   She
emigrated to the United States and settled in Philadelphia in
1866.
    The voice in singing is an early pedagogic work grounded
in scientific investigation.   Madame Seiler quotes Garcia often.
In turn, this work is one of the most quoted by contemporary
authors.   Seiler may be the originator of the five-register
theory.

Seitz, Hans.   A method of singing ... with numerous plates of the
    vocal organs, prepared by the author as an aid in teaching.
    Translated from the German by Dr. Th. Baker.   Cincinnati:
    John Church Co. , 1896.   Another ed. : ca. 1899.

Selle, Emma.   Voice preservation.   2nd rev. ed. [St. Louis]: Con-
    cordia Pub. House, 1926.   [NYPL] 1st ed. may have been
    printed in LaGrange, Ill. ca. 1924.

Seydel, Martin.   Grundfragen der Stimmkunde; für Sänger und
    Sprecher.   Leipzig: C. F. Kahnt, 1909.

Shakespeare, William.   The art of singing; based on the principles
    of the old Italian singing-masters.   London: Metzler & Co.;
    Boston: O. Ditson Co.; New York: C. H. Ditson & Co. , ca.
    1899.   Rev. ed. , entirely rewritten, printed in New York, ca.
    1921.   [NYPL]
    Shakespeare (1849-1931) was an English tenor vocalist, pia-
nist, composer and conductor.   He was a Mendelssohn scholar
at the Royal Academy of Music.   He studied piano with Reinecke
in Leipzig for a brief period, but left to study voice with Lamperti in Milan.   He made his concert and oratorio debut in
England in 1875.   In 1878 he was appointed professor of singing at the Royal Academy of Music.
    The art of singing is a complete vocal methodology, contain-
ing a summation of the prevalent thoughts of the time with no
unique theories.   The second half of the book contains 64 pages
of annotated exercises.

_____.   Plain words on singing.   London: G. P. Putnam's Sons,
    1924.   [NYPL]
    Shakespeare's second book repeats chapters of the first book
verbatim.   Part II outlines the teachings of some of the old
masters and adds essays on some famous singers of the author's era.

Shaw, W. Warren.   The lost art and its restoration, with practical
    exercises for the use of singers and teachers ... with intro-
    duction by David Bispham.   Philadelphia: J. B. Lippincott &
    Co. , 1914.   [NYPL]
    A psychological method is laid over the "natural" teachings
of the old masters.

Shryock, Daniel. The music teacher, comprising a thorough course
of elementary instruction in vocal music. Pittsburgh: n. p. ,
1856. [PU]
Shryock was a music teacher living in Pittsburgh.
This book belongs to the class of music primer for the
novice. There are very few technical instructions; the voice
is cultivated by a set of graded exercises.

Sieber, Ferdinand. Kurze Anleitung zum gründlichen Studium des
Gesanges. Magdeburg: n. p. , 1858. 2nd rev. & enl'd ed. ,
Leipzig: L. H. Matthes, 1865.
This volume is basically a shortened version of the next
entry.

_____ . Vollständiges Lehrbuch der Gesangkunst zum Gebrauche
für Lehrer und Schüler des Sologesanges. Magdeburg: Hein-
richshofen'sche Musikalienhandlung, 1858. [NYPL] English
ed. entitled The art of singing; translated by Dr. F. Seeger.
New York: W. A. Pond & Co. , ca. 1872.
Sieber (1822-1906) was a noted Austrian singing-teacher.
He studied with Ronconi and sang opera briefly. He taught
singing in Dresden 1848-1854, then settled in Berlin. Sieber
also wrote the Handbuch des deutschen Liederschatzes, a
catalogue of 10,000 songs arranged according to vocal range.
The art of singing presents the traditionally-accepted maxims
of singing in a teacher-pupil dialogue format.

Silva, Giulio. Il canto ed il suo insegnamento razionale; trattato
teorico pratico, seguito da un'appendice continente brevi nozioni
sulle principali malattie vocali e sull'igiene del cantante.
Turin: Fratelli Bocca, 1913. [NYPL] The English translation
is entitled Advice to beginners in singing (first and second
years of study); general observations on the theory of singing,
followed by 50 exercises in vocalization. English translation
by Dr. Th. Baker. New York: G. Schirmer, ca. 1922.
[NYPL]

Simon, Otto Torney. Monograph on the art of singing. Washington,
D. C. : W. F. Roberts Co. , ca. 1907.

_____ . The study of vocal physiology and the use of the laryngoscope as valuable adjuncts to voice-training. Baltimore:
n. p. , 1890.

Smith, Joseph. Voice and song, a practical method for the study
of singing. New York: G. Schirmer, 1907. Another ed. ,
1909. [NYPL]

Sonki, Stanislav Maksimovich. Théorie de la pose de la voix, basée
sur la physiologie des organes qui participant à la formation
du son. Paris: Fischbacher, 1911. [NYPL]
This is a translation by Louise Marville of the 16th ed. of
this work, issued in Russian in St. Petersburg in 1909.

Soper, I. N. A word to singers; voice culture and sight reading. Brooklyn, N. Y. : 18--. [NYPL]

Southard, L. H. see Baker, Benjamin Franklin

Stanley, Douglas. A few remarks on voice production and the operatic timbre. Montclair, N. J. : n. p. , 1916. [PU]
 Stanley wrote many books and articles on the singing voice, but this pamphlet is the only work that dates before 1928.
 Stanley presents many ideas in the space of just 24 pages, the benefits of humming being one of them.

Stark, Ludwig. Deutscher Liederschule. Stuttgart: J. G. Gottz, 1861. [NYPL]

Starke, Hermann. Physikalische Musiklehre; eine Einführung in das Wesen und die Bildung der Töne in der Instrumentalmusik und im Gesang. Leipzig: Quelle & Meyer, 1908. [NYPL]

Stebbins, Genevieve. Society gymnastics and voice-culture; adapted from the Delsarte system. New York: E. S. Werner, 1893. [NYPL]

Steinmann, Heinrich Ferdinand. Geschichte, Geist und Ausübung des Gesanges von Gregor dem Grossen bis auf unsere Zeit. Leipzig: B. G. Teubner, 1845.

_____ . Die grosse italienische Gesangschule, nebst praktischen Uebungstücken, klassischen, bisher ungedrückten Singübungen von Meistern aus derselben Schule, und Arien für den Unter- richt. Dresden: Arnoldische Buchhandlung, 1848. [NYPL]

Stephenson, Robert. How to breathe, speak and sing. New York: F. A. Stokes Co. , 1914. [NYPL]

Stevin, Simon. Vande spiegeling der singconst et Vande molens; deux traités inédits. Amsterdam: D. Bierens de Haan, 1884.

Stewart, Harriet Wainewright. Critical remarks on the art of sing- ing. London: G. Ellerton, 1836. [NYPL]

Stock, George Chadwick. Guiding thoughts for singers, dedicated for those who love to sing. New Haven, Conn. : Harty- Munsch Press, ca. 1912. [NYPL]

_____ . Helpful suggestions to young singers. [New Haven, Conn. : Tuttle, Morehouse & Taylor Co. , ca. 1916].

Stockhausen, Julius. Julius Stockhausen's Gesang-methode. Leip- zig: C. F. Peters, 1884?. English translation, A method of singing. London: Novello, 1884. [PU]
 Stockhausen (1826-1906) was a German baritone, born in Paris. He was considered among the finest of Lieder and

288 / Annotated Bibliography

oratorio singers. Stockhausen was a pupil of the Paris Conservatory and of Manuel Garcia in London. In 1862 he became
music-director at Hamburg (Opera?). From 1862 to 1867 he
was the conductor of the Philharmonic Concerts and the Sing-
akademie at Stuttgart. He also conducted and taught in Berlin
and Frankfurt.

This volume alternates explanations and instructions with
exercises. Many of the exercises are passages taken from
standard classical literature. Stockhausen introduces his
Sängeralphabet in this volume, which is an ordering of vowel
families by tongue position. He later developed this idea into
a pamphlet entitled Das Sängeralphabet; oder, Die Sprach-
elemente als Stimmbildungsmittel, 1901.

_____. Julius Stockhausen's Gesangtechnik und Stimmbildung;
ausgabe für hohe Stimme. Leipzig: C. F. Peters, 18--.
[NYPL]
This volume is missing from NYPL.

Strakosch, Moritz. Ten commandments of music for the development, perfection, and preservation of the voice, compiled and
edited by M. Leroy. London: publishers of Magazine of
Music, 1888. French translation, same publisher and date,
Les Dix Commandements de Maurice Strakosch, pour le
développement, le perfectionnement et la conservation de la
voix.

Straub, Solomon W. The singing teacher's helper, containing general directions and suggestions to teachers, and model lessons
referring to illustrations and exercises. Chicago: S. W.
Straub, ca. 1885.

Street, George Hotchkiss. Pure and easy tone production; fundamental principles of singing. New York: H. R. Eliot & Co.,
Inc., 1927.

Streeter, Horace R. Voice building. A new and correct theory
for the mechanical formation of the human voice. Boston:
White & Goullaud, 1871.

Stubbs, George Edward. The adult male alto or counter-tenor voice.
New York: H. W. Gray Co. for Novello & Co., London, ca.
1908.

Sturm, W. Gesangstudien für Mittel- und Oberschulen in methodisch
geordneter Reihenfolge. 2 parts in 1. Berlin: F. Luckhardt,
18--. [NYPL]

Sullivan, John Francis. Low loss voice. Boston: J. F. Sullivan,
1925.

Sutro, Emil. The basic law of vocal utterance. New York: E. S.
Werner, 1894. [PU]

Taylor, David Clark. New light on the old Italian method; an outline of the historical system of vocal culture, with a plea for
its revival. New York: The H. W. Gray Co. , 1916.
  Taylor (1871-1918) was an American singing-teacher. He
was a graduate of the College of the City of New York (1890).
He contributed the chapters on voice culture to The Art of
Music, 14 vols. , New York, 1917.
  "In all the confusion of methods of singing one fact stands
out clearly. There was a time when the study of voice culture was a matter of as much certainty as the study of any
other branch of music" [Preface].
  Taylor counsels the natural use of the voice, and investigates
the history of the bel canto era in an effort to uncover the
meaning of "natural singing."

   . The psychology of singing; a rational method of voice
culture based on a scientific analysis of all systems, ancient
and modern. New York: Macmillan Co. , 1908. Other eds. :
1910, 1917.
  Taylor exhorts the use of the ear as the total guide to correct singing. Imitation is recommended. He discusses the
old Italian school and the nineteenth-century changeover in
method from empiricism to scientific investigation.

   . Self-help for singers; a manual for self-instruction in
voice culture based on the old Italian method. New York: H.
W. Gray Co. , 1914.
  "... [A] theoretical work like the 'Psychology' is not adapted
to the needs of the vocal student. What the student wants is
a practical work, a text-book for use in self-instruction.
'Self-help' is now published to meet this need" [ix]. The
same philosophy is presented, with directions on ear training
and a few local effort ideas and guiding principles that Taylor
claims came to him from the old Italian schools.

Temple, Rosabella. Young singers, what they should know; a simple
course in elementary theory, with suggestions for beginners
in singing. Boston: the author, 1916.

Tenducci, Guisto Ferdinando. Instruction of Mr. Tenducci to his
scholars. London: Longman and Broderup, 1785?.
  Tenducci (1736-1800) was a celebrated Italian male soprano.
He toured England in 1785, and because of an especially enthusiastic reception remained there for most of his life. He
sang professionally until 1791.
  In one page (page 2), Tenducci lists 21 "Necessary Rules
for Students and Dilettanti of Vocal Music. " This is followed
by graded exercises.

Tetrazzini, Luisa, and Enrico Caruso. The art of singing. New
York: Metropolitan Co. , 1909. Reprinted, New York: Da
Capo Press, 1975.
  The second half of this book was written by Caruso.

Tetrazzini (1871-1940) was a celebrated Italian coloratura
soprano. She studied at the Liceo Musicale in Florence with
Ceccherini. Her operatic debut also took place in Florence
in 1895. During her career she sang in Europe, South America, Mexico and the United States. In 1907, while in England,
she was engaged by Hammerstein for the Manhattan Opera
House. After that time she remained largely in the United
States. Her last American concert took place in New York
in 1931.
Madame Tetrazzini's contribution to The art of singing is
a compendium of hints and traditional precepts on singing.
She spends little time on theory, but suggests physical actions
to bring about correct tone production.

_____. How to sing. New York: George H. Doran Co. , ca.
1923. Reprinted with The art of singing, New York: DaCapo
Press, 1975.
Madame Tetrazzini adds to her first publication information
on contracts, concert touring and other non-technical matters.
The art of singing and How to sing together represent the
best effort at help for the student from any singer of the time.

Thausing, Albrecht. Die Sängerstimme, ihre Beschaffenheit und
Entstehung, ihre Bildung und ihr Verlust. Stuttgart: Cotta,
1924.

Theirs, Albert Gerard. Technique of musical expression; a text
book for singers. New York: T. Rebla Pub. Co. , 1903.
[NYPL]

Thomas, E. Standard. Scientific singing; a study of the voice from
a logical common-sense basis. San Francisco: P. Elder and
Co. , 1916. [NYPL]

Thompson, Mary Sophia. Rhythmical gymnastics, vocal and physical.
New York: E. S. Werner, 1892. [NYPL]

Thorp, George E. , and Nicholl, William. A text book on the nat-
ural use of the voice. London: R. Cooks & Co. , 1896.
[NYPL]
Nicholl was a professor of singing in the Royal Academy of
Music.
Some important concepts of this volume are breath control
with the false vocal bands, upper range vowel modification,
the nature of vowels and consonants and their production.

Tilla, Haydon. Why we sing and where the voice is formed and
placed. The most extraordinary, comprehensive and original
work ever written on the singing voice. New York: J. Pol-
hemus, ca. 1886. Rev. and enl'd ed. , New York: Brentano
Bros. , 1887.

Tomeoni, Floridio. Théorie de la musique vocale; ou, Des dix règles qu'il faut connaître et observer pour bien chanter ou pour apprendre a juger par soi-même du degré de perfection de ceaux que l'on entend. Paris: chez l'auteur, 1799.

Trajetta, Philipo. Rudiments of the art of singing, written and composed for the American Conservatorio of Boston. Book II. Philadelphia: C. W. Murray & Co., 1843. [NYPL]
  Also known as Philip Traetta (1777-1851), the author was an Italian voice teacher. The son of Tommaso Traetta, he studied with Piccinni at Naples. Captured as a patriot in a civil conflict, he escaped from prison and sailed to Boston in 1799. He settled in Philadelphia in 1828 and founded the American Conservatorio.
  Heavy emphasis is placed on knowledge of which register to use and how to blend registers, but Book II is basically exercises. The lack of maxims and guidelines is probably due to the fact that they were placed in Book I, which is unavailable for this study.

Tree, Charles. How to acquire ease of voice production. The preservation of the voice. London: J. Williams, ca. 1911.

Trompeo, Benedetto. Memoria sulla voce considerata nel triplice rapporto fisiologico-patologico-pratico. Turin: Pomba, 1822. [NYPL]

Tubbs, Frank Herbert. Hints to my pupils. New York: n. p., ca. 1887.

_____. Science and art of breathing. 2nd ed. New York: F. H. Tubbs, 189-.

_____. Seed thoughts for singers. New York: the author, 1897.

Ulrich, Bernhard. Die Grundsätze der Stimmbildung während der Acappella-periode und zur Zeit des Aufkommens der Oper, 1474-1640. Leipzig: A. Theuerkorn, 1910.

Vaccai, Niccolò. Metodo pratico di canto italiano per camera, diviso in quindici lezioni. n. p.: n. p., ca. 184-.
  Freely translated into German by C. Wiseneder: Praktische Übungen des italienischen Gesanges in fünfzehn mit Text untergelegen Lectionen. Braunschweig: C. Weinholtz, ca. 1848. [NYPL] First English translation, by J. C. D. Parker: Practical method of Italian singing. Boston: O. Ditson & Co., ca. 1865. Another ed., ca. 1925. [NYPL]
  Second English translation: Practical Italian vocal method. Rev. ed. New York: G. Schirmer Inc., ca. 1894. [BPL] Third English translation, by Dr. Theodore Baker: Practical Italian method of singing; for medium voice. Boston: Oliver Ditson Co., 191-. [BPL]
  Vaccai (1790-1848) was an Italian composer and singing-teacher. He studied with Jannaconi and Paisiello. He wrote

about 12 operas, most of them failures. His career as a voice teacher took him from Venice (1818-27) to Trieste, Vienna, Paris (1829-31) and London (1829 or 1832 variously). He served as a professor of composition at the Milan Conservatory (1838-44).

Vaccai's very popular work teaches singing almost exclusively by means of 15 lessons that are skill-developing etudes. Such subjects as skips, semitone runs, syncopation, and the major graces and embellishments are presented in vocalise form. Range and diction are discussed briefly.

Vaille, Agnes Goodrich. Vocal science. Boston: O. Ditson Co., ca. 1889.

Vannini, Vincenzo. Delle voce umana, ma principalmente delle voce del soprano. Florence: Tip. Barbera, 1924. [NYPL]

Vié, Therese M. Notes sur l'art du chant. Paris: Heugel, ca. 1925.

Vincent, Mary E. How to sing; how to speak. Louisville, Ky. : n. p., 1895. 1st ed. pub. 1888.

Vitelli, Giovanni. A treatise on the formation, cultivation and development of the voice, with general directions for singing, according to the physical principals [sic] of the art, as adopted by Jenny Lind. London: the author, 185-. [NYPL] 2nd ed., London: published for author by Levesque & Co., 185-.

Vogler, G. J. Die Scale; oder, Personifizirte Stimmbildungsund Singkunst. Offenbach: M. J. Andre, 18--. [NYPL]

Voit, Carolus. Music and singing made easy. London: G. Sleder, 18--. [NYPL]

Vorhees, Irving Wilson. Hygiene of the voice. New York: Macmillan Co., 1923. [NYPL]

Wagenmann, Josef Hermann. Enrico Caruso und das Problem der Stimmbildung. Altenburg: S.-A. J. Räde, 1911. [NYPL] Another ed., Leipzig: A. Felix, 1924. [NYPL]

_____. Lille [sic] Lehmann's Geheimnis der Stimmänder. Leipzig: A. Felix, 1926.

_____. Umsturz in der Stimmbildung (Lösung das Stimmbildungs- und Carusoprobleme). Schrift für Sänger, Schauspieler, Redner und Jedermann. Leipzig: A. Felix, 1922. [NYPL]

Wallnöfer, Adolf. Resonantztonlehre. Berlin: Verlag Dreililien, 1911.

Walshe, Walter Hayle. Dramatic singing physiologically estimated. London: K. Paul, Trench & Co., 1881. [NYPL]

Walter-Hähnel, Elise. Das menschliche Schallgehäuse, die Gesetze der Wahrheit in Sprache und Gesang. Berlin: H. Rosenberg, 1913.

Wannstein, M. Die grosse italienische Gesangschule. Dresden: n. p. , 1848. [NYPL]

Wanrell, Joaquin Sastre. The art of singing, a collection of rules for singing, by celebrated teachers and artists. Fresno, Calif. ?: n. p. , ca. 1907.

Ward, Whitfield. The throat in its relation to singing. New York: C. A. Welles, 1881.

_____ . The singing voice and its preservation. Boston: O. Ditson Co. , ca. 1887.

Warren, Frederic. The philosophy of vocal fatigue; a synopsis of a lecture given before the New York Singing Teachers' Association on Nov. 14th, 1922. New York: n. p. , 1922?. [PU]

Weaver, Andrew Thomas. Experimental studies in vocal expression. Baltimore: n. p. , 1924.

Webb, George James, and Allen, C. G. Voice culture: a complete method of theory and practice for the cultivation and development of the voice. New York: Bigelow & Main, ca. 1871. [NYPL] Rev. ed. , ca. 1884. [NYPL]

Weiske, A. C. Beitrage zur Theorie der Künste... . Berlin: E. G. Schone, 1815. [NYPL]

Weiss, C. A. Kleine Gesangschule; zum Gebrauch für Lehrer und Schüler. St. Louis, Mo: A. Wiebusch & Son Printing Co. , 1882.

White, Ernest G. The voice beautiful in speech and song; a consideration of the capabilities of the vocal cords and their work in the art of tone production. London: J. M. Dent & Sons, 1918. [NYPL] Also pub. in 1927, 1931, 1938. First pub. as Science and singing, 1909; rev. and reprinted three times as The voice beautiful; 5th ed. , rev. and reset as Science and singing, 1938.
    White (1863-1940) was an English singing-teacher and writer. "Is the art of teaching singing in a state of chaos? I reply, yes, most certainly. Surely it is high time that some very real effort was made to put the art of singing upon a distinctly scientific basis" [p. 4]. White's scientific basis includes the conscious employment of the sinuses and the theory that the vocal cords do not produce vocal sound.

Widmann, Benedikt. Gehor- und Stimmbildung. Eine auf physiologische, psychologische und pädagogische Untersuchung. Leipzig: C. Merseburger, 1874.

Wieck, Friedrich. Clavier und Gesang. Leipzig: F. Whistling,
1853. The English translation, by H. Krueger, is entitled
Piano and singing. 2nd ed. Aberdeen: H. Krueger, 1875.
Another translation: Piano and singing. Boston: Ditson &
Co., ca. 1875.
Wieck (1785-1873) was a German pianist and teacher.
Before he began teaching, Wieck established a piano factory
and a circulating music library. He was the father of Clara
Wieck and father-in-law to Schumann.
Wieck does not recommend lessons for children. Breathing
and range receive the most emphasis.

Wilcox, John C. Simplified practice manual for vocal students.
Denver, CO: The Wilcox Studio, ca. 1915.

_____. Vocal guide for song and speech. Denver: Wilcox
Studies, ca. 1926. [PU]

Wilkenson, George Perkins. The voice; a musical instrument, as
by disease affected; some papers on applied acoustics. Omaha?:
n.p., 187-. [NYPL]

Williams, J. Hugh. Voice production and breathing for speakers
and fundamental studies for singers. London: Sir I. Pitman
& Sons, 1923.

Williams, Thomas E. A treatise on singing; by which a person,
though possessed but of limited power, may, with a correct
ear and some degree of voice to execute difficult passages
with facility, become a scientific singer. An analysis of the
vocal powers of the celebrated singers Incledon and Braham, in
the two distinct schools or opposite styles of singing, that of
the former originating with himself, and the latter, founded
on the best Italian system, are contrasted and considered.
London: the author, 1834.

Winter, Peter von. Sing-Schule. Leipzig: C. F. Peters, 1824?.
[NYPL]

_____. Vollständige Singschule, in vier Abtheilungen mit teutschen,
italienischen und französischen Vorbemerkungen und Erläuter-
ungen. Mainz: B. Schott Söhne, 1824?.

Wirz, Georg. Neue Wege und Ziele für die Weiterentwicklung der
Sing- und Sprechstimme, auf Grund wissenschaftlicher Ver-
suche. Leipzig: Breitkopf & Härtel, 1911.

Witherspoon, Herbert. Singing: a treatise for teachers and stu-
dents. New York: G. Schirmer, ca. 1925.
Witherspoon (1873-1935) was an American bass singer.
He studied with Horatio Parker at Yale University and Mc-
Dowell in New York before turning to singing. His voice
teachers were Bouhy in Paris, Henry Wood in London and G.

B. Lamperti in Berlin. He made his debut in the United
States in 1895 and was successful in recital, oratorio and in
opera with the Metropolitan Opera House. Around the year
1910 he turned to teaching; in 1925 he became president of
the Chicago Musical College; in 1931, the president of the
Cincinnati Conservatory of Music. In 1935 he was chosen to
succeed Gatti-Casazza as general manager of the Metropolitan
Opera Company, but died suddenly of a heart attack.

"There would seem, therefore, to be a need of a book,
somewhat in the nature of a textbook, useful to teacher and
pupil, which will show the natural laws governing the voice
organs, the established and accepted facts upon which these
laws depend the best means of insuring obedience to these
laws, and the faulty results due to disobedience" [p. 2]. In
the search for a satisfactory method, Witherspoon devotes
much of the book to a survey of various "schools," local
effort, scientific, psychological, empirical, etc.

Withrow, Marie. Some staccato notes for singers. Boston: Oliver
Ditson Co., 1915. [PU]

Wolf, Artur. Criticism of one-sided singing methods: problems
of voice building and their solution. Translated from German
by Bert Jahr. n. p. : n. p. , ca. 1916. [WCC]

_____. Gymnastik des Gesangs-apparates; der Weg zur Klang-
schönheit. Leipzig: L. Doblinger, 1927. [NYPL]

Wolf, Georg Friedrich. Georg Friedrich Wolf's Unterricht in der
Singkunst. Halle in Sachsen: J. C. Hendel, 1784.

Wolff, Eugène. Der Niedergang des Bel-canto und sein Wieder-
aufblühen durch rationelle Tonbildung. 2 vols. Leipzig: O.
Junne, 1896.

Wood, Sir Henry Joseph. The gentle art of singing. 4 vols. London: Oxford University Press, ca. 1927. [NYPL]

Woodbury, Isaac Baker. The cultivation of the voice without a
master. New York: F. J. Huntington, 1853. [NYPL]

Wright, William C. Golden precepts for vocal art. [St. Joseph,
MO]: the author, ca. 1895.

Wronski, Thaddeus. The singer and his art ... including articles
on anatomy and vocal hygiene by John F. Levbarg, M. D.
New York: D. Appleton and Co., 1921. [NYPL]
According to the author, this work was first published in
Italian.

Wronski was an operatic bass. He sang in Europe and
then in the United States with the Boston Opera Company.

"The three parts of the book--voice, mimicry (art of acting), and art of make-up--form a unit of great interest to the

singer. On the professional stage they constitute the 'singer's art,' and no one of the three should be neglected or sacrificed for the sake of the others" [Preface]. The first section presents a lengthy and valuable compendium of singing maxims, including a section on hygiene.

De Zangkunst gemaklyk gemaakt; of, Musykaal handboek. Amsterdam: H. Gartman, 1788.

Zanten, Cornelie van. Leitfaden zum Kunstgesang. Leipzig: Breitkopf & Härtel, 1903.

Zay, William Henri. Practical psychology of voice and life. Boston: G. Schirmer, ca. 1918. [NYPL]

Zopff, Herman. Practical advice for singers and singing teachers, with special consideration for voices that are poor or spoiled and of the diseases of the vocal organs. English translation by Edward Remack. Leipzig: J. Schuberth & Co. , 1867. [NYPL]

Zucconi, Louis. L'Art du chant. Paris: Vuibert, 1922.

Zuchtmann, Friedrich, and Kirtland, Edwin L. Teacher's manual; the American music system. Springfield, Mass. : King, Richardson & Co. , 1893. [NYPL]

CHRONOLOGICAL BIBLIOGRAPHY

For the sake of space, short titles only are given and first names (except where needed) and all publication information have been omitted in the following chronological bibliography. Those entries marked with an asterisk represent the primary sources used in the main body of the work. Only the earliest available edition and only the original language edition of a work have been entered here.

1777

Hansen, Musikens fórste grundsaetninger anvendte paa syngekonsten i sdelshed

1780

*Hiller, Anweisung zum musikalisch-zierlichen Gesange

1782

*Corrette, Le Parfait Maître a chanter

1784

Wolf (Georg Friedrich), Georg Friedrich Wolf's Unterricht in der Singkunst

1785

*Tenducci, Instruction of Mr. Tenducci to his scholars

1787

Danby, La guida alla musica

1788

De Zangkunst gemaakt

1792

*Hiller, Kurze und erleichterte Anweisung zum Singen

Martini, Mélopée moderne

1793

Durieu. Nouvelle méthode de musique vocale, concernant les principes de cet art ...

Kuerzinger, Getreuer Unterricht zum Singen mit Manieren

1798

Ebers, Vollständige Singschule

1799

Tomeoni, Théorie de la musique vocale

18--

*Anfossi, Trattato teorico pratico sull'arte del canto/ A theoretical and practical treatise on the art of singing

Benelli, Regien für den figurirten Gesang

Bennett, An introduction to the art of singing

Busse, Der Singemeister

*Corfe, A treatise on singing

Crivelli, The art of singing

*Furtado, General observations on the vocal art

Kingsbury, The voice and the structure and management of the vocal organ

Paris, Conservatoire National de Musique et de Déclamation, Méthode de chant ...

Soper, A word to singers

Sturm, Gesangsstudien für Mittel- und Oberschulen in methodisch geordneter Reihenfolge

Vogler, Die Scale;

Voit, Music and singing made easy

1800

*Duval, Méthode agréable et utile pour apprendre facilemente a chanter juste

1803

*D'Aubigny von Engelbrunner, Briefe an Natalie über den Gesang

1804

Schubert, Neue Singe-schule

1805

*Lasser, Vollständige Anleitung zur Singkunst

1807

Mengozzi, Méthode de chant du Conservatoire de Musique

1809

Garaudé, Nouvelle Méthode de chant et de vocalisation

1810

*Corri (Domenico), The singers' preceptor

Pellegrini-Celoni, Grammatica, o siano regole de ben cantare

*Pfeiffer and Nägeli, Gesangbildungslehre nach Pestalozzischen Grundsätzen pädagogisch begründet

1813

*Lanza (Gesualdo), Lanza's elements of singing

1815

The Gamut; or, Rules of singing

*Minoja, Über den Gesang

Persichini, Anfangsgründe des Gesanges

Weiske, Beitrage zur Theorie der Künste

1818

*Ferrari, Breve trattato de canto italiano

Schaul, Über Tonkunst

1819

Hastings, The musical reader

1820

*Corri (Philip Antony), New vocal instructor by Arthur Clifton

1821

Kitchener, Observations on vocal music

Roucourt, Essai sur la theorie du chant

1822

Fröhlich, Systematischer Unterricht zum Erlernen und Behandeln der Singkunst

Parry, The vocalist

Pastou, École de la lyre harmonique

Trompeo, Memoria sulla voce considerata nel triplice rapporto fisiologico-patologico-pratico

1823

King, An introduction to the theory and practice of singing ...

*Nathan, An essay on the history and theory of music

1824

*Bacon, Elements of vocal science

*Costa, Considerations on the art of singing in general

von Winter, Sing-schule

_____, Vollständige Singschule

1825

Garaudé, Méthode complète de chant

Rennie?, The art of improving the voice and ear

1826

*Marx, Die Kunst des Gesanges

1827

Markwort, Gesang-, Ton- und Rede- vortraglehre

Rush, The philosophy of the human voice

1828

*Cooke, Singing simplified in a series of solfeggios and exercises

Dyer, Vocal preceptor

183-

*Lanza (Francesco Giuseppe), Lanza's abridgement of his work on the art of singing

Massimino, Nouvelle Méthode pour l'enseignement de la musique [183- or 184-]

1830

Grosheim, Über Pflege und Anwendung der Stimme

*Pfeiffer and Nägeli, Auszug aus der Gesangbildungslehre nach Pestalozzischen Grundsätzen

Philipps, Elementary principles and practices for singing

1833

Bagioli, New method of singing with an accompaniment for the piano or harp

1834

Dingley, The intellectual and practical singing book

Williams (Thomas E.), A treatise on singing

1836

*Mason, Manual of the Boston Academy of Music for instruction in the elements of vocal music ...

Rodolphe, Solfège de Rodolphe

Stewart, Critical remarks on the art of singing

1838

*Costa, Analytical considerations on the art of singing

*Ferrari, Giacimo [sic] G. Ferrari's celebrated instruction book for the voice

1839

*Day, The vocal school

Fabio, Teorica del canto per servire al Musicale istituto ...

Hastings, Elements of vocal music

*Panseron, Méthode de vocalisation

Perino, Nouvelle Méthode de chant

Sconcia, An introduction to the art of singing

184-

*Ferrari, Instruction book for the voice

*Lablache, A complete method of singing for the bass voice

Massimino see under 183-

1840

Madelaine, Physiologie du chant

1842

Bronson, Abstract of elocution and music

1843

*Trajetta, Rudiments of the art of singing

1844

Barnett, School for the voice

Nehrlich, Gesang-Schule für gebildete Stände

1845

*Romer, The physiology of the human voice

Russell (William), Elements of musical articulation

Steinmann, Geschichte, Geist und Ausübung des Gesanges ...

1846

Chevé and Chevé, Méthode elémentaire de musique vocale

*Clifton, Clifton's vocal instruction

Segond, Hygiène du chanteur

1847

Fontana, The musical manual

*Garcia (Manuel), A complete treatise on the art of singing

1848

Casella, Compendia dell'opera sulle teorica per l'arte del canto

Steinmann, Die grosse italienische Gesangschule

*Vaccai, Metodo pratico di canto italiano per camera

Wannstein, Die grosse italienische Gesangschule

1849

Adams (Frederic Augustus), The singer's manual for teachers, pupils, and private students

*Garcia (Manuel), Memoire sur la voix humaine ...

*Panseron, Méthode de vocalisation pour soprano et tenor ...

185-

Vitelli, A treatise on the formation, cultivation and development of the voice

1850

Damoreau, Méthode de chant

Scudo, "L'Art du chant in Italie," Critique et Littérature Musicales

1851

Duca, Conseils sur l'étude du chant

1852

Baker and Southard, A complete method for the formation and cultivation of the voice

Bradbury, The singing bird

La Madelaine, Théories complètes du chant

1853

Nehrlich, Die Gesangkunst physiologisch, ästhetisch und pädagogisch dargestellt

*Wieck, Clavier und Gesang

Woodbury, The cultivation of the voice without a master

1854

Eirel, Die Stimmfähigkeit des Menschen ...

1855

Panseron, Méthode complète de vocalisation pour mezzo-soprano

1856

*Novello, Voice and vocal art

*Shryock, Daniel. The music teacher

1857

*Bassini, Bassini's art of singing

Mainvielle-Fodor, Réflexions et conseils sur l'art du chant

1858

*Sieber, Kurze Anleitung zum gründlichen Studium des Gesanges

* _____, Vollständiges Lehrbuch der Gesangkunst zum Gebrauche ...

1859

Müller, Theoretisch-praktische Anleitung zum Studium des Gesanges

Nehrlich, Der Kunstgesang physiologisch, psychologisch, pädagogisch
und ästhetisch dargestellt

*Panofka, Gesangs A B C

Schwarz, System der Gesangkunst nach physiologischen Gesetzen

186-

Cooke (Thomas Simpson), Cooke's method

1860

Döring, Aphorism vom Felde der Kunst des Gesanges

*Lablache, Lablache's complete method of singing

Schwarz, Die Musik als Gefühlssprache im Verhältniss zur Stimm-
und Gesangbildung

1861

Cazalet, The voice

Debay, Hygiène et gymnastique des organes de la voix parlee et chantée

*Everest, Everest's vocal instructor

Schmidt, Gesang und Oper

*Seiler, Altes und Neues über die Ausbildung des Gesangorganes

Stark, Deutscher Liederschule

1864

*Lamperti (Francesco), Guida teorico-pratico-elementare per lo studio del canto

1865

*Bassini, Bassini's education for the young voice

Graben-Hoffmann, Die Plege der Singstimme und die Gründe von der Zerstörung ...

Hopkins, A method for teaching Orpheus singing classes ...

1866

Hauser, Gesanglehre für Lehrende und Lernende

1867

Celentano, Intorno all'arte del cantare in Italia nel secolo decimonono

Zopff, Practical advice for singers and singing teachers

1868

Chevé, Science et art de l'intonation

Lefort, De l'émission de la voix

1869

*Bassini, Bassini's new method for soprano and mezzo-soprano

Monroe, Manual of physical and vocal training

187-

Nava, Method of instruction for a baritone voice

*Oliver, The vocalist's companion

Wilkenson, The voice; a musical instrument, as by disease affected

1870

Delprat, L'Art du chant et l'école actuelle

Duschnitz, Theorie der Tonerzeugung und der Gesangkunst

1871

Baxter, Technics for voice

Gaertner, The art of singing

Ludden, School for the voice

Streeter, Voice building

Webb and Allen, Voice culture

1872

Pruckner, Theorie und Praxis der Gesangkunst

1873

*Daniell, The voice and how to use it

Medini, The what and how of vocal culture

Merkel, Der Kehlkopf

1874

Osgood, Guide in the art of singing ...

Widmann, Gehor- und Stimmbildung

1875

*Bishenden, The voice and how to use it

How to cultivate the voice

1876

Abt, Practical singing tutor

Audubert, L'Art du chant

*Bishenden, How to sing

Lacombe, La Science du mécanisme vocale et l'art du chant

Orsin, Considerazioni generali sull'arte del canto

Sedie, Arte e fisologia del canto

1877

*Browne, Medical hints on the production and management of the singing voice

Goodrich, How to sing

Langethal, Elementare Gesanglehre nach Grundsätzen der neueren Pädagogik

1878

Howard, Papers illustrating the revolutionary principles of the Howard method

*Lunn, The philosophy of the voice

Manuale dell'artista de canto ...

Pattou, The voice as an instrument

1879

Davis, The voice as a musical instrument

*Holmes, A treatise on vocal physiology and hygiene

188-

Hey, Deutscher Gesang-Unterricht

*Stockhausen, Julius Stockhausen's Gesangtechnik und Stimmbildung

1880

*Bach, On musical education

Bozzelli, Brevi considerazioni sull'arte del canto

Federlein, Common sense in singing

_____, Gottlieb Federlein's practical school of voice culture

*Holmes, The science of voice production and voice preservation

*Lunn, Vox populi

1881

Lemaire, and Lavoix, <u>Le chant, ses principes et son histoire</u>

Walshe, <u>Dramatic singing physiologically estimated</u>

Ward, <u>The throat and its relation to singing</u>

1882

Duprez, <u>Sur la voix et l'art du chant</u>

Howard, <u>Respiratory control for vocal purposes</u>

Pattou, <u>The art of voice-production</u> ...

Weiss, <u>Kleine Gesangschule</u>

1883

Belari, <u>The secrets of the voice in singing</u>

Dow, <u>Artistic singing</u>

*Lamperti (Francesco), <u>L'arte del canto in ordine alle traditioni classiche</u> ...

Mills (Thomas Wesley), <u>An examination of some controverted points of the physiology of voice</u>

*Myer, <u>Truths of importance to vocalists</u>

1884

Stevin, <u>Vande spiegeling der singconst et Vande molens</u>

*Stockhausen, <u>Julius Stockhausen's Gesang-Methode</u>

1885

Formes, <u>Karl Formes' method of singing for soprano and tenor</u>

*Guttmann, <u>Key to the Guttmann tables</u>

Straub, <u>The singing teacher's helper</u>

1886

Barnette, <u>Talks about singing</u>

Coletti, <u>La scuola de canto in Italia</u>

Faure, <u>La Voix et le chant</u>

Howard, The physiology of artistic singing

*Mackenzie, The hygiene of the vocal organs

*Myer, The voice from a practical standpoint

Rand, Practical method of singing

Tilla, Why we sing and where the voice is formed and placed

1887

Dowd, Science and vocal culture

*Guttmann, Gymnastics of the voice

Helmore, The Italian registers

Michael, Die Bildung der Gesangsregister

Tubbs, Hints to my pupils

Ward, The singing voice and its preservation

1888

Miller (Olin W.), Miller's thorough vocal instruction, issued semi-
monthly ...

Strakosch, Ten commandments of music for the development, perfection, and preservation of the voice

Vincent, How to sing; how to speak

1889

Arthur, 70 lessons in voice training for medium voice

_____, 79 short studies for alto or bass

*Kofler, Die Kunst des Atmens als Grundlage der Tonerzeugung
für Sänger, Schauspieler, Redner, Lehrer

* _____, Take care of your voice

Vaille, Vocal science

189-

*Behnke (Emil), The mechanism of the human voice

Dunn, The solo singer

Tubbs, Science and art of breathing

1890

Carozzi, Guida ant'igenica de ginnastica vocale

Chater, Scientific voice, artistic singing and effective speaking

Emerson (Luther Orlando), Emerson's method for contralto, baritone and bass voice

Fauré, Aux jeunes chanteurs

Kohut, Johannes Miksch, der grösste deutscher Singmeister und sein Gesangsystem

Mueller-Brunow, Tonbildung oder Gesangunterricht

Schmauk, The voice in speech and song

Simon, The study of vocal physiology and the use of the laryngoscope ...

1891

Edgerley, Lessons in voice culture

*Myer, Vocal reinforcement

Rosewald, How shall I practice?

1892

Engel, A few hints on the foundation of the voice in song and speech

Gervinus, Naturgemässe Ausbildung in Gesang und Clavierspiel

Goldschmidt (Hugo), Der Vokalismus des neuhochdeutschen Kunstgesanges und der Bühnensprache

Henning, Die Unterscheidung der Gesangregister auf physiologisch Grundlage

Leslie; Shaw; and Jacobs, The teacher's manual

Maurel, Le Chant rénové par la science

Pratt, Outline study-notes in elocution and singing

Thompson, Rhythmical gymnastics, vocal and physical

1893

*Garcia (Manuel), École de Garcia, traité complet de l'art du chant

Hiebsch, Methodik des Gesangunterrichts

Maurel, Un Problème d'art

*Rogers, The philosophy of singing

Stebbins, Society gymnastics and voice-culture

Zuchtmann, and Kirtland, Teacher's manual

1894

*Bach, The principles of singing

Booth, Everybody's guide to music

Castex, Hygiène de la voix parlée et chantée

DeRialp, The legitimate school of singing

*Garcia (Manuel), Hints on singing

Meyer-Teeg, Concerning the psychological system of voice-culture and the exercises pertaining thereto

Rockstro, Jenny Lind

Sutro, The basic laws of vocal utterance

1895

Aldrich, Vocal economy and expressiveness

Croker, Handbook for singers

Dodge, The care of the voice

Iffert, Allgemeine Gesangschule

Joal, On respiration in singing

Meyer, A treatise on the origin of a destructive element on the female voice ...

Parker, The voice in speaking and singing

Wright, Golden precepts for vocal art

1896

Arlberg, Eine natürliche und vernünftige Tonbildungslehre für Sänger und Sängerinnen

Barlow, The balance of act in singing

*Botume, Modern singing methods

Brand, Brand's system of voice building

Cheney, The tone-line

*Hallock, and Muckey, Rational scientific voice-production

Hodgdon, The teachers' manual

Muscat, Practical suggestions about voice culture and the art of singing

North, Voxometric revelation

Root, The polychrome lessons in voice culture

Seitz, A method of singing

*Thorp, and Nicholl, A text book on the natural use of the voice

Wolff, Der Niedergang des Bel-canto und sein Wiederaufblühn durch rationelle Tonbildung

1897

*Botume, Respiration for advanced singers

Guillemin, Sur la génération de la voix et du timbre

Häuptner, Aussprache und Vortrag beim Gesange

Hays, The principles of vocal science

Pfordten, Musikalische essays

Tubbs, Seed thoughts for singers

1898

*Bach, Musical education and vocal culture

Belari, An open letter to singers and vocal teachers concerning the modern or natural voice method

*Miller (Frank Ebenezer), and Wangemann, Observations on voice and voice fatigue

Rowley, The voice

1899

Arlberg, Theoretische und praktische Tonbildungslehre

Gill, Golden rules for singers

Gordon y de Acosta, Consideraciones sobre la voz humana

*Lankow (Anna) et al, Kunst-gesang Schule

Mastrigli, La respirazione nel canto

Nava, Practical method of vocalization for bass or baritone

Pynchon, The bête noir of the vocalist

*Shakespeare, The art of singing

190-

Engel, The spirit of the art of singing

Nozat, L'Art du faire une voix

Palmer, The tenor voice and its training

Stubbs, Supplementary exercises for the use of singers

1900

Aiken, The voice

Chevé, and Chevé, An elementary course of vocal music ...

Marcel, L'Art du chant en France

Reeves, Sims Reeves on "the art of singing"

1901

Howe, Voice culture and artistic singing

*Lankow (Anna), et al. , Supplement to vocal art

Lawton, The singing voice and its practical cultivation

*Marchesi (Mathilde), Ten singing lessons

Röhrke, Tonbildung und Aussprache

Rosenberg, Stimme und Gesang; eine Studie

1902

Guetta, Il canto nel suo meccanismo

*Marchesi (Salvatore), A vademecum for singing-teachers and pupils

*Myer, The renaissance of the vocal art

Ranske, Health, speech and song

Rockwood, Foundation stages of tone production ...

Roeder (Karl), Vorbereitungen auf die Gesangstunde

1903

Flatau, Das habituelle Tremoliren der Singstimme

Grant, Vocal art as nature intended

Herrmann (Heinrich), Die Bildung der Stimme

*Hulbert, Breathing for voice production

James, Scientific tone production

Lankow (Anna) and Garcia (Manuel), The science of the art of singing

*Marchesi (Mathilde), The Marchesi school

Neidlinger, A primer on voice and singing

Thiers, Technique of musical expression

van Zanten, Leitfaden zum Kunstgesang

1904

Barth, Über der Bildung der menschlichen Stimme und ihres Klanges
    beim Singer und Sprecher ...

Breare, Vocalism, its structure and culture ...

*Browne and Behnke (Emil), Voice, song and speech

Howard, Expression in singing

*Lunn, The voice

Mahlendorff, The science and art of adjustment between the produc-
    tion and reflecting vocal apparatus

*Russell (Louis Arthur), The body and breath under artistic control

*_____, A plain talk with American singers

*_____, Some psychic reflections for singers

1905

*van Broekhaven, The tone producing functions of the vocal organs

Hacke, Lerne singen!

Heinrich (Traugott), Studien über deutsche Gesangsaussprache

*Lamperti (Giovanni Battista), The technics of bel canto

McCarty, The natural singing voice

Powell (Alma Webster), Advanced school of vocal art

1906

Bruns, Die Registerfrage in neuerer Forschung

*Ffrangçon-Davies, The singing of the future

*Henderson, The art of the singer

Héritte-Viardot, Die Natur in der Stimmbildung

*Lehmann, Meine Gesangkunst

Pownall, The singing voice and its development

Reinecke, Die Kunst der idealen Tonbildung

1907

Breare, Vocal faults and their remedies

Praetorius, The tone placed and developed

*Russell (Louis Arthur), The commonplaces of vocal art

Simon, Monograph on the art of singing

Smith, Voice and song

Wanrell, The art of singing

1908

Albert, Moderne Berliner Gesangspädagogen

Bonnier, La Voix professionnelle

*van Broekhaven, Some unfamiliar facts concerning the functions of the larynx in singing

* _____ , The true method of tone production

Cappiani, Practical hints and helps for perfection in singing

Garsó, Schule der speziellen Stimmbildung auf der Basis des losen Tones

Loebmann, Die "Gesangbildungslehre" nach Pestalozzischen Grundsätzen ...

Manchester, Twelve lessons in the fundamentals of voice production

*Rutz, Neue Entdeckungen von der menschlichen Stimme

*Santley, The art of singing and vocal declamation

Scheidemantel, Stimmbildung

Starke, Physikalische Musiklehre

Stubbs, The adult male alto or counter-tenor voice

*Taylor, The psychology of singing

1909

Adams (H. Travers), Physical development in relation to perfect voice production

Bonnier, La Voix

Brouillet, Artistic tone production through natural breathing

Girard, Vocal art

Mills (Charles Francis Henry), Voice and vocal exercises

_____ , Voice and vocalism

Pattou, The art of voice production established on a true scientific basis

Seydel, Grundfragen der Stimmkunde

*Tetrazzini and Caruso, The art of singing

1910

*Clippinger, Systematic voice training

Curry, Mind and voice

Feuchtinger, Die Kunststimme

Fischer, Neue Gesangschule

*Heinrich (Max), Correct principles of classical singing

Killermann, Stimme und Sprache

Kwartin, Der moderne Gesangunterricht

Lepanto, Sprech-und Gesangunterricht

MacKinlay, The singing voice and its training

*Miller (Frank Ebenezer), The voice

van Oldenbarnevelt, The art of breathing

Pinks, Atem-, Sprech- und Singtechnik

Reinecke, Die natürliche Entwicklung der Singstimme

*Rogers, My voice and I

Schilling, The upper soprano tones

Ulrich, Die Grundsätze der Stimmbildung während der Acappella-
periode ...

1911

Eitz, Bausteine zum Schulgesangunterrichte im Sinne der Tonwortmethode

*Fillebrown, Resonance in singing and speaking

Ganter-Schwing, The American method of tone production

Gib, Vocal science and art

Haslem, Style in singing

Horspool, The alpha and omega of voice production

Kwartin, Prinzipien für Stimmbildung und Gesang

*Myer, Position and action in singing

*Parisotti, A treatise on speaking and singing

*Rutz, Sprache, Gesang, und Körperhaltung

Sonki, Théorie de la pose de la voix

Tree, How to acquire ease of voice production

Wallnöfer, Resonantztonlehre

Wirz, Neue Wege und Ziele für die Weiterentwicklung der Sing- und Sprechstimme

1912

Garcia (Gustave), A guide to solo singing

Greene (Harry Plunket), Interpretation in song

Gutzmann, Stimmbildung und Stimmflege

Herman, An open door for singers

Hoche, Die Quintessenz des Kunstgesangunterrichts

*Miller (Frank Ebenezer), "Vocal art-science from the standpoint of the use and abuse of the voice"

*_____, and Merton, Vocal atlas

Noë, and Moser, Technik der deutschen Gesangkunst

*Randegger, Singing

Schilling, The upper tenor tones

Stock, Guiding thoughts for singers

1913

Brouillet, Science of tone production

Bryant, The voice instrument

*Caruso, How to sing

Cassius, Die Erziehung der Stimme und Atmung durch Artikulation der Konsonanten und Biegung der Vokale

Gib, The art of vocal expression

Hild, Our modern school of singing

von Höpflingen, and Bergendorf, Renaissance der Gesangs- und Sprechkunst

Mills (Thomas Wesley), Voice production in singing and speaking

*Myer, The vocal instructor

Perkins, Physiological voice culture

Silva, Il canto ed il suo insegnamento razionale

Walter-Hähnel, Das menschliche Schallgehäuse

1914

*Crowest, Advice to singers

*Curtis, Voice building and tone placing

Eitz, Der Gesangunterricht als Grundlage der musikalischen Bildung

*Frossard, La Science et l'art du chant

Goldschmidt (Bruno), Ein ärztlicher Ratgebar für Gesangstudierende

Granier, Le chant moderne

Kirkwood, A simple and practical method for obtaining correct voice
    production ...

Larson, Everybody's self-culturing vocal method

Miles (Walter R.), "Accuracy of the voice in simple pitch singing,"
    Psychological Monographs

*Shaw, The lost art and its restoration

Stephenson, How to breathe, speak, and sing

*Taylor, Self-help for singers

1915

Calicchio, The secret of how to become a great singer

Emerson (Charles Wesley), Psycho-vox

Feuchtinger, The vocal organ

*Muckey, The natural method of voice production in speech and song

Ranske, Voice and nerve control

Wilcox, Simplified practice manual for vocal students

Withrow, Some staccato notes for singers

1916

Averkamp, Vit mijn practijk

*Botume, Voice production today

Brouillet, Science in vocal tone production

Cooke (Clifton), Practical singing

Fellows, The art of singing

van Gelder, The foundation of artistic singing

Hurlbut, Voice fundamentals

*Kirkland, Expression in singing

Lyman, Self-instruction in voice training

Miller (George Harold), Tone production

Price, Self-help in voice production

*Stanley, A few remarks on voice production and the operatic timbre

Stock, Helpful suggestions to young singers

*Taylor, New light on the old Italian method

Temple, Young singers

Thomas, Scientific singing

Wolf (Artur), Criticism of one-sided singing methods

1917

*Clippinger, The head voice and other problems

Haywood, Universal song

Heller, The voice in song and speech

*Miller (Frank Ebenezer), Vocal art-science and its application

Zay, Practical psychology of voice and of life

1918

*Curtis, Thirty years' experience with singers

Lankow (Edward), How to breathe right

Magrini, Il canto

Povani, Five lessons in voice culture

Preston, Foundation facts in the development of the voice

*White, The voice beautiful in speech and song

1919

Benedict, A scientific system of voice culture without exercises

De La Marca, Important advice to singing students

*Duff, Simple truths used by great singers

Reichart, Die Lösung des Problems eines freien Tones auf Anatomisch-physiologischer Basis

192-

Borese, Emission esthétique et santé vocales résument tout l'art du chant

1920

*Brower, Vocal mastery

Dannenburg, Handbuch der Gesangkunst

*Greene (Herbert Wilbur), The singer's ladder

Hahn, Du chant

Larkcom, The singer's art

McLellan, Voice education

Martienssen-Lohmann, Die echte Gesangkunst dargestellt an Johannes Messchaert

1921

Benjamin, The singing voice

*Cooke (James Francis), Great singers on the art of singing

Edward, How to develop the voice for song

Forchhammer, Theorie und Technik des Singen und Sprechens ...

*Hulbert, Eurhythm

*Wronski, The singer and his art

1922

Bruns, Carusos Technik in deutscher Erklärung

Burritt, A process of vocal study

Duval, The secrets of Svengali on singing ...

Field, Five years of study under Fernando Michelena

*Fucito and Beyer, Caruso and the art of singing

Gib, Vocal success

*Marafioti, Caruso's method of voice production

Miles (Charles Chester), Basic elements of speech, song and melody

Powell (Ella May), Psychology and technique of speech and song

Schmid-Kayser, Der Kunstgesang auf Grundlage der deutschen Sprache

Schwartz, Die natürliche Gesangtechnik

Silva, Advice to beginners in singing

Wagenmann, Umsturz in der Stimmbildung

Warren, The philosophy of vocal fatigue

Zucconi, L'Art du chant

1923

Bedford, An essay on modern unaccompanied song

Fles, Spreken en zingen

Klein, The bel canto

Marchesi (Blanche), Singer's pilgrimage

*Martens, The art of the prima donna and concert singer

Martienssen-Lohmann, Das bewusste Singen

*Nordica, Lillian Nordica's hints to singers ...

Petit, La Fonction vocale et l'art du chant

*Proschowsky, The way to sing

Roeder (Marlin), Fundamental vocal exercises known as the Italian method of singing

Schilling, Unique voice training studies

*Tetrazzini, How to sing

Vorhees, Hygiene of the voice

Williams (J. Hugh), Voice production and breathing for speakers and fundamental studies for singers

1924

Arger, Initiation à l'art du chant

Blackman, Mind vs. practice

Bradley, Science of voice placement simplified for universal home study

Breare, Vocal analyses

Broad, How to attain the singing voice

*Douty, What the vocal student should know

*Drew, Voice training

*Garcia (Manuel), Garcia's treatise on the art of singing

Lagourgue, The secret

Litvinne, School of singing

Neuner, Gesanglehre für Alle

Scholes, Crotchets

Selle, Voice preservation

*Shakespeare, Plain words on singing

Thausing, Die Sängerstimme

Vannini, Delle voce umana

Wagenmann, Enrico Caruso und das Problem der Stimmbildung

Weaver, Experimental studies in vocal expression

1925

Baratoux, The voice

*Buzzi-Peccia, How to succeed in singing

*Dodds (George Robert) and Lickley, The control of the breath

Duhamel, Technique rationelle du chant

Feuchtinger, A manual for the study of the human voice

Gautier, Principes et techniques du chant

Hall, Hall's rudiments of music

Liévens, Le Vérité vocale sur la voix humaine

_____, Méthode de voix labiale idéale

McKerrow, The vocal movements and some others

*Marafioti, The new vocal art

Melchissédec, Le Chant

Pestalozzi (Heinrich), Kehlkopfgymnastik

*Rogers, Your voice and you

Sullivan, Low loss voice

Vié, Notes sur l'art du chant

*Witherspoon, Singing

1926

Adams (H. Travers), The "central point" in beautiful voice production

Behnke (Kate Emil), Singers' difficulties

Glubka, Secrets of correct and beautiful singing

Herrmann (Georg), Die Stimmkrise

Jacubert, Der Schlüssel zum Naturgesetz des Singers

Leipoldt, Stimme und sexualität

Massell, To sing or not to sing

*Melba, Melba Method

Ruff, Vocal fundamentals for speech and song

Wagenmann, Lille [sic] Lehmann's Geheimnis der Stimmbänder

Wilcox, Vocal guide for song and speech

1927

Adler-Selva, Wie steuern wir dem weiteren Verfall der Gesangkunst?

*Dodds (George), Practical hints for singers

*Downing, Vocal pedagogy for student, singer, and teacher

*Frossard, La Science et l'art de la voix

Hess, Die Behandlung der Stimme vor

Labriet, Le Chant scientifique

Martienssen-Lohmann, Stimme und Gestaltung

Moll, Singen und Sprechen

Pestalozzi (August), Bewegungphysiologische Voraussetzungen zur technischen Beherrschung der Musikinstrumente und des Gesangs ...

*Proschowsky, The singing school of Frantz Proschowsky

Scheel, Lösung des Stimmproblems

Scripture, Anwendung der graphischen Methode auf Sprache und Gesang

Street, Pure and easy tone production

Wolf (Artur), Gymnastik des Gesangs-apparatus

Wood, The gentle art of singing

BIBLIOGRAPHY OF
SECONDARY SOURCES

Baker, Theodore. A biographical dictionary of musicians. New York: G. Schirmer, 1900.

_____. Baker's biographical dictionary of musicians. 5th ed. Rev. by Nicolas Slonimsky. New York: G. Schirmer, 1958.

Baltzell, W. J. Baltzell's dictionary of musicians. Boston: O. Ditson Co., 1911.

Barnett, John. Systems and singing masters: an analytical comment upon the Wilhelm system ... with letters ... and critical remarks, upon Mr. John Hullah's manual. London: W. S. Orr & Co., 1842.

Brown, J. Stanford. "The literature of voice production and the art of singing...; a bibliography," Musician (Philadelphia), vol. 3 (1898), pp. 45, 73, 101, 133.

Brown, James D. Biographical dictionary of musicians. London: Alexander Gardner, 1886.

_____, and Stratton, Stephen S. British musical biography; a dictionary of musical artists, authors and composers born in Britain and its colonies. Birmingham, England: Chadfield and Son, 1897.

Burgin, John Carroll. Teaching singing. Metuchen, N. J. : Scarecrow Press, 1973. (Revised version of 1971 doctoral dissertation, "An analysis of the working concepts contained in contributions to vocal pedagogy, 1943-68. ")

Burney, Charles. A general history of music from the earliest ages to the present period (1789). New ed. 2 vols. New York: n. p. , 1935.

Clayton, Ellen Creathorne. Queens of song; being memoirs of the most celebrated female vocalists. London: Smith, Elder and Co. , 1863.

A dictionary of modern music and musicians. London: J. M. Dent & Sons, 1924.

Duey, Philip A. Bel canto in its golden age; A study of its teaching concepts. New York: King's Crown Press, 1951.

Duncan, Edmondstoune, ed. Reeve's dictionary of musicians. London: William Reeves, n. d.

Edwards, Henry Sutherland. The prima donna, her history and surroundings from the 17th to the 19th century. London: Remington and Co. , 1888.

Encyclopédie de la musique. Paris: Fasquelle, 1958.

Fields, Victor Alexander. Training the singing voice; An analysis of the working concepts contained in recent contributions to vocal pedagogy. New York: King's Crown Press, 1947.

Gatti, Guido M. La musica. 2 vols. Turin: Unione Tipografico, 1968.

Geering, Arnold. "Gesangspädagogik," in Die Musik in Geschichte und Gegenwart, edited by Friedrich Bloom. Kassel: Bärenreiter-Verlag, 1955.

Goldschmidt, Hugo. Die Italiensche Gesangmethode des XVII Jahrhunderts und ihre Bedeutung für die Gegenwart. Breslau: Schlesische Buchdruckerei, 1892.

Grove, G. Grove's dictionary of music and musicians. Edited by Eric Blom. 5th ed. New York: St. Martin's Press Inc. , 1954.

Helmholtz, Hermann L. F. Die Lehre von der Tonempfindungen als physiologische Grundlage für die Theorie der Musik. 4th ed. Braunschweig: Druck und Verlag von Friedrich Vieweg und Sohn, 1877. English version: On the sensations of tone as a physiological basis for the theory of music. The second English edition, translated, thoroughly revised and corrected, rendered conformed to the fourth (and last) German edition of 1877 ... by Alexander J. Ellis. New York: Dover Publications, 1954 (a reprint).

Henderson, William James. Early history of singing. New York: Longman's, Green & Co. , 1921.

Herbert-Caesari, Edgar F. Tradition and Gigli 1600-1955; a panegyric. London: R. Hale, 1958.

Hughes, Rupert. The biographical dictionary of musicians, completely revised and newly edited by Deems Taylor and Russell Kerr. New York: Blue Ribbon Books, 1940.

Kelly, Michael. Reminiscences/ Michael Kelly. Reprint. London: Oxford University Press, 1975.

Klein, Hermann. Thirty years of musical life in London. 1870-1900. New York: Century Co. , 1903.

Moore, John W[eeks]. A dictionary of musical information. Boston: Oliver Ditson & Co., 1876. Reprinted, New York: AMS Press, 1977.

Orrey, Leslie. The encyclopedia of opera. New York: Scribner's Sons, 1976.

Pratt, Waldo Selden, ed. The new encyclopedia of music and musicians. New York: Macmillan Co., 1941.

Rushmore, Robert. The singing voice. New York: Dodd, Mead & Co., 1971.

Sainsbury, John S., ed. Dictionary of musicians from the earliest ages to the present time. 2 vols. London: Sainsbury and Co., 1825. Reprinted, New York: Da Capo Press, 1966.

Sands, Mollie. "The teaching of singing in eighteenth century England," in Royal Musical Association Proceedings, 1944, 70th session, London, p. 11-31.

Tosi, Pietro Francesco. Observations on the florid song, translated by Mr. Galliard. London: J. Wilcox, 1743.

Appendix One:

WORKS NOT EXAMINED

None of the titles listed below appeared in the catalogs
of the seven libraries used for this study.   They do exist
in print, however, in at least one of the primary or
secondary sources consulted (of which the relevant work
is given in parentheses after each entry).   While the
existence of these works was not verified by additional
research, the author wished to include them in an appendix to make the bibliography as complete as possible.
The two most valuable sources from which the following
titles were taken were J. Standford Brown's "The literature of voice production and the art of singing...;
a bibliography," in Musician, 1898, abbreviated BRO,
and Arnold Geering's "Gesangspädagogik," in Die Musik
in Geschichte und Gegenwart, 1955, abbreviated MGG.

Arnim, G. Automatisches Stimmbildung. Leipzig, 1911. (MGG)

Battaille, C. De l'enseignement du chant. Paris, 1863. (MGG)

Behnke, Kate Emil, and Pearce, Charles W. Voice training primer
    and examination catechism of vocal physiology, voice training,
    and musical theory. (BRO)

Belari, Emilio. Vocal teaching is a fraud. 1892. (BRO)

Botume, J. F. Vocal technique. (Botume, J. F. , Respiration for
    advanced singers, 1897)

Brinkerhoff, Clara. The voice. (Myer, E. J. The voice from a
    practical standpoint. 1886).

Cirillo, Vincenzo. The Neopolitan school. Boston: Geo. H. Ellis,
    ca. 1896. (Botume, J. F. , Modern singing methods, 1896)

Courtney, Louise Gage. Hints about my singing method. 1896.
    (BRO)

Curwen, John Spencer. The voice in singing. (BRO)

Dama, Luigi. The Dama theory of voice cure. (Myer, E. J. ,
    Position and action in singing, 1897)

Daniell, W. H. "The value of the falsetto in developing the male voice. " [A paper read before the Music Teachers' National Association, 1883.] (Baker's Biographical Dictionary of Musicians)

Florimo, F. Breve metodo di canto. Before 1864. (MGG)

Goldschmidt, H. Handbuch der deutschen Gesang-Pädagogik. Leipzig, 1896. 2nd ed. , 1911. (MGG)

Hamilton, J. A. Hamilton's modern instructions for singing. (BRO)

Hast, Harry Gregory. The singer's art. London: Methuen & Co. , 1925. (Rushmore, Robert, The singing voice, 1971)

Hennig, K. Deutsche Gesang-Schule. 1889. 2nd ed. , 1903. (MGG)

Hey, Julius. Deutscher Gesangs-Unterricht. Mainz: B. Schott's Söhne. (Lankow, Anna, Supplement to vocal art, 1901)

Jordan, Julian. Some ideas about singing. (BRO)

Kelly, T. First principles of voice production in song and speech. (BRO)

Kennedy, John. Common sense and singing. London?: Joseph William, Ltd. (White, Ernest G. , The voice beautiful, 1918)

Kofler, Leo. The old Italian school of singing. Albany, N. Y. , 1882. (Fillebrown, Thomas, Resonance in speaking and singing, 1911)

Kuijpers. Anleitung zur Stimmbildung. 3rd ed. Leipzig, 1902. (MGG)

Lunn, Charles. Artistic voice in speech and song. (BRO)

_____. The management of the voice. (BRO)

Mackenzie, M. Singen und Sprechen; Pflege und Ausbildung der menschlichen Stimmorgans. Translated by J. Michael. Leipzig, 1887. (MGG)

Mannstein, H. F. Katechismus des Gesang im Lichte der Naturwissenschaft, Sprache und Logik. Leipzig?, 1864. (MGG)

_____. Die sogenannte Praktik des klassische Gesangschule. Leipzig, 1839. (MGG)

_____. Das System der grossen Gesang-Schule des Bernacchi von Bologna. Leipzig, 1834. 2nd ed. , Dresden, 1848. (MGG and Bach, Albert, Musical education and voice culture, 1884)

Meignen, L. Meignen's vocal method. (BRO)

Minoja, Ambrosio. Lettere sopra il canto. Milan, 1812. (Baker's
    Biographical Dictionary of Musicians)

Monroe, L. B. Vocal gymnastics. (BRO)

Nava, Gaetano. Elements of vocalization. (BRO)

Novello, Sabilla. Vocal school. (BRO)

Palmer, Edward Davidson. The rightly-produced voice. London,
    1898. (Fillebrown, Thomas, Resonance in speaking and sing-
    ing, 1911; and Lankow, Anna, Supplement to vocal art, 1901)

Perino, Marcello. Osservazioni sulcanto. Naples: Terni, 1810.
    (Bach, Albert, Musical education and voice culture, 1884)

Pinsuti, Ciro. Hints to students of singing. (BRO)

Quarterly Musical Magazine and Review (Bacon, Richard Mackenzie,
    Elements of vocal science, 1824) [this is a periodical].

Randegger, Alberto. Method of singing. 1897. (BRO)

_____. Singing primer. (BRO)

Ricci, V. La tecnica del canto in rapporto con la pratica antica e
    le teorie moderne. Livorno, 1920. (MGG)

Rimbault. Rimbault's singing tutor, chiefly selected from the cele-
    brated work of Lablache, comprising directions for the forma-
    tion and cultivation of the voice after the best Italian method
    ... for soprano, contralto, tenor and bass. (BRO)

Roderick, Emma. A revolution in the art of voice education result-
    ing from the new scientific discoveries made by the eminent
    vocal physiologist, Emilio Belari. 1890. (BRO)

Röhner, G. W. The art of singing concisely and fully explained,
    with a complete view of the classification of voices. (BRO)

Romer, Frank. Romer's school of singing. (BRO)

Root, Frederick W. Italian and German schools of vocal culture.
    (BRO)

Santley, Charles. The singing master. (2 parts). London, 1900.
    (Baker's Biographical Dictionary of Musicians and BRO)

Shaftesbury, Edmund. Lessons in voice culture. (BRO)

Sola. Grosse's method of singing, containing the necessary directions towards obtaining a perfect intonation and flexibility of the voice, exercises on graces and cadences; also a method of teaching how to sing a second, and to an accompaniment of any instrument. (BRO)

Sonky, S. Théorie de la musique vocale. Paris, 1911. (MGG)

Stoerk, Karl. Sprache und Gesang. 1881. (BRO)

Stone, William H. Singing, speaking and stammering. (BRO)

Suffern, J. William. The true art of singing. (BRO)

Sulzer. Theorie der schönen Künste. (BRO)

Sutro, Emil. Duality of voice and speech. London: Dryden House, 1904. (Rushmore, Robert, The singing voice, 1971)

Thorp, George E. Colour audition and its relation to voice production. (BRO)

_____. Twelve lessons in breathing and breath control. (BRO)

Tubbs, Frank Herbert. Expression in singing. (BRO)

Turner, John. Instructions in vocal music. 1833. (BRO)

Urling. Vocal gymnastics. (BRO)

Viardot, Pauline. An hour of study. 1897. (BRO)

Vogel, G. Italienische und deutsche Gesang-Kunst. 1901. (MGG)

Warman, Edward Barrett. The voice, how to train it. Boston, 1890. (Fillebrown, Thomas, Resonance in speaking and singing, 1911)

Wass, John. Wass's singing tutor. (BRO)

_____. The complete singing method. (BRO)

Weiss, G. Allgemeine Stimmbildungslehre für Gesang und Rede mit anatomisch-physiologischer Begründung dargestellt. Braunschweig, 1868. (MGG)

Wheeler, J. Harry. Vocal physiology, voice culture·and singing. (BRO)

Wing, Clinton E. The abdominal method of singing and breathing as a cause of 'female weakness' [A paper read before the Boston Society for Medical Improvement, November 22, 1880 and communicated to the Boston Medical and Surgical Journal.] (Botume, J. F., Modern singing methods, 1896 and BRO)

Winter, P. Celebrated vocal tutor: new edition with explanations in German and English by Dr. L. Benda. (BRO)

Appendix Two

THE PERIODICAL LITERATURE

From a practical standpoint, the gathering and analysis
of all vocal pedagogy materials printed between 1777
and 1927 is impossible. In order to delimit the study
to manageable proportions, it was necessary to pass
over the rich source of information available in more
than 80 periodicals published during the period. Each
of the periodicals in the listing to follow contains at
least one article related to the field of vocal pedagogy.
The list was gathered from the following sources:

Biographie der Deutschen Zeitschriften-Literatur, edited by
  F[elix] Dietrich. Vols. 1-60. Reprinted, New York:
  Kraus Reprint Corp. , 1961.

Biographie der fremdsprachigen Zeitschriftenliteratur.
  Vols. 1-20 and, in the new series, vols. 1-3. Reprinted, New York: Kraus Reprint Corp. , 1961.

The Center for Research Libraries Catalogue. 2 vols.
  Chicago: The Center for Research Libraries, 1972.

International Index to Periodicals, edited by Anna L. Guthrie
  et al. Minneapolis: H. W. Wilson Co. , 1907-1927.

Library of Congress card catalogue.

New York Public Library card catalogue.

Nineteenth Century Reader's Guide to Periodical Literature:
  1890-1899, with supplementary indexing: 1900-1922,
  edited by Helen Grant Cushing and Adah V. Morris. 2
  vols. New York: H. W. Wilson Co. , 1944.

Poole's Index to Periodical Literature, edited by William
  Frederick Poole et al. Rev. ed. , 1 vol. in 2 parts,
  with 5 supplements. New York: Peter Smith, 1938.

Reader's Guide to Periodical Literature, edited by Anna
  Lorraine Guthrie. Vols. 1-7. Minneapolis: H. W.
  Wilson Co. , 1905-1929.

Union List of Serials in Libraries of the United States and
Canada, edited by Edna Brown Titus. 3rd ed. 5 vols.
New York: H. W. Wilson Co. , 1965.

Allgemeine Musik-Zeitung (Berlin)

American Journal of Education (Hartford)

American Journal of Science (New Haven)

Les Annales Politiques et Littéraires (Paris)

Archiv für Laryngologie und Rhinologie (Berlin)

Art in Australia (Sydney)

Atlantic Monthly (Boston)

Bookman (New York)

Century Magazine (New York)

Christian Examiner (Boston)

Christian Magazine (New York)

Chronique Musicale (Paris)

Church Quarterly Review (London)

Colburn's New Monthly Magazine (London)

Critic (New York)

Current Literature (New York)

Deutsche Gesangkunst (Leipzig)

Education (Boston)

Educational Review (New York)

English Illustrated Magazine (London)

English Review (London)

The Etude (Philadelphia)

Every Saturday (Boston)

Fortnightly Review (London)

Forum (New York)

Galaxy (New York)

Gesundheitslehrer (Warnsdorf)

Idler (London)

Independent (New York)

Institut de France. L'Académie des Sciences (Paris)

International Music Soc. Zeitschrift (Leipzig)

Jahresberichte über das höhere Schulwesen (Berlin)

Journal of the Society of Arts (London)

Ladies' Home Journal (Philadelphia)

Living Age (Boston)

London Magazine (London)

Magazin der Musik (Hamburg)

Mercure de France (Paris)

Monatshefte für Musikgeschichte (Leipzig)

Monthly Musical Record (London)

Monthly Review (London)

Murray's Magazine (London)

Music (New York)

Music News (Chicago)

Music Teachers' National Association Proceedings (Hartford)

Musical America (New York)

Musical Courier (New York)

Musical Herald (Chicago)

Musical Leader and Concert-goer (Chicago)

Musical Observer (New York)

Musical Quarterly (New York)

Musical Times (New York)

Musical World (Boston)

Musician (Boston)

The Musician (Philadelphia)

Die Musik (Berlin, Leipzig, Stuttgart)

Musikalisches Wochenblatt (Leipzig)

Musikpädagogische Blätter (Berlin)

Nation (New York)

National Education Association of the United States. Journal of Proceedings and Addresses (Chicago)

Nature (London)

Neue Musik-Zeitung (Leipzig, Stuttgart)

New Music Review (New York)

Nineteenth Century (London)

North American Review (New York)

Pädagogisches Jahrbuch (Berlin)

Phonetische Studien (Marburg)

Die Redenden Künste (Leipzig)

Review d'Art dramatique (Paris)

Review of Reviews (New York)

Rivista musicale italiana (Turin, Florence)

Sängerhalle (Leipzig)

La Scena (Trieste)

Science (Lancaster, Pa.; New York)

Scribner's Magazine (New York)

Signale (für die musikalische Welt):(Leipzig)

Sitzungsberichte der kaiserliche Akademie der Wissenschaft (Vienna)

Spectator (London)

The Touchstone (New York)

Vereeniging voor Nederlandsche muziekgeschiedenis. Tijdschrift (Amsterdam)

Vierteljahrsschrift für Musikwissenschaft (Leipzig)

Westminster Review (London)

World Review (Mount Morris, Ill)

Zeitschrift für Musikwissenschaft (Leipzig)

Zeitschrift für Turnen und Jugendspiel (Leipzig)

Zeitschrift internationale Musikgesellschaft (Leipzig)

INDEX

Abdominal breathing, 63
Accompaniment, dependency
   upon, 42
Ah vowel, 197
Articulation, defined, 185
Attack, defined, 92; described,
   92
Audience, considered in song
   selection, 213

Beginners, first lessons, 38;
   handling, 36
Benefits of vocal study, 17
Bibliography, annotated, 233;
   chronological, guide to,
   231; secondary sources, 326
Body as resonator, 119
Bone conduction, 177
Breath, economy of, 66;
   pressure and support, 66;
   renewel, 67
Breath control, by phrasing,
   56; interpretational, 56;
   miscellaneous devices, 58;
   natural, 54; psychological
   approach, 54; synchronization with music, 58;
   technical approach, 59
Breathing, defined, 46; developed by singing, 56;
   exercises, 48; mouth, 64;
   mouth and nose, 65; nose,
   64; physiological factors,
   51; postural controls, 59;
   pre-vocal training, 48;
   as primary consideration,
   46; psychological factors,
   54; respiratory function

described, 51; volun-
   tary, 61
Breathing action, 65; ab-
   dominal, 63; diaphrag-
   matic, 63; silent, 68;
   speed of, 67

Categories, total number
   of, 10
Chanting, 194
Chest cavity, 117; position,
   60; register, 141; resonance, 117
Citations, mode of, 11
Classifying voices, criteria
   for, 36
Coloring, 200
Comparison of statement
   totals with Burgin and
   Fields, 8
Compass, 128
Consonants, as antivocal
   elements, 201; avoiding
   early training with,
   192; defined, 191; ex-
   aggeration of, 203;
   rhythm markers, 202;
   tone interrupters, 202;
   use of, 192
Coordination, its importance,
   24
Coup de glotte, 93, 100, 198

Diaphragm, action of, 51;
   control, 63
Diction, defined, 185; general considerations,